"One of our best and most underappreciated historians takes a hard look at the truth of our empire, both its covert activities and the reasons for its impending decline."

   —OLIVER STONE, Academy Award-winning director of *Platoon*

"*In the Shadows of the American Century* persuasively argues for the inevitable decline of the American empire and the rise of China. Whether or not one is a believer in American power, the case that Alfred McCoy makes—that much of America's decline is due to its own contradictions and failures—is a sad one. He provides a glimmer of hope that America can ease into the role of a more generous, more collaborative, if less powerful, world player. Let's hope that Americans will listen to his powerful arguments."

   —VIET THANH NGUYEN, Pulitzer Prize-winning author of *The Sympathizer*

"'What is the character of this American empire?' Alfred McCoy asks at the outset of this provocative study. His answer not only limns the contours of the American imperium as it evolved during the twentieth century but explains why its days are quite likely numbered. This is history with profound relevance to events that are unfolding before our eyes."

   —ANDREW J. BACEVICH, author of *America's War for the Greater Middle East: A Military History*

"Al McCoy has guts. . . . He helped put me on the path to investigative journalism."

   —JEREMY SCAHILL, founding editor of the *Intercept* and author of *Blackwater* and *Dirty Wars*

"Alfred McCoy offers a meticulous, eye-opening account of the rise, since 1945, and impending premature demise of the American Century of world domination. As the empire's political, economic, and military strategies unravel under cover of secrecy, America's neglected citizens would do well to read this book."

   —ANN JONES, author of *They Were Soldiers*

"Sobering reading for geopolitics mavens and *Risk* aficionados alike."

   —*KIRKUS REVIEWS*

"McCoy's detailed, panoramic analysis of the past, present, and future of the American empire covers all spheres of activity including not just land, sea, air, space, and cyberspace but also the netherworld of covert operations—and seasons all of this with some fascinating personal vignettes. His new book, *In the Shadows of the American Century*, joins the essential short list of scrupulous historical and comparative studies of the United States as an awesome, conflicted, technologically innovative, routinely atrocious, and ultimately hubristic imperial power."

—JOHN DOWER, Pulitzer Prize-winning author of *Embracing Defeat* and *The Violent American Century*

In the Shadows of the American Century

The Rise and Decline of US Global Power

Alfred W. McCoy

Dispatch Books

Haymarket Books
Chicago, IL

Published in 2017 by
Haymarket Books
P.O. Box 180165
Chicago, IL 60618
773-583-7884
www.haymarketbooks.org
info@haymarketbooks.org

ISBN: 978-1-60846-773-0

Trade distribution:
In the US, Consortium Book Sales and Distribution, www.cbsd.com
In Canada, Publishers Group Canada, www.pgcbooks.ca
In the UK, Turnaround Publisher Services, www.turnaround-uk.com
All other countries, Ingram Publisher Services International,
intlsales@perseusbooks.com

This book was published with the generous support of Lannan Foundation
and Wallace Action Fund.

Cover Photo: The Boeing Company's "Phantom Ray" Unmanned Combat
Air System making its maiden flight in April 2011 at Edwards Air Force Base,
California. Courtesy of the Boeing Company. Cover design by Eric Kerl.

Printed in Canada by union labor.

Library of Congress Cataloging-in-Publication data is available.

10 9 8 7 6 5 4 3 2 1

For Mary, who inspired these thoughts

Contents

Maps and Graphs

Introduction

US Global Power and Me

Throughout my long life in this country, America has always been at war. Short wars, long wars, world war, Cold War, secret war, surrogate war, war on drugs, war on terror, but always some sort of war. While these wars were usually fought in far-off countries or continents, sparing us the unimaginable terrors of bombing, shelling, and mass evacuation, their reality invariably lurked just beneath the surface of American life. For me, they were there in the heavy drinking and dark moods of my father and his friends, combat veterans of World War II; in the defense industries that employed him and most of the men I knew growing up; in the state surveillance that seemed to follow my family; in the bitter antiwar protests that divided the country during my college years; and in the endless war on terror that has stumbled ever onward since 2001.

I was born in 1945 at the start of an "American Century" of untrammeled global dominion. For nearly eighty years, the wars fought to defend and extend that vision of world power have shaped the American character—our politics, the priorities of our government, and the mentality of our people. If Americans aspired to govern the world like ancient Athenians, inspiring citizens and allies alike with lofty ideals, we acted more like Spartans, steeling our sons for war from childhood and relegating their suffering to oblivion as adults. Yet it was that Athenian aspiration to dominion that led this country into one war after another. It was that unbending ambition for a global Pax Americana that has allowed war to shape this country's character.

At great personal cost for those who fought such wars, this country has won not only a kind of security but unprecedented power and prosperity. At the end of World War II, the United States, alone among the planet's developed nations, had been spared its mass destruction. America emerged from history's most destructive conflict as an economic powerhouse responsible for more than half the world's industrial output, consuming much of its raw materials, possessing its strongest currency, and girding the globe with its armed forces and their garrisons. The Soviet Union's implosion at the close of the Cold War in 1991 again left America the richest, most powerful, most productive nation on the planet.

Though we would live our lives in the shadow of war and empire, my postwar "baby boom" generation was also privileged to grow up in a relatively safe society with a superior education system, excellent health care, affordable food, and opportunities once available only to aristocrats. None of this happened by accident. Every advantage came with a price paid at home and abroad by Americans and many others. Our country's global power was first won in a world war that left fifty million dead. It was maintained throughout the Cold War by covert interventions to control foreign societies, a global military presence manifest in hundreds of overseas bases, and the rigorous suppression of domestic dissent. In the quarter century since the Cold War's end, however, America's social contract has frayed. The old bargain, shared sacrifice for shared prosperity, has given way, through Washington's aggressive promotion of a global economy, to a rising disparity of incomes that has eroded the quality of middle-class life.

As an aspiring historian since seventh grade, I have remained more observer than actor, trying to make sense of the changing relationship between America and the world, attempting to understand our complex form of state power and our distinctive way of governing the globe. I consider myself fortunate to have grown up among middle-class families that served this state as soldiers, engineers, and later, on occasion, senior officials.

I was also privileged to attend schools that trained our future leaders, allowing me to observe firsthand the ethos that shaped those at the apex of American power, their character and worldview. For five years in the 1960s, I went to a small boarding school in Kent, Connecticut, that steeled its boys through relentless hazing and rigorous training for service to the state. Admiral Draper Kauffman (class of '29), founder of the navy's underwater demolition teams (forerunner of the SEALs), was the father of a classmate. Cyrus Vance (class of '35), the future secretary of state, was a commencement speaker. Sir Richard Dearlove (class of '63), later head of Britain's MI-6, was a year ahead of me. Countless alumni were known to be in the CIA. Through its defining rituals, this small school tried to socialize us into a grand imperial design of the kind once espoused by East Coast elites back when America was first emerging as a world power. On Sundays after mass celebrated with Anglican high-church liturgy, the cascading sounds of English change ringing pealed for hours from the chapel bell tower. Every class had one or two British exchange students provided by the English-Speaking Union. Our curriculum followed the classical form of English boarding schools, with Latin or Greek required subjects. The school crew made periodic trips to the Henley Royal Regatta. All this was aimed at instilling a cultural affinity between American and British elites for shared global dominion.

Both family and school taught me that criticism was not only a right but a responsibility of citizenship. So it has been my role to observe, analyze, and, when I have something worth sharing, to write and sometimes to criticize. This is a complex society, elusive in its exercise of world power. It has taken many years of education and much of my life experience to gain some insight into the geopolitical dynamics that propelled the United States to global hegemony and are undoubtedly condemning it to decline.

Only days after my father's graduation from the US Military Academy at West Point in June 1944, my parents married. That December, when he shipped out with the Eighty-Ninth Division for the war in Europe, my mother was pregnant with me. As an artillery forward observer, he was on the front lines in the Moselle, the Rhineland crossing, and onward through central Germany where his unit was the first to liberate a Nazi death camp. Typical of the veterans of that conflict, he only mentioned the war once, telling me in an offhand way when I was old enough to understand that the infantry company he fought with crossing the Rhine lost most of its two hundred men that day.

My birth coincided with the last months of World War II, just as the United States was ascending to unprecedented world power. As I grew up and we moved from one quiet street to another across America, war was always with us, just beneath the surface of family life. When my father wasn't away at war in Europe or Korea, we lived mainly at Fort Sill, Oklahoma, home of the US Field Artillery. There his promotions finally got us out of squalid army housing and into pleasant quarters on a tree-lined street opposite the parade ground. I can still remember visiting the grave of Geronimo, the Apache chief whose capture in the 1880s and life sentence at Fort Sill ended the "Indian wars" in the Southwest. Climbing the stone marker above his grave at age five was my introduction to the past and its occupants as I touched those stones wondering about the great chief who lay below.

A few months after the Korean War started in June 1950, my father shipped out again with the field artillery for a yearlong combat tour, and we moved to Florida to be with my mother's parents. In first grade, I had a map of Korea posted on my bedroom wall. Silver stars glued on it showed the position of my father's unit as it moved around the peninsula. For the first time, I learned that the world actually had other countries. One memorable morning, I woke to find my father magically home from war. Allowed to skip school for the first and only time in my life, I sat with him in the breezeway that warm Florida morning as he showed me photos he had taken with his new Japanese camera of far-off battlefields—howitzer batteries firing, tents in the snow, and, most memorably, a disheveled Korean woman squatting in a field before a pile of rubble and staring directly into the lens. "Her house," was my father's only comment. It would remain an indelible image of war for the rest of my life.

After that combat tour, we returned to Fort Sill where, among other duties, my father was range officer for artillery training. Once during a night-firing exercise, he took me along, though I was only seven. I watched beneath the eerie white light of falling flares as his words into a phone unleashed barrages that exploded tanks and trucks on faraway hills—a memorable lesson in the power of America's military arsenal.

After my father resigned his commission to become an electronics engineer, we followed him from one defense contract to another. Sperry Gyroscope on Long Island near New York City, Raytheon near Boston, and Aerospace Corporation in Los Angeles. Wherever we went, our neighbors were more or less like us—dad, the war veteran, mom, the suburban housewife, two or three kids, a dog, a small house, a mortgage, a car, a local church, crowded schools, and, of course, scouts. When I was in elementary school, it all felt pretty nice. Nobody had much money, but everyone seemed happy. The dads had good jobs. When you got sick, a doctor came to the house. The cafeteria food at school was fine. I got new bikes on my seventh and eleventh birthdays. There were always kids on the street to play with. Safety wasn't even a concept, just a given. Looking back, it seemed as if America had won more than a war.

Not long after we bought a house in Sudbury, a Boston suburb, in the mid-1950s, the Katzenbachs moved in next door. Their son Larry was a year older and already in high school, but he soon became my best friend (for life, as it turned out). Their daughter Matilda was my younger sister's playmate. Maude Katzenbach became my mother's confidante and close friend. Even after both families moved away, they carried on a correspondence that continued for nearly fifty years about children, divorces, careers, retirement—

Woman with remains of house, South Korea, 1951. (Photo by Alfred M. McCoy, Jr.)

and, let's face it—the suffering they shared as wives of those warrior males.

Like my father, Ed Katzenbach was a combat veteran of World War II. As a marine officer, he had fought for four years through nineteen blood-soaked landings on Japanese-occupied islands across the Pacific.[1] Every day, my dad drove to the Raytheon Laboratory in a nearby suburb to design radar for the country's missile defense system. And every morning, Larry's dad took the train into Boston where he was director of defense studies at Harvard University, planning strategy for the nation's military.

Though they lived next door and looked like us, the Katzenbachs were different. They had an aura of American aristocracy about them. Ed went to Princeton; his father had been New Jersey's attorney general; his uncle was a justice on that state's supreme court.[2] They had some money, not much, but enough to do things we couldn't afford, like lease a fishing cabin in Maine. One memorable spring when I was thirteen, the Katzenbachs took me along for ice-out fishing—hikes through the melting snow, splitting wood for the stove, and endlessly trolling the lake, which had water so clear that you could actually see the trout swim right up to examine the lure and then never quite bite.

Beneath his faint smile, Ed Katzenbach was troubled, fighting serious depression and an ambitious colleague named Henry Kissinger who was maneuvering for his job. Sometimes, after a night of drinking and arguing with his wife, he would retreat to the basement and fire his service pistol into the wall. When John F. Kennedy was elected president, the family moved to Washington and he became deputy assistant secretary of defense for education. His brother Nicholas would serve in Robert Kennedy's Justice Department, becoming famous in June 1963 for confronting Governor George Wallace on the steps of the University of Alabama in the struggle over integration. Visiting Larry in Washington during high school holidays left me with memories of dinner table stories about the Katzenbach brothers working alongside the Kennedy brothers. Larry's cousins went to parties at the White House. His classmates at the elite Sidwell Friends School were the children of ambassadors and cabinet officials.

Two years after the Katzenbachs went to Washington, our family moved to Los Angeles. Though just a few years out of the army, my father, with an IQ of 195 and an advanced engineering degree from the Illinois Institute of Technology, was climbing fast in the world of the military-industrial complex. He had become chief systems engineer for Aerospace Corporation's Defense Communications Satellite System, a half-billion-dollar effort to launch the world's first global satellite network. In contrast to the dirt floors or repurposed barracks of our old army housing, we now lived on a street of movie-star mansions in Pacific Palisades, right around the corner from Ronald Reagan. When a Titan III-C rocket blasted off from Cape Canaveral in 1966 carrying a payload of eight satellites, engineers from Aerospace Corporation crowded our living room awaiting news. After one of them stood up to read the telegram from Cape Canaveral confirming the system was live, the room rang with martini-soaked cheers.[3]

Many years later when I would start writing about the architecture of US global power, turning to the recondite aerospace technology for drones, satellites, and space warfare would seem intuitive. This family background would lead me to recognize, unlike many scholars, that a satellite system was a central pillar in that architecture.

Prosperity's glow turned out to have a darker side. My father had suffered more in two wars than we knew. During our first years in Los Angeles, he drank, gambled, caroused, and racked up debts that nearly bankrupted us. Little more than a year after asking my mother for a divorce and walking out, he died in an alcohol-fueled accident at the age of forty-five. Meanwhile, Nicholas Katzenbach became attorney general under President Lyndon Johnson and went on to top jobs at IBM. But Ed himself struggled with depression, divorce, and thoughts of death, compounded by "an inconsolable heartbreak" over the sacrifice of so many soldiers' lives in the moral and strategic quagmire of the war in Vietnam. At the age of fifty-five, he pointed that service pistol at himself instead of the wall.[4] Larry, deeply scarred, grieved with a sonnet in the *New York Times*.[5]

> It's March. Outside, the snow tries yet once more
> To wrap the melting wounds of spring—the ruts,
> The footprints sunk in soggy ground. I pour
> Some tea to soothe a memory that cuts.
> Two years ago, in March, I phoned. We spoke.
> I knew his thoughts, but talked of hopes, of books,
> Of ice-out trout in Maine. I told a joke.
> "Let's fish," I said. "I'll bet they'll go for hooks." . . .
> His life was always fish who'd never bite.
> A suicide that spring, he said. "We'll see.
> Bye. Thanks." I wish this snow could bandage me.

Ed Katzenbach and my father were not exceptional. Every family I knew well enough to know what was going on behind the façade wives maintained in those days had similar problems. Most dads drank hard. At my parents' parties back in the 1950s, those veterans would down four or five drinks—not beer and wine but bourbon and vodka. Their wives pretended that an entire generation of veterans being on liquid therapy was perfectly normal. Those men, in turn, inflicted the war's trauma on their families. A study published right after World War II by two army doctors reported that sixty days of continuous combat turned 98 percent of soldiers into psychiatric casualties, vulnerable to what would later be called post-traumatic stress disorder.[6]

Watching the invisible wounds of war slowly destroy Ed Katzenbach and my father, who were as smart and strong as any men could be, taught me that Washington's bid for world power carried heavy costs. Years later when the fighting started in South Vietnam, I was not surprised that many in my generation did not seem eager to repeat their fathers' experience.

With the war in Vietnam escalating relentlessly, I joined the protesters who occupied campus buildings during my senior year at Columbia University in 1968. Beaten by the riot police, I spent a memorable night in a crowded cell at the Tombs, Manhattan's infamous municipal jail.

The next year, at Berkeley for a master's degree in Asian Studies, I experienced the People's Park demonstrations that brought tear gas, riot police, and the National Guard to campus. As I stepped out of a medieval Japanese literature class, a San Francisco motorcycle cop in full black leathers dropped to one knee, raised his shotgun, and pumped a few rounds of birdshot into my legs. Others, not so lucky, were hit by bigger, lethal buckshot, blinding one, killing another.

The next fall, I moved on to Yale for my doctorate, but the Ivy League in those days was no ivory tower. The Justice Department had indicted Black Panther leader Bobby Seale for a local murder, and the May Day protests that filled the New Haven green also shut down the campus for a week. Almost simultaneously, President Nixon ordered the invasion of Cambodia, and student protests closed hundreds of campuses across America for the rest of the semester.

Not surprisingly perhaps, in all this tumult the focus of my studies shifted from Japan to Southeast Asia, and from the past to the present war in Vietnam. Yes, that war. So what did I do about the draft? During my first semester at Yale, on December 1, 1969, to be precise, the Selective Service cut up the calendar for a lottery. The first one hundred birthdays picked were certain to be drafted and any dates above two hundred likely exempt. My birthday, June 8, was the very last date drawn, not number 365 but 366 (don't forget leap year)—the only lottery I have ever won, except for a Sunbeam electric frying pan in a high school raffle (still have it; it still works). Through a complex moral calculus typical of the 1960s, I decided that my draft exemption, although acquired by sheer luck, required that I devote myself, above all else, to thinking about, writing about, and working to end the war in Vietnam.

During those campus protests over Cambodia in the spring of 1970, our small group of graduate students in Southeast Asian history at Yale realized that the US strategic predicament in Indochina would soon require an invasion of Laos in an attempt to cut the flow of enemy supplies into South Vietnam. So, while protests over Cambodia swept campuses nationwide, we were huddled inside the library, preparing for the next invasion by editing a book of essays on Laos for the publisher Harper & Row.[7] A few months after that book appeared, one of the company's junior editors, Elizabeth Jakab, intrigued by an account we had included about that country's opium crop, telephoned from New York to ask if I could research and write a "quickie" paperback about the history behind the heroin epidemic then infecting the US Army in Vietnam.

I promptly started the research at my student carrel in the Gothic tower that is Yale's Sterling Library, tracking colonial reports about the Southeast Asian opium trade that ended suddenly in the 1950s, just when the story got interesting. So, quite tentatively at first, I stepped outside the library to do a few interviews and soon found myself following an investigative trail that circled the globe. First, I traveled across America for meetings with retired CIA operatives. Then, across the Pacific to Hong Kong to study drug syndicates. Next, I went south to Saigon, then the capital of South Vietnam, to investigate the heroin traffic that was targeting the GIs, and on into the hills of Laos to observe CIA alliances with opium warlords and the hill tribe guerrillas who grew the opium poppy. Finally, I flew from Singapore to Paris for interviews with retired French intelligence officers about their opium trafficking during the first Indochina War.

The drug traffic that supplied heroin for the US troops fighting in South Vietnam was not, I discovered, exclusively the work of criminals. Once the opium left tribal poppy fields in Laos, the traffic required official complicity at every level. The helicopters of Air America, the airline the CIA ran, carried raw opium out of the villages of its hill tribe allies. The commander of the Royal Lao Army, a close American collaborator, operated the world's largest heroin lab and was so oblivious to the implications of the traffic that he opened his opium ledgers for my inspection. Several of Saigon's top generals were complicit in the drug's distribution to US soldiers. By 1971, this web of collusion, according to a White House survey of a thousand veterans, ensured that heroin would be "commonly used" by 34 percent of American troops in South Vietnam.[8]

None of this had been covered in my college history seminars. I had no models for researching an uncharted netherworld of crime and covert operations. After stepping off the plane in Saigon, body slammed by the tropical heat, I found myself in a sprawling foreign city of four million, lost in a swarm of snarling motorcycles and a maze of nameless streets, without contacts or a clue about how to probe these secrets. Every day on the heroin trail confronted me with new challenges—where to look, what to look for, and, above all, how to ask hard questions.

Reading all that history had, however, taught me something I didn't know I knew. Instead of confronting my sources with questions about sensitive current events, I started with the French colonial past when the opium trade was still legal, gradually uncovering the underlying, unchanging logistics of drug production. As I followed this historical trail into the present, when the traffic became illegal and dangerously controversial, I began to use pieces from this past to assemble the present puzzle, until the names of contemporary dealers fell into place. In short, I had crafted a historical method that would prove, over the next forty years of my career, surprisingly useful in analyzing a diverse array of foreign policy controversies—CIA alliances with drug lords, the agency's propagation of psychological torture, and our spreading state surveillance.

Those months on the road, meeting gangsters and warlords in isolated places, offered only one bit of real danger. While hiking in the mountains of Laos, interviewing Hmong farmers about their opium shipments on CIA helicopters, I was descending a steep slope when a burst of bullets ripped the ground at my feet. I had walked into an ambush by agency mercenaries. While the five Hmong militia escorts whom the local village headman had prudently provided laid down a covering fire, my photographer John Everingham and I flattened ourselves in the elephant grass and crawled through the mud to safety. Without those armed escorts, my research would have been at an end and so would I.

Six months and 30,000 miles later, I returned to New Haven. My investigation of CIA alliances with drug lords had taught me more than I could have imagined about the covert aspects of US global power. Settling into my attic apartment for an academic year of writing, I was confident that I knew more than enough for a book on this unconventional topic. But my education, it turned out, was just beginning.

Within weeks, my scholarly isolation was interrupted by a massive, middle-aged guy in a suit who appeared at my front door and identified himself as Tom Tripodi, senior agent for the Bureau of Narcotics, which later became the Drug Enforcement Administration (DEA). His agency, he confessed during a second visit, was worried about my writing and he had been sent to investigate. He needed something to tell his superiors. Tom was a guy you could trust. So I showed him a few draft pages of my book. He disappeared into the living room for a while and came back saying, "Pretty good stuff. You got your ducks in a row." But there were some things, he added, that weren't quite right, some things he could help me fix.

Tom was my first reader. Later, I would hand him whole chapters and he would sit in a rocking chair, shirt sleeves rolled up, revolver in his shoulder holster, sipping coffee, scribbling corrections in the margins, and telling fabulous stories—like the time Jersey Mafia boss "Bayonne Joe" Zicarelli tried to buy a thousand rifles from a local gun store to overthrow Fidel Castro. Or when some CIA covert warrior came home for a vacation and had to be escorted everywhere so he didn't kill somebody in a supermarket aisle. Best of all, there was the one about how the Bureau of Narcotics caught French intelligence protecting the Corsican syndicates smuggling heroin into New York City. Some of his stories, usually unacknowledged, would appear in my book, *The Politics of Heroin in Southeast Asia.* These conversations with an undercover operative, who had trained Cuban exiles for the CIA in Florida and later investigated Mafia heroin syndicates for the DEA in Sicily, were akin to an advanced seminar, a master class in covert operations.[9]

In the summer of 1972, with the book at press, I went to Washington to testify before Congress. As I was making the rounds of congressional offices on Capitol Hill, my editor rang unexpectedly and summoned me to New York for a meeting with the president and vice president of Harper & Row, my book's publisher. Ushered into an executive suite overlooking the spires of St. Patrick's Cathedral, I listened to them tell me that Cord Meyer Jr., the CIA's assistant deputy director for plans (actually, covert operations), had called on their company's president emeritus, Cass Canfield, Sr. The visit was no accident, for Canfield, according to an authoritative history, "enjoyed prolific links to the world of intelligence, both as a former psychological warfare officer and as a close personal friend of Allen Dulles," the ex-head of the CIA. Meyer denounced my book as a threat to national security. He asked Canfield, also an old friend, to quietly suppress it.[10]

I was in serious trouble. Not only was Meyer a senior CIA official but he also had impeccable social connections and covert assets in every corner of American intellectual life. After graduating from Yale in 1942, he served with the marines in the Pacific, writing eloquent war dispatches published in *Atlantic Monthly*. He later worked with the US delegation drafting the UN charter. Personally recruited by spymaster Allen Dulles, Meyer joined the CIA in 1951 and was soon running its International Organizations Division, which "constituted the greatest single concentration of covert political and propaganda activities of the by now octopus-like CIA," including Operation

Mockingbird that planted disinformation in major US newspapers meant to aid agency operations.[11] Informed sources told me that the CIA still had assets inside every major New York publisher and it already had every page of my manuscript.

As the child of a wealthy New York family, Meyer moved in elite social circles, meeting and marrying Mary Pinchot, the niece of Gifford Pinchot, founder of the US Forestry Service and a former governor of Pennsylvania. Pinchot was a breathtaking beauty who later became President Kennedy's mistress, making dozens of secret visits to the White House. When she was found shot dead along the banks of a canal in Washington in 1964, the head of CIA counterintelligence, James Jesus Angleton, another Yale alumnus, broke into her home in an unsuccessful attempt to secure her diary. Mary's sister Toni and her husband, *Washington Post* editor Ben Bradlee, later found the diary and gave it to Angleton for destruction by the agency.[12]

Cord was in New York's *Social Register* of fine families along with my publisher, Mr. Canfield, which added a dash of social cachet to the pressure to suppress my book. By the time he walked into Harper & Row's office in the summer of 1972, two decades of CIA service had changed Meyer from a liberal idealist into "a relentless, implacable advocate for his own ideas," driven by "a paranoiac distrust of everyone who didn't agree with him" and a manner that was "histrionic and even bellicose."[13] An unpublished twenty-six-year-old graduate student versus the master of CIA media manipulation. It was hardly a fair fight. I began to fear my book would never appear.

To his credit, Mr. Canfield refused Meyer's request to suppress the book but did allow the agency a chance to review the manuscript prior to publication. Instead of waiting quietly for the CIA's critique, I contacted Seymour Hersh, then an investigative reporter for the *New York Times*. The same day the CIA courier arrived from Langley to collect my manuscript, Hersh swept through Harper & Row's offices like a tropical storm and his exposé of the CIA's attempt at censorship soon appeared on the paper's front page.[14] Other national media organizations followed his lead. Faced with a barrage of negative coverage, the CIA gave Harper & Row a critique full of unconvincing denials. The book was published unaltered.

I had learned another important lesson: the Constitution's protection of press freedom could check even the world's most powerful espionage agency. Meyer reportedly learned the same lesson. According to his obituary in the *Washington Post*, "It was assumed that Mr. Meyer would eventually advance" to head CIA covert operations, "but the public disclosure about the book deal . . . apparently dampened his prospects." He was instead exiled to London and eased into early retirement.[15]

Meyer and his colleagues were not, however, used to losing. Defeated in the public arena, the CIA retreated to the shadows and retaliated by tugging at every thread in the threadbare life of a graduate student. Over the next few months, federal officials from HEW (Health, Education, and Welfare) turned up at Yale to investigate my graduate fellowship. The IRS audited my poverty-level income. The FBI tapped my New Haven telephone, something I learned years later from a class-action lawsuit. At the height of this controversy in August 1972, FBI agents told the bureau's director they had "conducted [an] investigation concerning McCoy," searching the files compiled on me for the past two years and interviewing numerous "sources whose identities are concealed [who] have furnished reliable information in the past"—thereby producing an eleven-page report detailing my birth, education, and campus antiwar activities.[16] A college classmate I hadn't seen in four years, and who served in military intelligence, magically appeared at my side in the book section of the Yale Co-op, seemingly eager to resume our relationship. The same week a laudatory review of my book appeared on the front page of the *New York Times Book Review*, an extraordinary achievement for any historian, Yale's History Department placed me on academic probation. Unless I could somehow do a year's overdue work in a single semester, I faced dismissal.[17]

In those days, the ties between the CIA and Yale were wide and deep. The campus residential colleges screened students, including future CIA director Porter Goss, for possible careers in espionage. Alumni like Cord Meyer and James Angleton held senior slots at the agency. Had I not had a faculty adviser visiting from Germany, a stranger to this covert nexus, that probation would likely have become expulsion, ending my academic career and destroying my credibility. At a personal level, I was discovering just how deep the country's intelligence agencies could reach, even in a democracy, leaving no part of my life untouched—my publisher, my university, my taxes, my phone, and even my friends.

During these difficult days, New York representative Ogden Reid, a ranking member of the House Foreign Relations Committee, telephoned to say that he was sending staff investigators to Laos to look into the opium situation. Amid all this controversy, a CIA helicopter landed near the village where I had escaped that ambush and flew the Hmong headman who had helped my research to an agency airstrip where a CIA interrogator made it clear that he had better deny what he had said to me about the opium. Fearing "they will send a helicopter to arrest me, or . . . soldiers to shoot me," the Hmong headman did just that.[18]

Although I had won the first battle with a media blitz, the CIA was winning the longer bureaucratic war. By silencing my sources and denying any culpability, its officials convinced Congress that it was innocent of any direct complicity in the Indochina drug trade. During Senate hearings into CIA assassinations by the famed Church Committee three years later, Congress accepted the agency's assurance that none of its operatives had been directly involved in heroin trafficking (an allegation I had never made). The committee's report did confirm the core of my critique, finding that "the CIA is particularly vulnerable to criticism" over indigenous assets in Laos "of considerable importance to the Agency," including "people who either were known to be, or were suspected of being, involved in narcotics trafficking." But the senators did not press the CIA for any resolution or reform of what its own inspector general had called the "particular dilemma" posed by those alliances with drug lords—the key aspect, in my view, of its complicity in the traffic.[19] During the mid-1970s, as the flow of drugs into the United States slowed and the number of addicts declined, the heroin problem receded into the inner cities, and the media moved on to new sensations. The issue would largely be forgotten for a decade until the crack-cocaine epidemic swept America's cities in the late 1980s.

Almost by accident, I had launched my academic career by doing something a bit different. Back in the 1970s, most specialists in international studies went overseas for "fieldwork" focused on aspects of indigenous societies untouched by foreign influence, as if the globalization of the past two centuries had never happened. Instead, I had focused on interactions between American officials and their foreign allies—the lynchpin, in my view, of any empire. In one of life's small ironies, I would have to leave America to better understand the sources of American power.

Embedded within that study of drug trafficking was an analytical approach that would take me, almost unwittingly, on a lifelong exploration of US global hegemony in its many manifestations, including diplomatic alliances, CIA intervention, military technology, trade, torture, and global surveillance. Step-by-step, topic-by-topic, decade-after-decade, I would slowly accumulate sufficient understanding of the parts to try to assemble the whole—the overall character of US global power and the forces that would contribute to its perpetuation or decline. By studying how each of these current attributes was shaped by the actual exercise of this power overseas and over time, I slowly came to see a striking continuity and coherence in Washington's century-long rise to global dominion. Its reliance on surveillance, for example, first appeared in the colonial Philippines around 1900; CIA covert intervention and torture techniques emerged at the start of the Cold War in the 1950s; and much of its futuristic robotic aerospace technology had its first trial in the war in Vietnam of the 1960s.

The Cold War made this scholarly work difficult. For decades, its ideological constraints would bar most academics from even naming the topic that needed the most study. Once the Cold War ended in 1991, I could finally admit to myself that I had been researching the rise of the United States as history's most powerful "empire." Not only was this imperium the first to cover the entire globe, but it was also the only one in two centuries largely exempt from serious scholarly study. Since the Soviet bloc used the Marxist-inflected term "imperialist" to denigrate the United States, this country's diplomatic historians, operating in a Cold War mode, subscribed to the idea of "American exceptionalism." The United States might be a "world leader" or even a "great power," but never an empire. Our enemy, the Soviet Union, was the one with an empire.

Within the Cold War's not-so-subtle pressures for affirmation of American foreign policy, critical voices, even within the academy, were few. The handful of Marxist historians still teaching often reduced the study of empires—the most complex and multifaceted of all political organizations—to a narrow, rather dull analysis of their economic causation. By contrast, a small group of historians affiliated with the so-called Wisconsin school, led by the historian William Appleman Williams, developed a more nuanced critique of US diplomatic history. Like many graduate students during the 1960s, I immersed myself in his landmark text, *The Tragedy of American Diplomacy*, scribbling notes in the margins of a well-worn paperback that I still have on my bookshelf. But I could not see a way to apply his approach to my own study of Asia, a field whose leading academics were still scarred by Cold War accusations of subversion.

As a graduate student in history during the 1970s, I thus found myself caught in a political conundrum that precluded even naming my subject, much less theorizing about it. Yet Yale's graduate school, through its close ties to English universities where imperial history still thrived, offered a back door into this otherwise closed realm of inquiry. In my first year at Yale, I took a seminar on "comparative imperialism" from Oxford historian David Fieldhouse, later considered the world's "leading imperial economic historian," and another on British imperial diplomacy in East Asia with Ian Nish from the London School of Economics.[20]

Both were erudite, engaging men, but Fieldhouse made the concept of empire come alive for me with personal anecdotes, like one about a temperamental relative who sprayed ink from his pen across an overbearing supervisor's white shirt and wound up a lowly colonial official in West Africa. Yet at a conference of graduate students hosted by the antiwar group Committee of Concerned Asian Scholars, I recoiled from a proposed commitment to "anti-imperialism," even though I was then the organization's national coordinator. In the context of the Cold War, the very name of my field had become an unpalatable political epithet.

With the last US combat troops home from Vietnam and the war winding down, I needed to get my academic career back on track. So, having worked double-time to finish those overdue Yale degree requirements, I moved to the Philippines in the fall of 1973 for dissertation fieldwork. During the next three years in the central Philippines, I learned a local language and immersed myself in the country's social history. As it happened, the Philippines was the only place on the planet where almost a half century of US colonial rule made the study of the American empire a serious, non-polemical exercise.

Looking back, it was a lucky choice. Over the next forty years, Filipinos would prove excellent teachers when it came to their country's long, complex relationship with America. Often they cast aside my ill-informed questions and taught me about facets of power I didn't even know I needed to know.

My doctoral dissertation focused on what seemed like a purely academic topic: the impact of World War II on the Philippine response to US colonial rule. Yet only a few months after I started my work, President Ferdinand Marcos declared martial law and launched what became fourteen years of military dictatorship. To justify his ever-tightening grip on power, he insisted that his heroism as an anti-Japanese guerrilla had steeled him to lead the nation through troubled times. He would redouble these claims a decade later during his reelection campaign against Corazon Aquino. As that contest heated up in late 1985, I happened to be in Washington on sabbatical from an Australian university for further research to turn my dissertation on World War II into a book. There, in the National Archives, I tracked down some long forgotten US Army files that revealed just how fraudulent Marcos's tales of wartime heroism really were. Those revelations made it onto the front pages of the *New York Times* and the *Philippine Daily Inquirer* just two weeks before that historic election.[21]

Then, after a million Filipinos assembled on the streets of Manila to force Marcos into exile, I found myself back in the Philippines as a consultant for an HBO television miniseries on that event, and soon discovered that this mass uprising had, in fact, been sparked by an abortive military coup, influenced in part by the CIA's invisible hand.

It was a remarkable story, revealing to me another dimension of the covert power of the United States. Just weeks after Marcos won reelection through massive fraud in February 1986, his defense minister and a group of dissident colonels met in secret to set the date for a military coup. Only a few days later, two of these colonels received an urgent call from a US military attaché, Major Victor Raphael—a friend of the rebel officers and, they believed, the resident agent of the Defense Intelligence Agency. According to the colonels, Raphael had a message "from the highest level of the U.S. government," telling them, first, that it "will not recognize nor look kindly on any unconstitutional move. Two, in case you have to make moves along the line of enlightened self-defense, the U.S. will understand it." So, the rebel colonels persisted in their plans, interpreting his message simply as the Americans "betting on all the horses." Indeed, just before their projected coup, the chief of the CIA's Manila station, Norbert Garrett, warned Marcos's security officer, General Fabian Ver, to strengthen the presidential palace's defenses against a possible coup. Within hours, the palace guard went on full alert. The colonels' coup plot was blown, but the way was opened for that mass uprising labeled "people power."[22]

Listening to the colonels' tale of US double-dealing, I was impressed by the way the CIA had calibrated its every move to minimize the violence and maximize American influence, whatever the outcome. I had also gained firsthand a sense of how the agency controlled US surrogates in those Cold War years through covert operations, thereby maintaining Washington's dominion over half the globe.

As for Major Raphael, after I published his name in the Manila press, he was soon sent home amid accusations that he was now supporting rebel officers conspiring to overthrow the new democratic government. Twenty years later in 2006, I sat opposite Victor Raphael, then a senior analyst for the State Department's Bureau of Intelligence and Research, during a daylong briefing for the outgoing US ambassador to Manila. With protocol dictating best behavior on both sides of the table, neither of us acknowledged our shared past.

But there was also something a bit unsettling about those Filipino colonels who had been so open to being interviewed by me. The international press had lionized them as heroes in the overthrow of a brutal dictator. Maybe it was the tank of pet piranhas outside one colonel's office, or another's obsessive repetition of the word *blood*, but something about them sent me off on a yearlong search for their service records. What I found was that most of them had not served as line or staff officers. Most had worked in internal security, interrogating and, I discovered, torturing suspected anti-Marcos dissidents, thanks in part to some rather sophisticated US torture training.

While they launched another half-dozen coups over the next decade, I tracked down their victims and learned something of the transactional nature of the torture relationship: the victims suffered devastating psychological damage, but their interrogators, in almost equal measure, were empowered, their egos inflated beyond all imagining by their years breaking priests and professors for Marcos. Having shed their roles as uniformed servants of the state, they would, like latter-day Nietzchean supermen, now be its master.

These findings won an attentive audience in the Philippines. In America, however, the Cold War and its controversies about torture were over, limiting the audience for the book-length study I published in 1999.[23] Further research uncovered striking similarities between Philippine torture techniques and those used in Latin America, indicating the CIA had been training allied agencies in those skills worldwide. But my paper reporting these findings aroused little interest a year later at an international human rights conference in Capetown, where activists from Asia, Africa, and Latin America were focused on bringing their own perpetrators to justice. I must admit, though, that I was relieved to set the study of that sordid subject aside and move on to other topics.

In April 2004, however, CBS broadcast those disturbing photos of US soldiers abusing Iraqi detainees at Abu Ghraib prison, forcing me to resume this troubling work. Looking at the now-infamous photo of a hooded Iraqi prisoner standing on a box, electrical wires hanging from his arms, I could see quite clearly the basic tenets of the CIA's psychological torture doctrine of the Cold War era: the hood was for sensory deprivation and the arms were outstretched to cause self-inflicted pain. Just a few days later, I wrote in the *Boston Globe*: "The photos from Iraq's Abu Ghraib prison are snapshots not of simple brutality or a breakdown in discipline but of CIA torture techniques that have metastasized over the past 50 years like an undetected cancer inside the U.S. intelligence community. From 1950 to 1962, the CIA led secret research into coercion and consciousness that . . . produced a new method of torture that was psychological, not physical—best described as 'no touch' torture."[24]

I might be done with torture, but torture was not yet done with me. So I ended up writing a new book, *A Question of Torture*, about the CIA's central role in propagating such psychological techniques globally.[25] At the time, the

Bush administration was releasing a succession of official reports blaming the army's lowly "bad apples" for Abu Ghraib. My controversial interpretation would not be corroborated until December 2014 when the Senate Intelligence Committee finally released a report finding the CIA responsible for serious and systemic torture. At a cost of several thousand dollars for a research assistant, my historical approach had revealed a fifty-year trail of institutional continuity that led to the post-9/11 psychological torture at Abu Ghraib and elsewhere. A decade later, the Senate committee would spend $40 million to review six million pages of classified CIA documents and reach similar, albeit more detailed and definitive conclusions.[26]

While the painful US debate over torture was running its course, my work on the Philippine security services was moving from the army to the police, from external defense to internal security, focusing on the role of surveillance. Reviewing documents from the American pacification of the Philippines after 1898, I made an unexpected discovery: to defeat a determined Filipino resistance, the United States formed what was arguably the world's first surveillance state. As described in my book *Policing America's Empire*, the commander of army intelligence at Manila circa 1900, Captain Ralph Van Deman, later applied lessons learned from pacifying the Philippines to establishing this country's first internal security agency during World War I, making him "the father of U.S. Military Intelligence."[27]

After he retired at the rank of major general in 1929, Van Deman compiled a quarter million files on suspected subversives that he shared with the military, the FBI, and conservative Republicans—including Richard Nixon, who used this "intelligence" to smear rivals in his California congressional campaigns. Van Deman also represented the army at a closed-door conference in 1940 that gave the FBI control over all US counterintelligence, launching J. Edgar Hoover's thirty-year attempt to extirpate subversion, real and imagined, through pervasive surveillance and illegal agent provocateur operations involving blackmail, disinformation, and violence.[28]

Although memory of the FBI's excesses had largely been washed away by the wave of reforms that followed the war in Vietnam, the terror attacks of September 2001 sparked a "Global War on Terror" that allowed the National Security Agency (NSA) to launch renewed surveillance on a previously unimaginable scale. Writing for the online journal *TomDispatch* in November 2009, I observed that once again coercive methods tested at the periphery of US power were being repatriated to build "a technological template that could be just a few tweaks away from creating a domestic surveillance state."

Just as the Philippine pacification of 1898 had created methods for domestic surveillance during World War I, so sophisticated biometric and cyber techniques forged in the war zones of Afghanistan and Iraq were now making a "digital surveillance state a reality, changing fundamentally the character of American democracy."[29]

Four years later, Edward Snowden's leak of secret NSA documents revealed those "few tweaks" had, in fact, been more than tweaked and the US digital surveillance state, after a century-long gestation, had finally arrived. During World War I, General Van Deman's legion of 1,700 soldiers and 350,000 citizen-vigilantes had conducted an intense shoe-leather surveillance of suspected enemy spies among German Americans (including my grandfather, breaking into his military locker to steal "suspicious" letters his mother had written in her native German about knitting him socks for guard duty). In the 1950s, Hoover's FBI agents tapped several thousand phones and kept suspected subversives under close surveillance, just as they did my mother's cousin Gerard Piel, an antinuclear activist and the publisher of *Scientific American* magazine. Now in the Internet age, the NSA could monitor tens of millions of private lives worldwide through a few hundred computerized probes into the global grid of fiber-optic cables.

Such surveillance was by no means benign. My own writing on sensitive topics like torture and surveillance earned me, in 2013 alone, another IRS audit, TSA body searches at national airports, and, as I discovered when the line went dead, a tap on my telephone at the University of Wisconsin–Madison. If my family's experience across the span of three generations is in any way representative, state surveillance has been an integral part of American political life far longer than we might imagine. Beyond our borders, Washington's worldwide surveillance has become, at the cost of personal privacy, a weapon of exceptional power in a bid to extend US global hegemony far deeper into the twenty-first century.

After decades of thinking about specific aspects of American power, I was finally ready to consider the larger system that encompassed them all, to explore a distinctive form of empire—the US global presence. With the end of the Cold War in 1991, the term *empire* suddenly lost its subversive taint, though most historians of American foreign policy remained indoctrinated into denial. So the initial exploration of this country as an empire was largely conducted, in the early 1990s, not by the academy's many diplomatic historians but instead by a smaller number of literary scholars who specialized in cultural or postcolonial studies.[30] Then, in the aftermath of the 2001 terror attacks and the 2003 invasion of Iraq, policy specialists across the political spectrum embraced the concept of empire to ask whether or not US global power was in decline. But there was still little history, particularly comparative history, of the nature of this imperial power. At the peak moment of its global dominion, history's most powerful empire, now commonly called the planet's "sole superpower," was arguably its least studied.

To address this disparity, some colleagues at the University of Wisconsin–Madison, where a critical perspective had survived the Cold War, launched a project on "Empires in Transition" meant to incorporate America into the comparative history of world empires. Starting in 2004, our small group quickly grew into a network of 140 scholars on four continents who participated in a series of international conferences and published two essay collections bookending the rise and decline of US global power.[31]

To sum up America's rise to world power over the past 120 years, imagine three distinct phases precipitated by those endless wars: first, following the Spanish-American War, a brief yet transformative experience with colonial rule in the Caribbean and the Pacific from 1898 to 1935; next, a sudden ascent to global dominion in the decades after World War II; and, finally, a bid to extend that hegemony deep into the twenty-first century through a fusion of cyberwar, space warfare, trade pacts, and military alliances. In the century from the Spanish-American War to the end of the Cold War, Washington had developed a distinctive form of global governance that incorporated aspects of antecedent empires, ancient and modern. This unique US imperium was Athenian in its ability to forge coalitions among allies; Roman in its reliance on legions that occupied military bases across most of the known world; and British in its aspiration to merge culture, commerce, and alliances into a comprehensive system that covered the globe.

With that system came a restless, relentless quest for technological innovation that lent it a distinctive dimension. Not only did Washington strive for military superiority in the three conventional domains of air, land, and sea, but its fusion of science and industry opened new arenas for the exercise of global dominion. During the Cold War, the US intelligence community, led by the CIA and the NSA, became a supple, sophisticated instrument for projecting power on a global scale. The CIA's attempt to penetrate communist states failed abysmally in China, Russia, and Vietnam, but the agency proved far more skilled in manipulating allies on Washington's side of the Iron Curtain through coups and covert interventions, particularly among the myriad of new nations that emerged in Asia and Africa amid the collapse of the last of the European empires. By the end of the Cold War, clandestine operations had thus become such a critical instrument for power projection that they made up a new, fourth domain of warfare I call the covert netherworld.

During those years as well, Washington also competed in the "space race" with the Soviet Union in ways that, through the world's first system of global telecommunications satellites, added another novel dimension to its global power. In the decades that followed, Washington would militarize the stratosphere and exosphere through an armada of unmanned drones, making space a fifth domain for great power expansion and future potential conflict.

Finally, thanks to the web of fiber-optic cables woven around the globe for the Internet, the NSA was able to shift its focus from signals intercepts in the sky to probing those cables beneath the sea for surveillance and cyberwar. In this way, cyberspace became the newest domain for military conflict. At the dawn of the twenty-first century, Washington's bid for what it termed "full-spectrum dominance" across all six domains of warfare—both conventional (air, land, sea) and clandestine (aerospace, cyberspace, covert netherworld)—gave it a national security state of potentially exceptional strength with which to maintain its global power, despite fading economic influence, for decades to come.

The "American Century" that publisher Henry Luce had proclaimed in a *Life* magazine editorial in February 1941 seemed certain, until quite recently, to reach its full centennial. "As America enters dynamically upon the world scene," Luce wrote on the eve of World War II, "we need most of all to seek and to bring forth a vision of America as a world power which is authentically American and which can inspire us to live and work and fight with vigor and enthusiasm."[32] For the next fifty years, the United States had fulfilled those aspirations, ruling over much of the world outside the Iron Curtain with a distinctive mix of cultural attraction and covert manipulation, supple diplomacy and raw force, and generous aid and grasping profits.

After the Soviet Union imploded in the early 1990s, there seemed no power on the planet that could challenge Washington's dominion. With the country standing astride the globe like an indomitable titan and no credible challenge on the horizon, Washington's policy gurus imagined that the "end of history" had arrived, making American-style democracy "the final form of human government."[33] Yet only a decade later, that portentous "end of history" had been swept away and history was back with a vengeance. Washington found itself in a period of imperial transition like those that had spelled the end of earlier empires in centuries past. Suddenly, we could see the shape of a new great power conflict between Washington and Beijing that could deter-mine the course of this still young twenty-first century.

With the shock of the 9/11 terror attacks and the subsequent slide into the military miasma of Afghanistan and Iraq, there was a growing sense that America's global power had reached its limits. In a detailed 2012 report, the National Intelligence Council, Washington's supreme analytic body, warned: "By 2030, no country . . . will be a hegemonic power . . . largely reversing the historic rise of the West since 1750. Asia will have surpassed North Ameri-ca and Europe combined in terms of global power, based on GDP, popula-tion size, military spending, and technological investment. China alone will probably have the largest economy, surpassing that of the United States a few years before 2030."[34] If this prediction proves correct, then many of my baby boom generation, born at the start of the American Century, will likely be around to witness its end.

After two decades of extraordinary economic growth, in 2014 China started to reveal its strategy for challenging Washington's hegemony. Its plans included making massive infrastructure investments that would bind Europe and Asia into a "world island," the future epicenter of global economic power, while building military bases in the South China Sea that would sever US military encirclement of the sprawling Eurasian landmass. Refusing to cede its global dominion, the Pentagon responded to China's challenge by shifting some strategic assets to Asia and by launching new "wonder weapons" meant to check any rival power.[35]

Countless unforeseen factors can, of course, subvert these grand strate-gies. Any number of powerful new forces can suddenly change the trajectory of world history. Projecting present trends into the future is perilously close to a fool's errand. No methodology can possibly encompass the many mov-ing parts of a world empire, much less the ever-changing interactions among several of these behemoths.[36]

Still, in the first decade and a half of this century, a few key trends al-ready seem clear enough. While the United States enjoyed strong national unity and a bipartisan foreign policy during the first half century of its glob-al dominion, it now faces the challenge of maintaining stability in a time of deepening social divisions, exacerbated by the slow waning of its world power. In the quarter century since the end of the Cold War, the old bipar-tisan consensus over foreign policy has given way to entrenched partisan divisions. While Democrats Bill Clinton and Barack Obama tried to main-tain Washington's world leadership through multilateralism and diplomacy,

Republicans George W. Bush and Donald Trump have, in a patriotic reaction against a perceived loss of stature, favored unilateral action and military solutions. This conflict whipsaws the country's foreign policy in contradictory directions, alienating allies and accelerating the decline of its power.

We are undoubtedly at the start of a major transition away from untrammeled US hegemony. If the National Intelligence Council is to be believed, then the American Century, proclaimed with such boundless optimism back in 1941, will be ending well before 2041. After a quarter century as the world's sole superpower, Washington now faces an adversary with both the means and determination to mount a sustained challenge to its dominion. Even if Beijing falters, thanks to a decline in economic growth or a surge in popular discontent, there are still a dozen rising powers working to build a multipolar world beyond the grasp of any global hegemon.

As the patterns of world power shift in the decades to come, we will learn whether this imperial transition will be similar to any of the epochal events of the past two centuries—the global war that defeated Napoleon's First French Empire in the early nineteenth century, the diplomacy that broke up the Austro-Hungarian and Ottoman empires after World War I, the tempest that crushed the Axis empires during World War II, the quiet entente that marked the imperial handover from London to Washington in the 1950s, or the mass protests that shattered the Soviet Empire in the 1990s.

Whether by slow erosion or violent eruption, this ongoing shift in the balance of power bears watching. From everything I have learned over the past fifty years, we can count on one thing: this transition will be transformative, even traumatically so, impacting the lives of almost every American. In the years to come, these changes will certainly demand our close and careful attention.

PART I
Understanding the US Empire

Chapter One

The World Island and the Rise of America

For even the greatest of empires, geography is often destiny. You wouldn't know it in Washington, though. America's political, national security, and foreign policy elites continue to ignore the basics of geopolitics that have shaped the fate of world empires for the past five hundred years. As a result, they have missed the significance of the rapid global changes in Eurasia that are in the process of undermining the grand strategy for world dominion that Washington has pursued these past seven decades.

A glance at what passes for insider "wisdom" in Washington reveals a worldview of stunning insularity. As an example, take Harvard political scientist Joseph Nye Jr., known for his concept of "soft power." Offering a simple list of ways in which he believes US military, economic, and cultural power remains singular and superior, he argued in 2015 that there is no force, internal or global, capable of eclipsing America's future as the world's premier power. For those pointing to Beijing's surging economy and proclaiming this "the Chinese century," Nye offered up a roster of negatives: China's per capita income "will take decades to catch up (if ever)" with America's; it has myopically "focused its policies primarily on its region"; and it has "not developed any significant capabilities for global force projection." Above all, Nye claimed, China suffers "geopolitical disadvantages in the internal Asian balance of power, compared to America." Or put it this way (and in this Nye is typical of a whole world of Washington thinking): with more allies, ships, fighters, missiles, money, and blockbuster movies than any other power, Washington wins. Hands down.[1]

If Nye paints power by the numbers, former secretary of state and national security adviser Henry Kissinger's latest tome, modestly titled *World*

27

Order and hailed in reviews as nothing less than a revelation, adopts a Nietzschean perspective. The ageless Kissinger portrays global politics as highly susceptible to shaping by great leaders with a will to power. By this measure, in the tradition of master European diplomats Charles de Talleyrand and Prince Metternich, President Theodore Roosevelt was a bold visionary who launched "an American role in managing the Asia-Pacific equilibrium." On the other hand, Woodrow Wilson's idealistic dream of national self-determination rendered him geopolitically inept, just as Franklin Roosevelt's vision of a humane world blinded him to Stalin's steely "global strategy." Harry Truman, in contrast, overcame national ambivalence to commit "America to the shaping of a new international order," a policy wisely followed by the next twelve presidents. Among the most "courageous" of them was that leader of "dignity and conviction," George W. Bush, whose resolute bid for the "transformation of Iraq from among the Middle East's most repressive states to a multiparty democracy" would have succeeded, had it not been for the "ruthless" subversion of his work by Syria and Iran. In such a view, geopolitics has no place. Diplomacy is the work solely of "statesmen"—whether kings, presidents, or prime ministers.[2]

And perhaps that's a comforting perspective in Washington at a moment when America's hegemony is visibly crumbling amid a tectonic shift in global power. With its anointed seers remarkably obtuse on the subject of global political power, perhaps it's time to get back to basics, to return, that is, to the foundational text of modern geopolitics, which remains an indispensable guide even though it was published in an obscure British geography journal well over a century ago.

Halford Mackinder Invents Geopolitics

On a cold London evening in January 1904, Halford Mackinder, the director of the London School of Economics, "entranced" an audience at the Royal Geographical Society on Savile Row with a paper boldly titled "The Geographical Pivot of History." His talk evinced, said the society's president, "a brilliancy of description . . . we have seldom had equaled in this room."[3]

Mackinder argued that the future of global power lay not, as most British then imagined, in controlling the planet's sea lanes but instead inside a vast landmass he called "Euro-Asia." He presented Africa, Asia, and Europe not as three separate continents, but as a unitary landform, a veritable "world island." Its broad, deep "heartland"—4,000 miles from the Persian Gulf to the

Siberian Sea—was so vast that it could only be controlled from its "rimlands" in Eastern Europe or what he called its maritime "marginal" in the surrounding seas.[4]

The "discovery of the Cape road to the Indies" around Africa in the sixteenth century, Mackinder explained, "endowed Christendom with the widest possible mobility of power . . . wrapping her influence round the Euro-Asiatic land-power which had hitherto threatened her very existence."[5] This greater mobility, he later explained, gave Europe's seamen "superiority for some four centuries over the landsmen of Africa and Asia."[6]

Yet the "heartland" of this vast landmass, a "pivot area" stretching from the Persian Gulf across Russia's vast steppes and Siberian forests, remained nothing less than the Archimedean fulcrum for future world power. "Who rules the Heartland commands the World-Island," Mackinder later wrote. "Who rules the World-Island commands the world." Beyond the vast mass of that island, which made up nearly 60 percent of the Earth's landmass, lay a less consequential hemisphere covered with broad oceans and a few outlying "smaller islands." He meant, of course, Australia, Greenland, and the Americas.[7]

For an earlier generation of the Victorian age, the opening of the Suez Canal and the advent of steam shipping had, he said, "increased the mobility of sea-power relatively to land power." But now railways could "work the greater wonder in the steppe"—a reference to a historic event that everyone in his audience that night knew well: the relentless advance of the Trans-Siberian Railroad's track from Moscow toward Vladivostok and the Pacific Ocean. Such transcontinental railroads would, he believed, eventually undercut the cost of sea transport and shift the locus of geopolitical power inland. In the fullness of time, the "pivot state" of Russia might, in alliance with another land power like Germany, expand "over the marginal lands of Euro-Asia," allowing "the use of vast continental resources for fleet-building, and the empire of the world would be in sight."[8]

For the next two hours, as he read through a text thick with the convoluted syntax and classical references expected of a former Oxford don, his audience knew that they were privy to something extraordinary. Several stayed after his talk to offer extended commentaries. The renowned military analyst Spenser Wilkinson, the first to hold a chair in military history at Oxford, pronounced himself unconvinced about "the modern expansion of Russia," insisting that British and Japanese naval power would continue the historic function of holding "the balance between the divided forces . . . on the continental area."[9]

Pressed by his learned listeners to consider other facts or factors, including the newly invented "air as a means of locomotion," Mackinder responded: "My aim is not to predict a great future for this or that country, but to make a geographical formula into which you could fit any political balance." Instead of specific events, Mackinder was reaching for a general theory about the causal connection between geography and global power. "The future of the world," he insisted, "depends on the maintenance of [a] balance of power" between sea powers such as Britain or Japan operating from the maritime marginal and "the expansive internal forces" within the Euro-Asian heartland they were intent on containing.[10]

For publication in the *Geographical Journal* later that year, Mackinder redrew and even reconceptualized the world map by turning the globe toward Eurasia and then tilting it northward a bit beyond Mercator's equatorial projection. Not only did this rendering show Africa, Asia, and Europe as that massive, unitary "world island," but it also shrank Greenland and the Americas into inconsequential marginalia.[11] For Europeans, used to projections that placed their continent at the world's center, Mackinder's map was an innovation; but for Americans, whose big, brightly colored schoolroom maps fostered an illusory sense of their hemisphere's centrality by splitting the Eurasian landmass into two lesser blobs, it should have been a revelation.[12]

Apart from articulating a worldview that would influence Britain's foreign policy for several decades, Mackinder also created, in that single, semi-

MACKINDER'S WORLD ISLAND
THE NATURAL SEATS OF POWER, 1904

nal lecture, the modern science of "geopolitics"—the study of how geography can, under certain circumstances, shape the destiny of whole peoples, nations, and empires.[13]

That night in London was, of course, more than a hundred years ago. It was another age. England was still mourning the death of Queen Victoria. Teddy Roosevelt was America's president. The bloody, protracted American pacification of its Philippine colony was finally winding down. Henry Ford had just opened a small auto plant in Detroit to make his Model A, an automobile with a top speed of twenty-eight miles per hour. Only a month earlier, the Wright brothers' *Flyer* had taken to the air for the first time—120 feet of air, to be exact.

Yet, for the next 110 years, Sir Halford Mackinder's words would offer a prism of exceptional precision when it came to understanding the often obscure geopolitics driving the world's major conflicts—two world wars, a Cold War, America's Asian wars (Korea and Vietnam), two Persian Gulf wars, and even the endless pacification of Afghanistan. The question we now need to consider is this: How can Mackinder help us understand not only centuries past but also the half century still to come?

Britannia Rules the Waves

In the age of sea power that lasted just over four hundred years—from Portugal's conquest of Malacca in 1511 to the Washington Disarmament Conference of 1922—the great powers competed to control the Eurasian world island via the sea lanes that stretched for 15,000 miles from London to Tokyo. The instrument of power was, of course, the ship—first, caravels and men-of-war, then battleships, submarines, and aircraft carriers. While land armies slogged through the mud of Manchuria or France in battles with mind-numbing casualties, imperial navies skimmed the seas, maneuvering for the control of coasts and continents.

At the peak of its imperial power around 1900, Great Britain ruled the waves with a fleet of three hundred capital ships and thirty naval bastions—fortified bases that ringed the world island from the North Atlantic at Scapa Flow off Scotland through the Mediterranean at Malta and Suez to Bombay, Singapore, and Hong Kong. Just as the Roman Empire had once enclosed the Mediterranean, making it mare nostrum ("our sea"), so British power would make the Indian Ocean its own "closed sea," securing its flanks with army forts along India's North-West Frontier and barring both Persians and Ottomans from building naval bases on the Persian Gulf.

By that maneuver, Britain also secured control over Arabia and Mesopo-
tamia, strategic terrain that Mackinder had termed "the passage-land from
Europe to the Indies" and the gateway to the world island's "heartland." From
this geopolitical perspective, the nineteenth century was, in essence, a strategic rivalry, often called "the Great Game," between Russia "in command of
nearly the whole of the Heartland . . . knocking at the landward gates of the
Indies," and Britain "advancing inland from the sea gates of India to meet the
menace from the northwest." In other words, Mackinder concluded, "the final
geographical realities" of the modern age were land power versus sea power.[14]

Intense rivalries, first between England and France, then England and Germany, helped drive a relentless European naval arms race that raised the price
of sea power to nearly unsustainable levels. In 1805, Admiral Nelson's flagship,
the HMS *Victory*, with its oaken hull weighing just 3,500 tons, sailed into the
battle of Trafalgar against Napoleon's navy at nine knots, its hundred smooth-
bore cannon firing 42-pound balls at a range of no more than 400 yards.

Just a century later in 1906, Britain launched the world's first battleship,
the HMS *Dreadnought*, its foot-thick steel hull weighing 20,000 tons, its
steam turbines allowing speeds of 21 knots, and its mechanized 12-inch guns
rapid-firing 850-pound shells up to 12 miles. The cost for this Leviathan was
£1.8 million, equivalent to nearly $300 million today. Within a decade, half-
a-dozen powers had emptied their treasuries to build whole fleets of these
lethal, lavishly expensive battleships.

Thanks to a combination of technological superiority, global reach, and
naval alliances with the United States and Japan, a Pax Britannica would
last a full century, 1815 to 1914. In the end, however, this global system was
marked by an accelerating naval arms race, volatile great-power diplomacy,
and a bitter competition for overseas empire that imploded into the mindless
slaughter of World War I, leaving sixteen million dead by 1918.

As the eminent imperial historian Paul Kennedy once observed, "The rest
of the twentieth century bore witness to Mackinder's thesis," with two world
wars fought over "rimlands" running from Eastern Europe to East Asia.[15] Indeed, World War I was, as Mackinder himself later observed, "a straight duel
between land-power and sea-power."[16] At war's end in 1918, the sea powers—
Britain, America, and Japan—sent naval expeditions to Arkhangelsk, the Black
Sea, and Siberia to contain Russia's revolution inside its own "heartland."

During World War II, Mackinder's ideas shaped the course of the war
beyond anything he could have imagined. Reflecting Mackinder's influence
on geopolitical thinking in Germany, Adolf Hitler would risk his Reich in a

misbegotten effort to capture the Russian heartland as *lebensraum*, or living space, for his German "master race."

In the interwar years, Sir Halford's work had influenced the ideas of German geographer Karl Haushofer, founder of the journal *Zeitschrift für Geopolitik* and the leading proponent of lebensraum. After retiring from the Bavarian Army as a major general in 1919, Haushofer studied geography with an eye to preventing a recurrence of the strategic blunders that had contributed to Germany's defeat in World War I. Later, he would become a professor at Munich University, an adviser to Adolf Hitler, and a "close collaborator" with deputy führer Rudolf Hess, his former student. Through his forty books, four hundred articles, countless lectures, and frequent meetings with top Nazi officials including Hitler, Haushofer propagated his concept of lebensraum, arguing that "space is not only the vehicle of power . . . it is power." His teaching inspired what an investigator for the Nuremburg war crimes tribunal called "visions of Germany being transformed into an immense continental power and rendered impregnable against the seapower of England." In sum, Haushofer argued that "any power which controlled the Heartland (Russia plus Germany) could control the world." His son Albrecht, a "skilled geopolitican," took these ideas into the heart of the Third Reich as professor of political geography at Berlin University where he also ran "a training school for members of the Nazi diplomatic service."[17]

On the eve of World War II, Karl Haushofer observed that the locus of the continent's land-sea conflict had moved east into the Pacific. "Eurasia is still unorganized and divided—hence America's superiority," he wrote in his *Geopolitics of the Pacific Ocean*. "Eurasia has no unified geopolitics. Meanwhile, both the largest sea space, the Pacific, and the second largest land space, America, are about to encounter and confront it."[18]

In 1942, the führer dispatched a million men, 10,000 artillery pieces, and 500 tanks to breach the Volga River at Stalingrad and capture that Russian heartland for lebensraum. In the end, the Reich's forces suffered 850,000 casualties—killed, wounded, and captured—in a vain attempt to break through the East European rimland into the world island's pivotal region. Appalled by the attack on Russia, Albrecht made peace overtures to Britain, then joined the underground that tried to assassinate Hitler, and was imprisoned after hiding in the Alps. In the months before he was shot by Nazi security on the day the Allies captured Berlin, Albrecht composed mournful, metaphorical sonnets about the fiend of geopolitical power buried deep under the sea until "my father broke the seal" and "set the demon free to roam throughout the world." A few months later, Karl Haushofer and his Jewish wife committed suicide together when confronted with the possibility of his prosecution as a senior Nazi war criminal.[19]

A century after Mackinder's treatise, another British scholar, imperial historian John Darwin, argued in his magisterial survey *After Tamerlane* that the United States had achieved its "colossal Imperium . . . on an unprecedented scale" in the wake of World War II by becoming the first power in history to control the strategic axial points "at both ends of Eurasia." With fear of Chinese and Russian expansion serving as the "catalyst for collaboration," the United States secured sprawling bastions in both Western Europe and Japan. With these axial points as anchors for an arc of military bases around Eurasia, Washington enjoyed a superior geopolitical position to wage the Cold War against China and the Soviet Union.[20]

America's Axial Geopolitics

Having seized the axial ends of the world island from Nazi Germany and Imperial Japan in 1945, the United States would rely for the next seventy years on ever-thickening layers of military power to contain rival hegemons China and Russia inside that continental heartland—enjoying decades of unimpeded access to the trade and resources of five continents and thereby building a global dominion of unprecedented wealth and power. The current emerging conflict between Beijing and Washington is thus, in this sense, just the latest round in a centuries-long struggle for control over the Eurasian landmass between maritime and land powers—Spain versus the Ottomans, Britain versus Russia, and, more recently, the United States versus the Third Reich and then the Soviet Union.

Indeed, in 1943, two years before World War II ended, an aging Mackinder published his last article, "The Round World and the Winning of the Peace," in the influential US journal *Foreign Affairs.* He reminded Americans aspiring to a "grand strategy" that even their "dream of a global air power" would not change the world's geopolitical fundamentals. "If the Soviet Union emerges from this war as conqueror of Germany," he warned, "she must rank as the greatest land Power on the globe," controlling the "greatest natural fortress on earth."[21]

Mindful of these geopolitics, the US War Department in Washington was already planning its postwar position along the Pacific littoral in ways that would correct the defensive conundrum that had dogged Washington for decades. Inspired by the naval strategist Alfred Mahan who, as early as 1890, imagined the United States as a Pacific power, Washington had established military bases in the Philippines as anchors for an expanded defensive perimeter that would stretch from Cuba through the Panama Canal to Pearl Harbor and all the way to Manila Bay. At the end of World War I, however, the Versailles peace settlement conceded the Marianas and Micronesia to Tokyo. Suddenly, the Japanese navy was in a mid-Pacific blocking position, rendering the American defense of the Philippines a strategic impossibility. That geopolitical reality doomed General Douglas MacArthur's army to a humiliating defeat in the Battle of Bataan at the start of World War II.[22]

As bomber ranges increased from 1,100 miles for the B-17 at war's start to 3,200 for the B-29 by war's end, the War Department in Washington decided, in 1943, to coordinate its wartime liberation of the Philippines with postwar plans for two strategic bomber wings, the "Luzon Bomber Striking Force" and the "Mindanao Bomber Striking Force," protected by twenty-six air, land, and sea bases that would ring the entire archipelago. Fearing the loss of US military protection and desperate for reconstruction aid, in 1947 Manila gave the United States a ninety-nine-year lease on twenty-three installations with unrestricted use for offensive operations.[23]

To clamp a vice-grip of control over the vastness of Eurasia, these Philippine bases, along with dozens more along the length of Japan, became bastions for securing the eastern end of this sprawling landmass, while US forces in Europe occupied the continent's western axial point. With offshore military bases stretching for two thousand miles from Japan through Okinawa to the Philippines, Washington made the Pacific littoral its geopolitical fulcrum for the defense of one continent (North America) and the control over another (Eurasia).[24]

When it came to the establishment of a new postwar Pax Americana, first and foundational for the containment of Soviet land power would be the US Navy. Its fleets would come to surround the Eurasian continent, supplementing and then supplanting the British: the Sixth Fleet based at Naples in 1946 for the Atlantic and the Mediterranean; the Seventh Fleet at Subic Bay, Philippines, in 1947 for the Western Pacific; and the Fifth Fleet at Bahrain in the Persian Gulf since 1995.[25]

Next, American diplomats added a layer of encircling military alliances— from the North Atlantic Treaty Organization (NATO, 1949) and the Middle East Treaty Organization (1955), all the way to the Southeast Asia Treaty Organization (SEATO, 1954). NATO proved the most robust of these alliances, growing eventually to twenty-eight member nations and thereby providing a firm foundation for the US military position in Europe. By contrast, SEATO had only eight members, including just two from Southeast Asia, and quickly collapsed after the war in Vietnam. Absent a strong multilateral pact for Asia, Washington's position along the Pacific littoral rested on four bilateral alliances—the ANZUS Treaty with Australia and New Zealand (1951), the Philippines Mutual Defense Treaty (1951), the US-Japan Security Treaty (1951), and the US–Republic of Korea Mutual Defense Treaty (1953).

To anchor its geopolitical position, Washington also built massive air and naval bastions at the axial antipodes of the world island—notably at Ramstein Air Base in Germany, Subic Bay Naval Station, and multiple locations in Japan. For five years until its completion in 1952, Ramstein was the largest construction site in Europe, employing 270,000 workers.[26] Starting in 1952, the navy spent $170 million on a home port for its Seventh Fleet at Subic Bay—building a massive wharf for aircraft carriers, runways for a busy naval air station, and a sprawling ship repair facility that employed 15,000 Filipino workers. As home to the Thirteenth Air Force, nearby Clark Field had capacity for two hundred fighters and a bombing range bigger than the District of Columbia.[27]

During its postwar occupation of Japan, the United States acquired more than a hundred military facilities—largely by occupying and rebuilding imperial installations—that stretched from Misawa Air Base in the north, through Yokota Air Base and Yokosuka Naval Base in the center near Tokyo, to the Marine Air Station Iwakuni and Sasebo Naval Base in the south. With its strategic location, Okinawa had the largest concentration of American forces, with thirty-two active installations covering about 20 percent of the entire island. By 1955, the United States also had a global network of 450 military bases in thirty-six countries aimed, in large part, at containing the Sino-Soviet bloc behind an Iron Curtain that coincided to a surprising degree with Mackinder's "rimlands" around the Eurasian landmass.[28]

After Soviet challenges to US control of these axial antipodes were blocked by a hot war in South Korea (1953) and a near-war in Berlin (1961), the conflict shifted to the continent's rugged southern tier stretching for five thousand miles, from the eastern Mediterranean to the South China Sea. There the Cold War's bloodiest battles were fought in the passageways around the massive Himalayan barrier, six miles high and two thousand miles wide—first in the east in Laos and Vietnam (1961–75) and then west ward in Afghanistan (1978–92). With its vast oil reserves, the Persian Gulf region became the fulcrum for Washington's position on the world island, serving for nearly forty years as the main site of its overt and covert interventions. The 1979 revolution in Iran signaled loss of its keystone position in the Gulf, leaving Washington flailing about ever since to rebuild its geopolitical leverage in the region. In the process, it would, during the Reagan years of the 1980s, simultaneously back Saddam Hussein's Iraq against revolutionary Iran and arm the most extreme of the Afghan mujahedeen against the Soviet occupation of Afghanistan.

It was in this context that Zbigniew Brzezinski, national security adviser to President Jimmy Carter, unleashed his strategy for the defeat of the Soviet Union with a geopolitical agility still little understood today. In 1979, Brzezinski, an émigré Polish aristocrat who had studied and frequently cited Mackinder, persuaded Carter to launch Operation Cyclone with funding that reached $500 million annually by the late 1980s.[29] Its goal: to mobilize Muslim militants to attack the Soviet Union's soft Central Asian underbelly and drive a wedge of radical Islam deep into the Soviet heartland, inflicting a demoralizing defeat on the Red Army in Afghanistan and simultaneously helping to cut Eastern Europe's rimland free from Moscow's orbit. "We didn't push the Russians to intervene [in Afghanistan]," Brzezinski said in 1998, explaining his geopolitical masterstroke in the Cold War edition of the Great Game, "but we knowingly increased the probability that they would. . . . That secret operation was an excellent idea. Its effect was to draw the Russians into the Afghan trap."[30]

Even America's stunning victory in the Cold War could not change the geopolitical fundamentals of the world island. Consequently, after the fall of the Berlin Wall in 1989, Washington's first foreign foray of the new era would involve an attempt to reestablish its dominant position in the Persian Gulf, using Saddam Hussein's occupation of Kuwait as its pretext.

In 2003, when the United States invaded Iraq, historian Paul Kennedy returned to Mackinder's century-old treatise to explain this seemingly inexplicable misadventure. "Right now, with hundreds of thousands of U.S. troops in the Eurasian rimlands," Kennedy wrote, "it looks as if Washington is taking seriously Mackinder's injunction to ensure control of 'the geographical pivot of history.'"[31] Within a decade, however, this intervention wound up looking less like a bold geopolitical gambit and more like Germany's disastrous decision to attack the Russian heartland. The subsequent proliferation of US bases across Afghanistan and Iraq was visibly the latest imperial bid for a pivotal position at the edge of the Eurasian heartland, akin to those British colonial forts along India's North-West Frontier.

In the ensuing years, Washington would attempt to replace some of its ineffective boots on the ground with drones in the air. By 2011, the air force and CIA had ringed the Eurasian landmass with sixty bases for their armada of drones. By then, the workhorse Reaper drone, armed with Hellfire missiles and GBU-30 bombs, had a range of 1,150 miles, which meant that from those bases it could strike targets almost anywhere in Africa or Asia.[32] To patrol this sweeping periphery, the Pentagon has also spent $10 billion to build an armada of ninety-nine Global Hawk drones with high-resolution cameras and a range of 8,700 miles.[33]

As it moved to a more agile global posture of smaller, scattered bases and drone strikes, Washington remained determined to maintain its axial positions at both ends of the Eurasian landmass. Although responding minimally to Russian incursions into Ukraine, the Obama administration reacted strongly to its stepped-up submarine presence in the North Atlantic. As Moscow's revitalized fleet of forty-five attack submarines extended their patrols well beyond the Arctic Circle, Washington allocated $8.1 billion to upgrade its "undersea capabilities," reopening a base in Iceland and adding nine new Virginia-class submarines to an existing fleet of fifty-three. "We're back to great powers competition," announced Admiral John M. Richardson, chief of naval operations.[34] During his two terms in office, Obama also launched what was to be a protracted geopolitical pivot, from the Middle East to the Asian littoral through expanded bases and strategic forces, all aimed at checking China's rise and its attempt to hobble Washington's strategic position at the edge of Asia.

Decades of Debate over US Empire

Yet even as America faced the first real challenge to its hegemony in a quarter century, most Americans seemed somehow oblivious. During the endless debates of the yearlong 2016 presidential campaign, there was much criticism of trade pacts and some mention of the Middle East but surprisingly little discussion of the United States' position in Asia or the wider world. Unmindful of the strategic significance of the alliances that long anchored America's geopolitical position in Eurasia, Republican candidate Donald Trump wooed voters by insisting repeatedly that Tokyo should "pay 100 percent" of the costs for basing American troops in Japan and suggesting he would defend NATO allies against Russian attack only "if they fulfill their obligations to us" by putting up "more money."[35] The historian William Appleman Williams once identified such self-referential myopia as the country's "grand illusion," the "charming belief that the United States could reap the rewards of empire without paying the costs of empire and without admitting that it was an empire."[36]

This profound, persistent ambiguity about empire among Americans was not only evident during the Cold War when Williams was writing, but dates back to the 1890s when the United States first stepped on to the world stage. For well over a century, Americans have expressed significant reservations about their nation's rise to world power. Throughout the ever-changing crosscurrents of the country's politics, generations of citizens in what was becoming history's greatest empire would remain deeply conflicted over the exercise of power beyond their borders.

As the Spanish-American War of 1898 segued from military triumph into a bloody pacification of the Philippines, the Anti-Imperialist League attracted leading intellectuals who offered a withering critique of this imperial adventure. The issue of whether or not to expand loomed large in the presidential election of 1900. The most beloved writer of his generation, Mark Twain, charged that the conquest of the Philippines had "debauched America's honor and blackened her face before the world," and suggested the flag, Old Glory, should be modified with "white stripes painted black and the stars replaced by the skull and cross-bones."[37] Similarly, eminent Yale sociologist William Graham Sumner warned that "the inevitable effect of imperialism on democracy" was to "lessen liberty and require discipline. It will . . . necessitate stronger and more elaborate governmental machinery" and increase "militarism."[38]

A century later, influential Americans were still worried about empire, though less about the costs of conquest than the consequences of its loss. Speaking before Congress in 2010 in the midst of a searing economic crisis, President Barack Obama warned of serious challenges to America's global power. "China is not waiting to revamp its economy. Germany is not waiting. India is not waiting. . . . These nations aren't playing for second place." Then, in a rhetorical flourish that brought thunderous bipartisan applause, he announced, "Well, I do not accept second place for the United States of America."[39] Reprising that theme a few days later, Vice President Joe Biden rejected any comparison with fallen European empires, insisting, "We will continue to be the most significant and dominant influence in the world as long as our economy is strong."[40]

As commentators cited imperial analogies, usually with Rome or Britain, to warn against America's retreat from its global "responsibilities,"[41] neoconservative historian Robert Kagan argued in an influential essay that with its unrivaled military, diplomatic, and economic clout, the United States "is not remotely like Britain circa 1900 when that empire's relative decline began." America alone, he insisted, can decide whether its world power will "decline over the next two decades or not for another two centuries."[42]

Clearly, the word *empire* is a fraught one in the American political lexicon. So it is necessary to be precise at the outset: empire is not an epithet but a form of global governance in which a dominant power exercises control over the destiny of others, either through direct territorial rule (colonies) or indirect influence (military, economic, and cultural). Empire, bloc, commonwealth, or world order—they all reflect an expression of power that has persisted for much of the past four thousand years and is likely to continue into the foreseeable future. Many empires have been brutal, some more beneficent, and most a mix of both. But empires are an undeniable, unchanging fact of human history. After counting seventy empires in that history, Harvard historian Niall Fergusson noted wryly: "To those who would still insist on American 'exceptionalism,' the historian of empires can only retort: as exceptional as all the other sixty-nine empires."[43]

Indeed, for a full half century, historians of US foreign relations subscribed strongly, almost universally, to a belief in "American exceptionalism"—the idea that this country in its beneficence was uniquely exempt from the curse of empire. During the Cold War's ideological clash with communism, an influential group of "consensus" historians argued that the United States had avoided Europe's class conflicts, authoritarian governments, and empires, becoming instead "an example of liberty for others to emulate."[44] To explain away his country's brief dalliance with colonial rule after 1898, the dean of diplomatic historians, Richard W. Leopold, asserted that empire had little lasting impact on the nation because there was no territorial expansion beyond the conquest of a few islands (Puerto Rico and the Philippines); no cabinet-level department for those overseas territories, lending the project an aura of impermanence; and no increase in military spending to defend those otherwise potentially indefensible islands.[45]

There was, however, some notable dissent from this patriotic consensus. During the coldest of the Cold War decades, the 1950s, when pressure for affirmation of America was strong, the Wisconsin school of diplomatic history, led by William Appleman Williams and his colleague Fred Harvey Harrington, offered an unorthodox perspective on Washington's rise to world power. In his famous dissent, *The Tragedy of American Diplomacy*, Williams argued that America's "great debate of 1898–1901 over the proper strategy and tactics of . . . expansion" had forged a political consensus that "opposed traditional colonialism and advocated instead a policy of an open door through which America's preponderant economic strength would . . . dominate all underdeveloped areas of the world." In effect, this "classic strategy of non-colonial imperial expansion . . . became the strategy of American foreign policy for the next half-century," launching Washington on a relentless extension of its informal commercial empire.[46] Such expansion often gave birth to aggression, most importantly against the Soviet Union at the end of World War II when, Williams argued, Washington's concerns over access to Eastern Europe and its markets sparked the Cold War.[47]

Other prominent scholars in the Wisconsin school made influential contributions as well, notably Walter LaFeber in his seminal study of late nineteenth-century expansion, *The New Empire*. There he explored not only the social and economic motives for overseas conquest but also its colonial outcomes in the Caribbean and Pacific.[48] While Williams moved to Oregon for a quieter life at the height of Madison's violent campus protests in 1968, his critique continued to resonate. His students—LaFeber at Cornell, Lloyd Gardner at Rutgers, and Thomas McCormick at Wisconsin—would remain active in the profession for another forty years, collaborating closely to explore America's imperial designs and desires.[49]

Although this revisionist view of the nature of American power won a devoted audience in the Vietnam War years, the Wisconsin school later drew hostile fire from prominent historians. Not only was its critique of Washington's role in the Cold War bitterly attacked but so too was its emphasis on the expansion of US economic power as an imperial phenomenon. Arthur M. Schlesinger Jr., called it "ludicrous" and Ernest R. May, "an artifact of the past."[50]

In the quarter century since the collapse of the Soviet Union, as such patriotic passions subsided, historians and others began to confront the undeniable reality of a global behemoth that transcended past experience. Analysts of US global power, whether critics or advocates, now strained to find appropriate historical models. Some applied the Roman term *imperium*, meaning "dominion enforced by a single power." Others preferred the Greek-inflected *hegemony*, meaning a world order that "rests on consent and cooperation, not exclusively on force and domination," much as ancient Athens had once led a coalition of city-states.[51] Recent opinion, among both pundits and scholars, separates into an imperium school that sees Washington as a latter-day Rome, the command center of a centralized empire; a hegemonic school that views America as Athens, leading a coalition of willing allies; and a conservative coterie who believe that the United States, like Great Britain in its day, should use its awesome military power to defend freedom and civilization.

On the imperium side, the critic Chalmers Johnson argued that "our militarized empire is a physical reality" manifest in over seven hundred overseas military bases that facilitated the global deployment of its armed forces and "a network of economic and political interests."[52] Reviving the Williams critique of open-door imperialism, Andrew J. Bacevich argued that both the Cold War and the war on terror were manifestations of "the American project of creating an open and integrated world."[53]

Using the same concept of empire to celebrate rather than criticize, Niall Fergusson styled the United States as the much-needed successor to Great Britain's "liberal empire," which once used its military power to maintain a world order of free trade and civilized standards.[54] "If the United States retreats from global hegemony," Fergusson warned darkly, the planet might well plunge into "an anarchic new Dark Age; an era of waning empires and religious fanaticism; of endemic plunder and pillage in the world's forgotten regions; of economic stagnation and civilization's retreat into a few fortified enclaves."[55]

During the economic troubles of the 1980s, historian Paul Kennedy surveyed the rise and fall of empires over the past five hundred years and issued a dire warning that the United States' future as "*the* global superpower" was threatened by a growing imbalance between its expanding military commitments and its shrinking economic resources.[56] But after fifteen years of sustained economic expansion, Kennedy concluded in a 2002 essay that America no longer faced the threat of such fatal "imperial overstretch." Although spending only 3 percent of its gross domestic product on defense at the start of the war on terror, the United States accounted for 40 percent of the world's total military expenditures. This power was manifest in the dozen lethal aircraft carriers ceaselessly patrolling the world's oceans, each "super-dreadnought" carrying seventy "state-of-the-art aircraft that roar on and off the flight deck day and night." A typical carrier was escorted by fourteen ships—cruisers, destroyers, attack submarines, and amphibious craft with three thousand marines ready to storm ashore anywhere in the world. After revisiting his statistics on those five hundred years of imperial history, Kennedy concluded: "Nothing has ever existed like this disparity of power; nothing. The *Pax Bri-*

tannica was run on the cheap. . . . Charlemagne's empire was merely western European in its reach. The Roman Empire stretched further afield, but there was another great empire in Persia, and a larger one in China. There is, therefore, no comparison." So great was America's advantage in armaments, finance, infrastructure, and research that, said Kennedy smugly, "there is no point in the Europeans or Chinese wringing their hands about U.S. predominance."[57]

In an article splashed across the cover of the *New York Times Magazine* on the eve of the 2003 invasion of Iraq, commentator Michael Ignatieff celebrated America's global presence as "an empire lite, a global hegemony whose grace notes are free markets, human rights and democracy, enforced by the most awesome military power the world has ever known."[58] Harvard historian Charles Maier made a similar celebratory argument that "America has exercised an imperial hold . . . not merely through armed power or the CIA, but also through such institutions as the Council on Foreign Relations . . . and its frequent convocations" of world leaders. Their striking deference to "the political leadership of the dominant power" suggested that Washington presided over a distinctly hegemonic empire by leading a coalition of willing allies. Looking into the twenty-first century, Maier admitted somewhat ruefully that if "there are to be two or more imperial contenders, then I believe it valuable to have the United States remain one of them."[59]

Between hegemony and imperium lay a more pragmatic, quintessentially conservative school that embraced the unadorned reality of Washington's global dominion. "U.S. imperialism has been the greatest force for good in the world during the past century," wrote the military historian Max Boot. "It has defeated the monstrous evils of communism and Nazism and lesser evils such as the Taliban and Serbian ethnic cleansing."[60] To protect the "inner core of its empire, . . . a family of democratic, capitalist nations," Washington, he argued, must prepare for countless future wars along a volatile imperial periphery "teeming with failed states, criminal states, or simply a state of nature."[61] Similarly, Eliot Cohen, neoconservative counselor to George W. Bush's State Department, argued that the "age of empire" was over, but "an age of American hegemony has begun," and suggested that "U.S. statesmen today cannot ignore the lessons and analogies of imperial history" if they were to put together the coalitions of allied states required for successful global governance.[62]

In short, analysts across the political spectrum had come to agree that *empire* was the most appropriate word to describe America's current superpower status. At the close of the Cold War even Arthur M. Schlesinger Jr., counselor to presidents, critic of Williams, and liberal historian par excellence, conceded the imperial nature of the American stance in the world: "Who can doubt that there is an American empire?—an 'informal' empire, not colonial in polity, but still richly equipped with imperial paraphernalia: troops, ships, planes, bases, proconsuls, local collaborators, all spread around the luckless planet."[63]

In the end, facts simply overcame ideology. Calling a nation that controls nearly half the planet's military forces and much of its wealth an "empire" became nothing more than fitting an analytical frame to appropriate facts.[64] From Boot on the right to Bacevich in the political center, a surprising consensus among established scholars of US foreign policy had formed. The question was no longer whether the United States was an empire, but how Washington might best preserve or shed its global dominion.[65]

Yet if we step back a bit from this fifty-year debate and the decades of denial that went with it, there has been surprisingly little time for much genuine analysis of America's global dominion. Compared to the countless books and articles that crowd library shelves covering every imaginable aspect of European colonial rule, there is still surprisingly little serious study of history's most powerful empire. With remarkably few exceptions, all these commentators seemed unaware of the geopolitics that had facilitated America's ascent to global hegemony and may yet play a critical role in its decline. At a moment when Washington is facing the first serious challenges to its dominion in seventy years, it seems timely to ask: What is the character of this US empire? What attributes did it acquire during its ascent, how did it exercise global dominion, and what forces might precipitate its decline?

Addressing such questions is a tricky business. Empires are the most elusive, complex, and paradoxical of all forms of governance—strong yet often surprisingly fragile. At their peaks, empires can crush rival powers or curb subordinate states, yet their power is surprisingly vulnerable to erosion, to simply slipping away. Unlike conventional states whose defense, if well managed, is an organic, cost-effective extension of civil society, empires face exceptional costs in mounting risky military operations and maintaining a costly overseas presence. All modern empires are alike in the fundamental facts of their dominion over others. Yet in their particular exercise of power and policy, each empire is distinct.

Over the past five hundred years, empires have grown either through continental or overseas expansion. Continental empires (Hapsburg Europe, Mughal India, China, Russia, and the United States before 1867) spread by the overland conquest of contiguous territories that usually, though not always, centralized imperial governance within a unitary state. By contrast, maritime empires (Great Britain, the Netherlands, Spain, post-Napoleonic France, and the United States after 1898) necessarily decentralized their far-flung overseas rule through surrogate states called variously colonies, protectorates, dominions, mandates, trust territories, occupied lands, or even allies.[66]

From 1500 onward, each century brought a new layer to Europe's overseas expansion, culminating in the late nineteenth century when half-a-dozen powers carved up Africa and Asia.[67] Then, after four centuries of relentless imperial expansion that encompassed half of humanity, Europe's overseas empires were all erased from the globe in just a quarter of a century, giving way between 1947 and 1975 to nearly a hundred new nations, over half of today's sovereign states.

In the twenty years after World War II, the population of the British Empire fell from seven hundred million to only five million in conjunction with the full-scale appearance of the United States on the world stage.[68] Over the past 120 years, Washington has moved to global power through three distinct phases, each one sparked by wars large and small. Stepping onto that stage for the first time during the Spanish-American War of 1898, America acquired a string of tropical islands stretching for 10,000 miles from the Atlantic to the Western Pacific, which plunged it into the transformative experience of colonial rule. Then, in the decades after World War II, it ascended suddenly to global dominion amid the collapse of a half-dozen European empires and the start of the Cold War with a rival global hegemon, the Soviet Union. Most recently, using technologies developed for the war on terror, Washington is making a determined bid to extend its dominion as the world's sole superpower deep into the twenty-first century through a fusion of cyberwar, space warfare, trade pacts, and military alliances.

Empire of Tropical Islands

Small though it was, the Spanish-American War had large and lasting consequences. It took just three months and caused only 345 American combat deaths, yet it changed America from an insular, inward-looking nation into a colonial power with island territories that extended 7,000 miles beyond its shores. Not only did this scattered empire require a mobile army and a blue-water navy but it also helped foster the modernization of the federal government.

After three years of diplomatic tensions over Spain's harsh pacification of the Cuban revolution, the explosion of the battleship USS *Maine* in Havana

Harbor in February 1898 sparked hostilities that were greeted with a burst of patriotic frenzy across America. During the fifteen weeks of war, the navy, with its modernized fleet, quickly sank two antiquated Spanish squadrons in Cuba and the Philippines. The regular army, numbering only 28,000 men, had to mobilize National Guard units and volunteer regiments to reach the requisite strength of 220,000 troops. The fighting in Cuba was comparatively bloody, with 1,400 American casualties in the capture of Santiago alone. But Philippine revolutionary forces had already confined Spanish troops inside Manila by the time the first army transports arrived, making the capture of that capital a virtual victory parade. This easy triumph was, however, followed by four years of demoralizing pacification efforts. In the end, it took 75,000 troops to defeat the nascent Philippine republic and establish colonial rule.

With the annexation of Hawaii in 1898 and the acquisition of the Panama Canal Zone in 1903, the United States suddenly had an island empire that stretched along the Tropic of Cancer nearly halfway around the globe. Washington then developed a distinctive form of imperial rule for its new colonies in the Canal Zone, Puerto Rico, and the Philippines that left a lasting imprint on governance, at home as well as abroad.

Eschewing the visible grandeur of the great European empires, the United States ruled its disparate arc of islands through a nimble nexus of public-private alliances. Lacking a European-style colonial ministry, Washington held its overseas territories lightly through a small Bureau of Insular Affairs buried in the bowels of the War Department, while outsourcing overseas rule to low-cost surrogate governments in Manila and San Juan. Instead of dedicated colonials such as the legendary British or Dutch savants who trained at Oxford and Leiden for lifelong colonial careers, American overseas territories relied on short-term consultants and contractors, experts like urban planner Daniel Burnham and forester Gifford Pinchot who framed templates for colonial policy. Within a few years of capturing Manila in 1898, the US colonial state had mobilized a transitory A-to-Z army of consultants in fields ranging from agronomy to zoology.[69]

The omnipresent yet invisible architect of this unique American imperial state was Elihu Root, a New York lawyer who served successively as secretary of war and secretary of state from 1899 to 1909. As the prototype of the "wise man" who shuttles between corporate law offices in New York and federal posts in Washington, Root formalized this system of ad hoc imperial rule by reorganizing key elements of the government and later establishing a network of public-private linkages as president of the Carnegie Endowment for International Peace (1910–25) and founder of the Council on Foreign Relations (1921). Unlike Europe's closed policymaking by cabinet and civil servants captured in those metonyms Whitehall or Quai d'Orsay, Washington's foreign policy formation would operate as "an empire without an emperor," reaching consensus through a "political free-for-all—parties, interest groups, entrenched bureaucracies, and the media."[70]

In this first phase of imperial evolution, those running America's scattered empire of islands conducted ad hoc experiments in policing, public health, and national defense that would have a significant impact on the development of the federal bureaucracy. On the eve of empire in 1898, the United States had what one landmark study called a "patchwork" or weak state with a loosely structured administrative apparatus, leaving ample room for the innovation and modernization that came, with stunning speed, in these imperial decades.[71] Ruling over subjects instead of citizens with civil rights, these colonies became laboratories for the perfection of state power—both the control over nature and the coercion of natives. Important innovations in governance and environmental management would migrate homeward from the imperial periphery, expanding the capacities of America's fledgling federal government.[72]

In Manila, the new colonial regime, confronted with intractable Filipino resistance, married advanced US information technologies to centralized Spanish policing to produce a powerful hybrid, the Philippine Constabulary, whose pervasive surveillance slowly suffocated both the armed resistance and political dissent. Through a small cadre of constabulary veterans, this innovative experiment in police surveillance migrated homeward during World War I to serve as a model for a nascent domestic security apparatus.

To cut a canal across the Isthmus of Panama, America's supreme imperial triumph, the United States faced almost insurmountable challenges in civil engineering and public health. During the ten years of construction, the canal became the world's most costly civil engineering project, moving mountain-sized excavations four times those needed to build the Suez Canal. The result was an engineering marvel that would perform flawlessly for the next century, with artificial lakes, electrical tow trucks, and precision locks that transported both tramp steamers and behemoth battleships, accident free, between the Atlantic and Pacific Oceans. To control the yellow fever that had defeated an earlier French attempt to cut a canal across Panama's isthmus, American officials eradicated almost all the mosquito breeding pools left by that country's torrential tropical rains. This new expertise in public health was then applied successfully to military bases across the American South and later would play a part in the formation of the Centers for Disease Control and Prevention.[73]

In this age of empire, the American conquest of cholera, malaria, and yellow fever made the man of science into a new kind of hero—notably, Walter Reed, who identified mosquitoes as the means of yellow fever transmission in Havana; William Gorgas, who conquered the same scourge in Cuba and Panama; and Walter Heiser, who purged cholera from Manila.[74] Indeed, General Leonard Wood's transformation of Santiago de Cuba from "its reeking filth, its starvation, its utter prostration" into a "clean, healthy, orderly city" catapulted this obscure army surgeon from a provincial command to the governor-generalship of Cuba and consideration for the presidency.[75]

Empire transformed the military. Amphibious operations spanning half the globe and the protracted pacification of the Philippines had a lasting impact on the army's overall organization and command. From America's founding, national defense had been the responsibility of a small standing army backed by state militia. The conquest of a sprawling overseas empire, however, changed these military realities. As secretary of war in these challenging years, Elihu Root reformed the army's antiquated structure, creating a centralized general staff and a modern war college, while expanding professional training for officers at every echelon. As a result, a modern imperial army, shorn of its traditional mission of domestic defense, took form.

Empire also challenged the basic design of national defense, pushing America's frontiers far beyond the chain of harbor fortifications along the eastern seaboard that had been the nation's front lines for a full century. That insular mindset was fully replicated even in the first major modernization of the military under the Navy Act of 1890, which produced only a defensive fleet of "short-range torpedo boats" and "sea-going coastline battleships."[76] Indeed, Congress restricted their range by limiting their coal capacity. Now, however, to defend a far-flung empire, Washington removed its "range restrictions on battleships" and in 1906 started construction of the "most powerfully armed and longest-range battleships afloat." To announce the country's arrival as a world power, President Theodore Roosevelt sent that "Great White Fleet" of sixteen battleships on an epic voyage that, as he said to the sailors upon their return in 1909, had "steamed through all the great oceans" and "touched the coast of every continent." They were, he told them, "the first battle fleet that has ever circumnavigated the globe." Within four years, the United States had launched an impressive armada of thirty-nine dreadnought-class battleships, including the USS *Pennsylvania*, which was three times the size of the older coastal warships.[77]

Empire, in other words, pushed American defenses deep into the world's oceans, requiring its first sustained projection of military power beyond its borders. In addition to a global navy, Washington now had its first experience of overseas military bases. Starting in 1907, it used scarce funds to fortify Pearl Harbor, the start of a long-term creation of an expansive Alaska–Hawaii–Caribbean defensive perimeter. When the Panama Canal finally opened in 1914, Woodrow Wilson tried to secure the country's southern flank by an escalating set of military interventions in the Caribbean and Central America—at Nicaragua from 1912 to 1933, Veracruz in 1914, Haiti from 1915 to 1934, and the Dominican Republic from 1916 to 1924. By 1920, the United States had a half-dozen major installations, with troops permanently deployed at them, stretching halfway round the globe—including a naval base at Guantánamo Bay, Cuba; army posts in Puerto Rico; coastal artillery at the entrances to the Panama Canal; the Pacific Fleet's home port at Pearl Harbor, Hawaii; and the Asiatic Fleet's headquarters at Manila Bay (with a nearby army base at Clark Field).

Ascent to Global Dominion

World War II and the Cold War transformed Washington into the preeminent world power and plunged it into an epochal struggle for global dominion with the Soviet Union. In marked contrast to the glorious little war against Spain, World War II was a global firestorm that left more than fifty million dead, swept away the Axis empires that ruled much of Eurasia, and exhausted the European imperial powers. By mobilizing sixteen million troops for combat and expanding its manufacturing base for war production, America emerged from that conflagration as a global superpower in a ruined world—its navy master of the oceans, its armies occupying much of Asia and Europe, and its expanded economy by far the world's largest.

The aftermath of war only amplified its global power. Although a rival Soviet Empire had acquired a dozen satellite states in Eastern Europe and a communist revolution soon closed China to the West, the rapid postwar decolonization of Europe's overseas empires opened nearly half of humanity to US influence. Those fading dominions became the foundation for an expanding American presence, allowing Washington to extend its hegemony across four continents with surprising speed and economy of force. Despite its rapid retreat, the British Empire left behind both models and methods that would influence this emerging hegemony.

At its peak circa 1900, Britain had managed its global empire with an effective array of hard and soft power, both the steel of naval guns and the salve of enticing culture. With strong fiscal fundamentals, Great Britain would dominate the world economy through London's unequaled foreign investments of £3.8 billion, the country's trade treaties with sovereign states, and global economic leadership through the gold standard and the pound sterling. Multilingual British diplomats were famously skilled at negotiating force-multiplier alliances with other major powers, including at various times France, Japan, Russia, and the United States, while ensuring its commercial access to secondary states like China and Persia that made up its informal empire.[78] Its colonial officers were no less skilled at cultivating local elites from Malay sultans to African chiefs that enabled them to rule over a quarter of the globe with a minimum of military force. Both forms of British diplomacy were eased by the cultural appeal of the English language, highlighted through its literature, the Anglican religion, sports (cricket, rugby, soccer, and tennis), and mass media (Reuters news service, newspapers such as the *Times*, and the later BBC Radio).

As the steel behind this diplomacy, the British navy controlled maritime chokepoints from Gibraltar through the Suez Canal to the Straits of Malacca.[79] Reflecting British innovation, its industries built the world's first true battleship, the earliest tanks, and a diverse modern arsenal. With a standing army of only 99,000 men, its entire defense budget consumed just 2.5 percent of Britain's gross domestic product, an extraordinary economy of global force.[80]

Britannia may have ruled the waves, but when it came ashore for either formal or informal rule it needed local allies who could serve as intermediaries in controlling complex, often volatile populations. These "subordinate elites"—so essential to the rise of any empire—can also precipitate its decline if they move into opposition. With its contradictory motto "Imperium et Libertas," the British Empire necessarily became, as the London *Times* said in 1942, "a self-liquidating concern."[81] Indeed, historian Ronald Robinson has famously argued that British imperial rule ended "when colonial rulers had run out of indigenous collaborators," with the result that the "inversion of collaboration into noncooperation largely determined the timing of decolonization."[82] The support of these local elites sustained the steady expansion of the British Empire for two hundred years, just as their later opposition assured its rapid retreat in just twenty more.

At the start of its rise to dominance after 1945, the United States had a comparable array of assets for the exercise of global dominion. Although Washington had no counterpart to the Colonial Office and would never admit to possessing anything like the British Empire, it quickly assembled a formidable bureaucratic apparatus for the exercise of world power.

Militarily, Washington had a brief monopoly on nuclear weapons and a navy of unprecedented strength. Diplomatically, it was supported by allies from Europe to Japan, an informal empire in Latin America secured by the Rio mutual-defense treaty of 1947, and an official anticolonial foreign policy that eased relations with the world's many emerging nations. The foundation for all this newfound power was the overwhelming strength of the American economy. During World War II, America's role as the "arsenal of democracy" meant massive industrial expansion, no damage to domestic infrastructure given that fighting only occurred elsewhere, and comparatively light casualties—four hundred thousand war dead versus seven million for Germany, ten million for China, and twenty-four million for Russia. While rival industrial nations struggled to recover from the ravages of history's greatest war, America "bestrode the postwar world like a colossus." With the only intact industrial complex on the planet, the US economy accounted for 35 percent of gross world output and half of its manufacturing capacity.[83]

At the end of World War II, the United States invested all this prestige and power in forming nothing less than a new world order through permanent international institutions—the United Nations (1945), the International Monetary Fund (1945), and the General Agreement on Tariffs and Trade (1947), predecessor to the World Trade Organization.[84] Continuing and deepening its commitment to the rule of law for resolution of disputes among nations, Washington convened international tribunals at Nuremburg and Tokyo to try the Axis leaders. It also helped establish the International Court of Justice at The Hague, empowered to issue rulings for enforcement by the UN Security Council.[85] Moving beyond London's ad hoc economic leadership, Washington forged formal international controls at the Bretton Woods conference of forty-four allied nations in 1944 to direct and dominate the global economy through the IMF and the World Bank. Despite such exceptional internationalism, the US imperium exhibited many essential attributes of its British and European predecessors. In the years that followed, Washington built "a hierarchical order with liberal characteristics" based on "multilateral institutions, alliances, special relationships, and client states."[86]

It was the Cold War that translated all this influence into an architecture for the actual exercise of world power. Within a decade, Washington had built a potent four-tier apparatus—military, diplomatic, economic, and clandestine—for the maintenance of its expansive hegemony. At its core was the unmatched military that circled the globe with hundreds of overseas bases, a formidable nuclear arsenal, massive air and naval forces, and client armies. Complementing all this steel was the salve of an active worldwide diplomacy, manifest in close bilateral ties, multilateral alliances, economic aid, and cultural suasion. Just as America's public sector had long created conditions for private prosperity at home, so its global extension promoted trade and security pacts that allowed its burgeoning multinational corporations to operate profitably. Adding a distinct, even novel dimension to US global power was a clandestine fourth tier that entailed global surveillance by the NSA and covert operations on five continents by the CIA, manipulating elections, promoting coups, and, when needed, mobilizing surrogate armies. Indeed, more than any other attribute, it is this clandestine dimension that distinguishes US global hegemony from earlier empires.

From the beginning, military power was at the heart of America's global presence. The three thousand installations its armed forces had operated during World War II shrank rapidly in the postwar demobilization to just ninety-eight overseas air and naval bases. But with the start of the Cold War in the late 1940s, Washington shelved its plans for a largely hemispheric defense and began acquiring hundreds of foreign military bases.[87] In geopolitical terms, Washington had become history's most powerful empire because it was the first, after a millennium of incessant struggle, to control "both ends of Eurasia."[88] With 2.6 million active-duty troops in 1958, its military could maintain 300 overseas installations, many of them ringing that landmass from Britain through Southeast Asia to Japan. Its navy had 2,650 ships in service, including 746 warships, as well as 7,195 combat aircraft; the air force had nearly 15,000 bombers, fighters, and transports.[89]

By 1960, the Pentagon also had built a triad of nuclear weapons that constituted "a virtually invulnerable strategic deterrent for decades to come." With the launch of the USS *George Washington* in 1959, the navy's new squadron of five nuclear-powered submarines cruised the ocean depths incessantly, each outfitted with sixteen nuclear-armed Polaris missiles. All of the navy's fourteen attack carriers, including the new atomic-powered USS *Enterprise*, were equipped for nuclear strikes. By 1960 as well, the Strategic Air Command had 1,700 intermediate- and long-range bombers ready for nuclear payloads, including six hundred of the behemoth B-52s with a range of 4,000 miles. The air force had also developed the Atlas and Titan ballistic missiles that could carry nuclear warheads over 6,000 miles to their targets.[90]

To soften all this abrasive hard power, Washington formed the Voice of America (1942) and Radio Free Europe (1949) for worldwide radio broadcasts, supplementing the undeniable global appeal of the Hollywood film industry. Culturally, the United States exceeded Britain's former influence thanks to its feature films, sports (basketball and baseball), and news media (newspapers, newsreel, and radio).

Both global regimes, British and American, promoted a "liberal international order" founded on free trade, free markets, and freedom of the seas.[91] By putting its Philippine colony on a path to independence in 1935, Washington had ended a brief flirtation with formal empire; but its later global hegemony seemed similar to Great Britain's informal imperial controls over countries like China and Persia.[92] Just as British diplomats were skilled at negotiating alliances to confine rivals France and then Germany to the European continent, so Washington contained the Soviet Union and China behind the Iron Curtain through multilateral alliances that stretched across the Eurasian landmass.

Yet there were also some significant differences in the ways London and Washington exercised global power. After completing his ten-volume history of human civilizations in 1961, Arnold Toynbee observed that the "American Empire" had two features that distinguished it from Great Britain's: military bases galore and its emphasis on offering generous economic aid to allies. Following the Roman practice of respecting "the sovereign independence" of weaker allies and asking only for a "patch of ground for . . . a Roman fortress to provide for the common security," Washington sought no territory, instead signing agreements for hundreds of military bases on foreign soil. The half-dozen naval bastions that the United States had acquired in 1898 grew into a matrix of three hundred overseas bases in 1954 to nearly eight hundred by 1988. In addition, in a policy "unprecedented in the history of empires," said Toynbee, America was making "her imperial position felt by giving economic aid to the peoples under her ascendancy, instead of . . . exploiting them economically."[93] Indeed, in the aftermath of World War II the State Department added an economic development branch, starting with the Economic Cooperation Administration to administer the Marshall Plan for the reconstruction of Europe, and then expanding, after 1961, into a wider global effort through the Agency for International Development.

With the accelerating pace of decolonization during the 1950s, the administration of President Dwight Eisenhower was forced to develop a new system of global dominion involving a worldwide network of national leaders—autocrats, aristocrats, and pliable democrats. In effect, the fulcrum for imperial controls had moved upward from the countless colonial districts to the national capitals of a hundred new nations. From his experience commanding allied forces during World War II, President Eisenhower revitalized the national security apparatus. Under the National Security Act of 1947, Washington had already forged the basic instruments for its exercise of global power—the Defense Department, the air force, the National Security Council (NSC), and the CIA. Through parallel changes in signals intelligence, the NSA emerged by 1951, completing the apparatus of covert power. Under Eisenhower, an expanded NSC would serve as his central command and brain trust for fighting the Cold War, meeting weekly to survey a fast-changing world and plan foreign policy. At the same time, the expanding CIA became his executive strike force for securing the new system of subordinate elites. With experienced internationalists Allen Dulles heading the CIA and John Foster Dulles at State, the security agencies, filled with veterans of World War II, proved apt instruments for implementation of these expansive policies.

After shifting the CIA's focus from an attempt to penetrate the Soviet bloc, which had failed badly, to controlling the emerging nations of Asia, Africa, and Latin America, which succeeded all too brilliantly, Eisenhower authorized 170 major covert operations in forty-eight nations during his eight-year term. In effect, clandestine manipulation became Washington's preferred mode of exercising old-fashioned imperial hegemony in a new world of nominally sovereign nations. In industrial societies, the agency cultivated allies with electoral cash, cultural suasion, and media manipulation, thereby building long-term alliances with the Christian Democrats in Italy, the Socialist Party in France, and above all the ruling Liberal Democratic Party in Japan, recipient of "millions of dollars in covert C.I.A. support." In the developing world, the agency brought compliant leaders to power through a string of coups from Iran in 1953 to the Congo and Laos in 1960. Under the Eisenhower administration's Overseas Internal Security Program, the CIA also served as lead agency in strengthening the repressive capacity of Washington's Third World allies, creating secret police units for a dozen such states and, in 1958 alone, training 504,000 police officers in twenty-five nations.[94]

During these Cold War years, the United States favored military autocrats in South America, monarchs across the Middle East, and a mix of democrats and dictators in Asia. In a top-secret analysis of Latin America in 1954, the CIA suggested "long-standing American concepts of 'fair play' must be reconsidered" if the United States were to halt the region's move toward "irresponsible and extreme nationalism, and immunity from the exercise of U.S. power." In a logic that would guide its dominion for the next forty years, Washington would quietly set aside democratic principles for a realpolitik policy of backing reliable pro-American leaders. According to a compilation at Carnegie Mellon University, between 1946 and 2000 the rival superpowers intervened in 117 elections, or 11 percent of all the competitive national-level contests held worldwide, via campaign cash and media disinformation. Significantly, the United States was responsible for eighty-one of these attempts (70 percent of the total)—including eight instances in Italy, five in Japan, and several in Chile and Nicaragua stiffened by CIA paramilitary action.[95]

In Asia, Latin America, and the Middle East, US military aid increased the institutional strength of local armed forces while American advisers trained more than three hundred thousand soldiers in seventy countries during the quarter century after World War II, acquiring access to this influential elite in emerging nations worldwide. Having formally established in 1968 that "Latin American military juntas were good for the United States," the CIA supported the right-wing leaders of eleven such nations with intelligence, secret funds, and military aid. When civilian leaders became disruptive, Washington could help install a sympathetic military successor, whether Colonel Joseph Mobutu in Congo, General Suharto in Indonesia, or General Augusto Pinochet in Chile. As its chief of station in Turkey put it, the agency saw every Muslim leader in the Middle East who was not pro-American as "a target legally authorized by statute for CIA political action." The sum of these policies fostered a distinct global trend between 1958 and 1975—a "reverse wave" away from democracy, as military coups succeeded in more than three dozen nations, a full quarter of the world's sovereign states.[96]

As economic competitors grew rapidly in the prosperous years after World War II, the US share of the world's gross product slipped from an estimated 50 percent in 1950 to only 25 percent by 1999.[97] Even so, at the close of the Cold War, American multinational corporations were still the engines of global growth, its inventors led the world in patents, and its scientists had won over half the Nobel Prizes.[98]

Sustained by this economic and scientific strength, the military then maintained more than 700 overseas bases, an air force of 1,763 jet fighters, an armada of over 1,000 ballistic missiles, and a navy of 600 ships, including 15 nuclear carrier battle groups—all linked by the world's only global system of communications satellites.[99] Testifying to the success of this strategy, the Soviet Empire imploded circa 1991 amid a coup and secession of satellite states but without a single American shot fired. By then, however, global defense was consuming a heavy 5.2 percent of the country's gross domestic product—twice the British rate at its peak.[100]

Securing the American Century

Just as the conjuncture of World War II and the Cold War made America a nuclear-armed superpower, so the war on terror developed new technologies for the preservation of its global hegemony via space, cyberspace, and robotics, levitating its military force into an ether beyond the tyranny of terrestrial limits.

In the aftermath of the 2001 terrorist attacks, Washington pursued perpetrators across Asia and Africa through an expanded information infrastructure with digital surveillance, biometric identification, and agile aerospace operations. After a decade of this war with its voracious appetite for information, a 2010 *Washington Post* investigation found that the intelligence community had fleshed out into a veritable "fourth branch" of the federal government—a national security state with 854,000 vetted officials, 263 security organizations, and over 3,000 intelligence units.[101]

Though stunning, these statistics only skimmed the visible surface of what had become history's largest and most lethal clandestine apparatus. According to NSA documents that Edward Snowden leaked in 2013, the nation's sixteen intelligence agencies had 107,035 employees and a combined "black budget" of $52.6 billion, equivalent to 10 percent of the vast defense budget.[102] By sweeping the skies and penetrating the World Wide Web's undersea cables, the NSA was capable of capturing the confidential communications of any leader on the planet while monitoring countless millions of their citizens. For classified paramilitary missions, the CIA and its Special Activities Division also had access to the Pentagon's Special Operations Command, with 69,000 elite troops (rangers, SEALs, air commandos) and their agile arsenal.[103] Adding to this formidable paramilitary capacity, the CIA operated thirty Predator and Reaper drones responsible, from 2004 to 2016, for 580 strikes in Pakistan and Yemen with at least 3,080 deaths.[104] In effect, this covert dimension had grown from a distinctive feature of US global hegemony back in the 1950s into a critical, even central factor in its bid for survival.

Starting in 2002, President George W. Bush gave the NSA secret orders to monitor domestic communications, and the agency later launched its top-secret "Pinwale" database to scan countless millions of electronic messages.[105] In 2009, digital surveillance grew into "cyberwarfare" after the formation of the Cyber Command (CYBERCOM), with headquarters at Fort Meade and a cyberwar center at Lackland Air Base staffed by seven thousand air force employees.[106] Two years later, the Pentagon moved beyond conventional combat on air, land, or sea to declare cyberspace an "operational domain," involving both the defense of the military's seven million computers and the deployment of cyberwarriors for offensive operations.[107] Washington's formidable capacity was manifest in the computer viruses it unleashed against Iran's nuclear facilities from 2006 to 2010, destroying 20 percent of that country's critical centrifuges. Four years later, Obama, realizing conventional antimissile systems would fail, ordered "left of launch" cyberstrikes against North Korea's missile program, causing its rockets "to explode, veer off course, disintegrate in midair and plunge into the sea."[108]

Meanwhile, the pressure to pacify foreign societies again produced innovation in the information infrastructure. The occupation of Iraq from 2003 to 2011 served as a crucible for counterinsurgency, creating a new fusion of biometric surveillance and digital warfare. Advanced biometrics first appeared in 2004 in the aftermath of the bitter battle for the city of Fallujah when marines stopped 250,000 returning residents at desert checkpoints for fingerprinting and iris scans.[109] By mid-2008, the army was checking the identities of Baghdad's population via satellite link to a biometric database in West Virginia that had a million Iraqi fingerprints and retinal scans on file.[110] Starting in 2010, the Pentagon deployed an upgraded identification system in Afghanistan as well, allowing US patrols to scan Afghan eyes into the Biometric Automated Toolset (BAT)—a laptop computer equipped with "separate plug-in units that record mug shots, fingerprints and retinal characteristics" for instantaneous identity checks via satellite.[111]

It was in Afghanistan that the remotely piloted vehicle first became a potent offensive weapon in Washington's aerospace arsenal, accelerating drone development largely suspended since early versions were first introduced during the war in Vietnam. Launched as an experimental craft in 1994, the Predator drone was deployed that year in the Balkans for photo reconnaissance, adapted in 2000 for real-time surveillance under the CIA's Operation Afghan Eyes, and armed with the tank-killer Hellfire missile for its first lethal strike at Kandahar, Afghanistan, in October 2001.[112] In July 2008, the air force released the larger MQ-9 "Reaper" drone with "persistent hunter killer" capabilities—including sixteen hours of nonstop flying time, sensors for "real time data," and fourteen air-ground missiles.[113]

Between 2004 and 2010, total flying time for all unmanned aerial vehicles rose sharply from just 71 hours to 250,000.[114] Launched in 1994 without weapons or even GPS (global positioning system), the drones were eventually equipped with sensors so sensitive they could read disturbed dirt at 5,000 feet and backtrack footprints to an enemy bunker.[115] By 2011, the air force was planning to quadruple its drone fleet to 536 unmanned aircraft and was training 350 drone pilots, more than all its bomber and fighter pilots combined, to operate an armada ranging from the hulking Global Hawk with a 116-foot wingspan to the hand-launched RQ-11 Raven with a five-foot span.[116]

In its planning for future wars, the air force has determined that the full weaponization of space is key to the next generation of combat. In 2004, an air force strategic study defined space assets as "critical to achieving information superiority."[117] Two years later, experience in Afghanistan convinced the air force to develop a strategy for "Battlespace Awareness (space and terrestrial)." Soon, the Pentagon established the Joint Functional Component Command for Space to manage military operations in what was fast becoming the ultimate strategic high ground.[118] Adding some weight to such words, in 2010 and 2012 the Defense Department conducted successful test flights of its X-37B Orbital Test Vehicle, an unmanned space shuttle that flew successfully for fifteen months at 250 miles above the earth.[119] To facilitate intelligence integration across multiple platforms, the Defense Department has, since 2004, expanded the National Geospatial-Intelligence Agency into a super-secret bureau. From its nearly $2 billion headquarters, the third-biggest federal building in Washington, this newest member of the intelligence community now deploys sixteen thousand employees to coordinate a rising torrent of surveillance data from spy planes, drones, and orbital satellites.[120]

Looking into the future, the core of these innovative technologies for an advanced information regime will come online around 2020, about the same time that China will be ready to contest American dominion over space and cyberspace, making both likely domains for international conflict. A 2010 Pentagon study reported that China has launched "a comprehensive transformation of its military," focused on improving the ability of the People's Liberation Army (PLA) "for extended-range power projection." With the world's "most active land-based ballistic and cruise missile program," Beijing could target "its nuclear forces throughout . . . most of the world, including the continental United States." Moreover, accurate missiles will, said the Pentagon, provide "the PLA the capability to attack ships, including aircraft carriers, in the western Pacific Ocean." China was also contesting American dominion over space and cyberspace, with plans to dominate "the information spectrum in all dimensions of the modern battlespace." With the development of the Long March V booster rocket and the launch of five satellites by mid-2010, China was building "a full network" of thirty-five satellites for command, control, and communications operational by 2020—thereby breaking Washington's fifty-year near-monopoly on the militarization of space.[121]

The vulnerability of the US satellite system, critical for all military communications, became painfully obvious in 2007 when China used a ground-to-air missile to shoot down one of its own.[122] Concerned about the "escalating threat of cyberattacks," in 2015 the Naval Academy required, for the first time since the air force launched two dozen GPS satellites in the 1990s, that its cadets learn to navigate by sextant. "We went away from celestial navigation because computers are great," said Lieutenant Commander Ryan Rogers, of the academy's navigation department. "The problem is, there's no backup."[123]

After human space flight in 2003, a spacewalk in 2008, and module docking in 2011, China was also on track to launch its own space station by 2020, just about the time the US-led International Space Station will be retired without replacement, making Beijing the sole power with a manned presence in space.[124] In the years following 2020, both Beijing and Washington will have the capability for space warfare, creating the potential for armed conflict in the heavens.

In the first decades of the twenty-first century, the relentless advance of military technology has created the potential for great power conflict across all five domains of modern warfare—air, land, sea, space, and cyberspace. Yet despite all these developments, the geopolitics that Sir Halford Mackinder defined over a century ago still remain determinative, with the tensions between Beijing and Washington arising from a classic imperial struggle over military bases in the South China Sea. After a fifty-year ascent to world power through its rule over tropical colonies followed by seventy years as a global hegemon in the aftermath of World War II, Washington is now facing multiple challenges that might well bring an untimely and early end to the American Century.

Chapter Two

"Our S.O.B.s"–America and the Autocrats

I n one of history's lucky accidents, the juxtaposition of two extraordinary events suddenly stripped the architecture of American global power bare for all to see. Between November 2010 and January 2011, WikiLeaks activists splashed snippets from 2,017 purloined US embassy cables, loaded with scurrilous comments about national leaders from Argentina to Zimbabwe, on the front pages of newspapers worldwide. Then, just a few weeks later, the Middle East erupted in pro-democracy protests against the region's autocratic leaders, many of whom were close US allies whose foibles had been detailed in those same cables.

Suddenly, it was possible to see the foundations of a world order that rested significantly on national leaders who served Washington as loyal subordinate elites that were, in reality, a motley collection of autocrats, aristocrats, and uniformed thugs. Then, in September 2011, the picture became clearer still when WikiLeaks accidentally released its entire cache of 251,287 confidential cables from 274 US embassies and consulates worldwide. At long last, we could grasp the larger logic of otherwise often inexplicable American foreign policy choices over the past half century.[1]

Why would the CIA risk controversy in 1965 at the height of the Cold War by overthrowing an accepted leader like Sukarno in Indonesia? Why would the US embassy encourage the assassination of the Catholic autocrat Ngô Đình Diệm at Saigon in 1963? The answer—and thanks to WikiLeaks and the "Arab spring" this is now so much clearer—is that each became insubordinate and so expendable.

Why, half a century later in 2011, would Washington betray its stated democratic principles by backing Egyptian president Hosni Mubarak against millions of demonstrators and then, when he faltered, use its leverage to encourage his replacement, at least initially, with his own intelligence chief Omar Suleiman, a man best known for running Cairo's torture chambers (and lending them out to Washington)? The answer again: because both were agile political operatives skilled in serving Washington's interests while simultaneously servicing the needs of their constituents in this key Arab state.[2]

Across the greater Middle East from Tunisia and Egypt to Bahrain and Yemen, the democratic protests of the Arab spring were suddenly threatening to sweep away figures crucial to the wielding of American power. Of course, all modern empires have relied on dependable surrogates to translate their global power into local control—and for most of them, the moment when those elites began to stir, talk back, and assert their own agendas was also the moment when you knew that imperial collapse was in the cards.

If the "velvet revolutions" that swept Eastern Europe in 1989 tolled the death knell for the Soviet Empire, then the "jasmine revolutions" that spread fitfully, painfully, violently across the Middle East after 2011 may well contribute, in the fullness of time, to the eclipse of American global power.

Putting the Military in Charge

To understand the importance of such subordinate elites, look back to the Cold War's early days when a desperate White House was searching for something, anything that could halt the seemingly unstoppable spread of what Washington saw as anti-American and pro-communist sentiment.

In December 1954, the NSC met in the White House to stake out a strategy that could tame the powerful nationalist forces of change then sweeping the globe. Across Asia and Africa, a half-dozen European empires that had guaranteed global order for more than a century were giving way to new nations, many—as Washington saw it—susceptible to "communist subversion." In Latin America, there were stirrings of leftist opposition to the region's growing urban poverty and rural landlessness. To make it "absolutely clear we will not tolerate Communism anywhere in the Western Hemisphere," influential Secretary of the Treasury George Humphrey advised his NSC colleagues that they should "stop talking so much about democracy" and instead "support dictatorships of the right if their policies are pro-American." At that moment, Dwight Eisenhower interrupted to observe, with a flash of strategic insight, that Humphrey was, in effect, saying: "They're OK if they're *our* s.o.b.'s." The secretary agreed, adding: "Whatever we may choose to say in public about ideas and idealism, among ourselves we've got to be a great deal more practical and materialistic."[3]

It was a moment to remember. The president had just articulated, with crystalline clarity, the system of global dominion that Washington would implement for the next fifty years—setting aside democratic principles for a tough realpolitik policy of backing any reliable leader who backed us, building a worldwide network of national (and often nationalist) leaders who would nonetheless put Washington's needs above local ones. To consolidate its dominion, Washington would build a worldwide system of subordinate elites that became nothing less than an Archimedean lever to shift the globe in its direction.

In 1958, military coups in Iraq, Pakistan, and Thailand suddenly focused the NSC's attention on the Third World's militaries as forces to be reckoned with. At one meeting, NSC officials agreed that "it was desirable to encourage the military to stabilize a conservative system" by providing "at least a minimum of military assistance to these backward and undeveloped countries." To maximize such leverage, Allen Dulles, director of the CIA, "stressed the need for our military attachés and for the personnel of our Military Assistance Advisory Groups to be carefully selected so that they could develop useful and appropriate relationships with the rising military leaders and factions in the underdeveloped countries." Expressing "vigorous support" for this CIA suggestion, President Eisenhower added that "the trend towards military take-overs in the underdeveloped countries of Asia and Africa was almost certainly going to continue," making it important "to orient the potential military leaders of these countries in a pro-Western rather than in a pro-Communist direction." Bringing foreign military leaders to the United States for further "training" would, it was suggested, facilitate "management of the forces of change released by the development" of these emerging nations.[4] In another moment of clarity, the administration now realized that military juntas could, if cultivated, serve as an important bulwark against communist takeovers.

Worldwide, Washington would pour massive military aid into cultivating the armed forces across the planet by using "training missions" to create crucial ties between American advisers and the officer corps in country after country. If subordinate elites did not seem subordinate enough, then these American advisers could help identify alternative leaders who would skip the ballot box and seize power by coup d'état.

When civilian presidents proved insubordinate, the CIA went to work promoting such coups that would install reliable military successors. In the first decade of the twenty-first century, America's trust in the militaries of its client states would only grow. Washington, for example, gave Egypt's military a solid subsidy of $1.3 billion annually, but provided lesser amounts, ranging from $250 to $500 million, for the country's economic development. As a result, in January 2011 when demonstrations in Cairo rocked the Mubarak regime, the *New York Times* reported that "a 30-year investment paid off as American generals . . . and intelligence officers quietly called . . . friends they had trained with," successfully urging the army's support for a "peaceful transition" to civilian rule that would soon fall to, yes, a military coup.[5]

Elsewhere in the Middle East, Washington has, since the 1950s, followed the British imperial preference for Arab aristocrats by cultivating allies that included a shah (Iran), sultans (Abu Dhabi, Oman), emirs (Bahrain, Kuwait, Qatar, Dubai), and kings (Saudi Arabia, Jordan, Morocco). Across this vast, volatile region from Morocco to Iran, Washington courted these royalist regimes with military alliances, weapons systems, CIA support for local security, a safe American haven for their capital, and special treatment for those favored, including access to educational institutions in the United States or Department of Defense overseas schools for their children.[6]

America was, of course, by no means the first hegemon to build its global power on the gossamer threads of personal ties to local leaders. In the eighteenth and nineteenth centuries, Britain may have ruled the waves, but when it reached land, like empires past, it needed local allies who could serve as intermediaries in controlling complex, volatile societies. These relations were the only realistic way that a small island nation of just forty million could rule a global empire of some four hundred million, nearly a quarter of all humanity.

From 1850 to 1950, Britain governed its formal colonies through alliances with an extraordinary array of local elites—from Fiji Island chiefs and Malay sultans to Indian maharajas and African emirs. Simultaneously, Britain reigned over an even larger "informal empire" through subordinate elites that encompassed emperors (from Beijing to Istanbul), kings (from Bangkok to Cairo), and presidents (from Buenos Aires to Caracas). At the peak of its informal empire circa 1880, Britain's domain in Latin America, the Middle East, and China was larger in population than its formal colonial empire in India and Africa. Its entire global empire, in other words, rested on the slender ties of cooperation from loyal local elites.[7]

Throughout Britain's century of world dominion, 1815 to 1914, its self-confident agents of empire, from imperial viceroys in ostrich-plumed hats to district officers in khaki shorts, ruled much of Africa and Asia through protectorates and direct colonial rule. In the succeeding half century of American hegemony, Washington substituted its ambassadors, CIA station chiefs, and military advisers as envoys to the presidents and prime ministers of the new nations that had emerged from Europe's faded empires.

When the Cold War coincided with an era of rapid decolonization, the world's two superpowers turned to the same methods, regularly using their espionage agencies to manipulate the leaders of newly independent states. The Soviet Union's KGB and its surrogates—like the Stasi in East Germany and the Securitate in Romania—enforced political conformity among the fourteen Soviet satellites in Eastern Europe and competed with the United States to win allies across the Third World. Simultaneously, the CIA monitored the loyalties of national leaders on four continents, employing coups, bribery, and covert operations to control and, when necessary, change nettlesome national leaders.

In an era of nationalist feeling, however, the loyalty of those elites proved a complex matter. Many of them were driven by their own deep feelings of nationalism, which meant that they had to be closely monitored. So critical were these subordinate elites, and so troublesome was their urge toward insubordination, that the CIA repeatedly launched risky covert operations to bring them to heel, sparking some of the great crises of the Cold War.

Since its global dominion emerged in a postcolonial era of national independence, Washington had little choice but to work not simply with surrogates or puppets but with allies who still sought to maximize what they saw as their nation's interests (as well as their own). Even at the apex of its global power in the 1950s, when its domination was relatively unquestioned, Washington was forced into hard bargaining with prickly allies like South Korean autocrat Syngman Rhee and South Vietnam's Ngô Đình Diệm. In South Korea during the 1960s, its president, General Park Chung-hee, typically bartered troop deployments to Vietnam for billions of US development dollars, which helped spark the country's economic "miracle." In the process, Washington paid up, but got what it wanted most of all: fifty thousand Korean troops as guns-for-hire helpers in its unpopular war in Vietnam.[8]

Our Man in Saigon and the "Mayor of Kabul"

A closer examination of Washington's relations with two of those handpicked allies, Ngô Đình Diệm of Saigon and Hamid Karzai of Kabul, though separated by nearly half a century, illustrates the enormous difficulties the United States faced in managing these often insubordinate subordinate elites.

The sorry history of the autocratic regime of Ngô Đình Diệm in Saigon from 1954 to 1963 offers a cautionary tale about Washington's authoritarian allies. Even in the early years of the Cold War, American envoys found out how uncomfortable it could be to tolerate an ally's corruption and election fraud. Washington's support, however grudgingly given, soon came to seem like an endorsement of a loyal surrogate's self-destructive policies that were greasing the slippery slide toward a foreign policy debacle.

From the very beginning of America's intervention in South Vietnam in mid-1954, the limitations of its chosen leader were readily apparent. After years of exile in the United States and Europe, Diệm had a narrow political base among Vietnamese, but could count on powerful patrons in Washington, notably Democratic senators Mike Mansfield and John F. Kennedy, and an influential ally in Saigon, the legendary CIA operative Edward Lansdale, Washington's master of political manipulation in Southeast Asia. Landing at Saigon from France where he had been appointed Vietnam's prime minister, Diệm was bundled into a black limousine escorted by "motorcycles in a police phalanx" that whizzed past a large crowd of "whole families . . . clustered together, children riding on backs" who had waited at the airport for hours under a tropical sun, leaving the people, as Lansdale noted, "disappointed" and "in a disgruntled mood." The limousine swept toward the prime minister's official residence downtown where a crowd of overseas Chinese and civil servants, released early from their desks, dutifully applauded his promises to "act decisively."[9] As narrow as that support might seem, Diệm would never succeed in expanding it significantly during his decade in power.

Amid the chaos accompanying France's defeat in its long, bloody Indochina War (1946–54), Lansdale and the rest of the US mission would pull upon every lever of power, overt and covert, to secure Diệm's tenuous hold on Saigon. In November 1954, US diplomats maneuvered to send his chief rival, the commander of the Vietnamese Army, packing for Paris. Meanwhile, Lansdale's team provided Diệm with clandestine backing against residual French forces and well-armed regional militia, with tensions erupting into a bloody battle for Saigon in April 1955. Within a few months and with Lansdale's assistance, Diệm won an incredible 98.2 percent of the vote over the emperor Bảo Đại in a rigged presidential election and promptly promulgated a new constitution that ended the Vietnamese monarchy after a millennium.[10]

Channeling all its aid payments through Diệm, Washington managed to destroy the last vestiges of French colonial support for his rivals, while winning the president a narrow political base within the army, among civil servants, and in the minority Catholic community. Backed by a seeming cornucopia of American aid, Diệm then dealt harshly with South Vietnam's Buddhist sects and attacked former Viet Minh veterans of the war against the French. He also resisted the implementation of rural reforms that possibly could have won him a broader base among the country's peasant population but certainly risked alienating the upper-class landowners who were a more reliable source of support. When the US embassy pressed for such changes, he simply stalled, convinced that Washington had already invested too much of its prestige in his regime and would be unable to withhold support. Like Afghanistan's president Hamid Karzai decades later, Diệm's ultimate weapon was his mixture of strength and weakness—the determination to pursue his own policies and the threat that his regime might simply collapse if American officials pushed him too hard in other directions.

Invariably, the Americans backed down, sacrificing any hope of real change in order to maintain the ongoing war effort against the local Viet Cong rebels and their North Vietnamese backers. As rebellion and dissent grew in South Vietnam, Washington only ratcheted up its military aid to battle the communists, giving Diệm yet more weapons to wield against his own people, communist and noncommunist alike. Working through his brother Ngô Đình Nhu—and this would have an eerie resonance in America's future war in Afghanistan—Diệm's regime took control of Saigon's drug rackets, pocketing significant profits as it built up a nexus of secret police, prisons, and concentration camps to deal with suspected dissidents.[11] By the time of Diệm's downfall in 1963, there were some fifty thousand prisoners in his gulag.[12]

From 1960 to 1963, resistance sparked repression and repression redoubled resistance until South Vietnam was plagued by Buddhist riots in the cities and a spreading communist rebellion in the countryside. Maneuvering after dark, Viet Cong guerrillas slowly began to encircle Saigon, assassinating Diệm's unpopular village headmen by the thousands.

In this critical three-year period, the US military mission in Saigon tried every conceivable counterinsurgency strategy to eradicate the Viet Cong— bringing in helicopters and armored vehicles for conventional mobility, deploying the Green Berets for unconventional combat, building up regional militias for localized security, and constructing "strategic hamlets" to isolate eight million peasants inside fortified compounds theoretically controlled by Diệm's militia. Nothing worked. By 1963, the Viet Cong had grown from scattered bands of fighters into a guerrilla army that controlled more than half the countryside. Apart from impetus of Diệm's repression, much of that rebel expansion was now sustained by support from North Vietnam, led by the newly ascendant southerner Lê Duẩn, who was determined to protect loyal cadres from elimination by Diệm and fulfill Hanoi's dream of national reunification.[13]

When protesting Buddhist monk Quang Dúc assumed the lotus position on a Saigon street in June 1963 and held the posture while followers lit his gasoline-soaked robes that erupted in fatal flames, the Kennedy administration could no longer ignore the crisis. As Diệm's batons cracked the heads of Buddhist demonstrators and Nhu's wife applauded "monk barbecues," Washington began to officially protest the ruthless repression. Instead of responding, Diệm worked through his brother to open negotiations with the communists in Hanoi, threatening Washington with willing betrayal of the US war effort via a coalition government with communist North Vietnam.[14]

In the midst of this crisis, the newly appointed ambassador Henry Cabot Lodge arrived in Saigon and, within days, approved a CIA coup to overthrow Diệm. For the next few months, Lansdale's hard-bitten CIA understudy Lucien Conein met regularly with Saigon's generals to hatch an elaborate plot that would be unleashed with devastating effect on November 1, 1963. As rebel troops backing the plotters stormed the palace, Diệm and Nhu fled to a safe house in Saigon's Chinatown. Flushed from hiding by false promises of safe conduct into exile, Diệm climbed aboard a military convoy for what he thought was a ride to the airport. But CIA operative Conein told the Vietnamese generals that a US aircraft for his flight into exile was "not in the books," making execution the only viable option. When the convoy stopped at a rail crossing, a military assassin riding along sprayed Diệm's body with bullets and stabbed his bleeding corpse in a coup de grâce.[15]

Although Ambassador Lodge hosted an embassy celebration for the rebel officers and cabled President Kennedy that Diệm's downfall would mean a "shorter war," the country soon collapsed into further military coups and countercoups that crippled army operations. Over the next thirty-two months, Saigon had nine different governments and a change of cabinet every fifteen weeks—every one of them incompetent, corrupt, and ineffective. After spending a decade building up Diệm's regime and a day destroying it, the United States had seemingly linked its power and prestige irrevocably to the survival of the Saigon government. The "best and brightest" in Washington were convinced that they could not just walk away. So as South Vietnam slid toward defeat in the two years after Diệm's death, the first of what became

540,000 US combat troops arrived, ensuring that Vietnam would become not just an American-backed war but a full-scale American war.[16]

Washington then searched desperately for anyone who could provide sufficient stability to prosecute that war, eventually, with palpable relief, embracing a military junta headed by General Nguyễn Văn Thiệu. Sustained in power by American aid, Thiệu had a limited popular following at the outset, but squandered even that support over time by running virtually unopposed for reelection in 1971 and winning a risible 94.3 percent of the vote—repeating the same mistake that had weakened Diệm's legitimacy from the start.[17] But chastened by its experience in precipitating Diệm's assassination, the American embassy decided to ignore Thiệu's unpopularity and continue to build his army. When Washington finally began reducing its aid and withdrawing its troops after 1972, Thiệu found that his soldiers simply would not fight with sufficient determination to defend his unpopular government. With enemy forces encircling Saigon in April 1975, a CIA operative drove him to the airport for a flight into exile, noting the "reek of Scotch" on Thiệu's breath and the sound of "gold bars clinking against each other" in his luggage. Within a week, his army collapsed with stunning speed, suffering one of the more devastating defeats in modern military history.[18]

In pursuit of its Vietnam War effort, Washington required a Saigon government responsive to its demands yet popular enough with its own peasantry to wage the war in the villages. These proved to be impossibly contradictory political requirements. In the end, the Americans settled for authoritarian military rule, which, acceptable as it proved in Washington, was disdained by the Vietnamese peasantry. Supporting democratic alternatives to Diệm and Thiệu—and there were several candidates—admittedly entailed risks in the face of a relentless communist insurgency. So Washington sacrificed democratic principles for determined leadership, and in end secured neither.

In the more fluid, multipolar world that followed the Cold War's end, US relations with some of its embattled allies once again had a Vietnam flavor to them. Take Afghan president Hamid Karzai. With his volatile mix of dependence and independence, he seemed like the archetype of all the autocrats Washington has backed in Asia, Africa, and Latin America since European empires began fading. When the CIA mobilized Afghan warlords to topple the fundamentalist Taliban government in October 2001, the country's capital, Kabul, was Washington's for the taking—and the giving. In the midst of the chaos that came with the Taliban regime's headlong collapse, Karzai, an obscure exile living in Pakistan "with few contacts outside the CIA," gathered a handful of followers and plunged into southern Afghanistan on a doomed agency mission to rally the Pashtun tribes for revolt. It proved a quixotic effort. With the Taliban in hot pursuit, his team was forced to flee from village to village where "not a single local stepped forward to join them." Only extraction by navy SEALs saved him from certain death.[19]

Desperate for a reliable post-invasion ally, however, the Bush administration engaged in what one expert has called "bribes, secret deals, and arm twisting" to install Karzai in power as president. This process took place not through an election in Kabul, but by lobbying the foreign diplomats and Afghan leaders at a 2001 donors' conference inside Bonn's Hotel Petersberg where he was appointed interim president. When King Zahir Shah, a respected figure whose family had ruled Afghanistan for more than 150 years, offered his services as acting head of state, the US ambassador had a "showdown" with the monarch, quickly sending him back into exile. In this way, Karzai's "authority," which came directly and almost solely from the Bush administration, proved to be unchecked. (American security forces guarded President Karzai for his first months in office because he had so little trust in his nominal Afghan allies.)[20]

In the years that followed, his regime slid into an ever-deepening state of corruption and incompetence. As a flood of $114 billion in US development aid poured into Kabul between 2002 and 2015, a mere trickle escaped the capital's bottomless bureaucracy to reach impoverished villages in the countryside.[21] In 2009, Transparency International ranked Afghanistan as the world's second most corrupt nation, just one notch above Somalia.[22]

The August 2009 presidential elections were an apt index of the country's problematic "progress." Karzai's campaign team, dubbed "the warlord ticket," included Abdul Dostum, an Uzbek warlord who had slaughtered "several thousand" prisoners in 2001; vice presidential candidate Muhammed Fahim, a former defense minister linked to drugs and human rights abuses; Akhundzada, the former governor of Helmand Province, who was caught with nine tons of drugs in his compound in 2005; and the president's brother Ahmed Wali Karzai, reputedly the reigning drug lord of the southern city of Kandahar. "The Karzai family has opium and blood on their hands," one Western intelligence official told the *New York Times* during the campaign.[23]

Desperate to capture an outright majority in the first round of balloting, Karzai's coalition employed an extraordinary array of electoral chicanery. After two months of counting and checking, the UN's Electoral Complaints Commission announced in October that more than a million of Karzai's votes, 28 percent of his total, were fraudulent, pushing the president's tally well below a winning margin.[24] Calling the election a "foreseeable train wreck," deputy UN envoy Peter Galbraith said: "The fraud has handed the Taliban its greatest strategic victory in eight years of fighting the United States and its Afghan partners."[25]

Galbraith was soon sacked, as US pressure extinguished the simmering flames of electoral protest. The runner-up withdrew from the runoff election that Washington had favored as a face-saving compromise, and Karzai was declared the outright winner by default. In the wake of the fraudulent election, he tried to stack the five-man Electoral Complaints Commission, replacing three foreign experts with his own Afghan appointees.[26] When the parliament rejected his proposal, he lashed out with bizarre charges, accusing the UN of wanting a "puppet government" and blaming all the electoral fraud on "massive interference from foreigners."[27] In a meeting with members of parliament, Karzai reportedly told them: "If you and the international community pressure me more, I swear that I am going to join the Taliban."[28]

Meanwhile, escalating pressure from Washington for reform only inflamed Karzai and led to public tantrums. As Air Force One headed for Kabul in March 2010, national security adviser General James Jones said bluntly that President Obama would try to persuade Karzai to prioritize "battling corruption, taking the fight to the narco-traffickers."[29] But after a week of inflammatory outbursts from Karzai, the White House was forced to retreat from this attempt at reform, with General Jones saying soothingly that during his visit to Kabul President Obama was "generally impressed with the quality of the [Afghan] ministers and the seriousness with which they're approaching their job."[30]

Despite the billions in aid lavished on Kabul, Washington found it impossible to control Karzai. He memorably summed up his fractious relationship with Washington this way: "I will speak for Afghanistan, and I will speak for the Afghan interest, but I will seek that Afghan interest . . . in partnership with America. In other words, if you're looking for a stooge and calling a stooge a partner, no. If you're looking for a partner, yes."[31]

With Washington's reform initiative effectively neutered, much like Diệm had done decades earlier, Karzai was free to spend the next four years presiding, as the sardonically dubbed "mayor of Kabul," over the growth of the Taliban resistance movement. With its bloated bureaucracy in the capital and its coalition of warlords and drug lords in the countryside, the government failed to promote alternative crops or check the proliferation of opium cultivation, whose profits would come to sustain the spreading insurgency.

By the time Karzai left office in September 2014, after a fraud-ridden election that required American mediation to broker a viable coalition, the Taliban was poised for a sustained offensive that would shatter the Afghan army's tenuous control of the countryside, taking over half of the rural districts.[32] Instead of fading into quiet retirement, Karzai continued to hold court in his residence near the presidential palace, working, as the *New York Times* put it, "from the wings to destabilize the government and exploit a moment of national crisis to try to return to power." As terrorist bombs erupted in the capital and Taliban guerrillas advanced in the countryside, Karzai encouraged protests in Kabul and warlord opposition in provinces like Kandahar, destabilizing the government of Washington's favored new ally, President Ashraf Ghani.[33] Whether at Saigon in the 1960s or at Kabul after 2002, Washington's would-be subordinate elites had proved surprisingly insubordinate, creating not only weak, corrupt governance for their own countries but also a severe foreign policy crisis for the United States.

Middle East Crisis

During this diplomatic standoff in Kabul, WikiLeaks activists began releasing those 251,000 diplomatic cables making it clear that Washington's relationship with Karzai in all its complexities and contradictions was by no means exceptional. Indeed, the most revealing of those cables offered uncensored insights into Washington's weakening controls over the global system of surrogate power that it had built over the past half century.

In reading these documents, the Israeli journalist Aluf Benn of the newspaper *Haaretz* could see "the fall of the American empire, the decline of a superpower that ruled the world by the dint of its military and economic supremacy." No longer, he added, are "American ambassadors . . . received in world capitals as 'high commissioners' . . . [instead they are] tired bureaucrats [who] spend their days listening wearily to their hosts' talking points, never reminding them who is the superpower and who is the client state."[34] As its influence declined, Washington was finding many of its chosen local allies either increasingly insubordinate or irrelevant, particularly in the strategic Middle East.

After the Berlin Wall fell in 1989, Moscow quickly lost its satellite states from the Baltic Sea to Central Asia, as once loyal surrogates were ousted or leapt off the sinking ship of Soviet Empire. For the "victor" in the Cold War, soon to be the planet's "sole superpower," a similar erosion of loyalties also began but at a much slower pace.

In the two decades that followed, globalization fostered a multipolar system of rising powers in Beijing, New Delhi, Moscow, Ankara, and Brasilia, even as a denationalized system of corporate power reduced the dependency of developing economies on any single state, however imperial. With its capacity to control elites receding, Washington faced ideological competition from Islamic fundamentalism, European regulatory regimes, Chinese state capitalism, and Latin American economic nationalism.

Amid this ongoing decline in its influence, Washington's attempts to control its subordinate elites or create new ones began to fail, often spectacularly—including, its efforts to topple bête noire Hugo Chávez of Venezuela in a badly bungled 2002 coup, to detach ally Mikheil Saakashvili of Georgia from Russia's orbit in 2008, or to oust nemesis Mahmoud Ahmadinejad in the 2009 Iranian elections.

Indicative of such declining influence, in early 2011 Washington faced an eruption of protests against pro-American autocrats from North Africa to the Persian Gulf. According to the WikiLeaks cables, President Zine al-Abedine Ben Ali of Tunisia had long kept Islamic radicals at bay. Colonel Muammar Gadhafi of Libya had been "a strong partner in the war against terrorism." Hosni Mubarak had repressed the radical Muslim Brotherhood in Egypt. President Ali Abdullah Saleh of Yemen had allowed the United States an "open door on terrorism." King Abdullah II of Jordan was a key defender of Israel. King Hamad of Bahrain provided port facilities for the US Fifth Fleet in the oil-rich Persian Gulf and favored "his relations with the U.S. intelligence community above all others."[35]

While these leaders served Washington well, they also subjected their own peoples to decades of corruption and repression, a policy whose ultimate failure prompted a frank admission from Secretary of State Condoleezza Rice in 2005. "For 60 years," she told an audience in Cairo, "the United States pursued stability at the expense of democracy . . . in the Middle East, and we achieved neither."[36]

In this region, perhaps more than any other, stability was indeed a serious problem. As European empires carved up the Ottoman domains in the decades surrounding World War I, they drew colonial boundaries for geopolitical convenience, ignoring what the *New York Times* called the "extraordinarily complex tapestries of tribes and subtribes and clans, ancient social orders that remained the population's principal source of identification and allegiance." After that Great War, the British fused the Shia, Sunni, and Kurdish populations of three Ottoman provinces into a protectorate called Iraq, and papered over the divisions by placing a made-up monarchy at its head. Just to the west, the French expropriated two more Ottoman provinces, and ruled Syria and Lebanon through a mosaic of sectarian minorities such as the Alawites, the Druze, and Maronite Christians. Between 1911 and 1920, the Italians seized half a dozen cities along the coast of North Africa from the Ottoman Empire and, after a protracted pacification, merged them into a colony called Libya. Through this tangled imperial history, many if not most of the twenty-two nations in the modern Arab world took form as fragile states, prone to fighting, fragmentation, or both. As the region's great-power patron during the Cold War decades that followed, Washington eschewed major social change and simply tried to maintain the imperial structure it had inherited—intervening twice in Lebanon (1958, 1982) to stabilize the ethnic coalition France had left behind, strengthening the many monarchies fostered by the British, and taking over the Bahrain naval base from Britain in 1971 to protect the Persian Gulf and its small sheikhdoms.[37]

Whatever the merits or demerits of earlier US policy might have been, Washington's occupation of Iraq from 2003 to 2011 proved a catalyst for chaos, first for the country itself and then for the wider Middle East where the political balance was tenuous at best. After the US invasion of March 2003 captured Baghdad in just three weeks, Washington's empowered envoy L. Paul Bremer made a series of decisions for his occupation government that ranged, in the words of the *New York Times*, from the "deleterious" to the "calamitous." First, he fired eighty-five thousand members of the ruling Baath Party, producing "the instant impoverishment of entire clans and tribes." Then, he abolished the Iraqi military, largely controlled by the Sunni minority, dismissing "hundreds of thousands of men . . . with both military training and access to weapons." Finally, the US military under his command gave "little thought to the arsenals and munitions depots . . . scattered about the country" that were soon "systematically looted, sometimes under the gaze of coalition soldiers who did not intervene."[38]

Under what the *New York Times* called the collective "weight of these blunders" the US occupation erupted in a violent insurgency within a year. After auditioning a succession of diffident allies, the United States finally settled on the Shia sectarian leader Nouri al-Maliki, whose eight years of corrupt, repressive maladministration (2006–14) were crowned by the disastrous ISIS offensive of June 2014. For nearly a decade, the United States had spent $25 billion building a modern Iraqi army with the full panoply of armor, artillery, infantry, and special forces. Within a week, however, just five thousand Sunni guerrillas routed a hundred thousand of these Iraqi (largely Shia) troops, capturing billions of dollars of advanced weaponry, cities with five million people, and a full third of Iraq's sovereign territory. It would take two full years to rebuild this army sufficiently to retake many of these captured cities, and even then sectarian troops—Shia militia and Kurdish Peshmerga fighters—did much of the fighting.[39]

In retrospect, the critical variable for this imperial misadventure in Iraq was Washington's inability to find an effective ally as surrogate for its exercise of power. In its last years, the shockwaves from this bungled American occupation and the sustained jihadist resistance were soon felt across this volatile region.

By 2009, political tensions were rising across the Middle East, threatening Washington's subordinate elites. The US ambassador to Tunisia reported that "President Ben Ali . . . and his regime have lost touch with the Tunisian people," relying "on the police for control," while "corruption in the inner circle is growing" and "the risks to the regime's long-term stability are increasing." Even so, the envoy could only recommend that Washington "dial back the public criticism" and instead rely on "frequent high-level private candor"—a policy that failed to produce any reforms before demonstrations toppled the government eighteen months later.[40]

Similarly, in late 2008 the American embassy in Cairo feared that "Egyptian democracy and human rights efforts . . . are being suffocated," but still insisted that "we would not like to contemplate complications for U.S. regional interests should the U.S.-Egyptian bond be seriously weakened."[41] When President Hosni Mubarak visited Washington a few months later, the Cairo embassy urged the administration "to restore the sense of warmth that has traditionally characterized the U.S.-Egyptian partnership."[42] Consequently, President Obama hailed this dictator as "a stalwart ally" and "a force for stability and good in the region."[43] When massive demonstrations demanded Mubarak's ouster just eighteen months later, Washington discouraged democratic reforms and backed General Omar Suleiman, the president's "consigliere" and intelligence chief who, according to embassy cables, had a "strong and growing relationship" with the CIA.[44]

As mass protests filled Cairo's Tahrir Square for eighteen days in early 2011, Mubarak's stunning downfall and the sudden ouster of his chosen successor Suleiman represented, wrote a *New York Times* commentator, "an historic eclipse of U.S. power." Indeed, in the year that followed what came to be called "the Arab spring," Islamist leaders whom Washington had long disdained rode to power in Egypt, Tunisia, and elsewhere in the Middle East on a wave of anti-American rhetoric.[45] The all-powerful Egyptian military tolerated the fundamentalist rule of the Muslim Brotherhood under Mohamed Morsi for a little more than a year until July 2013 when a junta led by General Abdel al-Sisi seized power in a successful coup. After consolidating his control by taking 96 percent of the vote a year later, President Sisi was determined that he "never be viewed as the West's lap dog"—a loss of influence compounded as American aid slid from over $2 billion annually during two decades under Mubarak to just $1.4 billion by late 2016.[46]

Taking a broader view of this failure, Egypt's respected opposition leader Mohamed ElBaradei complained bitterly that, after forty years of US dominion, the Middle East was "a collection of failed states that add nothing to humanity or science" because "people were taught not to think or to act, and were consistently given an inferior education."[47]

Reflecting the pathology of imperial dominion that has complicated Washington's ability to maintain its vast informal empire, the WikiLeaks cables also revealed a condescending attitude among American diplomats toward their subordinate elites. With the hauteur of latter-day imperial envoys, those diplomats derided "Canada's habitual inferiority complex vis-à-vis the U.S.";[48] dismissed "the Turks' neo-Ottoman posturing around the Middle East and Balkans";[49] and indulged in snide smugness at the failings of would-be allies: Colonel Muammar Gadhafi's yen for a "voluptuous blonde" nurse, Pakistani president Asif Ali Zardari's morbid fear of military coups, or Afghan vice president Ahmad Zia Massoud's reported $52 million in stolen funds.[50]

In addition, the State Department instructed its embassies worldwide to play imperial policemen by collecting comprehensive data on local leaders like "biographic and biometric data, including health, opinions toward the US, training history, ethnicity (tribal and/or clan), and . . . email addresses, telephone and fax numbers, fingerprints, facial images, DNA, and iris scans."[51] Emphasizing the importance of incriminating information, the department pressed its Bahrain embassy for details—damaging in an Islamic society—on the kingdom's crown princes, asking: "Is there any derogatory information on either prince? Does either prince drink alcohol? Does either one use drugs?"[52]

The Age of American Decline

In Washington's relations with both Diệm and Karzai there lurked a self-defeating pattern in its alliances with autocrats and dictators throughout the Third World, then and now. Selected and often installed in office by Washington, or at least backed by its massive military aid, these client regimes often became desperately dependent, even as their leaders failed to implement the sorts of reforms that might enable them to build independent political bases. Torn between pleasing foreign patrons or their own people, these leaders wound up pleasing neither. As opposition to their rule grew, a downward spiral of repression and corruption often ended in collapse. At the same time, despite all its power, Washington descended into frustration and despair, unable to force its allies to adopt reforms that might allow them to survive.

There was—and is—a fundamental structural flaw in any American entente with such autocrats. Inherent in these unequal alliances is a peculiar dynamic that makes the eventual collapse of American-anointed leaders an almost commonplace occurrence. At the outset, Washington selects clients who seem pliant enough to do its bidding. They, in turn, opt for Washington's support not because they are strong, but precisely because they are weak and need foreign patronage to gain and hold office.

Once installed, clients have little choice but to make Washington's demands their top priority, investing their slender political resources in placating foreign envoys. Responding to an American political agenda on civil and military matters, these autocrats often fail to devote sufficient energy, attention, and resources to cultivating a popular following—with Diệm isolated in his Saigon palace, just as Karzai became "the mayor of Kabul." Caught between the demands of a powerful foreign patron and countervailing local needs and desires, both leaders let guerrillas capture the countryside, while struggling uncomfortably, even angrily, in Washington's embrace.

Since the end of World War II, many of the sharpest crises in US foreign policy have arisen from such problematic relationships with authoritarian client regimes. It was the similarly close alliance with General Fulgencio Bautista of Cuba in the 1950s that inspired the Cuban Revolution and culminated in Fidel Castro's rebels capturing the Cuban capital, Havana, in 1959. That, in turn, led the Kennedy administration into the catastrophic Bay of Pigs invasion of the island and then the Cuban missile crisis with Russia.

For a full quarter century, the United States played international patron to Mohammad Reza Shah of Iran, massively arming his police and military while making him Washington's proxy power in the Persian Gulf. His fall in the Islamic revolution of 1979 not only removed the cornerstone of American power in this strategic region but also plunged Washington into a succession of foreign policy confrontations with Iran and other entanglements in the Greater Middle East that have yet to end.

The regime of Nicaragua's Anastasio Somoza, a similarly loyal client in Central America, fell to the Sandinista revolution in 1979, creating a foreign policy problem that led to the CIA's controversial Contra operation against the new left-wing regime and the seamy Iran-Contra scandal that would roil President Ronald Reagan's second term.

More recently in April 2010, Washington's anointed autocrat in the former Soviet socialist republic of Kyrgyzstan, President Kurmanbek Bakiyev, fled the palace after his riot police fired into the crowds and killed seventy-seven, but failed to stop opposition protesters from taking control of the capital Bishkek. Just five years before, Bakiyev rode into power "flanked by the robber barons on horseback from the south," and then proceeded to plunder the country to enrich his family and his cronies, even manipulating the Pentagon into giving his son's company a $315 million contract to fuel US military aircraft. Although his rule was brutal and corrupt, the Obama administration courted Bakiyev sedulously to preserve American use of the old Soviet air base at Manas, critical for supply flights into Afghanistan. Even as riot police were beating the opposition into submission to prepare for Bakiyev's "landslide victory" in the July 2009 elections, President Obama sent him a personal letter praising his support for the Afghan war. With Washington's imprimatur, there was nothing to stop Bakiyev's political slide into murderous repression and his ultimate fall from power.[53]

Why have so many American alliances with autocrats and dictators collapsed in such spectacular fashion, producing divisive recriminations at home and policy disasters abroad? In the new world of sovereign states that emerged after World War II, Washington has had to pursue a contradictory policy—dealing with the leaders of nations as if they were fully independent while playing upon their deep dependence on US economic and military aid. After identifying its own prestige with these fragile regimes, Washington usually tries to coax or chide them into embracing needed reforms. When this counsel fails and prudence might dictate the start of a staged withdrawal of support, as it once did in Saigon and does now in Kabul, American envoys usually cling to even the most unrepentant ally for the long slide into disaster.

Absent a global war to sweep away an empire, the decline of a great power often proves to be a fitful, painful, drawn-out process. To Washington's never-ending wars in the Middle East, its crippling partisan deadlock, the economy's slow slide toward second place globally, and some of its longtime allies, including the Philippines, now forging economic ties with rival hegemon China, must now be added the loss of loyal surrogates across the Middle East. Egypt's transition from President Mubarak to General al-Sisi, for instance, might seem a small move from one military autocrat to another, but it also was accompanied by a decline in US influence as the new regime, like others in the Middle East, distanced itself from Washington.

For more than fifty years, this system of global power has served Washington well, allowing it to extend its influence worldwide with surprising efficiency and economy of force. So there can be little question that the weakening of this network of subordinate elites and the ending of ties to a range of loyal allies—and they are indeed ending—is a major blow to American global power.

Chapter Three

Covert Netherworld

O ver the past thirty years, the world has witnessed a succession of sensational events, revealing traces of a clandestine domain that, though generally overlooked by pundits and scholars, has nonetheless been central to the rise of US global power.

- In 1986–87, eleven senior officials in President Ronald Reagan's administration were convicted of selling Iran embargoed arms to finance Nicaragua's Contra guerrillas, while this CIA-sponsored anticommunist force was also implicated in smuggling cocaine into the United States.[1]
- A decade later, Congolese president Joseph Mobutu, a longtime CIA ally, fled into exile after thirty years of rapacious corruption as a rebel militia captured the capital Kinshasha and unleashed a ten-year civil war—fueled by trafficking in blood ivory and rare minerals that left an estimated three to five million dead.[2]
- In reporting the 2011 assassination of Ahmed Wali Karzai, the brother of Afghanistan's president Hamid Karzai, BBC News described him as "a warlord mired in corruption who was openly involved in the drugs trade"—charges American officials had been loath to investigate because he was, according to the *New York Times*, considered a critical asset for the CIA.[3]

To understand the significance of these and countless similar incidents over the past half century, it is necessary to look into a clandestine domain where secret services and criminal syndicates play a significant role in contemporary political life. "The living are above and the dead are below," explained Rome's reputed Mafia boss Massimo Carminati, "and we're in the middle."[4]

Combining the intelligence tradecraft term *covert* with the classical concept of a *netherworld*, which connotes a shadowy realm beneath the surface of everyday political life, it's possible to pull such sensational incidents into a single meaningful category that has been integral to the formation of modern empires. Using the concept of a *covert netherworld* can also rescue such happenings from the realm of action cinema or pulp fiction, while at the same time restraining them from floating untethered into the ether of conspiracy theory. Through this concept, we can gain a more three-dimensional view of contemporary politics and the way empires actually work. The recent history of this shadowy domain has been marked by millions of deaths, massive fiscal malfeasance, and epidemic drug addiction, which means understanding the covert netherworld couldn't be more crucial.

Both land and sea are ancient arenas for warfare, and airpower appeared during World War I. But the covert netherworld first emerged as a critical domain for conflict among the Great Powers during the Cold War. While NATO and Warsaw Pact tanks faced off along the Iron Curtain, submarine fleets prowled the North Atlantic, and intercontinental missiles stood ready for launch, rival clandestine intelligence services, the CIA and KGB, worked through their local assets worldwide in a relentless struggle for political influence. If conventional domains threatened a globe-destroying possibility of nuclear war, then this covert netherworld—in which criminal activities and Cold War skullduggery combined to produce a lethal form of surrogate warfare—engulfed entire countries and even continents in devastating violence.

During the forty years of the Cold War, all the major powers—Britain, France, the United States, and the Soviet Union—deployed expanded, empowered clandestine services, making covert operations a central facet of geopolitical power. Moscow and Washington also sponsored satellite states with clandestine coercive capacities manifest in secret police, prisons, systems of torture, and extrajudicial executions.

As Europe's empires dissolved after 1945, the United States, the Soviet Union, and their respective allies also launched covert operations to control the new nations that suddenly sprouted across what was then called the Third World. Throughout the Cold War, the major powers relied on their secret services to dominate these subordinate states, thereby forming ad hoc, postcolonial empires. Moscow used the KGB to yoke its chain of twenty-two surrounding satellite states. Paris dispatched undercover operatives to contain West Africa's fourteen Francophone nations within an imperium called "Françafrique." London relied on its overseas secret service MI-6 to manage an orderly imperial retreat and to check communist influence in both Europe and Asia. Washington deployed the CIA to contend for dominion over four continents. To maintain their control, these clandestine services conducted coups and covert interventions, or at times engaged in open combat, waging proxy wars through warlords, rebels, or client armies that devastated vast swaths of Asia and Africa.

At the peak of the Cold War, President Eisenhower avoided conventional combat yet authorized 170 CIA covert operations in forty-eight nations, while President Kennedy approved 163 more during his three years in office. This represented a significant shift in US force projection from the conventional to the covert.[5] By manipulating elections in Italy, overthrowing a populist regime in Iran, slaughtering a million communists in Indonesia, ousting a social reformer in Guatemala, toppling a Socialist government in Chile, and countless other less spectacular interventions, the CIA allowed Washington to impose its writ upon that vast part of the globe then called the Free World. In effect, this recurring reliance on covert intervention transformed secret services from manipulators at the margins of state power into major players in international politics.

Yet unlike conventional military operations, where the balance of forces often produces a predictable outcome, covert interventions, often conducted by just a handful of clandestine operatives working with imperfect information, proved surprisingly delicate, prone to unintended results. And when these covert operations become entangled with the criminal underworld to form a covert netherworld, the possibility of failure only multiplied. To understand why the CIA's Nicaragua operation overcame formidable odds and why Washington's current war in Afghanistan has been such a debacle, we must first understand the character of this clandestine demimonde.

Clandestine Social Milieu

Although local forms of criminality and clandestine intrigues can be found around the globe and across time, the rise of modern empires was the essential precondition for this covert domain's transformation from sordid social margin into a significant political space. Over the past century, European imperial states and the United States have created powerful police and clandestine forces and often linked them to criminal syndicates in the shadowy realm of the covert netherworld.

At the end of the Cold War, the sudden collapse of the Iron Curtain opened the globe to untrammeled illicit trafficking that fostered a surprisingly large criminal milieu. By the late 1990s, UN investigators would report that "highly centralized" transnational crime syndicates employed 3.3 million members worldwide for trafficking in arms, drugs, humans, endangered species, and copyrighted goods, giving these nonstate actors ample personnel for political or paramilitary operations.[6]

While the illegality of their commerce forces criminal syndicates to conceal their activities, associates, and profits, political necessity similarly dictates that secret services practice a parallel tradecraft of untraceable finances, concealed identities, and covert methods. Criminal and clandestine operatives live simultaneously in the overt and covert dimensions, shape-shifting seamlessly between legitimate businessmen and syndicate bosses, or minor diplomats and undercover operatives. In sum, both criminal and covert actors are practitioners of what CIA operative Lucien Conein once called "the clandestine arts"—the skills involved in conducting complex operations beyond the bounds of civil society.[7]

Throughout much of the twentieth century, there were recurring instances of affinity, even alliance, between covert and criminal actors. State security services around the globe have long found drug traffickers useful covert-action assets—from the Chinese Nationalist Party's reliance on Shanghai's Green Gang to fight communists in the 1920s to French president Charles de Gaulle's use of the country's criminal milieu to battle leftist demonstrators during the political tumult of the 1960s.[8] As our knowledge of the Cold War grows, the list of drug traffickers who served the CIA lengthens to include Corsican syndicates, Chinese Nationalist Party irregulars, Lao generals, Haitian colonels, Honduran smugglers, and Afghan warlords.

Illicit commerce serves as the economic foundation for the covert netherworld, allowing this realm a measure of political autonomy from individual nations as well as the international community. Throughout the twentieth century, states and empires used their growing coercive capabilities for moral prohibition campaigns that failed to suppress the vice trades and instead served to transfer alcohol, drugs, and gambling into an expanding criminal sector. Even routine taxation can sometimes help transform conventional commodities into contraband commerce, as happened with cigarettes in France and the Philippines after World War II. In recent decades, post–Cold War conflicts have done the same for "blood diamonds," rare minerals, and "blood ivory" in Africa or oil in the insurgent-controlled areas of Iraq.[9]

But nothing can approach the scale, scope, and significance of illicit drug trafficking. Over the past two centuries, the major imperial powers have moved from an aggressive promotion of a free trade in opium to a rigorous prohibition of all narcotics production, sale, and use—a succession of contradictory policies whose collision has transformed opium as well as coca from folk medicines into major illicit commodities offering extraordinary profits to those who trade in them. After more than a century enmeshed in the imperial opium trade, China harvested 35,000 tons of opium in 1906 and imported 4,000 more to supply 13.5 million users, or 27 percent of its adult males, a level of mass addiction never equaled before or since.[10] Amplifying its commercial resilience, opium consumption also grew rapidly in the West, with a fourfold increase per capita in the United States and a sevenfold surge in the United Kingdom. By the time imperial Britain began phasing out India's opium exports to China in 1907, this drug had become a global commodity with a resilient nexus of supply and demand capable of resisting any attempt at eradication.[11]

In a sharp policy reversal at the start of the twentieth century, the great powers launched drug programs meant to prohibit and suppress much of the global narcotics trade.[12] As the United States stepped onto the world stage during Theodore Roosevelt's presidency, one of his first diplomatic initiatives was convening the 1909 Shanghai Opium Conference that launched the global prohibition effort. The conference urged national governments to ban the export of opium and control nonmedical use of its derivatives like heroin—recommendations that were incorporated, at Washington's urging, into the 1912 International Opium Convention.[13]

After a League of Nations convention banned nonmedical narcotics in 1925, criminal syndicates quickly emerged to take control of the residual drug traffic in Asia and the West.[14] Following its founding in 1945, the United Nations continued the league's anti-narcotics mission by adopting a succession of drug prohibition conventions that formed an international narcotics control regime in 1961, banned psychotropic drugs in 1971, and attempted to suppress transnational organized crime in 2000.[15]

In the early 1970s, President Richard Nixon declared a "war on drugs," expanding prohibition efforts beyond American borders to the Mediterranean basin and Southeast Asia—an ill-fated effort that would ultimately serve to stimulate an increase in trafficking. While heroin supply in the United States was temporarily reduced, this "stimulus of prohibition" expanded drug trafficking on five continents, largely in response to unmet demand.[16] A decade later, President Ronald Reagan redirected the drug war toward coca eradication in South America, while intensifying domestic enforcement.[17] Through the unfortunate combination of narcotics suppression and covert operations in drug source regions, the global supply of illicit opium increased sevenfold from 1,200 tons at the start of the drug war in 1972 to 8,870 tons by 2007.[18]

Since the end of the Cold War, expanding narcotics trafficking has sustained criminal syndicates, rebel armies, and covert operations on five continents. After the collapse of the Iron Curtain removed a continent-wide barrier to global trafficking, the international community was suddenly forced to confront a proliferation of criminal actors threatening global stability. At the Special Session of the General Assembly in June 1998, the UN adopted the Convention against Transnational Organized Crime and formed the Office of Drugs and Crime to curtail a global drug traffic with 180 million users (4.2 percent of the world's adults) and $400 billion in illicit income—equivalent to 8 percent of world trade, or about the same as the global commerce in textiles.[19] A decade later, the UN reported that drugs were "the single most profitable sector of transnational criminality" with a value of $322 billion, ten times the next largest activity, human trafficking.[20] When covert elements achieve an economic scale sufficient to fuel major conflicts, as they have in Afghanistan and Colombia, this netherworld can attain both the autonomy and the power to influence the course of world events.

US Intervention in Central America

Two of the largest CIA covert operations during the Cold War in Central America and Central Asia reveal the complexities of politico-military operations in this murky netherworld. After Soviet troops occupied Kabul and leftist Sandinista guerrillas seized Managua in 1979, the White House responded, first under Jimmy Carter but more decisively under Ronald Reagan, with clandestine operations rather than conventional military intervention. By fighting through surrogates—the Nicaraguan Contras and the Afghan mujahedeen—and tolerating their involvement in the local drug traffic, the CIA catalyzed the formation of covert netherworlds astride the Nicaraguan-Honduran borderlands and the Afghan-Pakistan frontier.

When American-backed Contra guerrillas began attacking Nicaragua from camps inside Honduras in the early 1980s, that country was already serving as a major transit route for the Medellín cocaine cartel's flights north to the United States.[21] The Drug Enforcement Administration (DEA) opened a new office in the Honduran capital, Tegucigalpa, in 1981. Its chief agent there, Tomas Zepeda, soon found that the country's ruling military officers were implicated in narcotics trafficking. In June 1983, however, the DEA shut that office without consulting Zepeda and transferred him to Guatemala "where he continued to spend 70% of his time dealing with the Honduran drug problem."[22] Asked why this office was closed, another DEA agent replied, "The Pentagon made it clear that we were in the way. They had more important business."[23] In the late 1980s, a Senate subcommittee found that four Contra-connected corporations hired by the State Department to fly "humanitarian aid" to rebel forces in Honduras were also smuggling cocaine back into the United States, part of the flood of drugs that unleashed a crack epidemic inside American cities.[24]

Such charges of Contra trafficking were soon overshadowed by the larger Iran-Contra political scandal. Indeed, they were largely forgotten until 1996 when the *San Jose Mercury News* tried to establish a direct connection between Contra cocaine smuggling, the CIA, and street-level crack distribution in Los Angeles. In the intense controversy that followed, the *Mercury* was repeatedly criticized for linking the CIA to such drug smuggling, but a later report by CIA inspector general Frederick Hitz confirmed that the agency had colluded with traffickers in Central America.[25]

With extensive quotations from classified memoranda and interviews with top agency officials, volume 2 of the Hitz report offers forty-eight paragraphs of extraordinary detail—since suppressed on the CIA's website—about the agency's alliance with one of the Caribbean's top cocaine smugglers, and so offers an inside look at its management of the complex forces at play within a covert netherworld.[26] To facilitate its arms shipments to the Contras (complicated by a Congressional embargo), the CIA allied with Alan Hyde, then considered a notorious cocaine trafficker who controlled thirty-five ships crisscrossing the Caribbean, and so gained access to his port facilities in the strategic Bay Islands off Honduras.[27]

In the years before the CIA allied with Hyde, every US security agency active in Central America had intelligence that he was a major cocaine trafficker. During the 1980s, he had reportedly used his fishing fleet and processing plant at Roatán Island to emerge, in the words of the US Coast Guard, as the "godfather for all criminal activities originating in Bay Islands." In 1984, the Defense Department attaché at Tegucigalpa reported that Hyde "is making much money dealing in 'white gold,' i.e., cocaine."[28] Two years later, the coast guard reported that his "criminal organization" was smuggling cocaine from the Bay Islands on "fishing vessels bound for South Florida." In addition to his own ships, Hyde was also serving as master of the vessel M/V *Bobby* "as a favor to Pablo Escobar, a major Colombian cocaine trafficker."[29] In March 1988, a report from the CIA's directorate of intelligence, "Honduras: Emerging Player in the Drug Trade," stated that Hyde was smuggling chemicals for two cocaine-processing plants in the Bay Islands.[30]

Showing how local social conditions can shape the character of covert operations, geography circumscribed the CIA's choices along this part of the Caribbean coastline. Lying astride the main smuggling routes between Colombia and the Gulf Coast, Hyde's base was ideally sited not only for smuggling cocaine north but also for the transshipment of arms south to the Contra bases along the Honduras-Nicaragua border.

Consequently, the CIA found it convenient to collaborate with him to supply its Contra allies from 1987 to 1989, a critical three-year period in both the proxy war against Nicaragua's leftist Sandinista government and the smuggling of cocaine into the United States. It was in July 1987 that a CIA field operative first suggested that "using Hyde's vessels to ferry supplies would be more economical, secure and time efficient than using aircraft." Although the Central American Task Force (CATF) at CIA headquarters warned, for the record, that Hyde "might have ties to drug traffickers," it still permitted developing contacts with him pending higher approval of the proposed logistical alliance.[31] On July 14, CIA headquarters cabled field officers that "there is a very real risk that news of our relationship with subject, whose reputation as an alleged drug smuggler is widely known to various agencies, will hit the public domain— something that could bring our program to a full stop."[32]

Two weeks later, W. George Jameson, counsel to the CIA's director for operations, advised CATF head Alan Fiers that despite a congressional ban on ties to "any individual who has been found to engage in . . . drug smuggling," this contact could proceed since "neither the firm, nor its owner, Alan Hyde, is under indictment or investigation to your knowledge and the allegations of drug trafficking are not substantiated."[33]

Accordingly, on August 5, 1987, Alan Fiers advised his superior, CIA deputy director for operations Clair George, that they "had no choice but to use Hyde on the grounds of 'operational necessity,'" even though he was "not attractive." George, in turn, discussed Hyde with the CIA's deputy director, Robert Gates, saying, "We need to use him, but we also need to figure out how to get rid of him." After Gates approved the relationship at the agency's highest level, George, in a cable dated August 8, issued the authorization to use Hyde to "provide logistical services to complete a project, after which all contacts must cease."[34] During the inspector general's later investigation, Fiers recalled that Gates, as acting CIA director, had also given him verbal approval to use Hyde "on a highly restricted basis."[35]

During the first two years of this ad hoc alliance, CIA headquarters sent what one agent called "mixed signals" about "the relationship with Hyde" to its field operatives. One agent recalled that there was "a lot of pressure from Fiers and DCI [director of central intelligence William] Casey to get the 'job done.'" But other officials urged caution "to make sure that the agency would be protected in case the congressional intelligence oversight committees 'came calling.'"[36] Left to resolve these contradictory directives, one CIA logistics officer, illustrating the affinity that can form between clandestine and criminal actors, insisted that he "never believed the drug allegations against Hyde, whom he came to regard as a close friend," though he admitted "it might have been possible for an employee of Hyde to use one of the boats for smuggling."[37]

In March 1988, CIA headquarters authorized the leasing of additional storage facilities from Hyde despite recent internal intelligence that he was "the head of an air smuggling ring with contacts in the Tampa/St. Petersburg area."[38] Within several months, however, "the receipt of continuing allegations of Hyde's involvement in cocaine trafficking" pressured CIA headquarters to find an alternative, particularly once a resumption of arms shipments to the Contra guerrillas, briefly suspended in response to congressional sanctions, made the agency less dependent upon his storage facilities to "mothball" supplies. Even so, field officers resisted requests from headquarters to sever ties, arguing that Hyde was their only reliable "delivery mechanism."[39] By early 1989, however, these logistical problems had apparently been resolved, and CIA headquarters finally ordered its field operatives to break off all contact—just a year before the Sandinistas finally lost power in Nicaragua's February 1990 elections.[40]

Although the tactical alliance was over, the CIA apparently continued to shield Hyde's drug smuggling from investigation by both Honduran and American authorities for another four years. In March 1993, an internal CIA directive stated that it was agency policy to "discourage . . . counternarcotics efforts against Alan Hyde because 'his connection to [the CIA] is well documented and could prove difficult in the prosecution stage.'"[41]

In retrospect, it seems that the CIA had closed its covert war zone to narcotics enforcement from 1987 to 1993, thereby protecting a top drug smuggler from investigation for six years at the peak of the crack-cocaine epidemic. At the same time, while strongly supporting the CIA Contra campaign, President Reagan began to emphasize the importance of increased domestic enforcement efforts in the drug war, including draconian penalties for personal use. Such enforcement doubled the US prison population, which rose from 370,000 in 1981 to 713,000 in 1989. Driven by Reagan-era drug laws, the number of the nation's prisoners continued to climb to 2.3 million by 2008, with over half (53 percent) of all those in federal penitentiaries sentenced for drug offenses.[42]

Such mass incarceration led to significant disenfranchisement, starting a trend that would, by October 2016, deny the vote to 6.1 million people and nearly 8 percent of all African Americans, a liberal constituency that had voted overwhelmingly Democratic for more than half a century. In four states—Florida, Kentucky, Tennessee, and Virginia—more than 20 percent of all African Americans were disenfranchised for felony convictions. Moreover, this carceral regime concentrated its prison populations, both guards and prisoners (who were enumerated yet disenfranchised), in conservative rural districts, creating something akin to latter-day "rotten boroughs" that reliably supported the Republican Party.[43] By fusing covert and overt, foreign and domestic, the clandestine netherworld invested President Reagan's drug policy with an implicit synergy, strengthening his conservative political base at home while securing critical peripheries abroad.

Although successful from both a partisan and foreign policy perspective, this covert operation came with heavy costs through some divisive political controversies. While the operation was still ongoing in 1986–87, investigations of the Iran-Contra scandal discovered that the Reagan administration, in violation of congressional bans, had sold surface-to-air missiles to Iran and then diverted the proceeds to purchase arms for the Contras. Following sensational congressional hearings, fourteen senior administration officials, including Defense Secretary Caspar Weinberger, were indicted and eleven were convicted. The controversy was quickly forgotten after all were either exonerated on appeal or given presidential pardons.[44]

But then years later, in August 1996, the *San Jose Mercury News* revived the issue, igniting a political firestorm with its "Dark Alliance" series, charging, "the Contra-run drug network opened the first conduit between Colombia's . . . cartels and L.A.'s black neighborhoods," and adding, in an editorial, "It's impossible to believe that the Central Intelligence Agency didn't know."[45] By mid-September, daily Internet "hits" at the dedicated website for the *Mercury*'s story, one of the first to use that innovation, passed the million mark and anger among African Americans was rising. On talk radio, some Black callers—going far beyond what the *Mercury* had actually said—accused the CIA of willfully destroying their communities with crack. In Washington, the Congressional Black Caucus demanded an investigation.[46]

When those charges became the biggest news story of the year, the national press entered the debate on the side of the CIA, with the *Washington Post*, the *New York Times*, and the *Los Angeles Times* each publishing front-page investigations, attacking the *Mercury*'s story and accusing that paper of fanning the flames of racial discord.[47] Although the *Mercury*'s editor apologized and the lead reporter Gary Webb committed suicide after being fired from his job, the Clinton administration felt compelled to further repair relations with African Americans by ordering CIA inspector general Hitz's inquiry into the affair.

As a global hegemon, the United States intervened episodically on five continents during the Cold War to contain challenges to its world order, often successfully, sometimes disastrously. In Central America, at the price of domestic political controversy, the CIA achieved a convergence between its covert warfare and the illicit cocaine traffic that sustained this operation for the decade needed to precipitate the defeat of a hostile regime in Nicaragua. For American conservatives, this clandestine warfare also produced political synergies, not only facilitating control of an imperial periphery but also fostering political advantage back home through the mass incarceration among the rival party's key electoral constituency. That success, if we can call all that success, would stand in striking contrast to the later complications from covert and conventional operations in Afghanistan.

How a Pink Flower Defeated the World's Sole Superpower

After fighting the longest war in its history, the United States stands at the brink of defeat in Afghanistan. How could this be possible? How could the world's sole superpower have battled continuously for over fifteen years, deploying a hundred thousand of its finest troops, sacrificing the lives of 2,200 of those soldiers, spending more than a $1 trillion on its military operations,[48] lavishing a record $100 billion more on "nation-building"[49] and "reconstruction," helping raise, fund, equip, and train an army of 350,000 Afghan allies, and still not be able to pacify one of the world's most impoverished nations? So dismal is the prospect of stability in Afghanistan that, in 2016, the Obama White House canceled a planned withdrawal of its forces, ordering nearly ten thousand troops to remain in the country indefinitely.[50]

Were you to cut through the Gordian knot of complexity that is the Afghan war, you would find that in the American failure lies the greatest policy paradox of the century: Washington's massive military juggernaut has been stopped dead in its steel tracks by a small pink flower—the opium poppy. Though seemingly metaphoric, even somewhat hyperbolic, this statement nonetheless reveals the power of economic forces to restrain the US exercise of global power via the clandestine netherworld.

Throughout its more than three decades in Afghanistan, Washington's military operations have succeeded only when they fit reasonably comfortably into Central Asia's illicit traffic in opium—and suffered when they failed to complement it. The first intervention in 1979 succeeded in part because the surrogate war the CIA launched to expel the Soviet Red Army coincided with the way its Afghan allies used the country's swelling drug traffic to sustain their decade-long struggle. Just as the convergence between the Contra forces and the cocaine traffic helped assure the CIA's success in Central America, so a parallel involvement of its Afghan allies in the opium trade allowed the agency a similar outcome in Central Asia. Indeed, the operational imperative of containing these volatile covert elements, particularly the illicit income from narcotics trafficking, would become blindingly clear in both this initial success and the later failure of US intervention in Afghanistan.

Despite almost continuous combat since the invasion of 2001, pacification efforts have failed to curtail the Taliban insurgency largely because the United States simply could not control the swelling surplus from the country's heroin trade. As its opium production surged from 180 tons in 2000 to a staggering 8,200 tons during the five years of American occupation that followed, Afghanistan's soil seemed sown with the dragon's teeth of ancient Greek myth. Every spring as the snow melts, the poppy plants cover the fields with pink flowers, and the opium harvest fills the Taliban's coffers, a new crop of teenage fighters seems to rise fully armed from remote villages to fill the growing guerrilla army for the fighting season that follows.

At each stage in its tragic, tumultuous history over the past forty years—the covert war of the 1980s, the civil war of the 1990s, and its post-2001 occupation—opium has played a surprisingly significant role in shaping the country's destiny. In one of history's bitter ironies, the way Afghanistan's unique ecology converged with American military technology transformed this remote, landlocked nation into the world's first true narco-state—a country where illicit drugs dominate the economy, define political choices, and determine the fate of foreign interventions. In the dismal denouement of its long Afghan adventure, Washington would discover not only serious limits to its exercise of military power but some of the complex geopolitical forces likely to hasten the waning of its global hegemony.

The CIA's secret war against the Soviet occupation of Afghanistan during the 1980s helped transform the lawless Afghani-Pakistani borderlands into the seedbed for a sustained expansion of the global heroin trade. "In the tribal area," the State Department reported in 1986, "there is no police force. There are no courts. There is no taxation. No weapon is illegal. . . . Hashish and opium are often on display."[51] By then, the process of guerrilla mobilization was long under way. Instead of forming its own coalition of resistance leaders, the CIA had relied on Pakistan's crucial Inter-Services Intelligence agency (ISI) and its Afghan clients who soon became principals in the burgeoning cross-border opium traffic.[52]

Not surprisingly, the agency looked the other way while Afghanistan's opium production grew unchecked from about 100 tons annually in the 1970s to 2,000 tons by 1991.[53] In 1979 and 1980, just as the CIA effort was beginning to ramp up, a network of heroin laboratories opened along the Afghan-Pakistan frontier. That region soon became the world's largest heroin producer. By 1984, it supplied a staggering 60 percent of the US market and 80 percent of the European.[54] Inside Pakistan, the number of heroin addicts surged from near zero (yes, *zero*) in 1979 to five thousand in 1980 and 1.3 million by 1985—a rate of addiction so high the UN termed it "particularly shocking."[55]

According to a 1986 State Department report, opium "is an ideal crop in a war-torn country since it requires little capital investment, is fast growing, and is easily transported and traded." Moreover, Afghanistan's climate was well suited to this temperate crop, with average yields two to three times higher than in Southeast Asia's Golden Triangle region, the previous capital of the opium trade.[56] As relentless warfare between CIA and Soviet surrogates generated at least three million refugees and disrupted food production, Afghan farmers began to turn to opium "in desperation" since it produced "high profits" that could cover rising food prices. At the same time, the State Department reported that resistance elements engaged in opium production and trafficking "to provide staples for [the] population under their control and to fund weapons purchases."[57]

As the mujahedeen guerrillas gained ground against the Soviet occupation and began to create liberated zones inside Afghanistan in the early 1980s, the resistance helped fund its operations by collecting taxes from peasants who grew the lucrative opium poppies, particularly in the fertile Helmand Valley, once the breadbasket of southern Afghanistan.[58] Caravans carrying CIA arms into that region for the resistance often returned to Pakistan loaded down with opium—sometimes, reported the *New York Times*, "with the assent of Pakistani or American intelligence officers who supported the resistance."[59]

Once the mujahedeen fighters brought the opium across the border, they sold it to Pakistani heroin refiners operating in the country's North-West Frontier Province, a covert-war zone administered by the CIA's close ally General Fazle Haq. By 1988, there were an estimated one hundred to two hundred heroin refineries in the province's Khyber district alone.[60] Further south in the Koh-i-Soltan district of Baluchistan Province, Gulbuddin Hekmatyar, an Islamic fundamentalist and the CIA's favored Afghan asset, controlled six refineries that processed much of the opium harvest from Afghanistan's Helmand Valley into heroin.[61] Trucks of the Pakistan Army's National Logistics Cell that carried crates of weaponry from the CIA to these borderlands also left with cargos of heroin for ports and airports where it would be exported to world markets.[62]

In May 1990, as this covert operation was ending, the *Washington Post* reported that Hekmatyar was the rebels' leading heroin trafficker. American officials, the *Post* claimed, had long refused to investigate charges of heroin dealing by Hekmatyar as well as Pakistan's ISI, largely "because U.S. narcotics policy in Afghanistan has been subordinated to the war against Soviet influence there."[63]

Indeed, Charles Cogan, former director of the CIA's Afghan operation, later spoke frankly about the agency's choices. "Our main mission was to do as much damage as possible to the Soviets," he told an interv iewer in 1995. "We didn't really have the resources or the time to devote to an investigation of the drug trade. I don't think that we need to apologize for this. . . . There was fallout in term of drugs, yes. But the main objective was accomplished. The Soviets left Afghanistan."[64]

Over the longer term, this "clandestine" intervention (so openly written and bragged about) produced a black hole of geopolitical instability never again sealed or healed. Lying at the northern reaches of the seasonal monsoon, where rain clouds arrive already squeezed dry, Afghanistan could not readily recover from the unprecedented devastation it suffered in the years of the first American intervention. Other than irrigated areas like the Helmand Valley, the country's semi-arid highlands were already a fragile ecosystem straining to sustain sizeable populations when war first broke out in

1979. As that war wound down between 1989 and 1992, the Washington-led alliance essentially abandoned the country, failing either to sponsor a peace settlement or finance reconstruction.

While Washington turned away from Afghanistan to other foreign policy hot spots in Africa and the Persian Gulf, a vicious civil war broke out in a country that had already suffered 1.5 million dead, three million refugees, and a ravaged economy. During the years of devastating civil strife among the bevy of well-armed warlords the CIA had left primed to fight for power, Afghan farmers raised the only crop that ensured instant profits: the opium poppy. Having multiplied twentyfold to 2,000 tons during the covert-war era of the 1980s, the opium harvest would double during the civil war of the 1990s.[65]

In this period of turmoil, opium's ascent is best understood as a response to severe damage from two decades of destructive warfare.[66] With the return of some three million refugees to a war-ravaged land, the opium fields were an employment godsend, requiring nine times as many laborers to cultivate as wheat, the country's traditional staple.[67] In addition, only opium merchants were capable of accumulating capital rapidly enough to be able to provide poor poppy farmers with much-needed cash advances that were more than half their annual income. That credit would prove critical to the survival of many impoverished villagers.[68]

In the civil war's first phase from 1992 to 1994, ruthless local warlords combined arms and opium in a countrywide struggle for power. Determined to install its Pashtun allies in Kabul, Pakistan worked through ISI to deliver arms and funds to its chief client Hekmatyar. By now, he was the nominal prime minister of a fractious coalition whose troops would spend two years shelling and rocketing the capital in savage fighting that left the city in ruins and some fifty thousand more Afghans dead.[69] When Hekmatyar nonetheless failed to take Kabul, Pakistan threw its backing behind a newly arisen Pashtun force, the Taliban, a fundamentalist movement that had emerged from that country's militant Islamic schools.

After seizing Kabul in 1996 and taking control of much of the country, the Taliban regime encouraged local opium cultivation, offering government protection to the export trade and collecting much-needed taxes on both the opium produced and heroin manufactured.[70] UN opium surveys showed that, during their first three years in power, the country's opium crop rose to 4,600 tons, or 75 percent of world production.[71]

In July 2000, however, as a devastating drought entered its second year and hunger spread across Afghanistan, the Taliban government suddenly ordered a ban on all opium cultivation in an apparent appeal for international acceptance.[72] To shed the country's image as "a pariah state," the regime's commissioner for drug control explained the ban was an "obligation under the international treaties." A subsequent UN crop survey of 10,030 villages found that this prohibition had reduced the harvest by 94 percent to a mere 185 tons. The area of poppy cultivation fell sharply from 82,000 hectares in 2000 to only 8,000 a year later.[73]

Three months later in September 2000, the Taliban sent a delegation led by its deputy foreign minister, Abdur Rahman Zahid, to UN headquarters in New York to trade upon the country's continuing drug prohibition in a bid for diplomatic recognition. Instead, that body imposed new sanctions on the regime for protecting Osama bin Laden.[74] The United States, on the other hand, actually rewarded the Taliban with $43 million in humanitarian aid, even as it seconded UN criticism over bin Laden. Announcing this aid in May 2001, Secretary of State Colin Powell praised "the ban on poppy cultivation, a decision by the Taliban that we welcome," but still urged the regime to end "their support for terrorism; their violation of internationally recognized human rights standards, especially their treatment of women and girls."[75]

The War on Terror (2001–2008)

After largely ignoring Afghanistan for a decade, Washington "rediscovered" the country with a vengeance in the aftermath of the 9/11 terrorist attacks. Only weeks later, in October 2001, the United States began bombing the country, and then launched an invasion spearheaded by local warlords. Surprisingly, the Taliban regime collapsed with a speed, in the words of veteran *New York Times* reporter R. W. Apple Jr., "so sudden and so unexpected that government officials and commentators on strategy . . . are finding it hard to explain."[76] Although the US air attacks did considerable physical and psychological damage, many other societies have withstood far more massive bombardments without collapsing in this fashion. In retrospect, it seems likely that its opium prohibition had economically eviscerated the Taliban, leaving its theocracy a hollow shell that shattered with the first American bombs.

To an extent not generally appreciated, Afghanistan had, for two full decades, devoted a growing share of its resources—capital, land, water, and labor—to the production of opium and heroin. By the time the Taliban banned cultivation, its agriculture had become little more than an opium monocrop. The drug trade accounted for most of its tax revenues, much of its export income, and a significant share of its employment.

In this context, the Taliban's sudden opium eradication proved to be an act of economic suicide that brought an already weakened society to the brink of collapse. Indeed, a 2001 UN survey found that the ban had "resulted in a severe loss of income for an estimated 3.3 million people," 15 percent of the population, including 80,000 farmers, 480,000 itinerant laborers, and their millions of dependents.[77] A UN mission that May reported an "alarming situation in the former poppy-growing areas" marked by "hardship for many small farmers" and unemployment forcing itinerant workers to seek "refuge in major urban centres, in other countries or enlisting in the Afghan conflict."[78] As farmers had to sell cattle and trade daughters to pay their crop loans while going hungry through a long, cold winter, it became, according to the UN, "easier for Western military forces to persuade rural elites and the population to rebel against the regime."[79]

In little more than a month, the lethal US bombing campaign, combined with ground attacks by its warlord allies, smashed the Taliban's weakened defenses. After four weeks of eluding airstrikes on the front lines northeast of Kabul, one of the Taliban's toughest commanders, known as Mullah Cable, began to think "he had put too much stock in the Americans' technological prowess." One day, however, a jet shrieked from the skies and dropped bombs on his forward unit with deafening explosions. "There were severed limbs everywhere," the mullah was shocked to discover. "There were headless torsos and torso-less arms, cooked slivers of scalp and flayed skin. The stones were crimson, the sand ocher from all the blood." Everyone was dead. That night when news came that 880 Taliban fighters were missing along the front, the mullah asked himself: "What kind of unimaginable power was this?" Hearing that entire Taliban units were defecting, the mullah gathered his surviving men, saying: "Get yourselves away from here. Don't contact each other." Though once notorious for his militancy, the mullah now promised himself that, if he somehow survived, "he would abandon politics forever." He then fled toward Kabul, following the thousands of Taliban soldiers who were returning to their villages, planning to live in peace and "give up the fighter's life entirely." The Taliban's once-formidable army was broken, seemingly forever.[80]

Yet the other half of the US strategy would plant the seeds, quite literally, for the Taliban's surprising revival just four years later. While the American bombing campaign raged throughout October 2001, the CIA shipped $70 million in cash into the country to mobilize its old coalition of tribal war-lords for the fight against the Taliban, an expenditure President George W. Bush would later hail as one of history's biggest "bargains."[81] To capture Kabul and other key cities, the CIA put its money behind the leaders of the North-ern Alliance, which the Taliban had never fully defeated.[82] They, in turn, had long dominated the drug traffic in the area of northeast Afghanistan they controlled in the Taliban years. Just as it had once allied with the cocaine trafficker Alan Hyde in the Caribbean, so the CIA also turned to a group of rising Pashtun warlords along the Pakistan border who had been active as drug smugglers in the southeastern part of the country. As a result, when the Taliban collapsed, the groundwork had already been laid for the resumption of opium cultivation and the drug trade on a major scale.[83]

Once Kabul and the provincial capitals were taken, the CIA quickly ced-ed operational control to allied military forces and civilian officials whose inept drug suppression programs in the years to come would leave the heroin traffic's growing profits first to these warlords and, in later years, largely to the Taliban guerrillas.[84] In the year after the US invasion, before that movement had even reconstituted itself, the opium harvest surged to 3,400 tons. In a development without historical precedent, illicit drugs would be responsible for an extraordinary 62 percent of the country's 2003 gross domestic prod-uct (GDP).[85] But for the first few years of the occupation, Defense Secretary Donald Rumsfeld reportedly "dismissed growing signs that drug money was being funneled to the Taliban," while the CIA and military "turned a blind eye to drug-related activities by prominent warlords."[86]

In late 2004, after nearly two years of studied disinterest in drugs, out-sourcing opium control to its British allies and police training to the Ger-mans, the White House was suddenly confronted with troubling CIA intel-ligence suggesting that the escalating drug trade was fueling a revival of the Taliban. Backed by President Bush, Secretary of State Colin Powell then urged a forceful counter-narcotics strategy for parts of rural Afghanistan, including the aggressive aerial defoliation then being used against Colombia's illicit coca crop. But US ambassador Zalmay Khalilzad resisted this approach, seconded by his local ally Ashraf Ghani, then the country's finance minister (and, since 2014, its president), who warned that such an eradication program would mean "widespread impoverishment" in the country without $20 billion in foreign aid to create a "genuine alternative livelihood."[87]

As a compromise, Washington came to rely on private contractors like DynCorp to train Afghan teams for manual drug eradication. By 2005, however, that effort had, according to *New York Times* correspondent Carlotta Gall, already become "something of a joke."[88] Two years later, as the Taliban insurgency and opium cultivation both spread in what seemed to be a synergistic fashion,[89] the American embassy again pressed Kabul to accept the kind of aerial defoliation the United States had sponsored against coca cultivation in Colombia. President Hamid Karzai refused, leaving this critical problem unresolved.[90]

By 2007, the UN's *Afghanistan Opium Survey* found that the annual harvest was up 24 percent to a record 8,200 tons, or 53 percent of the country's GDP and 93 percent of the world's illicit heroin supply. Significantly, the UN stated that Taliban guerrillas have "started to extract from the drug economy resources for arms, logistics, and militia pay."[91] A study for the US Institute of Peace concluded in 2008 that this movement had fifty heroin labs in its territory and controlled 98 percent of the country's poppy fields. That year, the rebels reportedly collected $425 million in "taxes" levied on the opium traffic, and with every harvest gained the necessary funds to recruit a new crop of young fighters from the villages. Each of those prospective guerrillas could count on monthly payments of $300, far above the wages they would have made as agricultural laborers.[92]

To contain the spreading insurgency, Washington decided to commit forty thousand more American combat troops to the country in mid-2008, raising allied forces to seventy thousand.[93] Recognizing the crucial role of opium revenues in Taliban recruitment, the allied command was also fielding Provincial Reconstruction Teams that used development aid in poppy-rich provinces to encourage drug suppression efforts at what proved a fortuitous moment. That record harvest in 2007 had created an opium surplus that depressed prices to only $60 per kilogram from a peak of $700 in 2001, while simultaneous food shortages made wheat, for the first time, a competitive crop. As farmers used foreign aid to plant food crops in key areas of Helmand and Nangarhar Provinces, the country's poppy cultivation slipped from a record 200,000 hectares in 2007 to only 123,000 two years later—still sufficient, however, to sustain the Taliban.[94]

Complementing this effort, the US Treasury Department also formed the Afghan Threat Finance Cell and embedded sixty of its analysts in combat units charged with launching strategic strikes against the drug trade. Using quantitative methods of "social network analysis" and "influence network modeling," these instant civilian experts would, according to a former Defense Department analyst, often "point to hawala brokers [rural creditors] as critical nodes within an insurgent group's network," prompting US combat soldiers to take "kinetic courses of action—quite literally, kicking down the door of the hawala office and shutting down the operation." Such "highly controversial" acts might "temporarily degrade the financial network of an insurgent group," but those gains came "at the cost of upsetting an entire village" dependent on the lender for legitimate credit that was the "vast majority of the hawalador's business." In this way, support for the Taliban only grew.[95] By then, this unintended outcome for what had once seemed a sophisticated counterinsurgency tactic was but one of many signs that these operations, instead of supporting American goals, were headed for a disastrous outcome.

Obama's Afghan Adventure (2009–2016)

By 2009, the guerrillas were expanding so rapidly that the new Obama administration opted for a "surge" of US troop strength to 102,000 in a bid to cripple the Taliban. After months of rising deployments, President Obama's big, breakthrough strategy was officially launched in the darkness before dawn on February 13, 2010, at Marja, a remote market town in Helmand Province. As waves of helicopters descended on its outskirts spitting up clouds of dust, hundreds of marines sprinted through fields of sprouting opium poppies toward the village's mud-walled compounds.[96] Though their targets were the local Taliban guerrillas, the marines were in fact occupying the capital of the global heroin trade. Almost 40 percent of the world's illicit opium supply was grown in the surrounding districts and much of that was traded in Marja.[97]

A week later, General Stanley McChrystal choppered into town with Karim Khalili, Afghanistan's vice president. They were there for the media rollout of new-look counterinsurgency tactics that were, the general told reporters, rock-solid certain to pacify villages like Marja. The local opium traders, however, had other ideas. "If they come with tractors," one Afghan widow announced to a chorus of supportive shouts from her fellow farmers, "they will have to roll over me and kill me before they can kill my poppy."[98] Speaking by satellite telephone from the region's opium fields, one US Embassy official told me: "You can't win this war without taking on drug production in Helmand Province."

Watching these events unfold back in March 2010, I warned of a defeat foretold. "So the choice is clear enough," I said at the time. "We can continue to fertilize this deadly soil with yet more blood in a brutal war with an uncertain outcome . . . or we can help renew this ancient, arid land by replanting the orchards, replenishing the flocks, and rebuilding the farming destroyed in decades of war . . . until food crops become a viable alternative to opium. To put it simply, so simply that even Washington might understand, we can only pacify a narco-state when it is no longer a narco-state."[99]

By attacking the guerrillas but failing to eradicate the opium harvest that funded new insurgents every spring, Obama's surge soon suffered that defeat foretold. As 2012 ended, the Taliban guerrillas had, according to the *New York Times*, "weathered the biggest push the American-led coalition is going to make against them."[100] Amid the rapid drawdown of allied forces to meet President Obama's politically determined deadline of December 2014 for "ending" all combat operations, a marked reduction in air operations allowed the Taliban to launch mass-formation offensives in the North, Northeast, and South, killing record numbers of Afghan army troops and police.[101]

At the time, John Sopko, the special inspector for Afghanistan, offered a telling explanation for the Taliban's survival. Despite the expenditure of a staggering $7.6 billion on "drug eradication" programs during the previous decade, he concluded that, "by every conceivable metric, we've failed. Production and cultivation are up, interdiction and eradication are down, financial support to the insurgency is up, and addiction and abuse are at unprecedented levels in Afghanistan."[102]

Indeed, the 2013 opium crop covered a record 209,000 hectares, raising the harvest by 50 percent to 5,500 tons and holding the price per kilogram at $172, nearly three times the record low of $60 that had depressed production back in 2007. [103] This massive harvest generated some $3 billion in illicit income,[104] of which the Taliban's tax took an estimated $320 million—providing well over half its revenues.[105] The US Embassy corroborated this dismal assessment, calling the illicit income "a windfall for the insurgency, which profits from the drug trade at almost every level."[106]

As the 2014 opium crop was harvested, fresh UN figures suggested this dismal trend only continued, with areas under cultivation rising to a record 224,000 hectares and production at 6,400 tons approaching the country's historic high.[107] In May 2015, having watched this flood of drugs enter the global market as US counter-narcotics spending climbed to $8.4 billion, Inspector Sopko tried to translate these developments into a comprehensible all-American image. "Afghanistan," he said, "has roughly 500,000 acres, or about 780 square miles, devoted to growing opium poppy. That's equivalent to more than 400,000 U.S. football fields—including the end zones."[108]

During Afghanistan's 2015 fighting season, the Taliban decisively seized the combat initiative and opium seemed ever more deeply embedded in its operations. The *New York Times* reported that the movement's new leader, Mullah Akhtar Mansour, was "among the first major Taliban officials to be linked to the drug trade . . . and later became the Taliban's main tax collector for the narcotics trade—creating immense profits."[109] The group's first major operation under his command was the two-week seizure of the northern city of Kunduz, which just happened to be located on "the country's most lucrative drug routes . . . moving opium from the poppy prolific provinces in the south to Tajikistan . . . and to Russia and Europe."[110] Stunned by the Taliban's sudden success, Washington felt forced to slam the brakes on further planned withdrawals of its combat forces.[111]

Amid a rushed evacuation of its regional offices in the threatened northern provinces, the UN released a map in October 2015 showing that the Taliban had "high" or "extreme" control in more than half the country's rural districts, including many in which it had not previously had a significant presence.[112] Within a month, the Taliban unleashed offensives countrywide that aimed at seizing and holding territory, threatening military bases in northern Faryab Province and encircling entire districts in western Herat.[113]

Not surprisingly, though, the strongest attacks came in the poppy heartland of Helmand Province, where half the country's opium crop was then grown and, said the *New York Times*, "the lucrative opium trade made it crucial to the insurgents' economic designs." By December 2015, after overrunning checkpoints, winning back much of the province, and setting government security forces back on their heels, the guerrillas came close to capturing Marja, the site of Obama's surge rollout in 2010. Had American special operations forces and its airpower not intervened to relieve "demoralized" Afghan forces, the town and the province would undoubtedly have fallen.[114]

Further north in fertile poppy districts astride the Helmand River system, insurgents captured most of Sangin district by the end of December 2015, forcing the retreat of government soldiers who, hobbled by endemic local corruption, were reportedly "fighting with lack of ammunition and on empty stomachs." By 2016, fifteen years after Afghanistan was "liberated," and in a significant reversal of Obama administration drawdown policies, Washington launched a mini-surge by "hundreds" of new US troops into Helmand Province to deny insurgents the "economic prize" of the world's most productive poppy fields. Despite support from American airpower and seven hundred special operations troops, in February and March 2016 embattled government forces retreated from two more districts, Musa Qala and

Khan Neshin, leaving the Taliban largely in control of ten of the province's fourteen districts.[115] After suffering three thousand killed in this Taliban offensive, demoralized government forces hunkered down inside provincial and district capitals, leaving the countryside and combat initiative to the heroin-funded guerrillas.[116]

With government forces demoralized and the Taliban fielding aggressive fighters equipped with night-vision and sophisticated weapons, American airstrikes became the government's last, tenuous line of defense.[117] And in a tacit admission of failure, the Obama administration ended its planned withdrawal in June 2016, allowing US forces to move beyond advising to actual combat and announcing, a month later, that some 8,400 troops would remain there for the foreseeable future.[118]

In Helmand and other strategic provinces, the Afghan army seemed to be losing a war that was now driven—in ways that eluded most observers—by a battle for control of the country's opium profits. Take, for example, the drop in the 2015 poppy crop, with cultivation down by 18 percent to 183,000 hectares and the harvest off sharply to 3,300 tons.[119]

While the Afghan government and UN attributed the decline to their successful eradication efforts, British agronomist David Mansfield traced the reduction to long-term ecological trends that do not bode well for the Afghan government. Between 2003 and 2013, poor opium farmers, forced out of Helmand's prime irrigated lands by drug eradication efforts, had migrated into the desert areas of neighboring Helmand and Farah Provinces, sinking wells that irrigated some 260,000 hectares and sustained a population of 1.2 million, largely opium farmers who soon became the mass base for the Taliban's revival in this region. But in 2014–2015, five years of declining yields thanks to soil salination and bad farming practices forced some fifty thousand people back into Helmand's irrigated districts like Marja, bringing along their Taliban loyalties, poppy skills, and surplus labor for the guerrilla offensive now hammering government forces.[120] Dispatching a few hundred US troops to Helmand to hold back such a relentless demographic tide unleashed by the poppy crop was a feeble, even futile response.

In Helmand Province, both Taliban rebels and provincial officials are locked in a struggle for control of the lucrative drug traffic. "Afghan government officials have become directly involved in the opium trade," the *New York Times* reported in February 2016. In so doing, they expanded "their competition with the Taliban . . . into a struggle for control of the drug traffic," while imposing "a tax on farmers practically identical to the one the Taliban uses." In a process that implicated virtually the entire government, provincial officials then passed a portion of their illicit profits "up the chain, all the way to officials in Kabul . . . ensuring that the local authorities maintain support from higher-ups and keeping the opium growing."[121]

Simultaneously, a UN Security Council investigation found the Taliban had systematically tapped "into the supply chain at each stage of the narcotics trade"—collecting a 10 percent tax on opium cultivation in Helmand, fighting for control of heroin laboratories, and acting as "the major guarantors for the trafficking of raw opium and heroin out of Afghanistan."[122] No longer simply taxing the traffic, the Taliban was so deeply and directly involved that, according to the *New York Times*, it "has become difficult to distinguish the group from a dedicated drug cartel."[123] For the foreseeable future, opium will likely remain entangled in the rural economy, the Taliban insurgency, and government corruption whose sum is the Afghan conundrum.

While Helmand grabbed headlines, the dynamics of the opium traffic in other strategic provinces were also serving to undercut government control. At the start of the 2016 fighting season, agronomist Mansfield reported that Nangarhar Province, "one of the major entry points for the capture of Kabul," was "in complete disarray." Once "celebrated for its success in counter narcotics and counterinsurgency," Nangarhar had experienced, in just two years, spreading opium cultivation, the return of heroin processing, and the loss of the countryside to rival armed groups responsible for "a dramatic uptick in levels of violence." Areas such as the Mahmand Valley with large families and small landholdings found, during the decade of drug eradication that ended in 2013, that they "simply cannot subsist without recourse to drug crop cultivation" and so supported the rebels' return. As the Taliban took control of Nangarhar's southern districts, tribal elders grew "too fearful" of the guerrillas to back government opium suppression, opening the way for a rapid resurgence of the crop.[124]

While UN officials attributed much of that 2015 opium decline to drought,[125] as well as a poppy fungus that might not continue into future seasons,[126] long-term trends are still an unclear mix of positive and negative news. Buried in the mass of data published in the UN's annual drug reports is one significant trend: as Afghanistan's economy grew from years of international aid, opium's share of GDP dropped steadily from a daunting 63 percent in 2003 to a far more manageable 13 percent in 2014. Even so, says the UN, "dependency on the opiate economy at the farmer level in many rural communities is still high."[127] With ample revenues from future opium crops, the

Taliban will likely be ready for each new fighting season as long as American soldiers remain in Afghanistan.

Lessons of War

The failure of America's intervention in Afghanistan offers broader insight into the limits to its global power. The persistence of both opium cultivation and the Taliban insurgency suggest the degree to which the policies that Washington has imposed upon Afghanistan since 2001 have reached a dead end. For most people worldwide, economic activity, the production and exchange of goods, is the prime point of contact with their government. When, however, a country's most significant commodity is illegal, then political loyalties naturally shift to the economic networks that move that product safely and secretly from fields to foreign markets, providing protection, finance, and employment at every stage. "The narcotics trade poisons the Afghan financial sector and fuels a growing illicit economy," special inspector John Sopko explained. "This, in turn, undermines the Afghan state's legitimacy by stoking corruption, nourishing criminal networks, and providing significant financial support to the Taliban and other insurgent groups."[128]

After fifteen years of continuous warfare, Washington is faced with the same choice it had back in 2010 when Obama's generals airlifted those marines into Marja. Just as it has been over the past decade and a half, the United States can remain trapped in the same endless cycle. As snow melts from the mountain slopes and poppy plants rise from the soil every spring, there will be a new batch of teenage recruits from impoverished villages ready to fight for the rebel cause.

Even in that troubled land, however, there are alternatives to this Gordian knot of a policy problem. Investing even a small portion of all that misspent military funding in the country's agriculture can produce economic alternatives for the millions of farmers who depend upon the opium crop for employment. Ruined orchards could be rebuilt, ravaged flocks repopulated, wasted seed stocks regrown, and wrecked snow-melt irrigation systems that once sustained a diverse agriculture before these decades of war repaired. If the international community continues to nudge the country's dependence on illicit opium downward from the current 13 percent of GDP through sustained rural development, then maybe Afghanistan will cease to be the planet's leading narco-state. And just maybe the annual cycle of violence could at long last be broken.

The deft deployment of US airpower and special operations forces utterly obliterated the Taliban government back in 2002. But the burgeoning drug economy revived and then sustained an insurgency of such strength that it could not be stopped by even the most sophisticated weapons in the awesome American arsenal—armed drones, carrier airstrikes, culture-sensitive counterinsurgency, night commando raids, systemic torture, biometric identification, and computerized intelligence.

At the peak of its global power back in the 1980s, Washington was master of the covert netherworld, as it was for so much of the world, manipulating a fusion of Islamic fundamentalism and illicit opium to drive the Soviet Army from Afghanistan and riding a convergence of Contra resistance and cocaine trafficking to force regime change in Nicaragua. Now those same economic forces the United States once manipulated so masterfully to maintain its hegemony have eluded its control. Just as the pink poppy flower has stopped this massive US military juggernaut dead, so Washington's attempt to extend its global hegemony by substituting military power for its eroding economic strength may suffer a similar fate.

The Cold War proved to be a historic high tide for covert action, fostering secretive agencies of unprecedented power and extending their netherworlds to whole countries and continents. This clandestine domain will likely remain a central component of future US involvement in geopolitical conflict, whether against Russia, China, or lesser powers worldwide. The globalization that succeeded the Cold War's bipolar division has not been kind to Third World states, fraying their borders and enmeshing them in international economic circuits of corruption and illegality. If such trends continue, this clandestine domain may become even more central to great power conflict in the rest of the twenty-first century than it was in the twentieth. If so, the impending defeat of US intervention in Afghanistan may well serve as an indicator of not only Washington's waning ability to control the covert elements of global politics but its weakening hold on world power over the longer term.

PART II
US Strategies for Survival

Chapter Four

A Global Surveillance State

A lthough Washington began withdrawing many of its troops from the Greater Middle East in 2011, its sophisticated intelligence apparatus, built for the pacification of Afghanistan and Iraq, had already preceded them home, creating a US surveillance state of unprecedented power. Two years later, Edward Snowden's cache of leaked documents would reveal that the National Security Agency (NSA) was already using this technology to monitor the private communications of almost every American in the name of fighting foreign terrorists. But the roots of this domestic surveillance were, in fact, much deeper than anyone realized at the time. This kind of imperial blowback had been building a massive US internal security apparatus, step by step, war by war, for well over a century.

Just a decade after Washington finally pacified the Philippines in 1907 by forging the world's most advanced surveillance state, the illiberal lessons of that moment, too, migrated homeward during World War I to form America's first internal security apparatus. A half century later, as protests mounted against the war in Vietnam, the CIA and FBI built upon this system to conduct illegal counterintelligence operations to suppress or harass antiwar activists and American radicals.

In the aftermath of each of these wars, however, reformers pushed back against such secret surveillance, with Republican privacy advocates abolishing much of President Woodrow Wilson's security apparatus in the 1920s, and Democratic liberals creating the Foreign Intelligence Surveillance Courts (FISA courts) in the 1970s to prevent recurrences of Richard Nixon's illegal domestic wiretapping operations.

President Obama broke this bipartisan pattern for the first time in a century. Instead of retrenching the domestic surveillance built by his Republican predecessor, he seemed determined to maintain American dominion through a strategic edge in information control—and so continued to support construction of a powerful global panopticon capable of surveilling domestic dissidents, tracking terrorists, manipulating allied nations, monitoring rival powers, countering hostile cyber strikes, protecting domestic communications, and crippling essential electronic systems in enemy nations.

During his first months in office, I observed that the so-called war on terror had seemed close to "creating a domestic surveillance state—with omnipresent cameras, deep data-mining, nanosecond biometric identification, and drone aircraft patrolling the homeland."[1]

That prediction has, in fact, become our present reality with breathtaking speed, propelled by the bureaucratic momentum from a full century of state surveillance. Not only are most Americans living under the Argus-eyed gaze of a digital surveillance state, but drones are now in our skies, cameras are an everyday presence in our lives, and the NSA's net sweeps up the personal messages of millions of people worldwide, Americans included, and penetrates the confidential communications of countless allied nations. The past was indeed prologue.

From the start of colonial conquest in August 1898, the Philippines served as the site for a seminal experiment in the use of surveillance as an instrument of state power. To break a nationalist revolution, the US Army plunged into a protracted pacification program, forming its first field intelligence unit that combined voracious data gathering with rapid dissemination of tactical intelligence. At this periphery of empire, freed from the constraints of courts, the Constitution, or civil society, the US colonial regime fused new technologies, the product of America's first information revolution, to form a modern police force and fashion what was arguably the world's first full surveillance state.

Over the past century, this same process has recurred as three other overseas pacification campaigns have dragged on, skirting defeat if not disaster. During each of these attempts to subjugate an Asian or Middle Eastern society, the American military has been pushed to the breaking point and responded by drawing together all its extant information resources, fusing them into an infrastructure of unprecedented power and producing a new regime for data management. Forged in such crucibles of counterinsurgency, the military's information infrastructure has advanced through three distinct technological phases: manual intelligence collection during the Philippine

War; computerized data management in the war in Vietnam; and, most recently, integrated robotic systems in Afghanistan and Iraq.

This broad time frame indicates that, once introduced, state security becomes dependent on covert controls like surveillance, which prove remarkably resistant to reform and are easily revived in any crisis. Through such persistence, cyber operations have become a distinctive US strategy for the exercise of global power.

America's First Information Revolution

At the start of the nineteenth century, European states launched bureaucratic reforms that rendered land and society "legible" by external measurements like the metric standard and registered family names.[2] At the start of the twentieth century, however, America moved beyond such passive data collection to become the site of an accelerating information revolution whose capacity for mass political surveillance represented a new phase in the perfection of modern state power—not just reading the legible superficialities of name and address but reaching deep inside private lives for intimate or even incriminating information.

In one extraordinary decade, from the 1870s to the 1880s, that information revolution arose from a synergy of innovations in the management of textual, statistical, and visual data creating, for the first time, the technical capacity for surveillance of the many rather than just a few—a defining attribute of the modern state. During this transformative decade, Thomas Edison's quadruplex telegraph (1874), Philo Remington's commercial typewriter (1874), and Alexander Graham Bell's telephone (1876) allowed for the transmission and recording of textual data in unprecedented qualities, at unequaled speed, with unsurpassed accuracy.[3]

These dynamic years also saw parallel progress in the management of statistical and visual data. After engineer Herman Hollerith patented the punch card (1889), the US Census Bureau adopted his electrical tabulating machine in 1890 to enumerate 62,622,250 Americans within a few weeks—a stunning success that would later lead to the founding of International Business Machines, better known by its acronym IBM.[4] Almost simultaneously, the development of photoengraving (1881) and George Eastman's roll film (1889) extended this information revolution to visual data.[5]

Parallel innovations in data storage provided the means for reliable encoding and rapid retrieval. In the mid-1870s, Melvil Dewey cataloged the

Amherst College Library with his "Dewey decimal system" and Charles A. Cutter worked at Boston's Athenaeum Library to create what became the current Library of Congress system. In effect, these two librarians had invented the "smart number" to manage this rising tide of information.[6]

Within a decade, libraries, hospitals, and armed forces would apply this smart number to create systems that reduced diverse data to uniform alphanumeric codes for rapid filing, retrieval, and cross-referencing, allowing a fundamental modernization of the federal bureaucracy. In quick succession, the Office of Naval Intelligence created a card method for recording intelligence (1882), and the army's Military Information Division (MID) adopted a similar system three years later. Indicative of the torrid tempo of this information revolution, MID's intelligence information cards grew from four thousand in 1892 to over three hundred thousand just a decade later.[7]

The information revolution came to crime detection and policing via a mix of foreign and domestic sources. At Paris police headquarters in 1882, Alphonse Bertillon developed the first biometric criminal identification system with eleven cranial and corporeal measurements that would, within a decade, be adopted as the American standard.[8] During the 1890s, the inspector general of police for British India, Sir Edward Henry, finalized the modern system of fingerprint classification and then brought it home to Scotland Yard in 1901, from whence it migrated three years later to America at the St. Louis World's Fair. Major urban police departments soon adopted fingerprinting as their sole standard for criminal identification. Although the Bureau of Investigation (later the FBI) did not follow suit until 1924, within a decade its files passed the six million mark and its director was soon urging compulsory fingerprinting for all citizens. Only months after a young J. Edgar Hoover became head of the bureau's Radical Division in 1919, he could boast of eighty thousand file cards "covering the activities of not only the extreme anarchists but also more moderate radicals."[9]

While an imitator in criminal identification, America was an innovator in police and fire communications. Starting in the 1850s, the Gamewell Corporation adapted the telegraph and telephone to create centralized fire-alarm systems that became the world's standard.[10] By 1900, America's cities were wired with a total of 764 municipal fire-alarm systems and 148 police call-box networks handling a total of 41,000,000 messages in a single year.[11] On the eve of empire in 1898, however, Congress and the courts restrained any national application of these innovations, leaving the federal government with a limited capacity for law enforcement or domestic security.

Colonial Laboratory

The conquest of the Philippines unleashed the potential of these new technologies to form the country's first information regime as the army battled an extraordinary array of insurgents—national army, urban underground, militant unions, messianic peasants, and Muslim separatists. In the process, the colonial government formed three new services seminal for the creation of a counterintelligence capacity: a Division of Military Information, which developed internal-security methods later applied to the United States; the Philippine Constabulary that pacified the new colony's insurgency through pervasive surveillance; and the highly efficient Manila Metropolitan Police.

In retrospect, the sum of their surveillance activities provided the nascent imperial regime with key elements of colonial control: basic intelligence on Filipino leaders and nationalist movements, and scurrilous information about local elites useful in assuring their compliance. Through the clandestine accumulation of knowledge—routine, intimate, or scandalous—about native collaborators, American officials gained a sense of omniscience and also an aura of authority for the exercise of colonial dominion. The importance of controlling these local leaders cannot be overstated. The British Empire expanded steadily for two hundred years through alliances with such subordinate elites and then unraveled suddenly in just twenty years when, as historian Ronald Robinson has written, "colonial rulers had run out of indigenous collaborators."[12]

Arriving in the Philippine Islands without maps, a knowledge of local languages, or intelligence, the US Army was, as a senior intelligence officer put it, "a blind giant more than able to annihilate, to completely smash" anything it faced, but unable "to get any information" about where or when to unleash this lethal force.[13] As it struggled to uproot guerrillas immersed in rugged terrain and hostile populations, the army discovered the need for accurate intelligence and established the Division of Military Information, or DMI—the first field intelligence unit in its hundred-year history.

In early 1901, Captain Ralph Van Deman, who came to be known as "the father of U.S. military intelligence," assumed command of this unit and began developing procedures that would, fifteen years later, influence intelligence operations for the entire US Army.[14] His Manila command began combining reports from the army's 450 post intelligence officers with data from the colony's civil police, laying telegraph lines to encircle guerrilla zones, and pressing subordinates for fast, accurate information. In this way, the DMI's field units became far more agile in tracking rebel movements and identifying locations for timely raids.[15]

With a voracious appetite for raw data, DMI launched a "confidential" project to map the entire guerrilla infrastructure by compiling information cards on every influential Filipino—documenting physical appearance, personal finances, political loyalties, and kinship networks. For rapid retrieval, the DMI's clerks then transcribed these cards into indexed, alphabetized rosters for each military zone.[16] With few military precedents to guide him, Captain Van Deman soon was developing comprehensive doctrines for both intelligence and counterintelligence.[17]

During its pacification of the capital city, the army also created a metropolitan police force that would apply military intelligence and data management to domestic counterintelligence. When colonial rule by civil officials began in 1901, Manila's police added the most advanced American crime control technologies—a centralized phone network, the Gamewell system of police-fire alarms, incandescent electrical lighting for city streets, Bertillon's photo identification, and fingerprinting. Within just twenty years, they would amass two hundred thousand alphabetized file cards covering 70 percent of the city's population.[18]

The first US civil governor, William Howard Taft, oversaw the elaboration of these military intelligence methods into a modern surveillance state, creating a colonial regime that ruled by controlling information through draconian libel laws and pervasive counterintelligence. Only weeks after taking office in July 1901, Taft established the Philippine Constabulary with 325 officers, many of them Americans, and 4,700 constables, all of them Filipino. Taft assigned this new force the dual mission of counterinsurgency and colonial intelligence.

The constabulary's founder was Captain Henry Allen, a West Point graduate who, from an earlier assignment as military attaché at the czar's court in St. Petersburg, had come to understand the importance of intelligence and a secret police.[19] With its network of two hundred Filipino spies, the constabulary's information division drew its data from intensive surveillance, covert penetration, and the monitoring of the press and public discourse. All this intelligence flowed into the constabulary's headquarters where it was translated, typed, numbered, and filed in dossiers for ready retrieval.[20]

Within this police panopticon, the constabulary was systematic in its collection of incriminating information and selective in its release—that is, suppressing scandal to protect allies and releasing scurrilous information to destroy enemies. Among the tens of thousands of reports that crossed his desk, General Allen carried just one document with him through wartime service in France and into retirement near Washington, DC—a DMI report titled "The Family History of M.Q." Among its many scandalous tales, this report alleged that an influential Filipino politician identified only as "M.Q." had concealed a premarital liaison with his half-sister and future wife by arranging an abortion and had buried the fetus from a similar liaison with another half-sister in Manila's Paco Cemetery.[21]

During the first decade of his political career, M. Q., or Manuel Quezon, then an attorney, served the constabulary as a secret agent and was, in turn, protected from the taint of such scandal. In 1903, future constabulary chief Rafael Crame, then a lieutenant in its Information Division, retained the young Quezon as what he called a "private spy . . . used in all sorts of cases in the early days of the Constabulary."[22]

Since Quezon cooperated fully with the constabulary, the "The Family History of M.Q." remained safely buried in General Allen's private files until his death, thereby ensuring Quezon's unchecked rise to become the country's first president in 1935 and, after independence in 1946, the namesake for the new nation's capital, Quezon City.

Surveillance Comes Home

While the pacification of the Philippines was under way, Mark Twain wrote an imagined history of a future twentieth-century America, arguing that its "lust for conquest" had destroyed "the Great Republic . . . [because] trampling upon the helpless abroad had taught her, by a natural process, to endure with apathy the like at home; multitudes who had applauded the crushing of other people's liberties, lived to suffer for their mistake."[23] Indeed, just a decade after Twain wrote those prophetic words, colonial police methods migrated homeward from the Philippines to provide models for the creation of an all-American internal security apparatus.

The Philippines would prove to be the first manifestation of the repressive potential of this new information technology. On the eve of empire in 1898, the United States was still what political scientist Stephen Skowronek has termed a "patchwork" state with a loosely structured administrative apparatus of limited capacity for law enforcement and state security.[24]

When Washington entered World War I in April 1917, it had the only army on the battlefield without an intelligence service of any description. With surprising speed, however, these colonial police methods helped create two new army commands that would foster a future domestic security apparatus extending far beyond the armed forces. In effect, these colonial methods served as the model for formation of America's own manual information regime.

Only weeks after Washington declared war on Germany, Colonel Van Deman drew upon his experience in the Philippines to establish the Military Intelligence Section, quickly recruiting a staff that grew from one employee (himself) to 1,700, and devising the entire institutional architecture for America's first major internal security agency. Just as the Philippine Constabulary had used civilian operatives, so Van Deman designed his new command as a fusion of federal agencies and civilian auxiliaries that would mark its operations for the next half century. In collaboration with the FBI, he would preside over a wartime counterintelligence auxiliary, the American Protective League, with 350,000 civilian operatives who amassed more than one million pages of surveillance reports on German Americans in just fourteen months—arguably the world's most intensive domestic surveillance to date.[25]

Similarly, in the final months of World War I, General Harry Bandholtz, drawing on his "long experience in command of the Philippine Constabulary," established the army's military police, or MPs, charged with managing the chaos of postwar occupation and demobilization. Following its formation in October 1918, Bandholtz quickly built the MPs into a corps of 31,627 men stationed in 476 cities and towns across France, Italy, Belgium, Luxembourg, and the German Rhineland.[26]

Bandholtz later applied lessons learned from repressing Filipino radical movements to defeating the only major armed uprising that the American state faced in the twentieth century. In 1921, as ten thousand striking mineworkers armed with rifles battled with sheriffs and private security agents along a firing line across Mingo and Logan counties in West Virginia, General Bandholtz quelled the violence without firing a shot. Using the psychological tactics learned in the colonial constabulary, he deployed 2,100 federal troops to demobilize some 5,400 miners, confiscate 278 firearms, and send everyone home. Sixteen men died in the five-day Battle of Blair Mountain, but none was shot by army troops.[27]

With war's end in 1918, Military Intelligence revived the Protective League and organized the American Legion to engage in two years of repression against the socialist left, marked by mob action across the Midwest, the notorious Lusk raids in New York City, J. Edgar Hoover's "Palmer raids" across the Northeast, and the suppression of strikes from New York to Seattle. Once Congress and the press exposed the excesses involved in these activities, however, Republican conservatives quickly curtailed Washington's internal security apparatus. In May 1924, Attorney General Harlan Fiske Stone, worried that "a secret police may become a menace to free government," announced, "the Bureau of Investigation is not concerned with political or other opinions of individuals." Five years later, Secretary Henry Stimson abolished the State Department's cryptography unit with the stern admonition, "Gentlemen do not read each other's mail."[28]

If General Van Deman's wartime service won him the title as father of US military intelligence, his subsequent surveillance activities should earn him another honorific: the father of the American blacklist. After retiring from the army in 1929, he and his wife worked tirelessly for the next quarter century from their bungalow in San Diego, coordinating an elaborate information exchange among naval intelligence, police red squads, business security outfits, and citizen vigilante groups to amass detailed files on 250,000 suspected subversives. Through this hard-won influence, Van Deman attended a confidential meeting in 1940 between FBI director J. Edgar Hoover and the chief of army intelligence. There, the world was literally divided through a "Delimitations Agreement" that assigned counterintelligence for the Americas to the FBI and intelligence gathering for the rest of the world to Military Intelligence—an inheritance that would pass on to its lineal descendants, the Office of Strategic Services (OSS) and, postwar, the CIA. During World War II, the FBI would use warrantless wiretaps, "black bag" break-ins, and surreptitious mail opening to track suspects, while mobilizing over three hundred thousand informers to secure defense plants against wartime threats that ultimately proved, said a Senate report, "negligible."[29]

In the aftermath of war, the nation's public-private security alliance grew into the anticommunist movement identified with Senator Joseph McCarthy. In this period of "witch-hunting," General Van Deman would work closely with the FBI and the California Committee on Un-American Activities to expose the Communist Party and its supposed fellow travelers, particularly in Hollywood. In June 1949, that committee, headed by state senator Jack Tenney, drew upon General Van Deman's massive archive of intelligence to issue a sensational 709-page report denouncing hundreds of Hollywood luminaries as "red appeasers"—including silver-screen stars Charlie Chaplin, Katharine Hepburn, Gregory Peck, and Orson Welles, singer Frank Sinatra, and, significantly, California congresswoman Helen Gahagan Douglas.[30]

Van Deman's archive would serve as an informal conduit for moving security reports from closed, classified government files into the hands of citizen anticommunist groups for public blacklisting. In the 1946 congressional elections, Richard Nixon, then an obscure Los Angeles lawyer, reportedly used Van Deman's files to red-bait and defeat popular five-term Democratic congressman, Jerry Voorhis. Four years later, Representative Nixon supposedly used the same files and the same tactics to beat Representative Douglas in a race for the Senate, launching his path to the presidency.[31]

Nor did this archive die with its creator. Only hours after Van Deman passed away at his San Diego home in 1952, a team from the army counterintelligence corps secured his voluminous files and shipped them north to the Presidio, a military base in San Francisco. For the next twenty years, his records would be used by the army and then, in 1971, delivered to the Senate Internal Security Committee where they assisted in the investigation of suspected communists until the late 1970s.[32]

Meanwhile, General Van Deman's methods were perpetuated inside the FBI, particularly after 1940 when J. Edgar Hoover's bureau gained control of counterintelligence and used wartime conditions for illegal break-ins, wiretaps, and mail intercepts. To curtail enemy espionage, President Franklin Roosevelt authorized Hoover, in May 1940, to engage in a program of limited wiretapping that the bureau expanded into widespread surveillance. During the war, the bureau planted 6,769 wiretaps and 1,806 bugs that provided the president with transcripts of the conversations of his domestic enemies—notably, aviator Charles Lindbergh, Senator Burton K. Wheeler, and Representative Hamilton Fish. Upon taking office in early 1945, President Harry Truman soon discovered the extraordinary extent of FBI surveillance. "We want no Gestapo or Secret Police," Truman wrote in his diary that May. "FBI is tending in that direction. They are dabbling in sex-life scandals and plain blackmail."[33] Yet after only a few months in office, Truman himself ordered FBI phone taps on Thomas G. Corcoran, President Roosevelt's trusted aide whom Truman now regarded as "poison."[34]

The manual information regime reached its apotheosis during World War II when Washington established the Office of Strategic Services (OSS) as its first global espionage apparatus. Among this agency's nine branches, research and analysis recruited 1,950 academics who amassed 300,000 photographs, a million maps, and three million file cards—which they deployed to produce over 3,000 staff studies and to answer countless tactical questions.[35]

By early 1944, however, the OSS found itself, in the words of historian Robin Winks, "drowning under the flow of information" with documents stacking up, unread and unanalyzed. Absent technological change, this labor-intensive, manual version of data gathering and surveillance might have eventually collapsed under its own weight, imposing real limits on America's voracious imperial information apparatus.[36]

Computerized Information Regime

Under the pressures of a protracted counter-guerrilla campaign in South Vietnam from 1964 to 1973, the United States launched a computerized information revolution that soon became nothing less than a second American information regime.

In 1966, Defense Secretary Robert McNamara asked the CIA to "design me something that will tell us the status of control in the countryside." The agency then identified eighteen variables that would allow US military advisers to assess security in all of South Vietnam's twelve thousand hamlets on a scale ranging from "A" (secure) to "E" (Viet Cong controlled). Every month, US command's IBM computers arrayed the results of this Hamlet Evaluation Survey (HES) on a dot-matrix computer map meant to reflect spreading South Vietnamese control over the countryside. Unable to measure the all-important variable of "popular commitment," the HES, said American pacification czar Robert Komer, faced an impossible dilemma. "We were trying desperately to find countrywide indicators," he explained, "and naturally the only indicators we could use were those that were statistically comparable and measureable." This proved to be a fool's errand, even as the share of South Vietnam's population rated "secure" climbed relentlessly to 75 percent on the eve of the Tet Offensive of 1968, which would reveal the illusory nature of all this data.[37]

Six years later as the Saigon regime plunged toward defeat, the HES survey still found South Vietnam 84 percent "pacified." In the end, these automated indices led South Vietnam's government, said CIA director William Colby, "to delude itself about its standing with its own people."[38] Even though all this computerized data contributed to a soul-searing defeat in Vietnam, in retrospect it served as an important experimental step, creating innovations that would start Washington, decades later, on the path toward a third, robotic information regime.

During the Vietnam era as well, the FBI's Counterintelligence Programs (COINTELPRO) conducted illegal acts of domestic surveillance against the antiwar movement in particular. In response to the civil rights and the anti–Vietnam War protests of the 1960s, the FBI deployed COINTELPRO, using what a congressional committee chaired by Senator Frank Church would later call "unsavory and vicious tactics . . . including anonymous attempts to break up marriages, disrupt meetings, ostracize persons from their professions, and provoke target groups into rivalries that might result in deaths." In assessing the program's 2,370 illegal actions from 1960 to 1974, that senate committee branded them a "sophisticated vigilante operation" that "would be intolerable in a democratic society even if all of the targets had been involved in violent activity."[39]

In addition, after a quarter century of warrantless wiretaps, the FBI had built J. Edgar Hoover's "Sex Deviate Files" and "Official/Confidential" files, housed inside the director's office, into an archive of the sexual peccadilloes of America's most powerful political figures. Hoover used such material as blackmail, or slipped to the press revelations that he used to shape the direction of politics. He distributed a dossier on Democratic candidate Adlai Stevenson's alleged homosexuality to encourage his defeat in the 1952 presidential election, circulated audiotapes of Martin Luther King Jr.'s philandering, and told President Kennedy over lunch in March 1962 he knew of his affair with mafia mistress Judith Exner.[40]

"The moment [Hoover] would get something on a senator," recalled William Sullivan, then the bureau's third-ranking official, "he'd send one of the errand boys up and advise the senator that 'we're in the course of an investigation, and we by chance happened to come up with this data on your daughter. . .' From that time on, the senator's right in his pocket."[41] By Hoover's death in 1972, locked file cabinets in his office held 722 files on congressmen and 883 on senators, documenting their indiscretions.[42]

In 1974, after *New York Times* reporter Seymour Hersh exposed the CIA's illegal surveillance of antiwar activists, Congress investigated the agency's Operation Chaos, discovering a database with 300,000 domestic names that it was legally barred from collecting.[43] After the Senate's Church Committee and the president's Rockefeller Commission documented the excesses of this domestic surveillance, Congress passed the Foreign Intelligence Surveillance Act of 1978, creating so-called FISA courts to issue warrants for all future national security wiretaps. In effect, media exposé and legislative reform put limits on Cold War excesses, much as Republican conservatives had done in the aftermath of World War I.[44]

And then, of course, came the terror attacks of September 11, 2001. In an atmosphere of fear and panic, the way was opened again for excesses of information gathering and surveillance of every sort. As its occupations of Afghanistan and then Iraq encountered fierce resistance, Washington only accelerated its development of electronic surveillance, biometric identification, and unmanned aerial vehicles—creating new technologies that are now, after more than a decade of such covert operations, forming a third, robotic US information regime. The amorphous war on terror's voracious appetite for information soon produced a veritable "fourth branch" of the federal government with 854,000 vetted security officials and over 3,000 private and public intelligence organizations.[45]

The George W. Bush administration soon retreated into the shadows to launch a remarkable range of secret domestic surveillance programs run by the FBI and NSA.[46] In 2002, Congress erased the legal barrier that had long barred the CIA from domestic spying, granting the agency power to access US financial records and audit electronic communications routed through the country.[47] But the White House soon went much further by conducting widespread surveillance without sufficient legal authority.

Starting in October 2001, President Bush also ordered the NSA to begin covert monitoring of private communications through the nation's telephone companies without the requisite warrants.[48] Once the Bush administration decided "metadata was not constitutionally protected," the NSA launched Operation Stellar Wind, a sweeping attempt "to collect bulk telephony and Internet metadata."[49] The architect of this spreading surveillance was General Keith Alexander (a domestic spymaster to rival J. Edgar Hoover), who, from the time he took charge of the NSA in 2005, pushed the metadata program to track every phone call made in America.[50]

Armed with expansive FISA court orders permitting the collection of broad categories rather than information on specific individuals, the FBI's Investigative Data Warehouse acquired over a billion documents within five years—including intelligence reports, social security files, driver's licenses, and private financial information—accessible to 13,000 analysts making a million queries monthly.[51] In 2006, as the sheer masses of data strained computer capacities, the Bush administration launched the Intelligence Advanced Research Projects Activity, using IBM's Watson supercomputer to sift through the rising haystack of Internet data.[52]

In 2005, the *New York Times* exposed the NSA's illegal surveillance for the first time.[53] A year later, *USA Today* reported that the agency was "secretly collecting the phone call records of tens of millions of Americans, using data provided by AT&T, Verizon and Bell South." One expert called the result "the largest database ever assembled in the world," adding presciently that the agency's goal was "to create a database of every call ever made."[54]

With expanded powers under congressional legislation in 2007 and 2008 that legalized Bush's once illegal program, the NSA launched PRISM, a program that compelled nine Internet service providers to transfer what became billions of emails to its massive data farms.[55] And the FISA courts, originally created to check the national security state, instead became its close collaborator, approving nearly 100 percent of government wiretap requests and renewing the NSA's mass metadata collection of all US phone calls thirty-six consecutive times from 2007 to 2014.[56]

Surveillance under Obama

Unlike Republicans in the 1920s or Democrats in the 1970s who curtailed wartime surveillance, President Obama instead expanded the NSA's digital project as a permanent weapon for the exercise of global power. Under his administration, the NSA's foreign and domestic Internet data capture became so pervasive that the American surveillance state penetrated the private lives of individual Americans on a massive scale.

By the end of Obama's first term, the NSA's system of surveillance was simultaneously sweeping up billions of messages worldwide while monitoring dozens of specific international leaders. To achieve such an extraordinary capability, it developed access points for penetrating the worldwide web of fiber-optic cables; other ways in via special protocols and "backdoor" software flaws; supercomputers that could begin to crack the encryption of this digital torrent; and massive data farms to store the endless flood of purloined data.

What made the NSA so powerful was, of course, the Internet—that global grid of fiber-optic cables, which, as of 2013, connected some 40 percent of humanity.[57] By the time Obama took office, the agency had finally harnessed the power of modern telecommunications for near-perfect surveillance. Centralization, via digitization, of all voice, video, textual, and financial communications on the Internet allowed the NSA, circa 2013, to monitor the entire globe by penetrating just 190 data hubs—an extraordinary economy of energy for both political surveillance and cyberwarfare.[58]

With a few hundred cable probes and computerized decryption, the NSA could capture, circa 2013, the kind of gritty private details that J. Edgar Hoover so treasured when it came to only hundreds of individuals and simultaneously provide the sort of comprehensive surveillance of entire populations once conducted by secret organizations like East Germany's Stasi.

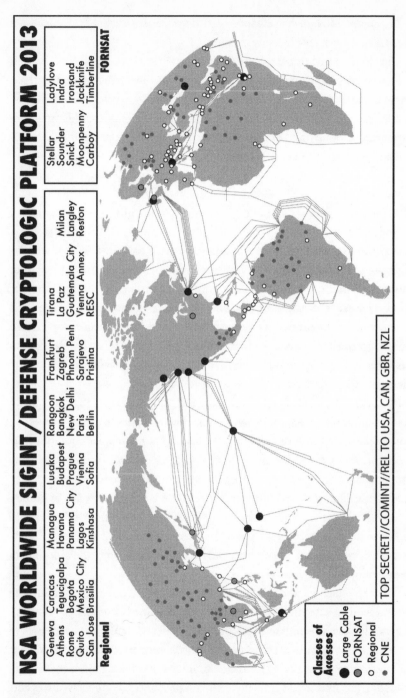

NSA WORLDWIDE SIGINT/DEFENSE CRYPTOLOGIC PLATFORM 2013

FORNSAT

Stellar	Ladylove
Sounder	Indra
Snick	Ironsand
Moonpenny	Jackknife
Carboy	Timberline

Tirana	Milan
La Paz	Langley
Guatemala City	Reston
Vienna Annex	
RESC	

Frankfurt	Rangoon	Geneva
Zagreb	Bangkok	Athens
Phnom Penh	New Delhi	Rome
Sarajevo	Paris	Quito
Pristina	Berlin	San Jose

Lusaka	Caracas
Budapest	Tegucigalpa
Prague	Bogota
Vienna	Mexico City
Sofia	Brasilia

Managua
Havana
Panama City
Lagos
Kinshasa

Regional

Classes of Accesses
- ● Large Cable
- ◐ FORNSAT
- ○ Regional
- · CNE

TOP SECRET//COMINT//REL TO USA, CAN, GBR, NZL

NSA Worldwide SIGINT/Defense Cryptologic Platform, 2013, showing 190 "access programs" for penetrating the Internet's global grid of fiber-optic cables for both surveillance and cyberwarfare

Yet the extent of NSA surveillance is so unprecedented that such historical precedents seem feeble by comparison.

The first round of mass surveillance came during World War I when the FBI and Military Intelligence swelled into all-powerful agencies charged with extirpating any flicker of disloyalty anywhere in America, whether by word or deed. Since only 25 percent of the country's households then had telephones, monitoring the loyalties of some ten million German Americans and countless suspect subversives proved incredibly labor intensive. Legions of postal workers had to physically examine the twelve billion first-class letters mailed in 1918 alone, while 350,000 badge-carrying vigilantes performed shoe-leather snooping on immigrants, unions, and socialists of every sort.[59]

In the next round of such surveillance during World War II, it was the telephone that made Hoover a Washington powerhouse. With 40 percent of the country and the entire political elite by then owning phones, FBI wiretaps at local switchboards could readily monitor conversations by both suspected subversives and the president's domestic enemies. Even with such centralized communications, however, the bureau's staff soared from just 650 in 1924 to 13,000 by 1943 to provide the massive manpower required for its wartime counterintelligence.[60]

Yet once FBI agents had tapped thousands of phones, stenographers had typed up countless transcripts, and clerks had stored this paper harvest in floor-to-ceiling file cabinets, J. Edgar Hoover still only really knew about the inner-workings of the elite in one city: Washington, DC. To gain the same intimate detail for an entire country, the Stasi would have to employ one police informer for every six East Germans—an unsustainable waste of human resources.[61] By contrast, the marriage of the NSA's decryption technology to the Internet's data hubs now allows the agency's 37,000 employees to monitor the entire globe with a highly efficient ratio of just one official for every 200,000 people on the planet.[62]

Since the start of the war on terror, the NSA has been relentless in pushing this powerful new technology to its limits to monitor influential political figures worldwide and simultaneously to sweep up data for almost every person on the planet. In August 2013, the *New York Times* reported that the FISA court had chastised the NSA two years earlier for intercepting some 250 million email messages from Americans annually while supposedly tracking foreign suspects and for maintaining a log of all domestic phone calls since 2006.[63] A month later, the same paper revealed that, since 2010, the NSA had applied sophisticated software to create "social network diagrams . . . to unlock as many secrets about individuals as possible . . . and pick up sensitive information like regular calls to a psychiatrist's office [or] late-night messages to an extramarital partner."[64]

Its "bulk email records collection" under the sweeping Patriot Act continued until 2011 when two senators protested that the agency's "statements to both Congress and the Court . . . significantly exaggerated this program's effectiveness"—eventually forcing Obama to curtail this particular operation.[65] Nonetheless, it continued to collect the personal communications of Americans by the billions under its PRISM program, authorized by a FISA court order requiring Verizon and other telecommunication companies to transfer records of all phone calls, foreign and domestic, on an "ongoing daily basis."[66] Beyond that "front-door access," the NSA's surreptitious MUSCULAR project, according to a January 2013 agency document, penetrated data transfers between Internet giants Google and Yahoo to capture 181 million new records in just thirty days.[67]

The ongoing war on terror provided both the political impetus and technical innovation for this rapid growth in surveillance. By the time the Obama administration withdrew from Iraq (for a time) in late 2011, the army's Biometrics Identity Management Agency (BIMA) had collected fingerprints and iris scans on three million people, or about 10 percent of that country's population. In Afghanistan by early 2012, US military computers held biometric data for two million Afghans, again about 10 percent of the country's population.[68] In 2009, the Pentagon's Homeland Security commander General Victor Renuart called for the domestic application of this technology. Two years later, a company called BI2 Technologies in Plymouth, Massachusetts, began marketing the Mobile Offender Recognition and Information System (MORIS), with smartphone-based iris recognition, to dozens of police forces nationwide.[69] Similarly, in 2010 the military transferred its experimental Biometric Optical Surveillance System (BOSS), first developed to spot suicide bombers in crowds of Afghans or Iraqis, to Homeland Security, which continued to develop facial recognition technology for future domestic use by local police.[70]

Despite a decade of relentless expansion, the full range of the NSA's operations remained one of Washington's best-kept secrets. So deeply classified was this operation that in March 2013 intelligence chief James Clapper could assure Congress, under oath, that the NSA did not collect "any type of data at all on millions of Americans." That knowing lie was so troubling for the young NSA contractor Edward Snowden that, just two months later, he fled to Hong Kong where he began leaking thousands of classified documents to the world's press, exposing for the first time the extraordinary extent of the NSA's spreading surveillance, both domestic and international.[71]

In addition to routinely sweeping up billions of communications made by ordinary Americans, the NSA, according to one of these leaked documents, "maintains relationships with over 100 US companies," facilitating a "home field advantage as the primary hub for worldwide telecommunications." As of April 2013, the NSA had 117,675 "active surveillance targets" at home—a figure that represents many if not most of those providing active leadership in American political life.[72] Think about it. If the NSA were to monitor the entire US cabinet and Congress as well as the governors and all 7,382 legislators in the fifty states, we would still have to account for another 109,782 targets. Even if we were to add an average of five students and faculty at every one of the 7,398 college campuses in America, we would still have 72,792 targets to go. Throw in the editor and four reporters at each of the country's 1,395 daily newspapers, and you would still have another 65,817 targets to account for. In sum, that number 117,675 is a reasonable approximation of almost every politically active leader in America.

The World Wide Web's centralization of most communications has given the United States a capacity for global surveillance far beyond the British Empire's yield from its control of transoceanic telegraph cables. Among the most revealing of those thousands of leaked documents, the NSA's 2012 schematic for its "Worldwide SIGINT/Defense Cryptologic Platform" indicates that it inserted malware on 50,000 computers worldwide through just twenty "covert, clandestine, or cooperative" cable access points, supplemented by 170 secondary and tertiary entries—an extraordinary economy of force for both worldwide surveillance and cyberwarfare.[73]

Other documents that Edward Snowden released to the press indicate that the agency's X-Keyscore program had collected 850 billion "call events" in 2007 and forty-one billion records for a single month in 2012 about "nearly everything a user does on the Internet," from chat rooms to online searches.[74] Through expenditures of $250 million annually under its Sigint Enabling Project, the NSA systematically and stealthily penetrated encryption designed to protect privacy. "In the future, superpowers will be made or broken based on the strength of their cryptanalytic programs," reads another 2007 document. "It is the price of admission for the U.S. to maintain unrestricted access to and use of cyberspace."[75]

Under President Obama as well, the NSA cooperated with its longtime British counterpart, the Government Communications Headquarters (GCHQ), to tap the dense cluster of transatlantic telecommunication fiber-optic cables that pass through the United Kingdom. During a visit to a GCHQ facility for high-altitude intercepts at Menwith Hill in June 2008, NSA chief General Keith Alexander asked: "Why can't we collect all the signals all the time? Sounds like a good summer project for Menwith." Two years after turning its gaze from sweeping the skies above to probing cables below the seas, GCHQ's Operation Tempora achieved the "biggest internet access" of any partner in a "Five Eyes" intelligence coalition that includes Great Britain, the United States, Australia, Canada, and New Zealand. After the operation went online in 2010, GCHQ sank probes into two hundred Internet cables and was soon collecting six hundred million telephone messages daily, all accessible to American security personnel.[76] During a single day, Operation Tempora processed thirty-nine billion pieces of information.[77]

Apart from tracking terrorists, the NSA has conducted extensive surveillance of allied nations, both their leaders and governments, to more efficiently control the nexus of subordinate elites that has been the fulcrum for US global power since the mid-1950s. What is the aim of such sensitive surveillance, which runs the risk of serious political repercussions if exposed? Here, the history of colonial policing provides a precedent that explains the strategic logic of current eavesdropping.

Just as colonial police forces once watched thousands of local elites to assure their continuing collaboration with European empires, so the CIA and the NSA have monitored several hundred national leaders worldwide who now play an analogous role in America's global dominion. Aggressive international surveillance provides Washington with the information needed to maintain its hegemony—operational intelligence on dissidents (once communists, now terrorists) to be countered with covert action or military intervention; basic political and economic intelligence to give American diplomats an advantage in bilateral or multilateral negotiations; scurrilous information about the activities of national leaders useful in coercing their compliance; and, perhaps most important, a sense of omniscience when it comes to independent foreign elites, from Berlin to Bogota, Jakarta to Johannesburg.

In deference to the historic Five Eyes alliance, which dates back to the dawn of the Cold War, the NSA has, since 2007, generally exempted close "2nd party" allies from surveillance programs. But, according to another leaked document, "we can, and often do, target the signals of most 3rd party foreign partners"—meaning thirty less reliable allies such as France, Germany, and Italy. On a busy day in January 2013, the NSA collected sixty million phone calls and emails from Germany, part of five hundred million messages purloined annually—with similar numbers for France, Italy, and Spain. To gain operational intelligence on these allies, the NSA tapped phones at European Council headquarters in Brussels and thirty-eight parallel "targets" in Washington and New York—including the European Union delegation at the UN.[78]

Revelations from the cache of documents that Edward Snowden leaked indicate that the NSA has conducted close surveillance on the leaders of some thirty-five nations worldwide—including Brazilian president Dilma Rousseff's personal phone; the cabinet communications of former Mexican president Felipe Calderón and the email of his successor, Enrique Peña Nieto; intercepts for Chancellor Angela Merkel's cell phone calls since 2002; taps on the phones of Indonesia's President Susilo Bambang Yudhoyono; and "widespread surveillance" of world leaders during the Group 20 summit meeting at Ottawa in June 2010.[79] In 2015, the activist news group WikiLeaks reported that the NSA had monitored three French presidents from 2006 to 2012, including some "highly sensitive conversations" of François Hollande. The group also released documents on the surveillance of three German chancellors over a fifteen-year period, including Angela Merkel's confidential conversations about the global financial crisis in 2009 and about Eurozone conflicts in 2011.[80]

In late 2013, the *New York Times* reported that there were "more than 1,000 targets of American and British surveillance in recent years," reaching down to mid-level actors in the international arena. Apart from obvious subjects like Israeli prime minister Ehud Olmert and Defense Minister Ehud Barak, the NSA and GCHQ monitored the vice president of the European Commission, Joaquin Almunia, who oversaw antitrust issues; the French energy company Total; and official German communications in Berlin and with Georgia, Rwanda, and Turkey.[81]

Such secret intelligence about its allies gives Washington a significant diplomatic advantage. According to surveillance expert James Bamford, "It's the equivalent of going to a poker game and wanting to know what everyone's hand is before you place your bet."[82] Indeed, during the diplomatic wrangling at the UN over the Iraq invasion in 2002–2003, the NSA intercepted Secretary General Kofi Annan's conversations and monitored the "Middle Six" Third World nations on the Security Council—"listening in as the delegates communicated back to their home countries . . . to discover which way they might vote," and offering "a highway, a dam, or a favorable trade deal . . . in a subtle form of bribery."[83] The NSA helped US ambassador Susan Rice "develop a strategy" for a UN Security Council vote on Iran sanctions in 2010 by monitoring members Gabon, Uganda, Nigeria, and Bosnia. And the agency assisted President Obama by gaining "access to U.N. Secretary General talking points prior to meeting" in 2013.[84]

In October 2012, another document quoted NSA director Alexander proposing that, in countering Muslim radicals, Washington should look to their "vulnerabilities, which if exposed, would likely call into question a radicalizer's devotion to the jihadist cause, leading to the degradation or loss of his authority." Citing the two timeless sources of scandal—sex and money—the director suggested that such vulnerabilities would likely include "viewing sexually explicit material online" or "using a portion of the donations they are receiving . . . to defray personal expenses." The document identified one potential target as a "respected academic" whose "vulnerabilities" are "online promiscuity." According to author James Bamford: "The NSA's operation is eerily similar to the FBI's operations under J. Edgar Hoover in the 1960s where the bureau used wiretapping to discover vulnerabilities, such as sexual activity, to 'neutralize' their targets." In response to this leaked NSA document, the deputy legal director of the American Civil Liberties Union, Jameel Jaffer, warned that the "president will ask the NSA to use the fruits of surveillance to discredit a political opponent, journalist or human rights activist. The NSA has used its power that way in the past and it would be naïve to think it couldn't use its power that way in the future."[85]

Indeed, in a December 2013 letter to the Brazilian people, Edward Snowden accused the agency of actually conducting such surveillance, saying: "They even keep track of who is having an affair or looking at pornography, in case they need to damage their target's reputation. . . . These programs were never about terrorism: they're about economic spying, social control, and diplomatic manipulation. They're about power."[86] In a 2014 interview, Snowden charged that the NSA passed unexpurgated messages from Palestinians to Israel's super-secret counterpart Unit 8200 for possible blackmail. In response to that revelation, forty-three members of the unit resigned in "moral protest," charging that information about "sexual orientations, infidelities, money problems" was being used "to apply pressure to people, to make them cooperate with Israel" as intelligence assets.[87]

Just as the Internet has centralized communications, so it has moved much of commercial sex off the mean streets and into cyberspace, providing easy surveillance of the embarrassing habits of targets anywhere. With an estimated twenty-five million salacious sites worldwide and a combined 10.6 billion page views per month at the top five sex sites in 2013,[88] online pornography has become a nearly $100 billion global business.[89]

Digital surveillance has tremendous political potency for scandal, exemplified by Eliot Spitzer's forced resignation in 2008 as governor of New York after phone taps revealed his use of escort services,[90] and the ouster of France's budget minister Jérôme Cahuzac in 2013 following phone taps that exposed his secret Swiss bank account.[91] Given the acute sensitivity of such executive communications, world leaders have reacted strongly to the reports of American surveillance—with potentially deleterious consequences for Washington's relations with key allies. Germany's Chancellor Merkel demanded, unsuccessfully, Five Eyes–exempt status.[92] France's President François Hollande insisted, "We cannot accept this kind of behavior between partners and allies."[93] After the European Parliament voted to curtail the sharing of bank data with Washington, its president Martin Shultz explained, "When you approach a negotiation and you need to be afraid that the other side . . . has already spied out what you are going to say in that negotiation, then we are not talking about equal partners any more."[94] Not only did Brazil's President Rousseff cancel a state visit to Washington in September 2013 after reports about NSA taps on her phone, but within two months the state telecom company Telebras announced a joint venture with Embraer for a $560 million satellite network meant to free Brazil from the US-controlled fiber-optic grid and thereby "ensure the sovereignty of its strategic communications."[95] Even in Canada, one of the Five Eyes coalition member countries exempt from surveillance, "boomerang routing" of communications through the United States allowed NSA surveillance, prompting the head of that country's Internet Registration Authority to call for Canada "to repatriate its internet traffic" for protection of privacy.[96]

Information and the Future of American Dominion

By leaking a trove of NSA documents, Edward Snowden has provided a rare glimpse into the changing architecture of US global power. At the broadest level, this digital pivot complements President Obama's overall defense strategy, announced in 2012, of keeping costs under control while conserving America's hegemony through a capacity for "a combined arms campaign across all domains—land, air, maritime, space, and cyberspace."[97]

Since 2009, digital surveillance has morphed into cyberwarfare through the formation of the US Cyber Command with operations housed in a cyber-combat center in Texas, initially staffed by seven thousand Air Force employees.[98] The Pentagon then concentrated power in a striking way by appointing NSA chief Alexander as CYBERCOM's concurrent commander and declaring cyberspace an "operational domain" for both offensive and defensive warfare.[99] Simultaneously, Washington deployed its first cyber-viruses with devastating effect against Iran's nuclear facilities from 2006 to 2010.[100]

President Obama has invested billions in building a new architecture for global information control. According to documents Snowden leaked to the *Washington Post* in August 2013, the United States had spent $500 billion on intelligence agencies in the dozen years since the 9/11 attacks, including 2012 appropriations of $10.3 billion for the National Reconnaissance Office, $10.8 billion for the NSA, and $14.7 billion for the CIA.[101] If we add the $791 billion expended on the Department of Homeland Security to this $500 billion for global intelligence in the dozen years since 9/11, then Washington has made a $1.2 trillion investment in hardware, software, and personnel to build a powerful security apparatus, including a formidable surveillance capacity, with enormous, unexplored implications for state controls at home and abroad.[102]

So formidable has this security bureaucracy proved that, in December 2013, Obama's executive review committee recommended not any real reforms but instead a regularization of current NSA practices, allowing the agency to continue tapping all domestic and international communications. From then on, any monitoring of foreign leaders would require presidential approval, a power Obama promptly exercised by promising Germany's Chancellor Merkel that her phone would not be tapped and by refusing to extend the same assurance to the presidents of Brazil and Mexico.[103]

This torrent of federal funding allowed, in just four years from 2012 to 2016, an unprecedented expansion in the scale and scope of the NSA's infrastructure. Complementing the agency's probes into the fiber-optic grid beneath the earth's surface, the National Reconnaissance Office launched, in June 2016, its seventh super-secret Advanced Orion satellite, the world's largest, equipped with a mesh antenna bigger than a football field to eavesdrop from a geostationary orbit 22,000 miles above the earth.[104]

To cover the globe with greater efficiency, the NSA also built a network of massive regional listening posts. For the Middle East, the agency completed, in 2012, a $286 million, 604,000-square-foot complex with four thousand employees in Savannah, Georgia. For Latin America, in 2013, the agency retrofitted a Sony chip facility in San Antonio, Texas, at a cost of $300 million. For Asia and the Pacific, the NSA opened a $358 million post on Oahu in January 2012. Simultaneously, at Menwith Hill in northern England, the NSA added supercomputers to process the two million intercepts an hour that its parabolic antennas sucked up from orbiting surveillance satellites.[105]

To store and process billions of messages collected worldwide, by June 2013 the NSA was employing eleven thousand workers to construct a data center in Bluffdale, Utah, at a cost of $1.6 billion, covering one million square feet and housing an immense storage capacity measured in "yottabytes," each the equivalent of a trillion terabytes—an unimaginably vast capacity when one realizes that just fifteen terabytes could store every publication in the Library of Congress.[106]

In its quest for ever more powerful supercomputers for processing data and decoding encryption, the NSA pushed far beyond the Cray Cascade that the Defense Advanced Research Projects Agency (DARPA) had developed in 2010, capable of a quadrillion calculations per second at a cost of $250 million.[107] In 2015, Obama authorized development of an exaflop computer that would operate at thirty times the speed of any current supercomputer. From its new 260,000-square-foot research facility in Oak Ridge, Tennessee, the agency is striving for superfast supercomputers, via breakthrough technologies such as "quantum computing," that will allow it to both crack ever-tougher encryption and master the "data tsunami" expected by 2020 when as many as two hundred billion devices will be networked globally.[108]

After Edward Snowden's revelations attracted sensational headlines worldwide, the NSA insisted its practices had blocked terror attacks on America. In numerous public statements, General Alexander claimed responsibility for stopping "54 different terrorist-related activities." When pressed for details during senate testimony in October 2013, the general could only cite a single San Diego taxi driver's cash transfer of $8,500 to the al-Shabab group in his native Somalia. Interviewed about the NSA's claims of success against terrorists, one member of Obama's review panel told NBC News, "We found none." This criticism prompted Congress to pass the USA Freedom Act in 2015, curtailing bulk collection inside America but preserving unchecked foreign surveillance. Within a year, the intercepts from Americans fell from "billions of records per day" to just 151 million phone messages per year, while warrantless overseas surveillance of foreigners climbed substantially to 106,000.[109] On balance, it seems the NSA's vast surveillance apparatus has been built for a mission other than domestic security.

By 2020, such massive surveillance will likely be integral to the US bid to perpetuate its waning global power. The Pentagon will deploy a triple-canopy aerospace shield, advanced cyberwarfare, and digital surveillance meant to envelop the earth in an electronic grid capable of simultaneously monitoring millions of private lives and blinding entire armies on the battlefield. Ultimately, this sophisticated technological regime, the third in America's century-long rise to global power, will require the integration of the Pentagon's evolving aerospace array into a robotic command structure that will coordinate operations across all combat domains—space, cyberspace, sky, sea, and earth. In this way, in its "Sigint Strategy 2012–2016" the NSA planned to "dramatically increase mastery of the global network" by integration of its systems into a national matrix of robotic sensors that will interactively "sense, respond and alert one another at machine speed."[110] In the future, Washington will require such an automated system capable of translating a babel of digital data captured from satellites in the skies and fiber-optic cables in the seas into actionable intelligence for the effective exercise of global power.

With the disparity growing between Washington's global reach and its withering mailed fist, the United States struggled, circa 2012, to maintain 40 percent of the world's armaments production with only 23 percent of its gross economic output.[111] As its share of world output fell further to just 17 percent by 2016, while its social welfare costs started climbing from 4 percent of GDP in 2010 to a projected 18 percent by 2050, savings were becoming imperative for Washington's survival as a world power.[112]

Compared to the trillion-dollar cost of conventional military intervention in Iraq, the NSA's 2012 budget of just $11 billion for worldwide surveillance and cyberwarfare looks like a cost savings the Pentagon cannot afford to forgo.[113] Cyberspace offers Washington a budget-priced arena of global power, albeit at the cost of the trust of its closest allies—a contradiction that will bedevil America's global leadership for years to come.

Surveying the past for recurring patterns, it seems that for well over a century innovative surveillance techniques forged during pacification campaigns at the periphery of US power have migrated homeward to provide both a blueprint for domestic surveillance and new technologies for the exercise of global hegemony. Through three sets of wars from 1898 to 2016, crucibles of counterinsurgency in the Philippines, Vietnam, and Iraq and Afghanistan have pushed Washington's pacification effort to its technological limits, forcing the formation of new systems for both surveillance and information warfare.

Looking inward for the domestic implications of this history, we can see that a global hegemon like the United States that exercises power beyond its borders over other societies soon begins to exhibit many of those same coercive features at home. To update Henry Stimson, in the age of the Internet, gentlemen don't just read each other's email, they now watch each other's porn and pry into each other's bank accounts. In the new world of national security surveillance, the US pursuit of global power seems to require, from Washington's perspective, that its citizens forgo any right to privacy, with other rights likely to follow. Clearly, Mark Twain may well have been right when he warned us, just over a hundred years ago, that this country could not sustain both empire abroad and democracy at home.

Chapter Five

Torture and the Eclipse of Empires

In the wake of the attacks on September 11, the White House made torture its secret weapon in the war on terror. Although Washington mobilized its military for conventional operations in Afghanistan and Iraq, the main challenge in this new kind of warfare would be "nonstate actors," terrorists who moved elusively across the Muslim world from Morocco to Manila in what one CIA veteran called "ad hoc networks that dissolve as soon as the mission is accomplished." With its countless Cold War victories, overthrowing enemies on five continents by coups and covert operations, the agency possessed an aura of invincibility that made it Washington's chosen instrument against al-Qaeda. Yet the CIA's reputation for clandestine derring-do had been grossly inflated and its qualifications for this new mission were few indeed.[1]

In the half century before 2001, the CIA had mounted a single security operation comparable to its pursuit of al-Qaeda, and the results of this earlier counterterror effort against communists in South Vietnam were decidedly mixed. In the new campaign against Islamic terrorists, the CIA soon found it had few, if any, covert assets inside militant Muslim circles, forcing the agency to revive the torture techniques it had developed for the Cold War.[2]

Facing a rival Soviet Empire that seemed to have cracked the code of human consciousness, Washington allied with Britain and Canada in 1951 for a massive mind-control effort whose budget reached a billion dollars annually.[3] After a decade of secret research, the CIA developed a coercive interrogation doctrine that the White House could deploy at times of extraordinary crisis. Across the span of three continents and four decades, there is then a striking similarity in torture techniques used against the Soviet Union and its satellite states in the 1950s, in South Vietnam during the 1960s, Central America in the 1980s, and Iraq after 2003.

At a deeper level, this recurring reliance on torture was a manifestation of America's long, largely forgotten history of involvement in coercive interrogation. During its rise to empire, Washington has encountered major mass revolutions just three times and responded with torture to all of them. In its conquest of the Philippines, the army used the "water cure" to extract information from Filipino peasants about omnipresent yet invisible guerrillas, sparking protests back home and courts-martial for military perpetrators. Confronting a similar form of guerrilla resistance during the Vietnam War, the CIA tried to pacify the countryside with a centralized torture-assassination apparatus called the Phoenix Program that, when revealed domestically, helped discredit the war effort. After the terror attacks of September 2001, the Bush administration revived CIA torture techniques developed for the Cold War and used them to pursue al-Qaeda's terrorist network.

Empire is the defining context that lends some larger meaning to these moments. After their triumphal entry into Manila in 1898 and Baghdad in 2003, US troops soon plunged into the pacification of societies with tight kinship ties that defied their superior firepower, prompting a reliance on torture for supposedly actionable intelligence. Yet if torture expresses a will to dominance for an empire on the rise, it also reveals a more complex pathology amid imperial retreat or defeat, involving as it does an unsettling mixture of arrogance and insecurity, a sense of superiority and savagery, as well as a legalistic mentality and an inescapable criminality. The repeated use of torture, despite the legal complications involved, seems more comprehensible when understood as an artifact of empire.

In their recourse to torture at times of crisis, three imperial powers—Britain, France, and the United States—moved through parallel phases with some revealing similarities. Each initially granted its security services a legal exemption, through formal procedures, for the use of extreme measures against restive populations on remote imperial frontiers. They all then suffered divisive, demoralizing controversy when journalists back home exposed the torture in all its savagery. Finally, each of them engaged in a protracted process of impunity, exempting both the perpetrators and the powerful from the consequences of their crimes. More ominously for the future of Washington's global hegemony, the use of torture by dying empires, and the moral damage that comes with it, seems like both a manifestation of and a causal factor for imperial decline.

A Short History of Psychological Torture

The roots of the continuing controversy over the abuse of detainees at the Abu Ghraib prison in Iraq and the Guantánamo prison in Cuba lie, most immediately, in the long history of the CIA's use of psychological torture. To counter Soviet advances in mind control at the start of the Cold War, the agency mounted a "Special Interrogation Program" whose working hypothesis was stated in a 1952 memo: "Medical science, particularly psychiatry and psychotherapy, has developed various techniques by means of which some external control can be imposed on the mind or will of an individual, such as drugs, hypnosis, electric shock and neurosurgery."[4]

The CIA tested all of these novel techniques covertly during the 1950s under a top-secret program, codenamed Project Artichoke, that aimed at the "development of any method by which we can get information from a person against his will and without his knowledge." When none of these exotic methods actually proved capable of breaking potential enemies or obtaining reliable information, the agency then collaborated with British and Canadian scientists on more conventional, and successful, academic research into "methods concerned in psychological coercion."[5]

This secret behavioral research produced two discoveries central to the CIA's emerging psychological paradigm for torture. Through classified experiments in collaboration with the agency from 1951 to 1954, renowned Canadian psychologist Donald Hebb found that he could produce a state akin to drug-induced hallucinations and psychosis in just forty-eight hours without drugs, hypnosis, or electric shock. For two days student volunteers at McGill University simply sat in a comfortable cubicle deprived of sensory stimulation by goggles, gloves, and earmuffs.[6] "It scared the hell out of us," Hebb said later, "to see how completely dependent the mind is on a close connection with the ordinary sensory environment, and how disorganizing to be cut off from that support." This discovery, soon confirmed by hundreds of scientific papers, led to the development of a torture technique called "sensory deprivation."[7]

During the 1950s as well, two researchers at Cornell University Medical Center, working under CIA contract, found that the most devastating form of torture used by the Soviet secret police, the KGB, was to force a victim to stand motionless for days while the legs swelled, the skin erupted in suppurating lesions, and hallucinations began. Later American versions of such a procedure came to be euphemistically called "stress positions."[8]

Four years into this secret research, American prisoners in North Korea suffered what was then called "brainwashing," prompting a sudden surge of interest in using such mind-control methods defensively. In August 1955, President Dwight Eisenhower ordered that any soldier at risk of capture must be given "specific training and instruction designed to . . . withstand all enemy efforts against him." Consequently, the air force developed a program it dubbed SERE (Survival, Evasion, Resistance, Escape) to train pilots in resisting psychological torture.[9] In this way, the United States soon developed two intertwined strands of mind-control research: aggressive techniques for breaking enemy agents and defensive methods for training Americans to resist enemy inquisitors.

In 1963, the CIA distilled this decade of research into the "KUBARK Counterintelligence Interrogation" manual, which stated that sensory deprivation was effective because it made "the regressed subject view the interrogator as a father figure . . . strengthening . . . the subject's tendencies toward compliance."[10] Refined through years of practice on human beings, the CIA's psychological paradigm came to rely on a mix of sensory overload and sensory deprivation via seemingly banal procedures—heat and cold, light and dark, noise and silence, feast and famine—meant to attack six basic sensory pathways into the human mind.

After codifying such methods in that manual, the CIA spent the next thirty years promoting them within the US intelligence community and among anticommunist allies worldwide. Along the global arc of containment that defined the Cold War, the CIA trained allied agencies in Iran, South Vietnam, and Latin America. During the war in Vietnam, the CIA's Phoenix Program deployed systematic torture and often brutal methods to dismantle communist networks in the countryside, producing 46,776 extrajudicial executions but little actionable intelligence. From 1966 to 1991, Military Intelligence also ran "Project X" to transmit these counterinsurgency tactics to Latin America via Spanish language training manuals, an elaborate interrogation curriculum, and field training programs.[11]

Training the Honduran military in psychological torture during the 1980s, for instance, the CIA taught local interrogators that they should "manipulate the subject's environment . . . to disrupt patterns of time, space, and sensory perception"—in short, assault the basic sensory pathways into human consciousness.[12] Significantly, the techniques described in this "Human Resources Exploitation Manual—1983" seem remarkably similar to those outlined twenty years earlier in the KUBARK report and those used twenty years later at Abu Ghraib prison in Iraq.

As torture proliferated during the Cold War, a countervailing movement, led by Amnesty International and like-minded organizations, gradually mobilized a civil society coalition that proved effective in publicizing and protesting these abuses. In December 1984, after years of such global, grassroots agitation, the UN General Assembly finally adopted the Convention Against Torture (CAT), defining this crime broadly, under Article I, as "any act by which severe pain or suffering, whether physical or mental, is intentionally inflicted on a person for such purpose as obtaining from him or a third person information or a confession."[13] Approved by a unanimous UN vote, the CAT created enormous international pressure for compliance. As a result, President Ronald Reagan sent the convention to Congress in 1988 with a ringing endorsement invoking "our desire to bring an end to the abhorrent practice of torture." Simultaneously, however, the administration proposed a record nineteen reservations that stalled its ratification in the Senate for the next six years.[14]

In 1994, four years after the close of the Cold War, Washington finally ratified the convention, seemingly resolving the tension between its anti-torture principles and the CIA's torture practices.[15] Yet when President Bill Clinton sent it to Congress, he included four little noticed diplomatic "reservations," drafted six years before by the Reagan administration, that were focused on just one word in the treaty's twenty-six printed pages: "mental." These reservations narrowed the definition of mental torture (just for the United States) to ban only four specific acts (physical pain, drugs, death threats, threats to harm another), thereby permitting methods such as sensory deprivation and so-called self-inflicted pain. Significantly, these were the very techniques the CIA had developed and propagated for the previous forty years. This exculpatory definition was later reproduced verbatim in Section 2340 of the US Federal Code and the War Crimes Act of 1996.[16]

Through all this legal legerdemain, Washington managed to ban physical abuse while exempting the CIA from the UN's prohibition on psychological torture. This exemption, buried like a landmine, would detonate with phenomenal force just ten years later at Abu Ghraib. Right after his public address to a shaken nation on September 11, 2001, President George W. Bush turned to his staff and gave them secret orders for torture, insisting emphatically, "I don't care what the international lawyers say, we are going to kick some ass."[17]

After months of recondite legal research, administration attorneys translated the president's eloquent but unlawful command into policy through three controversial, neoconservative legal findings: first, the president is above the law; next, torture is a legally acceptable exercise of presidential power; and, finally, the US Navy base at Guantánamo in Cuba is not US territory. These separate findings rested on a broader constitutional doctrine of overarching presidential power. In times of war, they argued, the president should be able to set aside all domestic laws or international treaties to defend the nation, correcting what Vice President Dick Cheney condemned as "the unwise compromises . . . over the last 30 to 35 years" that had eroded "the powers . . . of the president of the United States to do his job."[18] More fundamentally, administration attorneys argued that the presidency—what they called "the unitary executive"—was the preeminent branch of government, challenging the constitutional principle that the presidency is one of three coequal branches. John Yoo, a University of California law professor serving in the Bush Justice Department, asserted that "the founders intended that wrongheaded or obsolete legislation and judicial decisions would be checked by presidential action."[19]

Drawing on the advice of his neoconservative legal advisers, President Bush decided, in February 2002, that "none of the provisions of Geneva apply to our conflict with al-Qaeda in Afghanistan or elsewhere throughout the world," thereby removing any requirements for "minimum standards for humane treatment."[20] Much like the French had done in Algeria or the British in Kenya, the White House had, through formal procedures, exempted the CIA from legal restraints on torture.

By then, however, the agency no longer had any personnel experienced in coercive interrogation. Following a prisoner's death in custody in the mid-1980s, the CIA had purged torture techniques from its interrogation canon, concluding that they were counterproductive. After decades of training Latin American militaries in such techniques, the Defense Department under then Secretary Dick Cheney in the early 1990s recalled all copies of extant manuals that detailed these illegal methods.[21]

Twelve years later when the Bush administration opted for torture, the sole institutional memory of the CIA's psychological methods lay in the military's SERE training. Under a contract with the CIA, two retired military psychologists, James Mitchell and Bruce Jessen, reverse-engineered this defensive doctrine for offensive use on al-Qaeda captives. "They sought to render the detainees vulnerable—to break down all of their senses," one Bush administration official told *New Yorker* reporter Jane Mayer. "It takes a psychologist trained in this to understand these rupturing experiences." Inside CIA headquarters, officials felt a "high level of anxiety" about possible future prosecutions for methods defined as torture under international law. The presence of hired outside psychologists was considered a "way for CIA officials to skirt measures such as the Convention Against Torture."[22]

In a dramatic break with past policy, the White House also allowed the CIA to operate its own global network of prisons. Terror suspects would then be seized worldwide, subjected to "extraordinary rendition," and incarcerated endlessly inside a supranational agency gulag of eight secret "black sites" from Thailand to Poland and allied prisons and torture chambers from Morocco to Egypt to Uzbekistan.[23] The Bush administration also approved ten "enhanced" interrogation methods designed by the CIA's psychologists, including "waterboarding."[24] This use of cold water to block breathing triggers the "mammalian diving reflex," imprinted in the human brain to save infants from drowning, and thereby induces an unimaginable terror of impending death. Instead of simply outsourcing the abuse to allies as they had during the Cold War, CIA employees would now dirty their own hands with waterboarding and "wall slamming."

In response to White House inquiries about the legality of these techniques, Assistant Attorney General Jay Bybee and his subordinate John Yoo found grounds in a now notorious August 2002 memo for exculpating any CIA interrogator who tortured but later claimed his intention was to obtain information and not inflict pain. By parsing the definition of torture in Section 2340 of the Federal Code stating the physical or mental pain must be "severe," Bybee concluded that "physical pain amounting to torture must be equivalent in intensity to the pain accompanying serious physical injury such as organ failure," effectively allowing torture right up to the point of death. "For purely mental pain or suffering to amount to torture, it must result in significant psychological harm . . . lasting for months or even years"—a truly permissive standard that drew upon the elusive character of psychological torture.[25]

Not only were the Bush Justice Department lawyers aggressive in their advocacy of torture, they meticulously laid the legal groundwork for a future impunity. In a memo for the CIA in August 2002, Bybee cited the SERE training, which subjected US troops to a carefully controlled form of waterboarding, to advise the CIA that "the waterboard could not be said to inflict severe suffering." He found all ten of the agency's "enhanced techniques" legal because, under his convoluted interpretation of the Federal Code's Section 2340, "an individual must have the specific intent to cause prolonged mental harm in order to have the specific intent to inflict severe mental pain."[26]

In three detailed torture memos dated May 2005, drafted long after the worst abuse was over and apparently aimed at providing legal cover for Bush's counselors as they left office, Deputy Assistant Attorney General Steven Bradbury repeatedly cited the original American diplomatic "reservations" to the UN Convention, replicated verbatim in Section 2340, to argue that waterboarding was perfectly legal since the "technique is not physically painful."[27] All the enhanced techniques were, Bradbury counseled confidently, "unlikely to be subject to judicial inquiry."[28] Six months later in November 2005, the CIA, in a complementary move to conceal evidence of earlier abuse, destroyed ninety-two videotapes documenting the interrogation of top al-Qaeda suspects inside the agency black site in Thailand.[29]

From these same Justice Department memos, we now know that the CIA refined its psychological paradigm significantly under Bush. As described in a classified 2004 report titled "Background Paper on CIA's Combined Use of Interrogation Techniques," each detainee was transported to a black site while "deprived of sight and sound through the use of blindfolds, earmuffs, and hoods." Once inside the prison, he was to be reduced to "a baseline, dependent state" through conditioning by "nudity, sleep deprivation (with shackling . . .) and dietary manipulation." For "more physical and psychological stress," CIA interrogators were greenlighted to employ coercive measures such as "an insult slap or abdominal slap" and then "walling," that is, slamming the detainee's head against a cell wall.[30] If all these failed to produce the results being sought, interrogators escalated to waterboarding, as was done to Abu Zubaydah "at least 83 times during August 2002" and Khalid Sheikh Mohammed 183 times in March 2003.[31] Attorney General John Ashcroft approved "expanded use" of these techniques at meetings with CIA director George Tenet in July and September 2003, even when "informed that the waterboard had been used 119 times on an individual."[32]

In a parallel process at the Pentagon in late 2002, Defense Secretary Donald Rumsfeld approved fifteen aggressive interrogation techniques for the military prison at Guantánamo, authorizing harsh stress positions in a handwritten note reading: "I stand for 8–10 hours a day. Why is standing limited to 4 hours?"[33] Significantly, the Defense Department, like other Bush administration agencies, was careful to assure impunity for those who used its aggressive methods, even in the frenzied first months of the war on terror. In developing its expansive protocol, the Pentagon relied on the senior counsel at the CIA's Counterterrorism Center, Jonathan Fredman, who reportedly echoed the Bybee-Yoo August 2002 memo by advising that the legal definition of torture was "written vaguely" and "is basically subject to perception" by the perpetrator. He concluded that US law had no real restraints on interrogation, saying, "If the detainee dies, you're doing it wrong."[34]

Simultaneously, Rumsfeld gave General Geoffrey Miller command of the new American military prison at Guantánamo Bay with ample authority to transform it into an ad hoc psychology lab. There so-called Behavioral Science Consultation Teams of military psychologists probed detainees at Guantánamo for individual phobias such as fear of the dark. Interrogators strengthened the psychological assault by exploiting what they saw as Arab cultural sensitivities about sex and dogs.[35] In their three-phase attack on the senses, culture, and the individual psyche, Guantánamo interrogators perfected the CIA's psychological paradigm. After regular inspections of the facility from 2002 to 2004, the International Red Cross reported: "The construction of such a system . . . cannot be considered other than an intentional system of cruel, unusual and degrading treatment and a form of torture."[36]

After General Miller brought those methods to Iraq in September 2003, the US commander there, General Ricardo Sanchez, ordered Guantánamo-style abuse at Abu Ghraib prison. My own review of the 1,600 still-classified photos taken by American guards at Abu Ghraib prison, and later leaked to Australian reporters, reveals not random, idiosyncratic acts by individual "bad apples" but the repeated use of three core techniques in the CIA's psychological paradigm: hooding for sensory deprivation, shackling for self-inflicted pain, and nudity and dogs to exploit Arab cultural sensitivities. This was, for instance, why Private Lynndie England was so infamously photographed leading an Iraqi detainee leashed like a dog.[37]

According to the New York Times, these techniques escalated virally at five special operations field interrogation centers across Iraq where detainees were subjected to extreme sensory deprivation, beating, burning, electric shock, and waterboarding. Among the thousand soldiers serving in these units, thirty-four were later convicted of abuses and many more escaped prosecution only because records were officially "lost."[38]

As often happens in imperial wars, this attempt at pacification through harsh measures, mass incarceration, and systemic abuse simply intensified Iraqi resistance. Meeting in Kuwait in 2006, top US diplomats working on counterterrorism in the Middle East reported, "Detainee debriefs and intelligence reporting indicate that US treatment of detainees at Guantanamo Bay, Abu Ghraib and elsewhere is the single most important motivating factor for T/FFs [foreign jihadists] travelling to Iraq." Looking back on his combat service there, General Stanley McChrystal concluded: "In my experience, we found that nearly every first-time jihadist claimed Abu Ghraib had first jolted him to action."[39]

Indeed, the largest of American prisons, Camp Bucca in southern Iraq, became the training ground for the most radical of the jihadists, the future leaders of the Islamic State, or ISIS. By the time that prison closed in 2009, some hundred thousand detainees had passed through its barbed wire, including the main founders of the Islamic State—notably its head Abu Bakr al-Baghdadi, detained there for five years, and the nine members of his top command.[40] "We had so much time to sit and plan," a senior member of the Islamic State recalled. "It was the perfect environment. We all agreed to get together when we got out. The way to reconnect was easy. We wrote each other's details on the elastic of our boxer shorts." Released in 2009 and soon reunited, the Islamic State leaders expanded their movement steadily until 2013 when their militant followers attacked Abu Ghraib prison, fostering a mass breakout of five hundred inmates, including "senior jihadists." As the Islamic State seized cities and towns across northern Iraq in early 2014, the Baghdad government estimated that seventeen of its top twenty-five leaders had spent time in US military prisons.[41]

A History of Impunity

Even as they exercise extraordinary power over others, perpetrators of torture around the world are assiduous in their pursuit of impunity, constructing recondite legal justifications, destroying records of actual torture, and enacting legislation that will facilitate exoneration. Not only were the Bush administration's Justice Department lawyers aggressive in their advocacy of torture, they were meticulous from the start in laying the legal groundwork for later impunity.

Consequently, when Vice President Cheney presided over the drafting of the Military Commissions Act of 2006, he included clauses, buried in these thirty-eight pages of dense print, defining "serious physical pain" as "significant loss or impairment of . . . a bodily member, organ, or mental faculty"—a striking paraphrase of John Yoo's infamous August 2002 definition.[42] Above all, the Military Commissions Act protected the CIA's use of psychological torture by repeating verbatim the exculpatory language found in those Clinton-era, Reagan-created reservations to the UN Convention and still embedded in Section 2340 of the Federal Code. To make doubly sure of impunity, the 2006 Commissions Act made these definitions retrospective to November 1997, giving CIA interrogators immunity from any misdeeds under the Expanded War Crimes Act of 1997, which punished serious violations with life imprisonment or death.[43]

In June 2008, Major General Antonio Taguba, who had conducted the military's most thorough investigation of the abuse at Abu Ghraib, looked back on the past five years of "disclosures by government investigations, media accounts, and reports from human rights organizations." At this point, the general concluded, "there is no longer any doubt as to whether the current administration has committed war crimes. The only question that remains to be answered is whether those who ordered the use of torture will be held to account."[44]

In the transition from Bush to Obama, the dynamics of partisan wrangling over CIA interrogation produced a surprising bipartisan move toward impunity for past human rights abuse. Following the televised broadcast of photos from Abu Ghraib by the CBS News show *60 Minutes* in 2004, the United States had started moving, almost imperceptibly, through a five-step process of impunity quite similar to those experienced earlier by England and France. Through a process spun out over eight years, General Taguba's question would be answered decisively in the negative: none of those who ordered the tortures would be held accountable.

Step one toward impunity was a bipartisan effort. For a year after the 2004 Abu Ghraib exposé, Defense Secretary Rumsfeld's Pentagon claimed that the abuse was "perpetrated by a small number of U.S. military." Similarly, while announcing his refusal to release more torture photos in May 2009, President Obama echoed Rumsfeld, asserting that the abuse shown in these images "was carried out in the past by a small number of individuals."[45]

In early 2009, Republicans took the nation deep into the second stage with former vice president Cheney's televised statements that the CIA's methods "prevented the violent deaths of thousands, perhaps hundreds of thousands, of people." The Obama administration did not dispute this claim.[46]

On April 16, 2009, President Obama brought us to the third stage in the process when he released the four Bush-era memos detailing CIA torture techniques while insisting, "Nothing will be gained by spending our time and energy laying blame for the past."[47] During a visit to CIA headquarters four days later, Obama promised that there would be no prosecutions of its employees. "We've made some mistakes," he admitted; but he urged Americans to "acknowledge them and then move forward." In the furor surrounding the release of those memos, the Democratic Senate Judiciary Committee chairman Patrick Leahy called for an independent commission on interrogation. Even the House Minority Leader, Republican John Boehner, seemed open to such a course of action. But the White House press secretary announced,

"The president determined the concept didn't seem altogether workable" because such an inquiry "might just become a political back and forth." The president's position was in such blatant defiance of international law that the chief UN official on torture, Manfred Nowak, reminded him that Washington was legally obliged to investigate any violations of the Convention Against Torture.[48]

After the assassination of Osama bin Laden in May 2011, neoconservatives moved the nation to the next stage of impunity by forming an a cappella media chorus to claim, without any factual basis, that torture had led Washington to bin Laden. Within weeks, Attorney General Eric Holder ended the investigation of alleged CIA abuse, including the actual killing of prisoners, without a criminal indictment, exonerating both the interrogators and their superiors.[49]

In the months surrounding the tenth anniversary of the 9/11 attacks, the United States took the fifth and final step in the process of impunity: vindication before the bar of history. By censoring a critical memoir by a veteran FBI interrogator, while simultaneously facilitating laudatory accounts by former vice president Dick Cheney, CIA official Jose Rodriguez, and the makers of the film *Zero Dark Thirty*, the agency fostered the creation of a historical record suggesting that torture had been a significant and successful weapon in the war on terror.[50] In effect, the agency's defenders had won this political battle with the interrogation videos destroyed, a critical book censored, laudatory books launched, indictments quashed, lawsuits dismissed, imagined intelligence coups celebrated, medals awarded, bonuses paid, and promotions secured.

However, in December 2014, just when impunity seemed the order of the day, the Senate Intelligence Committee released a detailed, meticulously documented report that served as a powerful corrective to years of CIA disinformation. Instead of steely guardians willing to break laws, trample treaties, and dedicate their lives to the defense of America, this report reveals agency perpetrators as mendacious careerists willing to twist any truth to win a promotion or secure a lucrative contract.[51]

This report's executive summary, the only portion so far declassified, will likely remain an important historical document, defining these extraordinary events for years to come. At its most visceral level, the report's 524 pages of dense, disconcerting detail take us into a Dante-like hell of waterboard vomit, rectal feeding, midnight-dark cells, endless overhead chaining, sleep deprivation, death threats, humiliating nudity, savage beatings, and crippling cold. With its mix of capricious cruelty and systemic abuse, the CIA's Salt Pit prison in Afghanistan can now, for instance, join that long list of iconic cesspits for human suffering that would include Devil's Island, Château d'If, Côn Sơn Island, Montjuïc Castle, and Robben Island.[52] If nothing else, these details helped to purge that awkward euphemism "enhanced interrogation techniques" from our polite public lexicon. Now everyone, senator and citizen alike, can just say "torture."

In its most important contribution, the Senate report sifted through some six million pages of classified documents to rebut the CIA's claim that torture produced all-important intelligence. All the agency's assertions that torture stopped terrorist plots or led us to Osama bin Laden were false, and sometimes knowingly so. Instead of such spurious claims, CIA director John Brennan was finally forced to admit that any link between torture and actionable intelligence was, at best, "unknowable."[53]

The Senate committee's exhaustive review shattered the agency's myth of derring-do infallibility and exposed the bumbling mismanagement of its two main missions in the war on terror: incarceration and intelligence. Every profession has its B team, every bureaucracy has its bumblers. Instead of sending James Bond, Langley dispatched Mr. Bean and Maxwell Smart— in the persons of psychologists James Mitchell and Bruce Jessen. In a 2003 assessment, the CIA office supervising them criticized their "arrogance and narcissism" and their "blatant disregard for the ethics shared by almost all of their colleagues." In perhaps the single most damning detail of the Senate report, it was revealed that the CIA had paid those two Air Force retirees $81 million to create sophisticated enhanced interrogation techniques after they had spent their careers doing little more than administering the SERE torture-resistance curriculum—a mundane job tailor-made for mediocrities of modern psychology.[54]

For all its many strengths, the Senate report is not without serious limitations. Mired in detail, the committee's analysis of this rich data is often cursory or convoluted, obscuring its import for even the most discerning reader. This limitation is most apparent in the report's close case study of Abu Zubaydah, the detainee whose torture at a Thai black site in 2002 proved seminal, convincing the CIA that its enhanced techniques worked and giving these psychologists effective control over the agency's interrogation program for the next six years.[55] To its credit, the Senate report debunked both CIA claims that Abu Zubaydah was "bin Laden's senior lieutenant" and President Bush's 2006 statement that "he had run a terrorist camp in Afghanistan where some of the 9/11 hijackers trained." In fact, the Senate reported, such claims "significantly overstated Abu Zubaydah's role in al-Qa'ida and the information he was likely to possess." The CIA itself reported, in 2006, that al-Qaeda had rejected his membership application back in 1993 and his training camp had no connection to bin Laden.[56]

The Senate's mass of information about this incident is good as far as it goes, but a more extensive analysis in this critical section of the report might have yielded far more. Among countless thousands of interrogations during the war on terror, conservatives have repeatedly cited Abu Zubaydah's to defend the CIA's methods. In his memoirs, published on the tenth anniversary of 9/11, Dick Cheney claimed the CIA's methods had turned this hardened terrorist into a "fount of information" and thus saved "thousands of lives."[57] But just two weeks later, Ali Soufan, a former FBI counterterror agent fluent in Arabic, published his own book claiming he gained "important actionable intelligence" by using very different non-coercive, empathetic methods to interrogate Abu Zubaydah.[58]

If we juxtapose the many CIA-censored pages of Ali Soufan's memoir with his earlier, unexpurgated congressional testimony, this interrogation becomes an extraordinary four-stage scientific experiment in comparing the effectiveness of CIA coercion versus the FBI's empathic approach.[59]

Stage One. As soon as Abu Zubaydah was captured in 2002, FBI agent Ali Soufan flew to Bangkok where he built rapport with him in Arabic to gain the first intelligence about "the role of KSM [Khalid Sheikh Mohammed] as the mastermind of the 9/11 attacks." Angered by the FBI's success, CIA director George Tenet pounded the table and dispatched his contract psychologist James Mitchell, who stripped Zubaydah naked and subjected him to "low-level sleep deprivation."

Stage Two. After the CIA's harsh methods got "no information," FBI agents resumed their questioning of Abu Zubaydah to learn "the details of José Padilla, the so-called 'dirty bomber.'" Then the CIA team again took over and moved up the coercive continuum to loud noise, temperature manipulation, and forty-eight hours of sleep deprivation.

Stage Three. When this tough CIA approach again failed, FBI agents were brought back for a third time, using empathetic techniques that produced more details on the Padilla bomb plot.

Stage Four. When the CIA ratcheted up the abuse to outright and clear torture, the FBI ordered Ali Soufan home. With the CIA psychologist now in sole control, Abu Zubaydah was subjected to weeks of sleep deprivation, sensory disorientation, forced nudity, and waterboarding. But he gave no further information. Yet in a stunning bit of illogic, Mitchell claimed this negative result was, in fact, positive since these enhanced techniques showed that the subject had no more secrets to hide. Amazingly, the CIA bought this bit of flimflam.

Examined closely, the results of this ad hoc experiment were blindingly clear: FBI empathy was effective, while CIA coercion proved consistently counterproductive. But this fundamental yet fragile truth was obscured by repeated CIA claims of good intelligence from the torture of Abu Zubaydah and by its heavy-handed censorship of 181 pages in Ali Soufan's memoir that reduced his account to a maze of blackened lines that no ordinary reader can readily understand.

More broadly, the Senate committee's report also fails to ask or answer a critical question: If the intelligence yield from torture was so consistently low, why was the CIA so determined to persist in these brutal but unproductive practices for so long? Among the many possibilities the Senate failed to explore is a default bureaucratic response by an empowered security service flailing about in fear when confronted with an unknown threat. "When feelings of insecurity develop within those holding power," reported a CIA analysis of the Cold War Kremlin that couldn't be more applicable to the post-9/11 White House, "they become increasingly suspicious and put great pressures upon the secret police to obtain arrests and confessions. At such times police officials are inclined to condone anything which produces a speedy 'confession,' and brutality may become widespread."[60]

Moreover, the Senate report's rigorously pseudonymous format denies it the key element in any historical narrative, the actor, thereby making much of its text almost incomprehensible. Understanding the power of narrative, the CIA sedulously cultivated the makers of the feature film *Zero Dark Thirty*, encouraging the story of a heroic female operative whose single-minded pursuit of the facts, through the most brutal of tortures, supposedly led the navy SEALs to Osama bin Laden. While the CIA has destroyed videotapes of its interrogations and censored Ali Soufan's critical account, Langley gave that film's scriptwriter Mark Boal liberal access to classified sources.[61] The chair of the Senate Intelligence Committee, Dianne Feinstein, walked out of the resulting film after just twenty minutes, calling it "so false."[62]

Instead of a photogenic leading lady, the Senate report offers only opaque snippets about an anonymous female analyst who played a pivotal role in one of the CIA's biggest blunders—snatching an innocent German national, Khaled el-Masri, and subjecting him to four months of abuse in the Salt Pit prison in Afghanistan. That same operative later defended torture by telling the CIA's inspector general that the waterboarding of Khalid Sheikh Mohammed had extracted the name of terrorist Majid Khan—when, in fact, Khan was already in CIA custody. Hinting at something badly wrong inside the agency, the author of these derelictions was promoted to a high post in its Counterterrorism Center.

By quickly filling in the blanks, journalists have shed light on the real story of this operative that the Senate suppressed and Hollywood glorified with the CIA's eager collusion. This "torture queen," as Jane Mayer reported in the *New Yorker* just days after the Senate report's release, "dropped the ball when the C.I.A. was given information that might very well have prevented the 9/11 attacks; . . . gleefully participated in torture sessions afterward; . . . misinterpreted intelligence in such a way that it sent the C.I.A. on an absurd chase for Al Qaeda sleeper cells in Montana. And then she falsely told congressional overseers that the torture worked."[63]

After all that, this agent, whom journalist Glenn Greenwald identified as Alfreda Bikowsky, was rewarded with a high CIA salary that, reports an activist website, allowed her to buy a luxury home in Reston, Virginia, for $875,000.[64] In short, adding names and narrative reveals a consistent pattern of CIA incompetence, the corrupting influence of intelligence gleaned from torture, and the agency's perpetrators as self-aggrandizing incompetents.

Despite its rich trove of hard-won detail, the Senate report has, at best, produced a neutral outcome, a draw in this political contest over impunity. Even in the face of the Senate's sobering revelations, the allure of torture has refused to fade. In the long 2016 presidential race, Republican Party candidate Donald Trump stoked his insurgent campaign with fiery calls for waterboarding, saying he would approve it "in a heartbeat" because "only a stupid person would say it doesn't work." As his campaign gained momentum in early 2016, so did his repeated insistence, "Don't tell me it doesn't work—torture works."[65] After he suggested in March that the best way to stop terrorists would be to murder their families, a chorus of criticism arose from former national security officials, notably ex-CIA director Michael Hayden who said "the American armed forces would refuse to act" if given such illegal orders. He added Trump should "bring his own bucket" if he wanted to revive waterboarding.[66] Even after winning his party's nomination in July, Trump persisted in his torture advocacy, telling a press conference that the Geneva Conventions were outdated, adding: "I am a person that believes in enhanced interrogation, yes. And by the way, it works."[67]

With torture once again dominating political discourse, the *New York Times* invested scarce reportorial resources to publish, in October 2016, a searching review of Bush administration torture, crisscrossing three continents to track down dozens of former detainees once held in CIA black sites or at Guantánamo. The paper found "a disturbingly high number of these men were innocent," and that despite Bush administration assurances that enhanced interrogation would have "no negative long-term effects," years later many still suffered "flashbacks, nightmares and debilitating panic attacks."[68] In short, enhanced interrogation was clearly brutal torture, illegal under US law and the UN convention.

Right after his upset win in November 2016, Trump picked Mike Pompeo, a Kansas congressman known for vocal advocacy of torture, as his nominee for CIA director. Two years earlier, Pompeo had forcibly rejected the Senate's report on CIA torture, insisting that the agency's harsh methods were "within the law, within the constitution" and charging that this inquiry had "put American lives at risk" because "our friends and allies" in the fight against Islamic jihad now know Washington will not honor its commitments. He blasted Obama for "ending our interrogation program," saying the intelligence officials who ran it "are not torturers, they are patriots." Trump's choice for attorney general, former senator Jeff Sessions, was a passionate defender of waterboarding, and his first choice for national security adviser, General Michael Flynn, was on record favoring use of enhanced interrogation, a euphemism for torture.[69]

With most of his national security team open to using coercive interrogation, the Trump administration discussed, during its first week in office, a policy review that would allow the CIA to reopen its "black site" prisons and to resume use of harsh techniques. Asked in a television interview whether he favored waterboarding, President Trump said, "Absolutely, I feel it works," though he added he would heed the counsel of top officials. Should he ultimately opt for torture, Trump faced certain opposition in Congress, where Republican senator John McCain, backed by a 2015 law requiring that all interrogation comply with restraints in the army field manual, said: "I don't give a damn what the president of the United States wants to do. . . . We will not waterboard. We will not torture."[70]

While Trump's transition team was endorsing harsh interrogation, the prosecutor at the International Criminal Court in The Hague announced a formal finding that "as part of approved interrogation techniques . . . members of the CIA appear to have subjected at least 27 detained persons to torture" in Afghanistan from 2002 to 2008.[71] With his national security team unanimous on the issue, the Trump administration would, should the need arise, likely use techniques deemed torture under international law, damaging America's stature as a moral leader in the community of nations.

In the past forty years, there have been a half-dozen similar scandals over CIA torture or the agency's torture techniques in South Vietnam (1970), Brazil (1974), Iran (1978), Honduras (1988), Latin America (1997), and, most recently, its black sites and Guantánamo (2014). Each has followed a familiar cycle—revelation, momentary sensation, vigorous rebuttal, official inaction, and then oblivion. Why, we might well ask, have there been so many revelations with so little that we might call reform? A comparison with the experiences of imperial Britain and France offers insight into this troubling question.

Torture and Empire

In the long wind-down of their global empires, both Britain and France used torture against anticolonial resistance movements, producing divisive public controversies. In the aftermath of those media exposés, both London and Paris proved reluctant to punish their perpetrators, instead conducting formal inquiries that either sanctioned torture or facilitated impunity. Nonetheless, both the revelations and their inadequate resolutions served, over the longer term, to delegitimate imperial rule among their foreign subjects and damage the quality of democracy at home.

Facing a national revolution in its Algerian colony from 1954 to 1962, the French resorted to systematic torture that, as historian Marnia Lazreg reports in *Torture and the Twilight of Empire*, "normalized terror to forestall the collapse of the empire in an age of decolonization."[72] In a vain attempt to crush a nationalist movement with raw repression, France launched a massive pacification program that resulted in the forcible relocation of two million Algerians, the deaths of three hundred thousand more, and the brutal torture of thousands of suspected rebels and their sympathizers.

By branding the guerrillas "outlaws" and denying them the Geneva protections due lawful combatants, the French made such brutality quite legal throughout the seven years of war. In 1955, Interior Minister François Mitterand ordered his inspector-general Roger Wuillaume to investigate allegations of abuse. To contain the political damage, Wuillaume's report, foreshadowing the Bush administration's rhetorical devices, used clinical euphemisms ("procedures") to avoid the term *torture*, cited compliant experts to minimize the pain of the methods used, and asserted that these measures were unavoidably necessary to fight the insurgency.[73] In this way, the report excused the army's systematic torture of Algerian rebels, saying: "The water and electricity methods, provided they are carefully used, are said to produce a shock which is more psychological than physical and therefore *do not constitute excessive cruelty*." Forcing water down a victim's throat to simulate drowning, a technique then favored by the French Army and later used by the CIA, was, the report insisted, acceptable. "According to certain medical opinion, the water-pipe method," Wuillaume wrote, "involves no risk to the health of the victim."[74]

When the Front de Libération National (FLN) launched an urban uprising in the city of Algiers in 1956, the French military already had ample legal cover to apply torture without restraint. In the twisting streets of the old city's Casbah, the 10th Paratroop Division under Colonel Jacques Massu employed the water pipe, electric shock, beating, and burning to get information that would allow his men to track down Algerian guerrillas. Almost all the rebel suspects taken to the army's Villa des Tourelles safe house for interrogation under cover of darkness were dead by dawn, their bodies dumped in shallow graves outside the city. These "summary executions," which one senior officer called "an inseparable part of the task associated with keeping law and order," were so relentless that 3,024 of those arrested in Algiers went "missing"—a momentary setback for the FLN.[75]

"You might say that the battle of Algiers was won through the use of torture," observed British historian Sir Alistair Horne, "but that the war, the Algerian war, was lost."[76] Indeed, the French Army's campaign proved counterproductive as the revolt spread, thoroughly delegitimating their rule in the eyes of Algerians and transforming the FLN from a group of small cells into a mass party. Of equal import, France itself recoiled against the war's costs, both moral and material. The editor of an Algiers newspaper, Henri Alleg, who was tortured by the 10th Paratroop during the battle, wrote a moving memoir describing the pain of the army's water-pipe method as "a terrible agony, that of death itself." With an angry introduction by Jean-Paul Sartre, the book's publication in 1958 became a cause célèbre when the French government banned it, making it an underground bestseller in Paris.[77]

"The French army won an uncontested military victory," argued the French historian of the Algerian war, Benjamin Stora. "But in fact the political victory was far from being won because the use of torture heightened awareness among the French public. The society went through a serious

moral crisis." As the fighting ground on without end, the Paris press focused on the army's torture activities; and public support for the war effort,
once nearly unanimous, slowly eroded until France finally quit Algeria in
1962, after 130 years of colonial rule. In the painful aftermath—as Pierre
Vidal-Naquet explained in his study of the Algerian war, *Torture: Cancer
of Democracy*—an underlying public indifference to such systemic abuse
had the effect of eroding civil liberties and weakening the quality of French
democracy.[78]

In its long imperial recessional, Great Britain also used torture—
sporadically in Malaya, systematically in Aden and Kenya, and scandalously
in Northern Ireland and other places—finding in each case that exposés by
journalists and in Parliament weakened the moral legitimacy of its cause. As
part of its collaborative mind-control research with the United States and
Canada, Britain conducted tests in 1957 on human subjects at Lancaster
Moor Hospital, a mental institution. The tests replicated every detail of Dr.
Donald Hebb's findings about sensory deprivation, providing British intelligence ample evidence of its efficacy. In the early 1960s, Britain's military
began training its elite forces in these psychological methods, offensively for
counterinsurgency and defensively to survive the stress of capture.[79]

In the violent eclipse of the empire, these harsh interrogation techniques, as
a later official inquiry reported, "played an important part in counter insurgency
operations . . . in the British Cameroons (1960–61), Brunei (1963), British Gui-
ana (1964), Aden (1964–67), [and] Borneo/Malaysia (1965–66)." Determined to
defeat Kenya's Mau-Mau rebels, for example, British officials burned homesteads
housing a million people and opened fifty camps where many of the seventy
thousand detainees were subjected to "electric shocks, burnings, near-drown-
ings, mutilations, and sexual abuse." At the most notorious of these camps at
Hola, a mass murder was covered up by awarding its superintendent a knight-
hood. In February 1965, after allegations of such brutality by its forces, Britain
adopted a "joint directive on military interrogation" that cited the Geneva Conventions to bar any "violence to life and person" or "outrages upon personal dignity." Explaining the logic of these prohibitions, the directive stated that "torture
and physical cruelty of all kinds are professionally unrewarding since a suspect
so treated may be persuaded to talk but not to tell the truth."[80]

After further allegations of "cruelty and torture" at the British Army's
Interrogation Centre in Aden during a 1966 Arab terror campaign, an official inquiry by Roderic Bowen, QC, added some specific requirements for
external supervision during interrogation.[81] Despite these legal restrictions,

British intelligence evidently preserved the special psychological practices that were, under these tighter guidelines, at the cusp of illegality.

When 304 bombs erupted across Northern Ireland between January and June 1971, London employed extreme interrogation techniques against the underground Irish Republican Army (IRA). Like France had done in Algeria and America would do in Iraq, Britain felt compelled to fight terror with torture. In April of that year, the English Intelligence Centre gave Belfast's police, the Royal Ulster Constabulary, a top-secret training course in what were called the "five techniques" for "interrogation in depth." Although all instruction was done "orally" and no orders were "committed to writing or authorized in any official document," the British government later admitted that these abusive methods had been approved at a "high level." After investing its security forces with special powers of summary arrest and limitless internment, Belfast unleashed Operation Demetrius on August 9, quickly "sweeping up" some eight hundred suspected IRA terrorists.[82]

Among the hundreds of suspects arrested, fourteen were selected for a secret program to test the efficacy of psychological torture under actual field conditions. In the words of a later finding by the European Court of Human Rights, these fourteen subjects were taken to "unidentified centres" where they were subjected to "five particular techniques" that were "sometimes termed 'disorientation' or 'sensory deprivation' techniques." Showing the influence of Dr. Hebb's experiments and the CIA's methods, these, in the court's words, involved: self-inflicted pain—forcing detainees to remain immobile for hours while "spreadeagled against the wall, with their fingers put high above the head against the wall, the legs spread apart and the feet back, causing them to stand on their toes with the weight of the body mainly on the fingers"; and sensory deprivation—"putting a black or navy coloured bag over the detainees' heads and . . . keeping it there all the time except during interrogation."[83]

Within weeks, press reports detailing these harsh measures forced Britain's Conservative government to appoint a committee of inquiry, chaired by Sir Edmund Compton, to look into allegations of "physical brutality." In October 1971 while the committee was still investigating, the *Times* of London sparked a bitter debate in Parliament with an exposé of torture in Northern Ireland. Home Secretary Reginald Maudling defended the security forces, arguing that tough tactics were imperative since "intelligence is of enormous importance in defeating gunmen." But a member from Northern Ireland, Frank McManus, shot back that the case was going before Europe's Court of

Human Rights and the government was "in serious danger of coming into serious international disrepute."[84]

When released to the public four weeks later, the Compton Committee's report further stoked such partisan fires with its contorted justifications for each of the "five techniques." Wall-standing for up to forty-three hours was said to provide "security for detainees and guards," and the hood served a necessary "security" function. Such tough tactics were, Compton insisted, needed against terrorists since "information must be sought while it is still fresh . . . and thereby save the lives of members of the security forces and of the civil population." Although wall-standing did constitute "physical ill-treatment," the report maintained that there was "no evidence at all of a major trauma" from it. This extraordinary whitewash prompted a special parliamentary session, with the government justifying interrogation that "yielded information of great value . . . about individuals concerned in the IRA campaign, . . . about the location of arms dumps and weapons."[85] Responding to Compton and his defenders, Amnesty International explained, "The purpose and effects of these techniques is to disorientate and break down the mind by sensory deprivation," making them "as grave an assault on . . . the human person as more traditional techniques of physical torture."[86]

The Irish Republic later complained formally to the European Human Rights Commission, which in 1976 released an 8,400-page report finding that "the combined use of the five techniques . . . shows a clear resemblance to those methods of systematic torture which have been known over the ages." The commission ruled unanimously that the techniques were "a modern system of torture." In February 1977, the case advanced to the European Court of Human Rights, which would later find Britain guilty of "inhuman and degrading treatment" but not torture—a distinction, the judges said, that derived "principally from a difference in the intensity of the suffering inflicted." Nonetheless, Britain's attorney general had to appear before the court and offer an "unqualified undertaking that the 'five techniques' will not in any circumstances be reintroduced as an aid to interrogation."[87]

After sanctioning torture to secure their empires, both Britain and France found that the inevitable revelations of abuse not only intensified resistance among subject populations and discredited the military effort among their own citizenry but also damaged their international standing. The systemic use of torture is both the sign of a dying empire and a cause of imperial retreat, and that obviously applies to the United States as well.

By focusing its might and majesty on breaking hapless individuals through torture, any empire—whether British, French, or American—reveals the gross power imbalance otherwise concealed within the daily exercise of dominion. After centuries of cruel scourges by autocrats and absolute monarchs, Europe's Enlightenment had repudiated the practice, making the abolition of torture a sign of civilization and its use a mark of barbarism. Just as any modern government loses legitimacy among its citizens for such abuse, so an empire sacrifices its hard-won cultural suasion among both allies and subjects when it demeans its moral stature by torture.

Looking back on the occupation of Iraq a half century hence, historians may well find that the Abu Ghraib scandal was emblematic of the decline of US imperial power. From the perspective of informed opinion in Berlin, Beijing, Brasilia, Cairo, London, Mumbai, or Tokyo, America could not and cannot, now or in the future, simultaneously claim both moral leadership of the international community and the sovereign prerogative to torture at will in defiance of international law.

Chapter Six

Beyond Bayonets and Battleships: The Pentagon's Wonder Weapons

I t's 2030 and an American "triple canopy" of advanced surveillance and armed drones fills the heavens from the lower stratosphere to the exo-atmosphere. It can deliver its weaponry anywhere on the planet with staggering speed, knock out an enemy's satellite communications system, or follow individuals biometrically for great distances. It's a wonder of the modern age. Along with the country's advanced cyberwar capacity, it's also the most sophisticated militarized information system ever created and an insurance policy for global dominion deep into the twenty-first century.

That is the future as the Pentagon imagines it. Though it's actually under development, most Americans know little or nothing about it. They are still operating in another age. "Our Navy is smaller now than at any time since 1917," complained Republican candidate Mitt Romney during the 2012 presidential debates.

With words of withering mockery, President Obama shot back: "Well, Governor, we also have fewer horses and bayonets, because the nature of our military's changed . . . the question is not a game of Battleship, where we're counting ships. It's what are our capabilities." Obama then offered just a hint of what those capabilities might be: "What I did was work with our joint chiefs of staff to think about, what are we going to need in the future to make sure that we are safe? . . . We need to be thinking about cyber security. We need to be talking about space."[1]

Amid all the post-debate media chatter, few if any commentators had a clue when it came to the profound strategic changes encoded in the president's sparse words. Yet for the previous four years, working in secrecy, the Obama administration had presided over the earliest stages of a technological revolution in defense planning, moving the nation far beyond bayonets and battleships to cyberwarfare and the full-scale weaponization of space. With America's economic influence slowly waning, this breakthrough in "information warfare" may be significantly responsible if its global hegemony somehow continues to hold sway far into the twenty-first century.

While the technological changes involved are revolutionary, they have deep historical roots that reach back to the moment this nation first stepped onto the world stage during the Spanish-American War. Over the span of a century, as it plunged into three Asian crucibles of counterinsurgency—the Philippines, Vietnam, and Afghanistan—the US military has repeatedly responded by fusing the nation's most advanced technologies into new information infrastructures of unprecedented power.

During the Cold War, the Pentagon institutionalized its alliance with industry by forging a long-term partnership with defense contractors to create a formidable "military-industrial complex." In his farewell address to the nation in January 1961, President Dwight Eisenhower took the measure of America's progress and reflected soberly on his role in fostering a system of military procurements for what then seemed an endless Cold War. "Our military organization today bears little relation to that known by any of my predecessors in peacetime, or indeed by the fighting men of World War II or Korea," he told a national television audience. "Until the latest of our world conflicts, the United States had no armaments industry. But now we can no longer risk emergency improvisation of national defense; we have been compelled to create a permanent armaments industry of vast proportions. . . . Akin to, and largely responsible for the sweeping changes in our industrial-military posture, has been the technological revolution during recent decades. In this revolution, research has become central; it also becomes more formalized, complex, and costly."[2]

Eisenhower himself did more than any other president to forge this alliance between the Pentagon and private contractors. He responded to the profound shock in 1957, when Russia beat America in the race to launch the world's first orbital satellite (Sputnik), by creating NASA (National Aeronautics and Space Administration) and, even more importantly, a "high-risk, high-gain" research unit called ARPA (Advanced Research Projects Agency), that later added the word *Defense* to become DARPA. In the coming decades, these agencies would preside over a succession of technological triumphs, exemplified by NASA's moonwalk and ARPA's creation of ARPANET, the basis for the Internet.[3]

For seventy years, this close alliance between the Pentagon and a tight circle of major defense contractors has produced the world's largest and most powerful military arsenal. In 2010, the US defense budget of $700 billion represented nearly half (43 percent) of world military spending, compared with only 7 percent for China, while just forty-five American defense contractors accounted for 60 percent of the arms sales (worth $247 billion) by the world's one hundred leading military manufacturers.[4]

Apart from sheer scale, this arsenal's capacity for constant, cutting-edge technological innovation has been a key component in America's ascent to global dominion. Indeed, for the past five centuries shifts in military technology have contributed to both the expansion and eclipse of empires. From 1500 to 1930, European empires were synonymous with naval power. Hence, small states with weak armies—Portugal, Holland, and England—could parlay maritime prowess and technological advantage into vast overseas dominions. Though both small and poor, fifteenth-century Portugal combined its innovative caravel ship rigging, the first to allow a vessel to sail into the wind, with sophisticated navigation, the first to measure both longitude and latitude, to conquer a maritime empire spanning three continents. Britain's development of history's first four-ocean navy helped it defeat its Bourbon rivals, France and Spain, in the global Seven Years' War (1756–63) and slowly strangle Napoleon's continental empire (1803–15), leading to its century of global dominion. During World War II, Britain's skillful codebreaking gave it the edge over Nazi Germany's formidable air force, its U-boats, and its surface ships, while America's deployment of radar, submarines, and airpower swept Imperial Japan's navy from the Pacific.[5] In the postwar decades, the transfer of global hegemony from London to Washington was accompanied by a parallel shift in strategic dominion from the Royal Navy to the US Air Force.

Ever since construction of the Pentagon was completed in 1943, that massive bureaucratic maze—with seventeen miles of corridors, nearly four million square feet of office space, and over twenty thousand employees—has somehow managed, despite bloated budgets and problematic procurements, to preside over a creative fusion of science and industry. During the Cold War and its aftermath, Washington's military-industrial complex produced an unbroken succession of "wonder weapons" that gave it a critical technological advantage over its communist rivals in all major domains of military conflict. Even when defeated, as it would be in Vietnam, Iraq, and

Afghanistan, the Pentagon's research matrix would demonstrate, time and again, a recurring resilience that could turn battlefield disaster into techno-logical advance, almost as if it contained some embedded engineering for ever-increasing innovation.

Crucible of War

While ground combat in Vietnam was an unrelenting mix of failure and frus-tration, the sheer scale of air operations forged some important technological innovations. No matter how you measure it, the Vietnam conflict was the biggest air war in military history. By 1971, the United States had dropped 6.3 million tons of bombs on Indochina—double the total of 3.3 million tons the Allies dropped in all theaters during World War II. The air force and navy flew nearly two million combat missions, or sorties, in Indochina, more than the 1.7 million flown in World War II. Beyond these daunting numbers, the war also sparked important innovations in the use of airpower that would lead, decades later, to the formation of a new robotic information regime. Indeed, these nine years of air operations produced an amazing record of "firsts"—including, the first electronic battlefield, history's earliest use of airpower to take and hold ground without infantry, the first computerized bombing, the first use of communications satellites to support air combat, and perhaps most importantly, the initial impetus for the development of the unmanned aircraft that are now called drones.

Within this wider war, tiny, landlocked Laos, then rated the world's poorest nation, became the site of history's largest air war and a protracted experiment in the uses of airpower. The air force dropped 2.1 million tons of bombs on Laos alone—equal to its total for Germany and Japan combined in World War II. From a few dozen missions a day in 1965, air operations escalated steadily to reach two hundred combat sorties daily between 1968 and 1970.[6]

Even as the United States withdrew its ground forces from Vietnam after 1969, the air force bombardment of Laos continued and, in certain areas, in-tensified. Under the pressures of the general withdrawal from Vietnam, total air sorties for Indochina dropped from a peak of 20,000 per month in 1969 to 10,000 by 1971, and aircraft in theater declined from 1,800 to 1,100. But reflecting the supposed strategic significance of Laos, the air force shifted its residual capacity to focus overwhelmingly on this tiny country. From its four main bases just across the Mekong River in Thailand, it maintained, even in mid-1971, a fleet of 330 aircraft, including 125 workhorse F-4 fighter-bombers. Additional fighter aircraft from carriers off the coast and bases in South Vietnam, as well as B-52s based in Guam and Thailand, were also deployed against Laos. Even as the Nixon administration withdrew ground troops from South Vietnam, it tripled the bombing of Laos from an annual average of 129,482 tons (1965 to 1968) to 387,466 tons (1969 to 1972).[7]

Inside Laos, air activity was divided into two main arenas. Operation Barrel Roll in the North provided tactical air support for CIA paramilitary operations against Lao communist guerrillas. Operation Steel Tiger in the South deployed electronic sensors and massive bombardment in an attempt to cut North Vietnamese infiltration down the Ho Chi Minh Trail. Reflecting US strategic priorities, Steel Tiger received about 85 percent of all sorties flown over Laos circa 1970, while Barrel Roll received about 15 percent.[8]

Although the CIA's secret war in northern Laos was fought on the ground by thirty thousand Hmong tribal guerrillas, it gained both mobility and firepower from one of the most remarkable air armadas in the history of warfare. To tie their mountaintop villages together and arm the scattered Hmong hill tribes, the CIA's Air America had a fleet of agile Helio Couriers, with extended wingspans for maneuverability, to land on some two hundred dirt airstrips along the rugged ridges of northern Laos. As the war expanded, the CIA brought in helicopter gunships to increase Hmong air mobility and provide tactical air support. To air drop supplies to hill tribe villages, the CIA used C-130 transports with rear doors and cargo kickers. The Royal Lao Air Force operated squadrons of antiquated T-28s, single propeller trainers that were effective in close support bombing. Flying out of bases in northeast Thailand, an armada of air force F-4 fighter-bombers pounded northern Laos during daylight hours. After 1968, the air force introduced the night-flying AC-47 gunship, known as "Spooky"—a converted World War II–era C-47 cargo aircraft retrofitted with "urine sniffers" that could detect mammal ammonia and three navy mini-guns that could each rain 6,000 rounds per minute upon the countryside. Flying at 35,000 feet, B-52 strategic bombers dropped their racks of 500-pound bombs into fiery rectangles of sudden death across northern Laos.

Within that total of 2.1 million tons, some 321,000 tons, twice the conventional bombardment of Japan during World War II, were dropped on the Plain of Jars region, a highland valley with some 200,000 people and ancient Buddhist temples, a royal palace, market towns, and rice-growing villages.[9] During the years of peak bombing, its peasant population suffered heavy loss of life and property. Many were reduced to living in caves and working their fields in the few hours of twilight between the daylight tactical bombing and the nighttime strafing by AC-47 gunships.[10]

During a weeklong trek through northern Laos at the peak of this operation in the summer of 1971, I could not miss the omnipresent signs of the air-war canopy the air force maintained over this region. During daylight hours, jet fighters returning from bombing runs were always visible, weaving a dense cat's cradle of wispy white contrails in the skies above. One night, sleeping in a Hmong village on the edge of the free-fire zone, I could hear the incessant whine of an AC-47 gunship—fading, getting stronger, then fading again—and occasional far-off bursts of their mini-guns. The next morning, I woke to find a group of two dozen refugees, sitting dirty and tired beside bundles of their worldly goods, who had somehow emerged from that hail of gunfire. They were, they said, the remains of a larger group of ninety who had fled the Plain of Jars two weeks before to escape the air war. Those twenty-five that I met that morning, almost all women and children, were the only survivors.

After 1968, Barrel Roll's bombardment of northern Laos grew in both tonnage and lethal effect. By photo mapping the entire Plain of Jars, the main air force base in Udorn, Thailand, produced a detailed grid with coordinates for every feature, allowing transmission of target coordinates directly into the bombing computers of F-4 fighters for deadly accuracy.[11] But above all, the air force and its defense contractors introduced ever more efficient cluster bomb units for more lethal strikes against anyone on the ground, soldiers or civilians.[12]

Apart from the heavy loss of life, this aerial bombardment covered portions of northern Laos with countless thousands of unexploded antipersonnel bomblets that, nearly fifty years later, continue to maim and kill hundreds of residents yearly in the Plain of Jars area. Since the war in Vietnam ended in 1975, approximately twenty thousand Laotian civilians have been killed or maimed by these unexploded bombs, and the number continues to mount.[13] During his visit to Vientiane in September 2016, President Obama, in what he called a "spirit of reconciliation," offered $90 million to accelerate removal of these unexploded bombs, saying that under the American air war "villages and entire valleys were obliterated. Countless civilians were killed."[14]

Of the 2.1 million tons of bombs dropped on Laos by April 1973, the air force concentrated 85 percent, or 1.7 million tons of them, on the strategic bombing of the Ho Chi Minh Trail, an infiltration route through a narrow, lightly populated mountain corridor in southern Laos. As Hanoi's manpow-

Refugee from the Plain of Jars, northern Laos, August 1971. (Photo by John Everingham)

er and matériel flowed down the trail, Washington realized that victory in South Vietnam required cutting this vital route.

Creating a physical barrier between the Mekong River and South China Sea would have required a prohibitive 140,000 troops and ten million land mines. Instead, Secretary of Defense Robert McNamara was intrigued by the idea, suggested by scientists who advised DARPA, for "a barrier of electronic, acoustic, and pressure sensors and other devices to detect enemy movement." To turn this vague concept into a physical reality, he formed a high-powered task force under Lieutenant General Alfred Starbird, who cobbled together components from the military's most advanced technology—sensors from the navy, communications aircraft from the air force, and computers from contractor IBM—to assemble a $2 billion "electronic barrier" anchored by an "air-supported anti-infiltration subsystem" astride the Ho Chi Minh Trail in southern Laos.[15] In its technological sophistication, this system was a model for what the US commander in Vietnam, General William Westmoreland, called the "battlefield of the future" that would track enemy forces "through the use of data links, computer assisted intelligence evaluation, and automated fire control," reducing the need for conventional infantry.[16]

Under a program dubbed Operation Igloo White, the air force combined sensors, computers, and fighter-bombers in an electronic bombing campaign against truck convoys in southern Laos that dropped over a million tons of bombs from 1968 to 1973, equal to the total tonnage for the Korean War. To detect Hanoi's trucks, the air force, at a cost of $800 million a year, laced this forested mountain corridor with twenty thousand acoustic, seismic, thermal, and ammonia-sensitive sensors. The "Acoubuoy," a listening device, was parachuted into trees, while "Spikebuoy," meant to detect motion, was dropped into soil with antennae made to look like local weeds. Both sent signals to four EC-121 communications aircraft circling ceaselessly overhead.[17]

At the US air base in Nakhorn Phanom just across the Mekong River in Thailand, the Infiltration Surveillance Center used the four hundred airmen of Task Force Alpha and two powerful IBM 360/65 mainframe computers equipped with the company's first visual display monitors to translate all those sensor signals into "an illuminated line of light" called a worm, which "moved down the map at a rate equal to the computed target speed." After confirming coordinates, the center would launch its F-4 Phantom jets over the Ho Chi Minh Trail where LORAN radio signals guided them to the target and the IBM computers discharged laser-guided bombs automatically.[18] Concerned about losing the lumbering EC-121s to antiaircraft fire, the air force began to experiment with unmanned aircraft, retrofitting several Beechcraft Debonairs as "radio controlled drones" and testing Nite Gazelle helicopters "as hovering killer drones" to destroy trucks.[19]

Bristling with antennae and filled with the latest computer technology, Task Force Alpha's massive concrete bunker seemed like a futuristic marvel. "Just as it is almost impossible to be an agnostic in the Cathedral of Notre Dame," said a top Pentagon official after a 1968 visit, "so it is difficult to keep from being swept up in the beauty and majesty of the Task Force Alpha temple."[20]

In its initial assessments of this electronic barrier, the air force was resolutely sanguine. In 1969, a senior Pentagon official told Congress: "There has been no case where the enemy has successfully come through the sensor field." A year later, an internal evaluation found that "the Igloo White system was both effective and accurate," hitting 40 percent of enemy targets.[21] The program reported an incredible twenty-five thousand North Vietnamese trucks destroyed. The digital worm crawling across Igloo White computer screens identified a truck's coordinates, aircraft bombed that location, and the worm, after a twenty-minute lag, disappeared—data sufficient to convince the air force that the trucks were actually destroyed. Within the project's sealed information loop, there was no external check on such inflated estimates of success.[22]

Even when the war was raging, such optimism attracted sharp criticism. Skeptical CIA analysts reduced air force damage claims by 75 percent.[23] While the air force raised its estimates to 80 percent of enemy trucks destroyed in southern Laos, Hanoi reported only 15 percent lost.[24] After more than one hundred thousand North Vietnamese troops with tanks, trucks, and artillery successfully moved down the Ho Chi Minh Trail through the sensor field undetected for a massive offensive in South Vietnam in 1972, one analyst for the Pacific air force advised his commander: "Due to the duration, intensity, and geographical extent of the current NVN [North Vietnamese] offensive . . . everyone now recognizes that our estimates were in error." An air force historian called the program's calculations to determine enemy casualties "an exercise in metaphysics rather than mathematics." Hanoi's commander of the Ho Chi Minh Trail recalled that they drove trucks back and forth as decoys, herded cattle to simulate marching troops, and hung bottles of urine to confuse the sniffer sensors. An official history of the Igloo White operation later concurred, stating: "Thousands of North Vietnamese soldiers and local laborers kept the Ho Chi Minh Trail open by constructing, camouflaging, and repairing . . . the roads," thereby defeating the sophisticated sensors. In short, the air force's bold $6 billion attempt to build an "electronic battlefield" was an unqualified failure.[25]

Yet this bombing campaign is anything but a historical footnote to the war in Vietnam. Under the pressures of history's longest and largest air campaign, the air force experimented with technological innovations, including computer-directed bombing, new kinds of antipersonnel weaponry, aerial gunships with lethal firepower, and drone warfare. Under the pressures of fighting a ground war without effective infantry, the air force overturned established military doctrine that it "could not gain, hold, or occupy terrain; only ground forces could."[26]

Indeed, in the years since the bombing of Laos ended, the United States has increasingly relied on airpower as its main strike force in Bosnia, Kosovo, Kurdistan, Afghanistan, Libya, and Yemen (in part via Saudi Arabia's US-purchased and -resupplied air force). And in the future, Washington's operations overseas may rely heavily, possibly primarily or even solely, on airpower, making this long-forgotten air campaign over Laos the progenitor for wars that will be fought well into the twenty-first century.

In retrospect, Igloo White was but one example of the way that these massive air operations over Indochina encouraged innovation. In the pressure cooker of history's largest air war, the air force also accelerated the transformation of a new information system that would rise to significance three decades later: the "Firebee" target drone, first developed by Ryan Aeronautical of San Diego in 1955. During eight years of combat in Indochina, the air force deployed twenty variations of this unmanned aircraft, launching them from lumbering C-130 transports for photo reconnaissance over China and North Vietnam, for monitoring enemy communications, and for decoy flights to detect weakness in the air defenses of the northern capital, Hanoi. Indicative of rapid progress, the "Lightning Bug" series achieved a 2,400-mile range and flew 3,500 sorties in the Vietnam theater equipped with ever more sophisticated electronics. In 1965, a Lightning Bug intercepted the electronic signal from an enemy surface-to-air missile, allowing later US fighters to carry missile jammers, a success the Pentagon called "the most significant contribution to electronic reconnaissance in the last 20 years." By 1972, the air force could send an "SC/TV" model drone, equipped with a camera in its nose, distances of 2,400 miles while controlling it via a low-resolution television image. A year earlier, using one of the Firebee target drones modified for Vietnam, the air force made aviation history in a test at Edwards Air Base in California by firing the first missile from an unmanned aircraft.[27]

These early drones did, however, have some serious limits that precluded their inclusion in a peacetime arsenal. Once launched from beneath the wing of the C-130 transport, their recovery was tricky, requiring a lumbering "Jolly Green Giant" CH-3C helicopter to hook the drone mid-drop and reel it in with a thousand-foot steel cable. Not surprisingly, each drone averaged only four flights and half crashed or were shot down, making them a costly weaponry to field. In the war's aftermath, the Pentagon lost interest in planes without pilots, while the navy doubted their value given the difficulties of unmanned landings on its carriers.[28] Nonetheless, through the pressure of history's largest air war over Indochina, drones were transformed from dumb targets into reasonably agile surveillance aircraft and launched on a technological trajectory toward full weaponization that would be realized decades later in Afghanistan.

The air war in Vietnam was also impetus for development of the Pentagon's global telecommunications satellite system, another important first. In 1962, Bell Laboratories launched the successful Telstar satellite that "dazzled the world with live images of sports, entertainment and news" during its seven-month, low-altitude orbit. Meanwhile, in that same era ARPA had been working with contractors General Electric and Hughes Aerospace to develop larger military models for higher geosynchronous orbits with wide coverage and longer life.[29]

After the Initial Defense Satellite Communications System launched seven orbital satellites in 1966, ground terminals in Vietnam started transmitting high-resolution aerial surveillance photos to Washington, a "revolutionary development" that allowed analysts to conduct "near-real-time battlefield intelligence from afar." In this "first opportunity to use satellite communications from a real-world theater of operations," those satellites proved so useful for "emergency operational communications with Vietnam" that the Pentagon accelerated the launch of an additional twenty-one satellites over the next two years, giving it the first system that could communicate from anywhere on the globe.[30]

At great cost, the war in Vietnam thus marked a watershed for Washington's global information architecture. In the short term, the automated bombing in Laos created the illusion that North Vietnam's supply effort had been thwarted, while computerized data collection in South Vietnam similarly fostered the delusion that the pacification program was defeating the Viet Cong guerrillas—both harbingers of future information failures. In the medium term, the Vietnam debacle, at the cost of 58,000 dead and a $100 billion in wasted capital, was a sharp blow to American power, sparking domestic divisions for a generation and weakening Washington's global military posture for more than a decade.[31]

At a deeper level, however, those information failures proved self-correcting, leading to experiments that would result in major advances in military technology. Under the pressure of a protracted war in Vietnam, the Pentagon worked to improve individual components—satellite communications, remote sensing, computer-triggered bombing, aerial gunships, and unmanned aircraft—that would merge forty years later into a new system of robotic warfare. Within the longer arc of technological progress, Igloo White proved transformative, integrating electronic sensors in lieu of human intelligence and computerized targeting in lieu of visual contact, moving warfare toward a future electronic battlefield.

The War on Terror

A generation later—when Washington found itself facing defeat in its attempted pacification of two complex societies, Afghanistan and Iraq—the Pentagon responded in part by accelerating the development of new electronic technologies. After six years of a failing counterinsurgency effort in Iraq, the Pentagon discovered the power of biometric identification and electronic surveillance to pacify the country's sprawling cities.[32] When President Obama took office in 2009 and launched his "surge," escalating the US war effort in Afghanistan, that country too became a frontier for testing and perfecting biometric databases, as well as for drone warfare.

After developing drones into a surprisingly effective weapon during the war in Vietnam, the Pentagon largely ignored them until the end of the Cold War brought a succession of crises scattered about the globe that seemed ideal for an agile weapon that could cross borders silently and offer effective surveillance. Alone among the world powers, America had the global satellite system that could be used for the deployment of drones. Without geostatial satellites for over-the-horizon communication, drones lack the GPS navigation, guidance, and video monitoring for effective combat operations.

In the mid-1980s, the advent of the Global Positioning System (GPS) sparked renewed interest in drones at the Pentagon. After Soviet fighters shot down a Korean Airlines flight that had strayed into their airspace, President Ronald Reagan ordered the accelerated deployment of GPS systems to avoid any such future accidents, prompting the air force to launch ten satellites by 1985 and reach "initial operational capability" in December 1993 when its full complement of twenty-four satellites was orbiting. Inspired by the idea that an unmanned aircraft "equipped with a GPS receiver connected to an autopilot could be flown with great accuracy to any point on the globe," DARPA mobilized its nexus of private contractors, large and small, including Israeli immigrant engineer Abraham Karem, who was designing drones in his Los Angeles garage. After being acquired by General Atomic, his team won a $31 million Pentagon contract, in January 1994, just days after the GPS was fully operational, to deliver ten drones to the air force within six months. The prototype model, called Predator, that took its test flight in July looked rather mundane, with thin wings twice the length of its fuselage, a cruising speed of just 80 mph, and a bulge above the nose to house the satellite dish.[33]

But that unmanned aircraft far exceeded expectations during its first combat mission in mid-1995. Flying over Sarajevo in Bosnia, the Predator transmitted microwave signals that took one second to bounce 150 miles through the mountains to its base transmitter, then 25,000 miles up to a satellite, 25,000 more miles back down to Fort Belvoir, and 4,000 miles across the Atlantic to NATO headquarters in Naples, where officers were impressed with the constant stream of "crisp color video" from that drone over the Bosnian capital.[34]

Six years later in October 2001, a CIA Predator was hovering high above a three-car convoy carrying the elusive Taliban chief Mullah Omar as it sped through Kandahar, Afghanistan, and stopped at a mud-walled compound outside the city. While the Central Command chief watched on a screen in Tampa and the air force chief of staff followed the action on a monitor in Washington, the drone's pilot inside a trailer parked at CIA headquarters in Langley, Virginia, pulled the trigger on a joystick—a historic shot that was, in fact, the first missile fired from a drone in combat. As the "red bloom" of an exploding truck and glowing bodies of Taliban guards filled the video monitors, cheers erupted inside the CIA trailer. But the shouts and high-fives proved premature. According to a later interview with his driver, Mullah Omar had jumped out of that vehicle and fled on foot just before the missile struck his car, never to be seen again by Western intelligence.[35]

In 2005, Washington deployed a new drone, the advanced MQ-9 Reaper, with thirty hours flying time and the ability to detect disturbed dirt at 5,000 feet and track footprints back to enemy installations. Despite a price tag of $30 million each and annual operating costs of $5 million per plane—more than a manned F-16 fighter—the Reaper was soon "the backbone" of the US drone fleet.[36] Although these second-generation Reapers seemed to represent stunningly sophisticated technological advances, one defense analyst spoke of them as the equivalent of "Model T Fords."[37]

When former CIA director Robert Gates became secretary of defense in 2007, the drone revolution accelerated. Pushing aside what he called the "flyboys with silk scarves" who then filled the Pentagon, he fought to change priorities "so from now on, the watchword is: drones, baby, drones!"[38] Just as Gates fought for drone procurement, so CIA director Michael Hayden, a former air force general and NSA director, won White House agreement to put ever fewer restraints on lethal drone strikes in 2008 and soon made drone targeting one of the widest career tracks inside the agency. By 2009, the air force and the CIA had deployed a drone armada of at least 195 Predators and 28 Reapers inside Afghanistan, Iraq, and Pakistan, flying thirty-four patrols daily, transmitting 16,000 hours of video every month, and firing Hellfire missiles at confirmed targets.[39] From 2006 to 2016, according to one source, there were 392 attacks inside Pakistan, largely by CIA drones, that killed 2,799 insurgents and 158 civilians.[40] According to another tally, 424 strikes killed up to 3,035 insurgents and 966 civilians.[41] One marker of the torrid pace of drone development was total flying time for all unmanned vehicles. Between 2004 and 2010, it rose from just 71 hours to 250,000 hours.[42]

In 2011 there were already seven thousand drones in the American armada of unmanned aircraft, including: five hundred of the light, low-flying Shadow drones for infantry support, 250 of the missile-firing, mid-altitude Reaper and Predator drones, and fourteen of the high-flying Global Hawk surveillance drones. In those years, by funding its own fleet of thirty-five attack drones and borrowing others from the air force, the CIA moved from passive intelligence collection to a permanent capacity for extrajudicial executions on three continents. So central had drones become to its military power that the Pentagon was planning to expend $40 billion to expand its armada by 35 percent over the next decade.[43]

By 2011 as well, the air force and CIA had ringed the Eurasian landmass with a network of sixty bases for Reaper and Predator drones—all the way from the Sigonella naval station in Sicily[44] to the Incirlik Air Base in Turkey,[45] Djibouti on the Red Sea,[46] Qatar and Abu Dhabi on the Persian Gulf,[47] the Seychelles Islands in the Indian Ocean, Jalalabad, Khost, Kandahar, and Shindand in Afghanistan,[48] Zamboanga in the Philippines,[49] and Andersen Air Base on the island of Guam.[50] With a flying range of 1,150 miles when armed with its full payload of Hellfire missiles and GBU-30 bombs, the Reaper could now strike targets almost anywhere in Europe, Africa, or Asia. To fulfill its expanding global mission, the air force planned to have 346 Reapers in service by 2021, including eighty for the CIA.[51]

As of 2016, one of the Pentagon's prime contractors, AeroVironment of Monrovia, California, was producing an agile array of battlefield drones including the hand-launched, four-pound RQ-11B Raven, "the most widely used unmanned aircraft . . . for military applications requiring low-altitude surveillance"; the Wasp AE that "delivers, in a man packable asset, . . . superior imagery, increased endurance, and encrypted video"; and the Switchblade, "a back-packable, non-line-of-sight precision strike solution" with a five-mile range and "quiet motor . . . difficult to detect, recognize, and track."[52]

Miniature or monstrous, in the sky or the stratosphere, hand-held or runway-launched, drones were becoming so numerous, so critical for so many military missions that they emerged from the war on terror as America's ultimate wonder weapon for preserving its global power.

Even as Washington's reliance on unmanned aircraft expanded exponentially, however, there were ample signs of serious complications—practical, tactical, and strategic. At the practical level, American "pilots," seated before video monitors in Arizona or Nevada, suffered acute stress from twelve-hour shifts in windowless rooms where they witnessed close-up death and destruction wrought halfway around the world. Few air force pilots requested drone assignments. By 2013, resignations among them were three times higher than those of their conventional counterparts. Apart from post-traumatic stress disorder, drone pilots suffered from the "powerful perception" of low status within the service. Two years later, about 180 new drone pilots were graduating annually from air force training and 240 old ones were resigning, an outflow, said two top generals, that "will damage the readiness of the MQ1/9 enterprise for years to come."[53]

At a tactical level, there is mounting evidence to challenge early claims of immaculate intervention by drones. As Obama's escalation of drone strikes in Pakistan produced reports of civilian casualties, John Brennan, then White House counterterrorism adviser, insisted in mid-2011 that "there hasn't been a single collateral death because of the exceptional proficiency [and] precision of the capabilities we've been able to develop." The CIA supported that claim, saying its drones had killed six hundred terrorists to date "and not a single noncombatant."[54]

Yet the international press was starting to carry regular reports of increasing civilian casualties from air operations over both Afghanistan and

Pakistan. Journalist Tom Engelhardt would later count, from 2001 to 2013, eight instances in which US airpower had exterminated "wedding celebrants from the air," resulting in the deaths of three hundred Afghan, Iraqi, and Yemeni civilians. While seven of those strikes in Afghanistan and Iraq involved piloted aircraft, the latest in this sad count, in December 2013, was a drone attack on a caravan of vehicles in Yemen carrying wedding celebrants, leaving "scorched vehicles and body parts . . . scattered on the road." Although the two official inquiries ordered by the Obama White House found those killed were mostly "militants," Human Rights Watch concluded, after interviewing survivors in Yemen, that the twelve dead and fifteen wounded, including the bride, were probably innocent civilians.[55]

The military's most objective investigation of a drone-strike-gone-wrong corroborates these skeptical findings about the severe human limitations of this alluring technology. "Pilots" looking at human beings 12,000 miles away through a camera lens 12,000 feet above the ground saw what were essentially digital blips in a real-life video game. In those circumstances, innocent acts were easily misconstrued as worthy of an instant zap with a Hellfire missile. Among the hundreds of drone strikes in those years, only one has been subjected to a searching US investigation that allows us to grasp the full extent of these limitations.

In the early morning darkness of February 2010, a convoy of three small trucks was driving overland across Uruzgan Province, Afghanistan, carrying thirty passengers. Flying above the area at 14,000 feet, a Predator drone detected their warmth in the winter's cold and began streaming video, via satellite and transoceanic cable, to Creech Air Base, Nevada (where its crew was watching), Hurlburt Air Base, Florida (a control center for global drone operations), and two special forces posts in Afghanistan (where "battle captains" supervised combat operations). For the next four hours, this convoy would be the subject of close observation by four aircraft and incessant online chatter by military officials in Florida, Nevada, and Afghanistan, all aimed at sparing innocent civilians from the fiery death of a Hellfire missile strike.[56]

Overhead, the crew of an AC-130 gunship, the high-tech successor to the Vietnam-era AC-47 "Spooky," radioed at 4:54 a.m. local time, "We are now tracking three vehicles and standby we will give you an update." Within twelve minutes, the gunship crew saw the first suspicious signs, saying, "It appears the two vehicles are flashing lights signaling between."[57]

Over the next thirty minutes, evidence began piling up that could mean only one thing: an insurgent convoy. At 5:14 a.m., the Joint Terminal Attack

Controller reported "the individuals egressed the trucks holding cylindrical objects in their hands." To protect a joint operation by allied forces in a village just seven miles away, the special forces "ground force commander's intent is to destroy the vehicles."

A minute later, the drone pilot in Nevada blurted out, "Is that a fucking rifle?" His camera operator replied, "Can't really tell right now, but it does look like an object." At 5:24 a.m., the attack controller, after receiving a vague insurgent radio intercept, announced, "We believe we may have a high-level Taliban commander." The camera operator added, "Yeah, he's got his security detail."

Suddenly the screeners in Florida intervened, saying, "at least one child near SUV." The camera operator retorted, "Bullshit . . . where? Send me a fucking still [photograph]. I don't think they have kids out at this hour, I know they're shady, but come on." A few minutes later, his pilot offered reassurance, "We passed him [information about] potential children and potential shields, and I think those are pretty accurate now."

At 6:08 a.m., the pilot reported a suspicious activity common to Islamic insurgents, "They are outside the trucks praying at this time." The mission intelligence coordinator chimed in, "They're gonna do something nefarious."

As the passengers climbed back in the vehicles after pre-dawn prayers, the intelligence coordinator reported, "Adolescent near the rear of the SUV." But the camera operator rejoined, "Well, teenagers can fight," adding, "Oh sweet target, . . . put it [the missile] dead center of the [truck] bed." The intelligence coordinator agreed, saying, "Oh, that'd be perfect." An hour later as the convoy approached a small town, the camera operator reiterated: "Still a sweet fucking target, geez. Take out the lead vehicle on the run and then uhh bring the helos [helicopters] in."

At 8:42 a.m., as two light Kiowa helicopters armed with Hellfire missiles arrived on scene, the drone pilot radioed them: "Those are your three vehicles. Be advised we have about twenty-one MAMs [mature adult males], about three rifles PIDed [positively identified]."

Just a minute later, the helicopters were cleared for attack. Fifteen minutes after that, they fired the first missile at the lead pickup truck, killing eleven passengers on impact. A second missile hit the rear vehicle's engine block, blunting the blast and killing only four more. The last missile missed the middle truck.

At 8:52 a.m. as the smoke cleared, the camera operator said, "That's weird."

The pilot added, "Can't tell what the fuck they're doing."

The safety observer asked: "Are they wearing burqas?"

Camera operator, "That's what it looks like."

Pilot: "They were all PIDed [positively identified] as males, though. No females in the group."

After scanning the wounded, the camera operator said: "We looked at all of them and I don't think any of them have weapons."

At 9:10 a.m., the camera operator asked, "What are those? They were in the middle vehicle."

The intelligence coordinator replied, "Women and children."

At 9:15 a.m., the drone pilot told the helicopter crews still circling the area, "Just be advised, . . . potential 3 females and, uh, 2 adolescents, uh, near the center vehicle. . . . It looks like, uh, one of those in the, uh, bright garb may be carrying a child as well."

Within an hour, Taliban rebel radio announced "forty to fifty civilians" had been killed in a missile attack. In fact, twenty-three people had died, including two boys ages three and four. Instead of Taliban guerrillas, the thirty passengers were ordinary Afghan villagers, including unemployed men heading to Iran for work, shopkeepers on a buying expedition, and students returning to school. Activities that seemed so suspiciously malign when viewed on a video screen turned out to require a minimum of cultural knowledge, missing among all these military participants, to understand that Afghan women would remain out of sight in a vehicle away from home and millions of Muslims worldwide pray before dawn. When US helicopters arrived to evacuate the wounded, the special forces battle captain searched the scene desperately but unsuccessfully for a weapon that would make this a "legitimate target." After a Dutch military hospital treating the wounded confirmed that all were civilians, General Stanley McChrystal raced to the presidential palace in Kabul where he expressed "my deepest, heartfelt condolences." He also appointed a special inquiry under Major General Timothy McHale that discovered serious lapses in both drone technology and its management.[58]

After a six-week investigation, General McHale's executive summary criticized the "inaccurate and unprofessional reporting of the Predator crew operating out of Creech, [Air Base] Nevada" that led the ground force commander to believe the vehicles "contained a group of insurgents attempting to execute a flanking maneuver to reinforce insurgents" in a nearby village where allied forces were operating. Despite "ample evidence" of casualties, the commanders of both units involved only admitted a possible attack on innocent civilians after the Dutch "surgeon reported the casualties at the hospital."[59]

The general's full report singled out the Predator crew, calling them "almost juvenile in their desire to engage the targets" and condemning their "unprofessional conduct." Yet he also found that this supposedly wondrous technology transmitted blurry, unfocused images that made it difficult for anyone looking at the "intelligence, surveillance, reconnaissance" (ISR) on their video screens to know just what they were seeing. When the general grilled one special forces major about his tardiness in reporting the casualties, saying, "Your ISR knows there are civilians there," that officer shot back: "The ISR? Literally, look at this rug right here, sir, that's what an ISR looks like."[60]

Severe tactical complications were not limited to such spectacular blunders. A Stanford University study found that in remote rural areas of Pakistan and Yemen, the incessant drone overflights "terrorized" and "traumatized" local populations, building support for jihadists. An American correspondent held captive in Pakistan's tribal territories for seven months in 2008–2009 also reported that the incessant drone overflights were "terrifying" for villagers since "the buzz of a distant propeller is a constant reminder of imminent death." Not surprisingly, in mid-2012, polling in twenty-one nations including Brazil, Japan, Turkey, and Russia found strong, often overwhelming disapproval of American drone attacks on extremists in the Middle East.[61] Two years later, 70 percent of those surveyed across six Middle East nations opposed drone strikes against suspected terrorists, including 87 percent of Egyptians and 90 percent of Jordanians. Inside the battleground state of Pakistan, 66 percent were critical.[62]

In 2015, the *New York Times* reported that "proliferating mistakes have given drones a sinister reputation in Pakistan and Yemen and have provoked a powerful anti-American backlash in the Muslim world," making President Obama's aim of rebuilding relations with Islamic nations another "part of the collateral damage."[63] Washington was thus faced with a sharpening contradiction between its reliance on drones for global force projection and the rising opposition to their use among its would-be allies worldwide.

After five years of insisting that there was not "a single collateral death" from drone strikes, the Obama administration was finally forced to admit, in July 2016, that 473 attacks in Pakistan and Yemen from 2009 to 2015 had killed 116 civilians. (Human rights counts were seven times higher.) To prevent future innocent deaths, President Obama ordered that protecting bystanders should be a priority for future attacks.[64]

At the all-important strategic level, moreover, drones were supposed to be integrated into a wider global mission of working with allied armies for more effective counterterror security, often through joint special forces operations. In a postcolonial world of sovereign nations, nonstate actors such as rebels and terrorists became the main threat to global order, requiring almost perpetual deployments of adaptable forces. As part of a longer-term shift away from a reliance on the military bastions that had ringed Eurasia during the Cold War to a more agile global strike capability, special operations forces experienced a sustained growth. Building upon a relatively small force of 11,600 commandos in the army rangers and navy SEALs, Congress enacted legislation in 1987 forming the unified Special Operations Command (USSOCOM). After the 9/11 attacks, Defense Secretary Donald Rumsfeld gave it the lead role in planning the war on terror and executing special operations missions within that plan. Its budget climbed from $2.3 billion in 2001 to $10.3 billion a decade later, comparable to the funding for powerful agencies like the CIA and NSA. Apart from combat capability, its personnel were to serve as "forward-deployed warrior diplomats" working "in dozens of countries conducting theater security cooperation events to train host nations to eliminate terrorism."[65]

Indeed, by 2015 SOCOM had 69,000 elite troops in the Rangers, SEALs, and Air Commandos deployed to 147 countries, or 75 percent of the world, meaning on any given day they were operating in seventy to ninety nations. Between 2012 and 2014, these forces also ran five hundred Joint Combined Exchange Training exercises in sixty-seven nations. In Colombia, the program contributed to the formation of two elite battalions that served as the core for the Comando de Operaciones Especiales-Ejército and fought the FARC (Fuerzas Armadas Revolucionarias de Colombia—Ejército del Pueblo) guerrillas sucessfully, eventually forcing them into peace negotiations. In Syria, by contrast, the Green Berets ran a $500 million program that, instead of mobilizing the planned fifteen thousand troops against the regime of Bashar al-Assad, actually trained just five fighters before it was canceled.[66] What accounts for the difference? Cloaked in secrecy by host countries and strict security by the US military, these joint special operations have generally escaped scrutiny, precluding any insight into the elements that make for their success or failure. In 2015, however, the longest and arguably the most successful of these operations in the Philippines suffered an unexpected debacle, prompting revealing inquiries on both sides of the diplomatic divide that offer an answer to this critical question about the factors for success or failure.

For over a decade after the 9/11 attacks, conventional US programs like military training or USAID development were effective among the Muslim minority on the southern Philippine island of Mindanao, building local support and defusing conflict. But counterterror operations by the CIA, the FBI, and special forces sometimes proved problematic. In January 2015, these failings finally broke through the pervasive secrecy when forty-four Filipino commandos died during an abortive counterterror attack. Amid the "tsunami" of grief and anger that swept the country after live television coverage of the funerals, the Philippine government conducted several investigations that represent our most detailed public examination of these high-tech special forces operations, exposing some of their severe limitations.[67]

After four years and nine failed attempts to eliminate one of their top targets in Southeast Asia, American counterterror operatives began planning a bold night strike in the southern Philippines to capture two "internationally wanted terrorists and mass murderers." Target One: Marwan, a Malaysian bomb expert with a $5 million price on his head for masterminding the 2002 Bali bombing that killed more than two hundred people and for ten subsequent bombings that murdered forty-six more. Target Two: Usman, a "bomb-making trainer" who carried a $2 million bounty for his involvement in five bombings that had killed seventeen and wounded sixty-two.[68]

On the evening of January 24, 2015, some four hundred members of the Special Action Force (SAF), an elite unit of the Philippine National Police, plunged into the midnight-dark countryside of western Mindanao for a three-mile trek through rugged tropical terrain, across a deep river, and into a jungle camp where the targets were believed to be hiding. While half a dozen American advisers monitored a drone video feed at a nearby command post, the advance party of thirteen US-trained police commandos approached under cover of darkness. Just before dawn, they rushed a bamboo hut in a blaze of gunfire. From inside, the troops radioed the command post a coded message, "Bingo Mike One." Success. Marwan, a top terrorist target, was dead. To confirm the kill, the attackers cut off the dead man's index finger.[69]

According to a report by the Philippine Senate, just minutes later the mission, codenamed Oplan Exodus, started going badly wrong. The exchange of gunfire had alerted surrounding villages where many residents were members of the Moro Islamic Liberation Front (MILF) that supported the terror suspects. For the rest of the day, over a thousand hostile Muslim fighters from rebel groups and private armies attacked the Philippine police commandos. After twelve hours of shooting that pinned down both the police advance and rear units, inflicting heavy casualties, the fighting ended when artillery fire from a nearby Philippine Army unit finally forced the Muslim fighters to withdraw. By then, forty-four troops were dead, including thirty initially wounded who were reportedly finished off with bullets to the head. According to a separate investigation by the MILF command, seventeen of their fighters and three civilians also died in this "ferocious firefight."[70]

The Philippine Senate investigation of the incident found heavy American involvement in the debacle from start to finish. On the eve of the operation, the SAF chief brought three Americans into his command post, including one covert operative identified variously as "Al Katz," "Allan Konz," or "Alan Kurtz" who had previously trained the lead commando unit. Three more Americans arrived by helicopter and later joined the police commander "at his work table." During that long day of fighting, they viewed the battlespace via television monitors linked to an overhead drone. At one point, "Alan Kurtz" ordered the commander of the nearby Sixth Infantry Division, Major General Edmundo Pangilinan, to shell the Muslim attackers. The general angrily refused, saying, "Do not dictate to me what to do. I am the commander here!" Frustrated by the refusal of the SAF commander to provide further details about the American role, the senators could only wonder whether the operation was even "authored by Filipinos." That $5 million bounty for Marwan under the US Rewards for Justice program was, they observed, a "staggering amount [that] could have enticed law enforcers to conduct operations to support the interests of others despite the high risks involved."[71]

In their own investigation, the Philippine National Police reported their planning was bungled from the outset by the ill-considered decision, complicated by flawed American advice, to send just four hundred lightly armed SAF troops into a remote area protected by thousands of Muslim fighters. During the planning, American operatives had provided the SAF commander with all the "technical intelligence support [that] facilitated the formulation and execution of the Oplan Exodus."[72] As the attack unfolded, "six American nationals" at the Tactical Command Post in Mindanao provided what the police report called "real-time information on the actual movements of friendly and enemy forces" via "special technical equipment and aircraft, which they themselves operated"—an apparent reference to a drone and to satellite communications. In the debacle's aftermath, US helicopters evacuated wounded Filipino troops, while the Philippine police immediately turned over all evidence about Marwan, both photographs and that "severed left index finger," to two FBI agents waiting in nearby General Santos City to confirm his identity.[73]

After viewing video on the cell phone of an SAF officer, the *Philippine Daily Inquirer* reported that there was now "proof that a drone . . . believed to have originated from the US drone facility in Zamboanga City" was overhead during the fighting. That meant US Joint Special Operations Task Force-Philippines (JSOTF-P) was directly implicated in this mismanaged mission.[74] A source inside the SAF told the *Inquirer*: "The Americans started this. They funded the operation, including the intelligence. . . . The Americans dictated every move." Before the attack, they had reportedly trained the SAF's Eighty-Fourth Company at a beach resort in nearby Zamboanga. During the firefight, the lead American instructor, Alan Kurtz, remained at the command post. To position their handpicked Eighty-Fourth Company to secure Marwan, the Americans apparently compromised the Philippine chain of command, impeded coordination of the attack, and slowed support from nearby Philippine Army units.[75]

Amid the spreading controversy, JSOTF-P suddenly announced that, after thirteen years in Mindanao, it was shutting down its operations. Indicating the depth of damage to bilateral relations, two years later President Rodrigo Duterte would order a full investigation of the incident, charging that "actually it was an operation of the CIA."[76]

In retrospect, it seems that the US operatives manipulated their close relations with a client unit, used the lavish reward to encourage a risky operation, facilitated its planning with intelligence from satellites and digital intercepts, and provided real-time intelligence from a circling drone.[77] David Maxwell, a retired army colonel who once commanded the JSOTF-P in Mindanao, summed up matters this way: "It was a bungled operation and it has had major fallout." Not only did the controversy bring "an inglorious end" to thirteen years of joint counterterror operations, but it also damaged Washington's relations with Manila, delaying approval of key US bases at a critical juncture in President Obama's geopolitical pivot to Asia.[78] Maxwell later added a telling critique, saying, "Most US forces . . . are so focused on mission accomplishment they often lack the patience to let the host nation operate in accordance with its own capabilities as well as customs and traditions."[79]

Clearly, even the world's most sophisticated special operations forces and aeronautic technology were no substitute for the military fundamentals of effective alliances and accurate field intelligence. Whether in Uruzgan Province, Afghanistan, or Mindanao Island, Philippines, American war fighters, trapped inside their hermetic technology and mesmerized by their video screens, proved incapable of grasping the realities of local conditions, a critical factor in any combat operation. And as can often happen in an imperial relationship, the asymmetry of power between nominal allies accentuated American arrogance and contributed to these damaging debacles.

Technology's Triple Canopy

With remarkably little attention paid to such limitations, the American occu-pations of Iraq and Afghanistan have been catalysts for a new information re-gime, meant to fuse aerospace, cyberspace, biometrics, and robotics. In 2012, after years of ground warfare in both countries and a marked expansion of the Pentagon budget, the Obama administration announced a somewhat lean-er future defense posture. A sharp 14 percent cut in future infantry strength would be offset by increased investments in space and cyberspace, particular-ly in what the administration called "critical space-based capabilities."[80]

To effect this technological transformation of warfare, starting in 2009 the Pentagon spent $55 billion annually to replace piloted aircraft with drones and to develop robotics for a data-dense interface of space, cyberspace, and the terrestrial battle space.[81] Through an annual allocation for new technol-ogies reaching $18 billion in 2016, the Pentagon had, according to the *New York Times*, "put artificial intelligence at the center of its strategy to maintain the United States' position as the world's dominant military power." Under an emerging doctrine of "centaur warfighting," humans would in the future direct "autonomous weapons" like drones that could identify and eliminate enemy targets on their own.[82] By 2025, the United States will likely deploy advanced aerospace, cyberwarfare, and digital surveillance technology to envelop the earth in a robotic matrix theoretically capable of blinding entire armies or atomizing an individual insurgent.

Significantly, both space and cyberspace are still unregulated domains of military conflict beyond the writ of international law. Washington hopes to use both as strategic domains to exercise new forms of global hegemony, just as the British Empire once ruled from the seas and Cold War America exercised its reach via airpower. As the US intelligence community seeks to surveil the globe from space, the rest of the world might well ask: Just how high does national sovereignty extend?

Interestingly, the International Civil Aviation Convention signed at Chicago in 1944 gave every nation "exclusive sovereignty over the air space above its territory." But it did not specify whether "air space" meant seven miles high to the end of the troposphere (where propeller-driven aircraft have enough air to fly), thirty miles through the stratosphere (where some jets can travel), or three hundred miles to the thermosphere (where oxygen molecules are a half-mile apart and satellites orbit). Absent any internation-al agreement about the precise extent of "airspace" within the 6,000-mile breadth of the earth's atmosphere, some Pentagon lawyer might answer such a question about the height of sovereignty with a puckish reply: only as high as you can enforce it.[83]

For the past fifty years, Washington has filled this legal void by simply expropriating much of the air and space above the earth, the ultimate global commons, for its military operations. Just as Britannia once "ruled the waves" without any diplomatic niceties, so in 1966 the Pentagon, under its Defense Satellite Communications System I, started launching twenty-six satellites unilaterally into geosynchronous orbits above the earth. This network now provides, in the words of the official website for System III, secure command, control, and communications for "the Army's ground mobile forces, the Air Force's airborne terminals, Navy ships at sea, the White House Communications Agency, the State Department, and special users" (that is, CIA and NSA, among other agencies).[84]

The strategic analyst Barry Posen has argued that Washington's "command of the commons" has allowed it "more useful military potential for a hegemonic foreign policy than any other offshore power has ever had." While Britain's global power projection "ended at the maximum range of the Royal Navy's shipboard guns," the Pentagon's position in space let it see "across the surface of the world's land masses," its airpower "can reach targets deep inland," and its infantry can advance with "a great reserve of responsive, accurate, air-delivered firepower."[85] Or so, at least, as the fantasies of America's futuristic warriors would have it. Adding to all that, the Obama White House unilaterally expropriated the lower stratosphere as an ad hoc legal jurisdiction for its drones—operated by the CIA and the clandestine Special Operations Command—which deliver sudden death from the sky across the breadth of the Muslim world for terror suspects on its "kill list" (and far too often anyone else in the way).[86] And that is by no means the end of American plans for its command of space.

Although Washington's space warfare strategy remains highly classified, it is possible to assemble the pieces of a future aerospace puzzle by trolling the Pentagon's websites, finding many of the key components in technical descriptions at the DARPA home page and in publications by its stable of cutting-edge military contractors. By the mid-2020s, the Pentagon hopes to patrol the entire planet ceaselessly via its triple-canopy aerospace shield reaching from sky to space, secured by an armada of drones with lethal missiles or Argus-eyed sensors, linked by a resilient modular satellite system, monitored through an electronic matrix, and controlled by robotic systems.

During fifteen years of nearly limitless military budgets for the war on terror, DARPA has spent billions in an imaginative, often fantastical quest

for new wonder weapons. Among the many failed creations was a solar surveillance aircraft with a 400-foot wingspan for ceaseless flight, a hypersonic
missile meant to reach speeds of 13,000 miles an hour, and a laser death ray
capable of zapping launched missiles from the bulbous nose of a modified
747 jet.[87] The Pentagon's micro technologies are almost playful, such as the
$12 million air force scheme for dropping a swarm of "mirco UAVs" (aka
drones) from a jet fighter and thereby gaining "military advantage" over China and Russia; or the navy's Sea Mob of "small swarming boats" to protect its
ships during combat.[88] After pushing these innovative technologies beyond
their practical limits—some experimental aircraft have crashed during testing—Pentagon planners came, by trial and error, to the slow realization that
established systems, particularly drones and satellites, could in combination
create an effective aerospace architecture.

At the bottom tier of this emerging aerospace shield in the lower stratosphere (about 30,000 to 60,000 feet elevation), the Pentagon has been working
with its contractors to develop high-altitude drone models that will replace
manned aircraft. To succeed the Cold War–vintage manned U-2 surveillance
aircraft, the Pentagon since 2006 has been procuring a projected armada of
ninety-nine Global Hawk drones for the air force and navy at a mind-bog-
gling cost of $223 million each, seven times the price of a Predator. With its
extended 116-foot wingspan (bigger than that of a Boeing 737) for flights at
60,000 feet, the Global Hawk is equipped with high-resolution cameras capable of photographing individual soldiers within a hundred-mile radius "with
real-time speed and dramatic clarity"; electronic sensors for intercepting radio
and telephone communications with "unparalleled accuracy"; and efficient
engines for a continuous 32-hour flight, which would potentially mean surveillance of up to 40,000 square miles daily by a single drone. After six years
of operations restricted by this drone's inability to fly above the weather as a
human pilot would, the air force in 2012 recommended ending the program.
But its builders, powerful defense contractors Northrop and Raytheon, fought
back and saved it. With its enormous bandwidth to bounce a torrent of audio-
visual data between satellites and ground stations, the Global Hawk, like other
long-distance drones in America's armada, may prove vulnerable to a hostile
hack in some future conflict.[89]

The sophistication, and limitations, of this developing technology were
exposed in December 2011 when an advanced RQ-170 Sentinel drone suddenly landed in Iran, revealing a dart-shaped, 65-foot wingspan for flight
up to 50,000 feet. Under a super-secret "black" contract, Lockheed Martin

had built twenty of these advanced drones at a cost of about $200 million each. After the aircraft appeared mysteriously in Afghanistan in 2007 and was dubbed the "Beast of Kandahar," the air force released information about its radar-evading stealth capacity and advanced optics that provide "reconnaissance and surveillance support to forward deployed combat forces."[90]

So what was this super-secret drone doing in hostile Iran? "The GPS navigation is the weakest point," an Iranian engineer explained to a reporter from the *Christian Science Monitor*. "By putting noise [jamming] on the communications, you force the bird into autopilot. This is where the bird loses its brain." The next problem, he said, was persuading the drone's autopilot to land. "If you look at the location where we made it land and the bird's home base, they both have [almost] the same altitude," the engineer explained. "There was a problem [of a few meters] with the exact altitude so the bird's underbelly was damaged in landing; that's why it was covered in the broadcast footage." Transmitted from satellites 12,000 miles above the earth, GPS signals are notoriously weak, making it relatively easy, as the Los Alamos National Laboratory had reported in 2002, for an adversary to "send a false signal reporting the moving target's true position and then gradually walk the target to a false position"—just what the Iranians seemingly did nine years later. Although the Pentagon first denied the capture and then pooh-poohed it after Iran released photos, the event sent silent shock waves down its endless corridors.[91]

In the aftermath of this debacle, the Pentagon worked with one its top contractors, Northrop, to accelerate development of a super-stealth drone capable of penetrating hostile airspace without capture. As General Robert Otto, the air force deputy chief of staff for intelligence, surveillance, and reconnaissance, told Congress in September 2014, "We have to transform the force to fight and win in contested environments. We will seek a more balanced fleet of both manned and unmanned platforms that are able to penetrate denied airspace and provide unprecedented levels of persistence." After Northrop started test flights for the RQ-180 drone at Area 51, Nevada, in 2012, the Pentagon told CNN off the record that "its capabilities are now a top intelligence-gathering priority, especially after a less sophisticated drone went down in Iran in 2012." Detailing those capabilities, *Aviation Week* reported this new drone would be the biggest to date with a 130-foot wingspan, "advanced aerodynamics" for an extended range of 1,200 miles, 24-hour flying time, thermal imaging, audio intercepts, and an "advanced stealth" capacity greater than that of the F-35 fighter. The contract for the

RQ-180 would also be the most expensive for a drone to date, totaling an estimated $2 billion for aircraft costing $300 million each. Clearly, the era of lavishly expensive war-fighting drones had finally arrived.[92]

Simultaneously, the navy was testing a dart-shaped X-47B surveillance and strike drone that has proven capable of both in-flight refueling and carrying a ponderous payload of 4,000 pounds in bombs or missiles. In July 2013, this drone passed its most crucial test, from the navy's perspective, when it landed on the deck of the USS *George H. W. Bush* off the coast of Virginia. It performed so flawlessly in test flights that, in early 2016, the navy announced that an unmanned carrier-launched surveillance and re-fueling aircraft, dubbed the MQ-25 Stingray, would indeed enter service sometime after 2020.[93]

In its quest for dominance over the stratosphere, the Pentagon pushed its contractors to the technological edge, spending billions on futuristic air-craft that sometimes seem plucked from the pages of science fiction. As in any boldly experimental program, some prototypes like the solar-powered "Helios" drone suffered spectacular crashes and the failure of others con-tributed to subsequent research, but a very few succeeded sufficiently to join America's arsenal.[94]

For the upper stratosphere, DARPA and the air force have collaborated, since 2003, in developing the highly experimental Falcon Hypersonic Cruise Vehicle. Flying at an altitude of twenty miles, it was expected to "deliver 12,000 pounds of payload at a distance of 9,000 nautical miles from the conti-nental United States in less than two hours."[95] Although the first test launches in April 2010 and August 2011 crashed midflight, they did so after reaching an amazing 13,000 miles per hour, twenty-two times the speed of sound.[96]

Yet, as has often happened with the Pentagon's resilient institutional ar-chitecture, failure produced progress. After the Falcon's crash, the Defense Department shifted its hypersonic technology in two promising new direc-tions. With the emergence of China as a threat, DARPA has, since 2013, applied its hypersonics to shorter-range tactical weapons, using its more successful X-51A scramjet technology to develop a missile capable of pene-trating Beijing's air defenses at Mach 5 (about 3,300 miles per hour).[97]

Simultaneously, Lockheed's secret "skunk works" experimental unit, famed for building the U-2 for the CIA back in the 1950s, used the hyper-sonic technology to develop the SR-72 unmanned surveillance aircraft as a successor to its famed SR-71 Blackbird, the world's fastest manned aircraft with speeds up to 2,200 mph until it was retired in 1998. When tested by

2023 and operational by 2030, the SR-72 is supposed to fly at Mach 6 (about 4,500 mph) and an altitude of 80,000 feet, with a fuselage of titanium crystals wrapped in carbon fiber for extreme stealth, making it "almost impossible to shoot down" while it crosses any continent on the planet in an hour, scooping up electronic intelligence.[98]

In the exosphere 200 miles above Earth, the age of space warfare dawned in April 2010 when the Defense Department launched the robotic X-37B spacecraft, just 29 feet long, into orbit 250 miles above the earth for a seven-month mission. Although described as an "orbital test vehicle" or an unmanned space shuttle, the X-37B is actually the Pentagon's ultimate drone. A civilian agency, NASA, started developing it in 1999 to replace the manned space shuttle. After five years, however, the Pentagon saw the project's military potential and took charge. By removing pilots and their costly life-support systems, the air force's secretive Rapid Capabilities Office created a miniaturized, militarized space drone with thrusters for in-orbit maneuvers to elude missile attacks, solar batteries for extended flight, and a cargo bay for signals-intercept sensors, satellite launch, or possible air-to-air missiles.[99] By the time the second X-37B prototype landed at Vandenberg Air Force Base in June 2012 after a flawless fifteen-month flight, a "robotically controlled reusable spacecraft" had been successfully tested, establishing the viability of space drones.[100]

In the exosphere where the space drones will soon roam, orbital satellites will be their prime targets. At the start of the war on terror, the Pentagon had a hundred military satellites to handle all its secure communications. To protect this critical element in its space infrastructure, in its 2001 *Quadrennial Defense Review* the Pentagon allocated $165 billion for a five-year effort to achieve "space control" that would "deny such freedom of action to adversaries."[101] The vulnerability of its system became obvious in 2007, however, when China used a ground-to-air missile to shoot down one of its own satellites in orbit over five hundred miles above the earth. A year later, the Pentagon accomplished the same feat, firing an SM-3 missile from a navy cruiser to score a direct hit on a US satellite 150 miles high.[102]

After failing to fully develop the F-6 satellite that would "decompose" into microwave-linked components despite expenditures of over $200 million, the Pentagon has opted instead to upgrade its more conventional single-module satellites.[103] Between 2013 and 2016, the navy launched five interconnected Mobile User Objective Systems (MUOS) satellites into geostatial orbits for communications with aircraft, ships, and motorized infantry. With ground stations in Australia, Hawaii, and Sicily, the MUOS system has an exceptional global reach all the way to the poles, with strong coverage of the Arctic necessary now that global warming is opening the region to geopolitical competition for shipping lanes and resource exploitation.[104]

Reflecting the role of the heavens as a domain for future wars, the Joint Functional Component Command for Space, established at Vandenberg Air Force Base in 2006, has the mission of protecting "friendly space systems, prevention of an adversary's ability to use space . . . for purposes hostile to US national security interests, and direct support to battle management." This unique command operates the Space Surveillance Network, which is a worldwide system of radar and telescopes. From twenty-nine remote locations like Thule, Greenland, Ascension Island in the South Atlantic, and Kwajalein Atoll in the Pacific, it makes about four hundred thousand observations daily to monitor every object in the skies.[105] As its newest tool in this ambitious endeavor, DARPA has built, from 2002 to 2015, the wide-angle Space Surveillance Telescope for installation in Western Australia where it will monitor the Southern Hemisphere, scanning "the entire geosynchronous belt several times a night" with its wide-angle view of "10,000 objects the size of a softball at a time."[106]

Robotic Information Regime

Ultimately, the impact of America's third information regime will be shaped by the ability of the military to integrate its array of aerospace weaponry into a robotic command structure capable of coordinating operations across all combat domains—space, cyberspace, sky, sea, and earth.

Air force information specialists like Lieutenant General David Deptula have long been aware of the problem of intelligence integration, warning, "We will soon be swimming in sensors and drowning in data." Starting in 2005, he used his appointment as the first air force deputy chief of staff for intelligence, surveillance, and reconnaissance to build the Distributed Common Ground System to integrate all that data. At a cost of $4.2 billion for the air force, and $10.2 billion for the military as a whole, the system comprises five principal "nodes" at places like Hurlburt Air Base in Florida and Langley Air Base in Virginia—high-tech fusion hives, costing $750 million each, swarming with uniformed analysts turning the endless streams of data into a steady flow of operational intelligence. "I overhauled the system," Deptula recalled after his retirement in 2010, "made it global so that any station could be involved in any operation with a phone call." Yet even with all that technology at his command, he knew there was another critical step still to come: "Making this automatic is an absolute must."[107]

To manage the surging torrent of information within its delicately balanced triple canopy, the system will, in the end, have to become self-maintaining through "robotic manipulator technologies," such as DARPA's Front-end Robotics Enabling Near-term Demonstration, or FREND system, that someday could potentially deliver fuel, provide repairs, reposition satellites, or destroy dead ones.[108] In April 2016, DARPA took a step in that direction, announcing the Robotic Servicing of Geosynchronous Satellites program "to robotically inspect, autonomously grapple, reposition, repair, and upgrade cooperative GEO spacecraft."[109] Operation of this complex worldwide apparatus will require, as one DARPA official explained in 2007, "an integrated collection of space surveillance systems—an architecture—that is leak-proof."[110]

By 2010, the newest unit in the US intelligence community, the National Geospatial-Intelligence Agency, had sixteen thousand employees, a $5 billion budget, and a massive $2 billion headquarters at Fort Belvoir, Virginia—all aimed at coordinating the flood of surveillance data pouring in from Predators, Reapers, U-2 spy planes, Global Hawks, X-37B space drones, Google Earth, the Space Surveillance Network, and orbiting satellites.[111]

Yet the ultimate test of all this innovation will be an ability to stay one step ahead of its sole rival for control over space, China. Like many late adopters of technology, China has made a series of strategic choices by apparently identifying orbital satellites, among the many components in such a complex system, as its fulcrum for the effective weaponization of space. In August 2016, three years after the Pentagon abandoned its own attempt at satellite security through the disaggregated F-6 system, Beijing launched the world's first quantum communications satellite. By replacing radio waves with the transmission of entangled photons (light particles) through unique crystals, this new technology will, according to one scientific report, "create a super-secure communications network, potentially linking people anywhere." China would likely launch the twenty satellites needed for complete global communications coverage should the technology prove successful.[112]

Almost simultaneously, China lofted a prototype of the Long March 7 rocket with a massive 13.5-ton payload, for both satellite deployment and for components of a sixty-ton space station that is expected to be operational by 2022. Moreover, in the race to develop artificial intelligence for the robotics to operate such complex systems, China was closing on America. While Washington was cutting its 2018 budget for AI research to a paltry $175 million,

Beijing was launching "a new multi-billion-dollar initiative" linked to building "military robots."[113] In a move of potential strategic significance in the event of future conflict, China has, at least for the moment, taken the lead in securing its critical satellite communications system from cyber attack.

By 2020 or thereafter, the Pentagon's triple canopy should be able to atomize a single "terrorist" with a missile strike after tracking his eyeball, facial image, and heat signature for hundreds of miles through field and favela, or, with equal ease, blind an entire army by knocking out all its ground communications, avionics, and naval navigation. Through agile data management and a continuing ability to turn its failures into innovation, this system might allow the United States a diplomatic veto of global lethality, an equalizer for any further loss of international influence.

As we learned so painfully in Vietnam, however, history offers some pessimistic parallels when it comes to the ability of militarized technology alone to preserve regional or global hegemony. Even if this robotic information regime could in fact check China's growing military power, Washington might still have the same ability to control wider geopolitical forces with its aerospace technology as the Third Reich had of winning World War II with its "wonder weapons," including the devastating V-2 rocket, the unstoppable Me-262 jet fighter, and the ship-killing Hs-293 guided missile.[114]

Further complicating the future, the illusion of information omniscience might incline Washington to more military misadventures akin to Vietnam, Iraq, or Afghanistan, creating the possibility of yet more expensive and draining conflicts. Whatever the eventual outcome, Washington's dogged reliance on military technology to maintain its hegemony will mean endless combat operations with uncertain outcomes, whether the forever war against terrorists along the ragged edge of Asia and Africa, incessant low-level aggression in space and cyberspace, or the threat of actual armed conflict with rivals China and Russia.

Part III
Dynamics of US Decline

Chapter Seven

Grandmasters of the Great Game

Washington's moves, whether in Asia, the Greater Middle East, Europe, or for that matter space, and its attempts to control what Sir Halford Mackinder once called the "world island" represent something old and familiar in the history of empires, even if on a previously unimaginable scale. By contrast, the rise of China as the world's largest economy, inconceivable a century ago, represents something new and threatens to overturn a geopolitical balance that has shaped the world for the past five hundred years. Indeed in 2012, the National Intelligence Council, Washington's supreme analytic body, summarized this infinitely complex historical process in a single succinct chart. From 1820 to 1870, Britain increased its share of global gross domestic product by 1 percent per decade; the United States raised its share by 2 percent during its half-century ascent, 1900 to 1950; at a parallel pace, Japan's grew about 1.5 percent during its postwar resurgence, from 1950 to 1980. China, however, raised its slice of the world pie by an extraordinary 5 percent from 2000 to 2010 and is on course to do so again in the decade ending in 2020, with India not far behind. Even if China's growth slows by the 2020s, US economic leadership is expected to be decisively "overtaken by China."[1]

The impact of this economic juggernaut has been profound. As China's exports surged, its foreign exchange reserves soared from $100 billion in 1996 to $4 trillion in 2014, many times more than any other nation.[2] Once China joined the World Trade Organization in 2001, it soon became the largest US trading partner, with $500 billion in exports in 2015 alone. China's low-cost products devastated labor-intensive industries across America, destroying ten thousand apparel jobs in the South, shutting down paper mills in the country's midsection, and putting pressure on steel production nationwide.[3]

Instead of focusing purely on building a blue-water navy like the British or a global aerospace armada akin to America's, China is using its cash reserves to reach deep within the world island to the heart of Eurasia in an attempt to thoroughly reshape the geopolitical fundamentals of global power, using a subtle strategy that has so far eluded Washington's power elites. Following Hannah Arendt's dictum that there are two types of imperial expansion, overland like Russia's or overseas like Britain's, China is clearly of the landed variety, as it has attempted to expand its dominion into adjacent territories—first Tibet and now Central Asia, Southeast Asia, and the South China Sea.[4]

After decades of quiet preparation, Beijing has recently revealed its grand strategy for global power, move by careful move. Its two-step plan is designed to build a transcontinental infrastructure for the economic integration of the three continents that comprise the world island, while mobilizing military forces to surgically slice through Washington's encircling containment.

The initial step has involved a breathtaking project to put in place a costly infrastructure for Eurasia's economic integration. By laying down an elaborate and enormously expensive mesh of high-speed, high-volume railroads and petrochemical pipelines across the continent's vast, empty interior, China may realize Mackinder's vision, even if in a new way. For the first time in history, the rapid transcontinental movement of critical cargo—oil, minerals, and manufactured goods—will be possible on a massive scale, thereby potentially unifying that sprawling landmass into a single economic zone stretching 6,500 miles from Shanghai to Madrid. In this way, the leadership in Beijing hopes to shift the locus of geopolitical power away from the maritime periphery and deep into the continent's heartland.

"Trans-continental railways are now transmuting the conditions of land power," Mackinder told an attentive London audience back in January 1904 as the "precarious" single track of the Trans-Siberian Railway, then the world's longest, was reaching across the continent for 5,700 miles from Moscow toward Vladivostok—making Eurasia a meaningful entity for the first time in human history. "But the century will not be old before all Asia is covered with railways," he added. "The spaces within the Russian Empire and Mongolia are so vast, and their potentialities in . . . fuel and metals so incalculably great that a vast economic world, more or less apart, will there develop inaccessible to oceanic commerce."[5]

Mackinder was a bit premature in his prediction. The Russian Revolution of 1917, the Chinese revolution of 1949, and the subsequent forty years of the Cold War slowed much actual development for decades. In this way, the Euro-Asian heartland was denied economic growth and integration, thanks in part to artificial ideological barriers—the Iron Curtain and then the Sino-Soviet split—that stalled infrastructure construction across it. No longer.

Only a few years after the Cold War ended, former president Jimmy Carter's national security adviser, Zbigniew Brzezinski, by then a contrarian sharply critical of both Republican and Democratic political elites, began raising warning flags about Washington's inept style of geopolitics. "Ever since the continents started interacting politically, some five hundred years ago," he wrote in 1998, essentially paraphrasing Mackinder, "Eurasia has been the center of world power. A power that dominates 'Eurasia' would control two of the world's three most advanced and economically productive regions . . . rendering the Western Hemisphere and Oceania geopolitically peripheral to the world's central continent." With a global hegemony that was both wide and shallow, Washington faced enormous challenges in controlling Eurasia, which was "too large, too populous, culturally too varied . . . to be compliant." Yet, wrote Brzezinski, "America's global primacy is directly dependent on how long and how effectively its preponderance on the Eurasian continent is sustained." With 75 percent of the world's population, 75 percent of known energy reserves, and 60 percent of its productivity, Eurasia was "geopolitically axial" in ways that render the other continents "geopolitically peripheral."[6]

This Eurasian heartland is so vast, so empty that its development represents a daunting challenge too difficult to grasp by a mere glance at the map. For nearly a thousand years, the sheer scale of these steppes and deserts has served to separate what is in fact a unitary landmass into two continents, Europe and Asia. From the twelfth to the twenty-first century, the endless distances alone challenged any traveler who tried to cross them, rendering Eurasia's actual geographical unity, in human terms, meaningless. Leaving Venice in about 1270, Marco Polo became one of the first Europeans to travel overland to China, surviving bandits, sandstorms, and wilderness to complete the trek in three years. Some six hundred years later in 1907, another Italian aristocrat, Prince Scipione Borghese, won the first Peking to Paris auto race, driving his forty-horsepower Itala motorcar for sixty days to cover a distance of nine thousand miles and capture the prize fit for a prince—a magnum of Mumm's champagne.[7]

When the auto race was commemorated a century later, my wife's uncle, a retired schoolteacher from Iowa, drove his lovingly restored 1938 Ford Coupe in a fleet of 130 antique automobiles on a journey that still took thirty-six days. Somewhere in the Gobi Desert, he became separated from the pack. As he steered across the trackless terrain for hours without roads, signs, or landmarks, desperately scanning the horizon, his concern slowly turned to anxiety. Uncle David and his navigator were utterly alone in an endless emptiness that stretched to the sky in every direction. Finally, after what seemed like an eternity, he spotted a faint cloud of dust on a distant horizon. Flooring the accelerator, he pushed every one of that V-8 engine's ninety horsepower hard to catch up.[8]

Just about the time Uncle David cleared that wasteland and was safely on his way across Russia on an actual road to Paris, the Chinese leadership in Beijing was making investment decisions that would change that landscape forever in ways that represent a challenge to US dominion. Starting around 2007, China launched the world's largest burst of infrastructure investment, already a trillion dollars' worth and counting, since Washington began building its interstate highway system in the 1950s. Under its disarmingly named "Silk Road Strategy," the numbers for the rails and pipelines Beijing has been building are mind-numbing. The sum of these massive investments represents nothing less than a transcontinental engineering project of sufficient scale to realize Mackinder's original vision of harnessing the Eurasian heartland as an engine to drive the ascent of a new world power.

Between 2007 and 2014, China crisscrossed its own countryside with 9,000 miles of new high-speed rail, more than the rest of the world combined. That network now carries 2.5 million passengers daily at top speeds of 240 miles per hour.[9] By the time the system is complete in 2030, 16,000 miles of high-speed track at a cost of $300 billion will link all of China's major cities.[10]

Simultaneously, Beijing's leadership began collaborating with surrounding states on a massive project to integrate the country's national rail network into a transcontinental grid. Starting in 2008, the Germans and Russians joined with the Chinese in launching the "Eurasian Land Bridge." Two east–west routes, the old Trans-Siberian Railroad in the north and a new southern route along the ancient Silk Road through Kazakhstan, were meant to bind Eurasia together. On the quicker southern route, containers of high-value manufactured goods, like computers and auto parts, could travel 6,700 miles from Leipzig, Germany, to Chongqing, China, in just twenty days, far faster than the thirty-five days via ship.[11]

In 2013, Deutsche Bahn AG (German Rail) began preparing a third route between Hamburg and Zhengzhou that was expected to cut travel time to just fifteen days. Within a year, three trains a week with up to fifty containers each

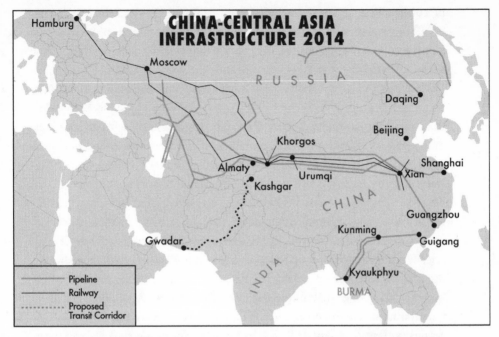

were covering the 6,800 miles between Chongqing, China, and Duisburg, Germany, via Kazakh Rail, in just sixteen days.[12] In October 2014, China announced plans for the construction of the world's longest high-speed rail line at a cost of $230 billion. According to plans, bullet trains will someday shoot across the 4,300 miles between Beijing and Moscow in just two days.[13]

In addition, China is building two major new railroads running south toward the world island's maritime "marginal." In April 2015, President Xi Jinping signed an agreement with Pakistan to spend $46 billion on a China–Pakistan Economic Corridor. Rail links, pipelines, and a highway will stretch nearly two thousand miles from Kashgar in Xinjiang, China's westernmost province, to a joint port facility at Gwadar, Pakistan, opened back in 2007. There, China had already invested more than $200 billion to transform a sleepy fishing village into a strategic megaport on the Arabian Sea, just 370 miles from the Persian Gulf.[14] Starting in 2011, China extended its rail lines through Laos into Southeast Asia at an initial cost of $6.2 billion. When completed, a high-speed train is expected to shoot passengers and goods south from Kunming, China, all the way to Singapore in just ten hours.[15]

In this same dynamic decade, China has constructed a comprehensive network of transcontinental gas and oil pipelines to import fuels from the whole of Eurasia for its swelling population centers. In 2009, after a decade of construction, the state-owned China National Petroleum Corporation (CNPC) opened the final stage of the Kazakhstan–China oil pipeline. It stretches 1,400 miles from the Caspian Sea to Xinjiang, where it feeds into domestic pipelines that flow eastward into the heart of central China.[16] Simultaneously in 2008, CNPC collaborated with Turkmenistan, Kazakhstan, and Uzbekistan to launch the Central Asia–China gas pipeline, a complex that will eventually extend more than four thousand miles. To give an idea of this project's scale, one Uzbek branch pipeline completed in late 2014 and covering just three hundred miles had an annual capacity of twenty-five billion cubic meters of gas and cost $2 billion to build.[17]

To bypass the Straits of Malacca controlled by the US Navy, CNPC opened the Sino-Myanmar pipeline in 2013 to carry both Middle East oil and Burmese natural gas for 1,500 miles from the Bay of Bengal to China's remote southwest region inhabited by a hundred million people.[18] To power the country's densely populated Northeast, the Chinese oil giant opened a 650-mile spur that tapped into Russia's 3,000-mile Eastern Siberia–Pacific Ocean oil pipeline, bringing fifteen million tons annually into its enormous refinery at Daqing. By 2016, Russia had become China's second largest source of crude oil and rising demand sparked plans to double shipments via an additional spur line, scheduled for opening within two years.[19] In May 2014, CNPC also signed a $400 billion, thirty-year deal with the privatized Russian energy company Gazprom to deliver thirty-eight billion cubic meters of natural gas annually by 2018 via a still-to-be-completed northern network of pipelines across Siberia and into Manchuria.[20]

Though massive, these projects are just part of an ongoing construction boom that has woven a cat's cradle of oil and gas lines across Central Asia and south into Iran and Pakistan. The result will soon be an integrated inland energy infrastructure, including Russia's own vast network of pipelines, extending across the whole of Eurasia, from the Atlantic Ocean to the South China Sea.

To capitalize such costly development plans, in October 2014 Beijing announced the establishment of the Asian Infrastructure Investment Bank. China's leadership sees this institution as a future Eurasian alternative to the US-dominated World Bank. Despite pressure from Washington not to join, fifty-seven countries—including close American allies such as Germany, Great Britain, Australia, and South Korea—signed on, contributing $100 billion in capital, which made the new institution half the size of the World Bank on its opening day in January 2016. Simultaneously, China began building long-term trade relations with resource-rich areas of Africa, with Australia, and with Southeast Asia. After a decade of such sustained development, in May 2017 China's president, Xi Jinping, convened an historic conference of sixty nations that make up the "world island" to proclaim Beijing's new trillion-dollar commitment to building the infrastructure—ports, pipelines, power plants, and rails—for the economic integration of Asia, Africa, and Europe. Despite reservations from India and the European Union, President Xi himself hailed it as the "project of the century" that would "add splendor to human civilization," while the *Los Angeles Times* headlined it as the "groundwork for a new global order." [21]

Finally, Beijing has begun to reveal the key components of its strategy for neutralizing the military forces Washington has long arrayed around the continent's perimeter. In mid-2015, Beijing escalated its claim to exclusive control over the South China Sea—expanding Longpo Naval Base on Hainan Island so

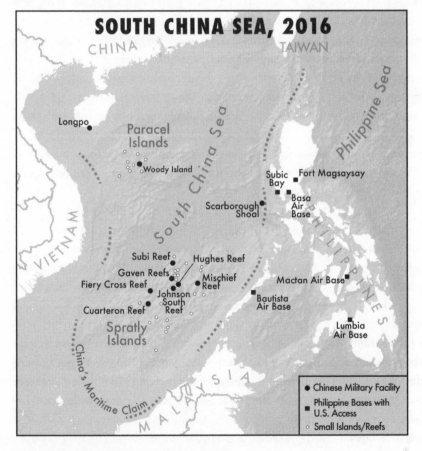

Military Situation in the South China Sea, 2016

that it could become the region's only nuclear submarine facility,[22] accelerating its creation of seven artificial atolls further south in the disputed islands that will undoubtedly someday become military airfields,[23] and formally warning off US Navy overflights.[24] Complementing its massive highway-rail-pipeline corridor to the port of Gwadar in Pakistan, Beijing began building, in 2016, a major base at Djibouti on the Horn of Africa, creating the basis for permanent Chinese naval deployments in the energy-rich Arabian Sea. With its naval bases spanning 5,000 miles across the Arabian and South China Seas while its submarines range as far as San Diego, China is forging a future capacity to strategically curtail America's military containment.[25]

In response to China's challenge, the Pentagon issued stern warnings about freedom of the seas and sent a succession of naval patrols through the South China Sea, a strategic waterway for $5.3 trillion in maritime trade, 30 percent of world total. But nothing could slow China's armada of dredges steadily churning the seabed to build permanent bases on those seven shoals. In January 2016, its first aircraft landed on a new 3,000-meter airstrip on Fiery Cross Reef in the Spratlys, prompting a formal protest from Vietnam.[26] A month later, China moved toward militarizing even more atolls by basing batteries of HQ-9 antiaircraft missiles on Woody Island in the Paracels—and did so just a day after Obama's summit with Southeast Asian leaders had issued a call for freedom of navigation in those disputed waters.[27] By installing a nominally defensive weapon rather than jet fighters, China quietly asserted its claim to control of the airspace in this part of the South China Sea with a minimum of diplomatic disruption.

In March 2016, however, US intelligence chief James Clapper told Congress that China had installed a powerful military radar system on the Spratlys' southernmost atoll, Cuarteron Reef, giving China's DF-21D carrier-killer missile batteries on the mainland the ability to strike American ships in the South China Sea. Washington responded by sending a carrier group headed by the USS *John Stennis* on a patrol across those waters while Chinese naval vessels cruised nearby in a "wary standoff."[28]

Continuing its stealth escalation, Beijing built hardened hangers for its largest military jets on three reefs—Fiery Cross, Subi, and Mischief—but did not throw down the gauntlet by actually deploying any fighters. Then in December 2016, China took decisive steps toward an exclusive zone by installing antiaircraft weapons on all seven of its artificial islands and, just days later, snatching a US "ocean glider" drone from waters near Scarborough Shoal—exploiting the unwritten rules that left drones "in a gray zone, just under the threshold of

AIR AND NAVAL FORCES
EAST AND SOUTHEAST ASIA 2015

| 1 Destroyer/Frigate | 1 Submarine | 1 Aircraft Carrier | 10 Fighter Jets |

China

73
58
1
2,100

U.S. Carrier Strike Group

9
2
1
54

Japan

47
16
353

Vietnam

7
217

Philippines

3
8

actual hostilities."[29] Simultaneously, a Pentagon study warned that, by 2030, China will have built so many aircraft carriers that one will always be close to these "contested waters," making them "virtually a Chinese lake." As if to corroborate that prediction, China's navy pronounced its refitted Soviet carrier the *Liaoning* "combat ready" in November and also laid the keel in its own Dalian dockyard for a second carrier, with sophisticated electromagnetic catapults to launch its complement of a dozen advanced J-15 Flying Shark fighters.[30]

Concealed in this strategic confrontation is China's determination to exploit the South China Sea's fishing grounds as a critical source of protein. With the world's population heading for nine billion by 2050, competition among rival powers will likely shift from the classic imperial issues of minerals and markets to elements more fundamental for human survival—energy, grains, fresh water, and fishing grounds. With its shallow continental shelf and circumferential breeding areas of mangrove deltas, the South China Sea ranks fourth among the planet's nineteen major fishing grounds, producing a full fifth of world maritime harvest in 2010 and providing critical nutrition for two billion people in the twelve surrounding nations.[31] After tripling its fish consumption to thirty kilograms per capita in just two decades, China will likely consume 38 percent of the world's fish catch by 2030.[32] To sustain that growth, its commercial fleet of 92,000 vessels in the South China Sea was pushing southward beyond their depleted home grounds into disputed waters near Malaysia and the Philippines.[33]

At the same time, Beijing is developing plans to challenge Washington's dominion over space and cyberspace. It expects, for instance, to complete its own global satellite system by 2020, offering the first real challenge to Washington's dominion over space.[34] Simultaneously, Beijing is forging a formidable capacity for cyberwarfare.[35] In a decade or two, China will have consolidated its control over the rich resources of Central Asia and also be ready, should the need arise, to slice through Washington's continental encirclement at a few strategic points in the Arabian and South China Seas.

Lacking the geopolitical vision of Mackinder and his generation of British imperialists, much of America's leadership in these years has generally failed to grasp the significance of the radical geopolitical change being worked inside the Eurasian landmass. If China succeeds in linking its rising industries to the vast natural resources of the Eurasian heartland, then quite possibly, as Sir Halford Mackinder predicted on that cold London night back in 1904, "the empire of the world would be in sight."[36]

Obama's Grand Strategy

In ways that eluded Washington pundits and policymakers, President Barack Obama deployed a subtle geopolitical strategy that, if adopted by his successors, just might give Washington a fighting chance to extend its global hegemony deeper into the twenty-first century. After six years of sometimes-secret preparations, the Obama White House, in its last months, unveiled some bold diplomatic initiatives whose sum was nothing less than a tricontinental strategy to check Beijing's rise. As these moves unfolded worldwide, Obama revealed himself as one of those rare grandmasters with an ability to go beyond mere foreign policy and play the Great Game of Geopolitics.

From the time he first took office in 2009, Obama faced an unremitting chorus of criticism, left and right, domestic and foreign, dismissing him as hapless, even hopeless. "He's a poor ignoramus; he should read and study a little to understand reality," said Venezuela's leftist president Hugo Chávez, just months after Obama's inauguration.[37] "I think he has projected a position of weakness and . . . a lack of leadership," claimed Republican senator John McCain in 2012.[38] "After six years," opined a commentator from the conservative Heritage Foundation in April 2015, "he still displays a troubling misunderstanding of power and the leadership role the United States plays in the international system."[39] Even former Democratic president Jimmy Carter has dismissed Obama's foreign policy achievements as "minimal."[40] Voicing the views of many Americans, Donald Trump derided Obama's global vision this way: "We have a president who doesn't have a clue."[41]

But let's give credit where it's due. Without proclaiming a presumptuously labeled policy like "triangulation," "the Nixon Doctrine," or even a "freedom agenda," Obama moved step-by-step to repair the damage caused by a plethora of Washington foreign policy debacles, old and new, and then maneuvered, sometimes deftly, sometimes less so, to rebuild America's fading global influence.

"I want a president who has the sense that you can't fix everything," a reflective Obama told the *Atlantic* magazine during his last months in office. "The world is ever-shrinking. Withdrawal is untenable . . . I suppose you could call me a realist in believing we can't, at any given moment, relieve all the world's misery. We have to choose where we can make a real impact." Yet, he added in an affirmation of America's primacy, "If we don't set the agenda, it doesn't happen. The fact is, there is not a summit I've attended since I've been president where we are not setting the agenda, where we are not responsible for the key results. That's true whether you're talking about nuclear security, whether you're talking about saving the world financial system, whether you're talking about climate." In exercising this leadership, America cannot, in his view, act unilaterally as a sole superpower. "One of the reasons I am so focused on taking action multilaterally where our direct interests are not at stake is that multilateralism regulates hubris."[42] Yet there was much more to Obama's foreign policy than he admitted even in these disarmingly frank statements.

Viewed historically, Obama set out to correct past foreign policy excesses and disasters, largely the product of imperial overreach, that could be traced to several generations of American leaders bent on the exercise of unilateral power. Within the spectrum of foreign policy options, he slowly shifted from the coercion of war, occupation, torture, and other forms of unilateral military action, toward the more cooperative realm of trade, diplomacy, and mutual security—all in search of a new version of American supremacy.

Obama first had to deal with the disasters of the post-9/11 years. Looking through history's rearview mirror, the administration of George W. Bush and Dick Cheney imagined the Middle East as the on-ramp to greater world power and burned through several trillion dollars and much US prestige in a misbegotten attempt to make that illusion a reality. Since the first day of his presidency, Obama tried to pull back from or ameliorate the resulting miasmas in Afghanistan and Iraq (though with only modest success), while resisting constant Republican pressure to reengage fully in the permanent, pointless Middle Eastern war that they consider their own.

Instead of Bush's endless occupations with 170,000 troops in Iraq[43] and 50,000 in Afghanistan,[44] Obama adopted a more mobile footprint of advisers, air strikes, drones, and special operations squads across the Greater Middle East and northern Africa. Rejecting the established "playbook" of Washington's foreign policy elites stipulating that the United States was the perpetual guardian of the Middle East, duty bound to intervene in every crisis, Obama refused, in 2013, to commit air or ground forces to the project of regime change in Syria. "When you have a professional army," he told the *Atlantic* in 2016, "that is well armed and sponsored by two large states"—Iran and Russia—"the notion that we could have—in a clean way that didn't commit U.S. military forces—changed the equation on the ground there was never true." Instead of bombing to punish the Assad regime for using chemical weapons, Obama negotiated with Russian president Vladimir Putin to force the removal of Syria's chemical arsenal.[45] On other matters, however, Obama has acted far more boldly.

Throughout his two terms, Obama's diplomats pursued reconciliation with three "rogue" states—Burma, Iran, and Cuba—whose seemingly implacable opposition to the United States sprang from some of the most disastrous CIA covert interventions of the Cold War. "We have history," Obama explained in 2016. "We have history in Iran, we have history in Indonesia and Central America. So we have to be mindful of our history when we start talking about intervening, and understand the source of other people's suspicions."[46]

In 1951, as the Cold War gripped the globe, Democratic president Harry Truman ordered the CIA to arm some twelve thousand Nationalist Chinese soldiers who had been driven out of their country by communist forces and taken refuge in northern Burma. The result: three disastrous attempts to invade their former homeland. After being slapped back across the Chinese border by mere provincial militia forces, the Nationalist troops, again with covert CIA support, occupied Burma's Northeast, prompting Rangoon to lodge a formal complaint at the UN and the US ambassador to Burma to resign in protest.

Not only was this operation one of the great disasters in a tangled history of such CIA interventions, forcing a major shake-up inside the agency, but it also produced a lasting breach in bilateral relations with Burma (now Myanmar), contributing to that country's sense of isolation from the international community. Even at the Cold War's close forty years later, Burma's military junta persisted in its international isolation while retaining a close dependency relationship with China, thereby giving Beijing special claim to its rich resources and strategic access to the Indian Ocean.

During his first term, Obama made a concerted effort to heal this strategic breach in Washington's encirclement of the Eurasian landmass. He sent Hillary Clinton on the first formal mission to Burma by a secretary of state in more than fifty years; appointed the first ambassador in twenty-two years; and, in November 2012, became the first president to visit what he called, in an address to students at the University of Yangon, the "crossroads of East and South Asia" that borders on "the most populated nations on the planet."[47]

Washington's Cold War blunders were genuinely bipartisan. Among the 170 CIA covert operations that President Dwight Eisenhower authorized, two must rank as major debacles, inflicting especially lasting damage on America's global standing.[48] In 1953, after Iran's populist prime minister Mohammad Mossadeq challenged Britain's imperial monopoly over his country's oil industry, Eisenhower authorized a covert regime change operation by the CIA and British intelligence. Though the agency came perilously close to failure, it did finally succeed in installing the young, untested shah in power. The agency then helped him consolidate his autocratic rule by training a secret police, the notorious Savak, in torture and surveillance techniques.

While Beltway insiders toasted the delicious brilliance of this secret-agent derring-do, Iranians seethed until 1979 when demonstrators ousted the shah and students stormed the US embassy, producing a thirty-five-year breach in relations that weakened Washington's strategic position in the region.

In September 2013, spurning neoconservative calls for a military solution to the "Iranian problem," Obama dramatically announced his brief phone conversation with President Hassan Rouhani, the first direct contact with any leader of that country since 1979. In this way, he launched two years of sustained diplomacy that culminated in a historic agreement halting Iran's nuclear weapons program.[49] From a geopolitical perspective, this entente, or at least truce, avoided the sort of military action Republicans have been regularly calling for that would have mired Washington in yet another Middle Eastern war. Such a conflict would also have voided any chance for what Secretary of State Clinton first termed in 2011 "a pivot to new global realities." She was, of course, speaking about "our strategic turn to the Asia-Pacific,"[50] a policy that in a 2014 Beijing press conference Obama would brand "our pivot to Asia."[51]

During his last months in office in 1960, President Eisenhower also authorized a disastrous CIA invasion of Cuba, confident that a thousand ragtag Cuban exiles backed by US airpower could somehow overthrow Fidel Castro's entrenched revolutionary regime. Inheriting this operation and sensing disaster, President John F. Kennedy forced the CIA to scale back its plans and yet did not stop the agency from proceeding. So it dumped those exiles on a remote beach fifty impassable miles of trackless, tangled swamp from the mountain refuge that had been planned for them and then sat back as Castro's air force bombed them into surrender.

For the next forty years, the resulting rupture in diplomatic relations and a US embargo of Cuba weakened Washington's position in the Cold War, Latin America, and even southern Africa. After decades of diplomatic isolation and economic embargo failed to change the communist regime, President Obama initiated a thaw in relations, culminating in the July 2015 reopening of the American embassy in Havana, closed for nearly fifty-five years.[52] Defying entrenched congressional opposition, in March 2016 Obama made a historic state visit to Havana where he declared an end to the "last remnant of the Cold War in the Americas" and called upon the Cuban people to embrace a democratic future. That diplomatic initiative signaled Washington's shift away from its domineering posture of past years, removing "a region-wide stumbling block" to marked improvement in relations with Latin America, one of Obama's prime objectives.[53]

Moving from repair to revival, from past to future, President Obama also used America's status as the planet's number one consumer nation to create a new version of dollar diplomacy. While he saw the Middle East as "a region to be avoided—one that, thanks to America's energy revolution, will soon be of negligible relevance to the U.S. economy," he was "fixated on turning America's attention to Asia" and thereby meeting the challenge posed by China. As his defense secretary Ashton Carter put it, Obama believed Asia to be "the part of the world of greatest consequence to the American future." As Obama himself put it, the Middle East has "countries that have very few civic traditions" roiled by all "the malicious, nihilistic, violent parts of humanity," while Southeast Asia "is filled with striving, ambitious people who are every single day scratching and clawing to build businesses. . . . The contrast is pretty stark."[54]

His strategic pivot was aimed at drawing China's Eurasian trading partners back into Washington's orbit. While Beijing was maneuvering to transform parts of Africa, Asia, and Europe into a unified "world island" with China at its economic epicenter, Obama countered with a bold geopolitical vision meant to trisect that vast landmass by redirecting its trade toward the United States.[55]

During the post-9/11 decade when Washington was spilling its blood and treasure onto desert sands, Beijing was investing its trillions of surplus dollars from trade with the United States in the economic integration of the Eurasian landmass. As an index of its influence, China as of 2015 accounted for 79 percent of all foreign investment in Afghanistan, 70 percent in Sierra Leone, and 83 percent in Zimbabwe.[56] Beijing managed to double its annual trade with Africa over just four years to $222 billion, three times America's $73 billion, thanks to a massive infusion of capital that is expected to reach a trillion dollars by 2025.[57] As China's economy grew, its defense budget, constant at 2 percent of GDP, increased fourfold from $52 billion in 2001 to $214 billion in 2015, second only to Washington's, allowing for a rapid modernization of the country's military.[58]

In his second term, however, Obama unleashed a countervailing strategy, seeking to split the world island economically along its continental divide at the Ural Mountains through two trade agreements that aimed to capture nothing less than "the central global pole position" for "almost two-thirds of world GDP and nearly three-quarters of world trade."[59] By negotiating the Trans-Pacific Partnership (TPP), Washington hoped to redirect much of the vast trade in the Asian half of Eurasia toward North America. Simultaneously, Washington also tried to reorient the European Union's portion of Eurasia—which still has the world's largest single economy[60] and another 16 percent of world trade[61]—toward the United States through the Transatlantic Trade and Investment Partnership (TTIP).

Finally, in a stroke of personal diplomacy that much of the US media misconstrued as a sentimental journey, Obama was aggressive in his diplomatic courtship of Africa—that third continental component of China's would-be world island—convening a White House summit for more than fifty of the continent's leaders in 2014 and making a state visit to East Africa in July 2015.[62] With its usual barbed insight, Beijing's *Global Times* accurately identified the real aim of Obama's Africa diplomacy as "off-setting China's growing influence and recovering past U.S. leverage."[63]

When grandmasters like Obama play the Great Game of Geopolitics, there is, almost axiomatically a certain sangfroid to their moves as well as an indifference to any resulting collateral damage at home or abroad. Should some version of these two treaties or successor agreements, so central to Obama's geopolitical strategy, ever be adopted, they will bring in their wake both diplomatic gains and high social costs. Think of it in blunt terms as the choice between maintaining the empire abroad and sustaining democracy at home.

In his first six years in office, Obama invested his diplomatic and political capital in advancing the TPP, a prospective treaty that carefully excluded China from membership. Surpassing any other economic alliance except the European Union, this treaty would have integrated the US economy with those of eleven nations around the Pacific Basin—including Australia, Canada, Chile, Japan, Malaysia, Mexico, and Vietnam—that represent $28 trillion in combined GDP or 40 percent of gross world product and a third of all global trade. By sweeping up areas like agriculture, data flows, and service industries, this treaty aspired to an unparalleled Pacific economic integration. In the process, it would decisively secure these highly productive nations in America's orbit.[64]

Not surprisingly, Obama faced ferocious opposition from progressive leaders within his own party, like Senator Elizabeth Warren, who were sharply critical of the highly secretive nature of the negotiations for the pact and the way it was likely to degrade American labor and environmental laws.[65] The left-leaning Economic Policy Institute estimated that the TTP would eliminate 370,000 jobs in the industrial heartland of the upper Midwest.[66] So scathing was this critique that, in June 2015, the president needed Republican votes to win Senate approval for "fast track" authority just to complete the final round of negotiations on the treaty.[67]

Obama also aggressively pursued negotiations for the TTIP with the European Union to similarly secure its $18 trillion economy.[68] The treaty sought fuller economic integration between Europe and the United States by meshing government regulations on matters such as auto safety in ways that might add some $270 billion to their annual trade.[69]

According to a coalition of 170 European civil society groups, the TTIP, like its Pacific counterpart, would damage democracy in participating countries by transferring control over consumer safety, the environment, and labor to closed, pro-business arbitration tribunals. Whatever one thinks about the ultimate impact of such trade pacts, the TTP treaty, propelled by Obama's singular determination, had moved at light speed compared to the laggard Doha round of World Trade Organization negotiations that had reached year twelve of inconclusive talks with no end in sight. And then, of course, Donald Trump formally quit the Trans-Pacific Partnership during his first week in office, sweeping all of Obama's trade plans into the dumpster of history.[70]

Grandmasters of Geopolitics

Nevertheless, in his pursuit of this grand strategy, Obama revealed himself as one of the very few US leaders, in the century-plus since America's rise to world power, who could imagine how to play the Great Game of Geopolitics with the requisite balance of vision and ruthlessness. Forget everyone's nominee for master diplomat, Henry Kissinger, who was as inept as he was ruthless—extending the Vietnam War by seven bloody years to mask his diplomatic failure, turning East Timor over to Indonesia for decades of slaughter until its inevitable independence, cratering US credibility in Latin America by backing a murderous military dictatorship in Chile, and mismanaging Moscow in ways that helped extend the Cold War by fifteen years. Kissinger's career, as international law specialist Richard Falk observed, has been marked by "his extraordinary capacity to be repeatedly wrong about almost every major foreign policy decision made by the U.S. Government over the course of the last half-century."[71]

Once we subject other American leaders to a similar calculus of costs and benefits, we are, surprisingly enough, left with just three grandmasters of geopolitics: Elihu Root, the original architect of America's rise to global power; Zbigniew Brzezinski, the national security adviser to President Carter who shattered the Soviet Empire and made Washington the world's sole superpower; and Barack Obama, who tried to defend that status by offering an imperial blueprint for how to check China's rise. In each case, their maneuvers have been supple and subtle enough to generally elude both contemporary observers and later historians.

Many American presidents—think Theodore Roosevelt, Franklin Roosevelt, Dwight Eisenhower, George H. W. Bush, or Bill Clinton—have been capable diplomats, skilled at negotiating treaties or persuading allies to do their bidding. But surprisingly few world leaders, American or otherwise, have had an intuitive feel for the cultural, economic, and military forces whose sum is geopolitics. Fewer still grasped both the temporal and spatial dimensions of global power—that is, the connections between present actions and often-distant results.

To borrow Brzezinski's favorite metaphor, most American presidents have been competent at moving pieces on the global chessboard. But a geopolitical grandmaster does not simply move a pawn or rook a few squares to counter an enemy's gambit; he breaks the "board" apart into coherent blocs of land, peoples, and resources that can be manipulated to effect major change. In the hands of skilled strategists, geopolitics involves the exercise of concerted coercion to turn that interface of land and society into manipulable counters whose maneuver can change the global balance of power—either deftly through diplomacy or crudely by force of arms. Thus, Root deployed Latin America diplomatically to intrude into Europe's power politics; Brzezinski covertly penetrated Central Asia to free Eastern Europe three thousand miles to the west; and Obama tried to split Eurasia economically at the Urals to contain China.

If they did not rise to the stature of Hegel's "world historical men," latter-day Napoleons capable of manipulating the dialectics of change to become the "heroes of an epoch," both Root and Brzezinski nonetheless manipulated their moments sufficiently to advance American interests while altering, often fundamentally, the future balance of global power.[72] Though little noticed in the avalanche of criticism that has all but buried his accomplishments in the Oval Office, Obama followed in their footsteps.

Elihu Root, Architect of American Power

All but forgotten today, Elihu Root, not Theodore Roosevelt, was the true architect of America's transformation from an insular continental nation into a major player on the world stage.[73] About the time Sir Halford Mackinder was imagining his new model for studying global power back in 1904, Root was actually building an institutional infrastructure at home and abroad for the exercise of that same power.

In the first thirty years of his career Root achieved fame, some would say infamy, as a New York corporate lawyer representing the richest of robber barons, the most venal of trusts, and the most corrupt of big city bosses, notably New York's notorious William "Boss" Tweed. This legal legerdemain let the "infamous" Havemeyer Sugar Trust increase its monopoly over the nation's market from 78 to 98 percent and facilitated the "financial abuses" of New York City's Whitney traction syndicate.[74] Yet after several decades of enriching the rich—and himself in the bargain—Root turned his talents to selflessly serving the nation.

After his appointment as secretary of war in 1899, he would devote the rest of his long life to modernizing the American state, and continue to do so in later years as secretary of war, secretary of state, senator, and finally envoy extraordinaire. Not only did he shape the conduct of foreign policy for the century to come, but he also played an outsized role, particularly for a cabinet secretary of a then-peripheral power, in influencing the character of an emerging international community.[75] By degrees, Root moved the United States and the world with it beyond the crude colonialism of military conquest and gunboat diplomacy to a new global system of sovereign states resolving disputes through international law.

As a prominent attorney, Root understood that the Constitution's protection of individual liberties and states' rights had created an inherently weak federal bureaucracy ill suited for the concerted projection of imperial power beyond the country's borders. To transform this "patchwork" state and its divided society—still traumatized by the Civil War—into a world power,[76] he spent a quarter century in the determined pursuit of three intertwined objectives: fashioning the fragmentary federal government into a potent apparatus for overseas expansion, building a consensus among the country's elites for such an activist foreign policy, and creating new forms of global governance open to Washington's influence.

As secretary of war from 1899 to 1904, he reformed the army's antiquated structure, creating a centralized general staff, establishing a modern war college, and expanding professional training for officers. In effect, he transformed the army from a small force focused on coastal defense into an agile apparatus for foreign intervention—in China, the Caribbean, the Philippines, and ultimately Europe. To resolve the knotty contradiction of a republic running an empire, he quickly established colonial regimes for Puerto Rico and the Philippines, while dictating the constitution for a nominally independent Cuba that conceded the United States a navy base on the island and the right to intervene whenever it chose. With his eye firmly fixed on America's ascent, he also covered up atrocities that accompanied the army's extraordinarily brutal pacification of the Philippines.[77]

As secretary of state from 1907 to 1909, senator from 1909 to 1915, and special envoy to Russia in 1917, Root then led a sustained diplomatic effort to make America a real presence in the community of nations. As the first secretary of state to take a grand diplomatic tour, he launched an unprecedented circumnavigation of Latin America in 1906 as step one in a bold geopolitical strategy to open a central place for Washington, still peripheral to a world politics centered on Europe, into the great game of international leadership. Steaming south aboard the cruiser USS *Charleston*, Secretary Root made a "triumphal visit" to Rio for the Inter-American Conference and then circled the continent, stopping at half a dozen capitals, greeted by wildly cheering crowds at every port. A year later at the Second Hague Peace Conference, Washington, with the backing of the seventeen Latin republics among the forty-four nations present, had sufficient geopolitical clout to conclude the first broad international legal agreement on the laws of war. To house the Permanent Court of Arbitration, the world's first ongoing institution for global governance, Root's good friend and steel baron Andrew Carnegie spent $1.5 million, a vast sum at the time, to build a lavish Peace Palace at The Hague in 1913. A year later Root helped establish the Academy of International Law, housed within that same palace.[78]

Simultaneously, he cemented a close alliance with Britain by promoting treaties to resolve territorial disputes that had roiled relations with the world's preeminent power for the better part of a century. That effort won him the Nobel Peace Prize in 1912. Even in retirement in his seventies, he served on a League of Nations committee that established the Permanent Court of International Justice and lobbied hard for Congress to approve it in 1926, realizing his long-held vision of an international community governed by the rule of law.[79]

Throughout these decades Root was careful, even methodical, in building social networks that joined New York financiers, Washington politicians, and their academic experts in a distinctively American apparatus for foreign policy formation. Through his "affectionate friendship" with Carnegie, he presided over the investment of a significant part of that tycoon's vast fortune, then the world's largest, in building an institutional architecture for America's unique way of engaging the world. In the process, he personally organized and chaired both the Carnegie Institution and the Carnegie Endowment for International Peace.

As the culmination of this effort, in 1921 Root led a group of financiers, industrialists, and corporate lawyers in establishing the Council on Foreign Relations in New York City, which soon became the country's most influential forum for promoting an expansive foreign policy. He also cultivated academic specialists at leading universities, using their expertise to shape and support his foreign policy ideas. In sum, Root recast key elements of American society to form a layered nexus of money, influence, and intellect, creating a foreign policy establishment that would define the country's diplomatic priorities for the century to come.[80]

Zbigniew Brzezinski, Destroyer of Empire

After a long period of indifferent international leadership, foreign policy came under the charge of an underestimated figure, Zbigniew Brzezinski, who served as national security adviser to President Jimmy Carter during the late 1970s. An émigré Polish aristocrat, professor of international relations, and autodidact when it came to geopolitics, Brzezinski was above all an intellectual acolyte of Mackinder. Through both action and analysis, he embraced Mackinder's conception of Eurasia as the "world island" and its vast interior heartland as the "pivot" of global power. He would prove particularly adept at applying Sir Halford's famous dictum: "Who rules East Europe commands the Heartland; Who rules the Heartland commands the World-Island; Who rules the World-Island commands the world."[81]

Wielding a multibillion-dollar CIA covert operation like a sharpened wedge, Brzezinski drove radical Islam from Afghanistan deep into the "heartland" of Soviet Central Asia, drawing Moscow into a debilitating decade-long Afghan war that weakened Russia sufficiently for Eastern Europe to finally break free from the Soviet Empire. With a calculus that could not have been more coldblooded, he understood and rationalized the untold misery and unimaginable human suffering his strategy inflicted through ravaged landscapes, millions of refugees uprooted from ancestral villages, and countless Afghan dead and wounded. Asked about this operation's legacy when it came to creating a militant Islam hostile to the United States, Brzezinski was coolly unapologetic. "What is most important to the history of the world?" he asked in 1998. "The Taliban or the collapse of the Soviet empire? Some stirred-up Moslems or the liberation of Central Europe and the end of the Cold War?"[82]

Even as the long-term damage from those "stirred-up Moslems" came to include the devastating Afghan civil war that followed the Red Army's withdrawal from the country and the rise of al-Qaeda, none of it added up to a hill of beans, as he saw it, compared to the importance of striking directly into that Eurasian heartland to free Eastern Europe, half a continent away, and shatter the Soviet Empire.[83] Under the strategy he launched, Afghanistan became, for over a decade, a training ground for global jihad, drawing in young recruits from across the Muslim world and sending them home hardened militants. Even as the toll rose to include the 9/11 attacks, America's second Afghan War, and the unsettling of the Greater Middle East, Brzezinski seemed stubbornly oblivious to the longer-term costs of his hour as a grandmaster on the world stage.

Twenty years after his geopolitical strike against the Soviet Union, Brzezinski resumed his study of Mackinder's theory in retirement, this time doing a better job with it as an armchair analyst than he had as presidential adviser. Although Washington was still basking in the pre-9/11 glow of being the world's sole superpower, Brzezinski used geopolitical analysis in his 1998 book *The Grand Chessboard* to warn of challenges to America's continuing global hegemony. The United States might appear a colossus bestriding the world, but Eurasia still remained, he said, "the globe's most important playing field . . . with preponderance over the entire Eurasian continent serving as the central basis for global primacy."

That Eurasian "megacontinent," Brzezinski observed, has "too many historically ambitious and politically energetic states to be compliant toward even the most economically successful and politically preeminent global power." Washington, he hypothesized, could continue its half-century dominion over the "oddly shaped Eurasian chessboard extending from Lisbon to Vladivostok" only as long as three critical conditions remained. First, the United States must preserve its unchallenged "perch on the Western periphery" in Europe. Second and most significantly, the vast "middle space" of Eurasia cannot become "an assertive single entity." Finally, the eastern end of this vast landmass in Asia should not unify itself in a way that might lead to "the expulsion of America from its offshore bases." Should any of these critical conditions change, then, Brzezinski predicted presciently, "a potential rival to America might at some point arise."[84]

Barack Obama, Defender of Global Hegemony

Less than a decade after Brzezinski specified these conditions, China emerged to challenge America's control of Eurasia and, much as he predicted, threaten

Washington's standing as the globe's great hegemon. While the US military was mired in the Middle East, Beijing quietly began working to unify that vast "middle space" of Eurasia and preparing to neutralize America's "offshore bases."

By the time Barack Obama entered the Oval Office in 2009, the first signs of a serious geopolitical challenge were already stirring in Asia, though only the president and his closest advisers seemed to recognize them. The media's obsession with Obama's African heritage blocked any focus on his formative mid-Pacific identity—birth and childhood in Hawaii, elementary schooling in Jakarta, and his mother's long academic career in Southeast Asia. Unlike the country's northeast political elites, wedded myopically to a mid-Atlantic view of the world, Obama came into office carrying vivid memories of "the trembling blue plane of the Pacific" with "thunderous waves, crumbling as if in a slow motion reel" pounding upon the shores of his tiny island, Oahu. His strongest childhood experiences were a pastiche of Pacific experience. Eating "poi and roast pig" with Hawaiians; watching old Filipino men play checkers while they "spat up betel-nut juice as if it were blood"; divers spearfishing in the "inky black waters" of Kailua Bay; and poverty that "twists the lives of children on the streets of Jakarta."[85]

Growing up on a speck of earth tossed by a sea that covered half the planet's surface, Obama seemed to acquire an intuitive feel for the shape of the globe. If his generation of world leaders had anything akin to a geopolitical grandmaster, then it would likely be him.

In a speech to the Australian parliament in November 2011, he announced his pivot to Asia. "Let there be no doubt," he said, "in the Asia Pacific in the twenty-first century, the United States of America is all in." After two long wars in Iraq and Afghanistan "that cost us dearly, in blood and treasure, the United States is turning our attention to the vast potential of the Asia Pacific region . . . the world's fastest-growing region—and home to more than half the global economy."[86]

In geopolitical terms, Obama was intent on withdrawing American troops from an endless, exorbitant war in the Middle East—a region Brzezinski had dubbed Eurasia's "central zone of instability"—while simultaneously deploying naval forces at "offshore bases" along the Pacific littoral to secure Washington's axial position for control of that continent. In a deft exercise of imperial management, this military pivot complemented Obama's focus on Asian trade. With North America's increasing energy independence via natural gas and alternative sources, Washington could, for the first time in fifty years, regard the "economic prize" of the Middle East's "enormous concentration of natural gas and oil reserves" as a marginal matter, no longer worth a massive price in blood and treasure.[87] Simultaneously, the economic significance of East and Southeast Asia's booming manufactures for the country's new economy of information and consumer goods made freedom of the seas for trans-Pacific commerce a critical strategic priority.

In the aftermath of that commitment to Asia, Obama's initial deployment of just 2,500 US troops to Australia seemed a slender down payment on his "strategic decision" to become his country's first "Pacific president," producing a great deal of premature criticism and derision.[88] Four years later, one CNN commentator would still be calling this "Obama's pivot to nowhere."[89] In early 2015, even seasoned foreign policy commentator Fareed Zakaria would ask, "Whatever happened to the pivot to Asia?" Answering his own question, Zakaria argued that the president was still mired in the Middle East and that the centerpiece of any true future pivot, the Trans-Pacific Partnership, seemed to face certain defeat in Congress.[90]

In March 2014, however, the Obama administration deployed a full battalion of marines at Darwin on the Timor Sea, an Australian base well positioned to access the strategic Lombok and Sunda straits.[91] Five months later, the two powers signed a US-Australia Force Posture agreement allowing for both the pre-positioning of equipment and the basing of US warships at Darwin. Just in time for Obama's April 2014 visit to Manila, the American ambassador there signed an Enhanced Defense Cooperation Agreement with a Philippine government angry at China over its recent seizure of Scarborough Shoal, a fishing ground the country claimed in the South China Sea. This bilateral accord paved the way for the future stationing of American forces and the pre-positioning of their equipment in the country. After the Philippine Supreme Court finally affirmed the legality of the agreement in 2016, Manila lifted a twenty-five-year ban on any permanent US presence, allowing the United States to build facilities inside five Philippine military bases, including two on the shores of the South China Sea.[92]

Through eight major air and naval bastions in Japan, the construction of a joint naval facility on Jeju Island in South Korea, and access to host-country naval bases in Australia, Singapore, and the Philippines, Washington had, by the end of Obama's second term, rebuilt its chain of military enclaves along the Asian littoral, positioning its forces to challenge China's navy in the East China and South China Seas.[93] To operate these installations, the Pentagon announced plans to "forward base 60 percent of our naval assets in the Pacific by 2020" along with a similar percentage of air force fighters and bombers, as well

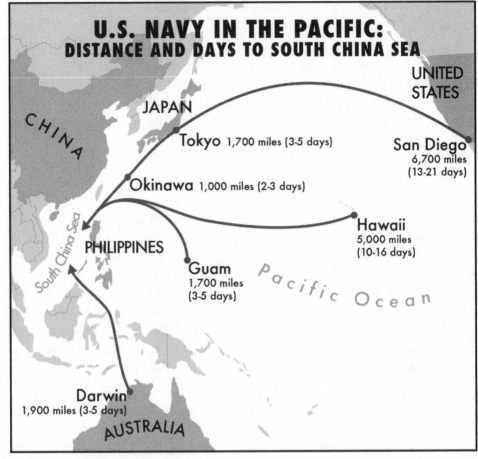

U.S. NAVY IN THE PACIFIC:
DISTANCE AND DAYS TO SOUTH CHINA SEA

UNITED STATES

CHINA

JAPAN

Tokyo 1,700 miles (3-5 days)

San Diego
6,700 miles
(13-21 days)

Okinawa 1,000 miles (2-3 days)

South China Sea

PHILIPPINES

Hawaii
5,000 miles
(10-16 days)

Guam
1,700 miles
(3-5 days)

Pacific Ocean

Darwin
1,900 miles (3-5 days)

AUSTRALIA

US Navy Positions in the Pacific, 2016

as "space and cyber capabilities."[94] As Obama himself observed in 2016, "If you look at how we've operated in the South China Sea, we have been able to mobilize most of Asia to isolate China in ways that have surprised China, frankly, and have very much served our interest in strengthening our alliances."[95]

By coordinating the economic and military components of his grand strategy, Obama sought to achieve a potential for geopolitical synergy. While his trade initiatives, embodied in that Trans-Pacific Partnership, aimed to direct the flow of commerce from Pacific littoral nations toward America, his chain of maritime bastions and naval patrols aspired, in coordination with Asia-Pacific allies, to secure the free movement of that same transoceanic trade. Yet Obama's grand strategy, like those of the grandmasters who preceded him, soon suffered from unforeseen complications.

The Limits of Vision

These grandmasters saw the possibilities of geopolitical change, but they also seemed to suffer from their singular focus, a form of tunnel vision that blinded them to the pitfalls of their bold maneuvers. Their strategies, so dazzling in the historical present, have often led remarkably quickly to unanticipated, even dismal outcomes over the longer term.

For all his skill in fostering Washington's ascent to global power and forging a complementary world order, Elihu Root, cosseted among wealthy elites, could not imagine the nativist reaction that would follow World War I, when Congress rejected the League of Nations proposed by his intellectual successor Woodrow Wilson and Root's antithesis Warren G. Harding led the country in an isolationist retreat from the international community. Half a century later, Zbigniew Brzezinski, obsessed with the liberation of Eastern Europe, proved deft in his mobilization of Islamic jihadists to break up the Soviet Union, but was myopic when it came to grasping the long-term threat that such Muslim militants might pose to America's position in the volatile Middle East. Similarly, Obama, determined to reestablish America as the dominant Asia-Pacific power, underestimated the difficulties of military withdrawal from the Middle East and the populist hostility to the trade treaties that were the centerpiece of his strategy. Just as early internationalists Root and Wilson prompted a nativist retreat led by Harding, whose insularity and cronyism mocked their idealism, so it has been Obama's fate to precipitate a populist reaction to globalization led by Donald Trump.

For all the boldness of his geopolitical vision, Obama faltered in its implementation as events, domestic and international, intervened decisively. The two trade pacts, TTP and TTIP, that promised to redirect Eurasia's economies toward America soon encountered formidable domestic political opposition on both continents from both left and right. Despite volumes of economic studies to the contrary, just 19 percent of Americans polled in July 2016 believed that trade creates more jobs, and an earlier survey of public opinion in forty-four countries found only 26 percent of respondents felt trade lowers prices. Between 1999 and 2011, Chinese imports eliminated 2.4 million American jobs, closing plants for furniture in North Carolina, glass in Ohio, and auto parts and steel across the Midwest.[96] After a half century of accelerating globalization, displaced or disadvantaged workers began mobilizing politically to oppose an economic order that privileged corporations and economic elites. As nations worldwide imposed a combined 2,100 restrictions on imports, world trade started slowing and actually fell during the second quarter of 2016 for the first time during a period of economic growth since World War II.[97]

As the most transcendent of these trade treaties, designed to supersede the sovereign authority of courts and legislatures, the TTP and TTIP became symbols of a globalization gone too far. Obama's promotion of these treaties coincided with a growing nativist reaction to globalization. Across Europe an increasing number of voters supported hyper-nationalist parties that included the Danish People's Party, the French National Front, the Alternative for Germany, Greece's Golden Dawn, Sweden Democrats, and the UK Independence Party. Simultaneously, a generation of populist demagogues gained popularity or power in nominally democratic nations around the world—notably, Norbert Hofer (Austria), Marine Le Pen (France), Viktor Orban (Hungary), Geert Wilders (Netherlands), Rodrigo Duterte (Philippines), Narendra Modi (India), Prabowo Subianto (Indonesia), Vladimir Putin (Russia), Recep Erdoğan (Turkey), and Donald Trump (United States). In June 2016, the British public voted to quit the European Union, eliminating its most forceful advocate for the TTIP, and two months later Germany's economy minister announced that these trade talks with Washington had failed.[98]

During the American election campaign that fall, Donald Trump was famously vociferous in his opposition to the TTP and, under the pressure from the progressive candidacy of Bernie Sanders, his Democratic rival Hillary Clinton soon followed suit.[99] Only days after Trump's unexpected win in November, the Obama White House conceded the deal was dead—a blow to US prestige that opened the way for Beijing to push its own Asian trade pact, the sixteen-nation Regional Comprehensive Economic Partnership, that excludes the United States.[100]

Moreover, Obama's long-heralded military pivot to Asia was slowed by competing American commitments in the Middle East, many of them of his own making, and adverse trends in Asia. With Syria's civil war destabilizing the region via millions of refugees, ISIS resilient in a struggling Iraq, and an open-ended commitment to keeping ground troops and airpower in Afghanistan, Washington's redeployment of its forces to military bases along the Pacific littoral slowed, sometimes drastically so. Despite announced long-term plans, the Pentagon's projected commitment of actual assets to Asia in 2015–16 was still exceedingly modest—those 2,500 marines to Australia, an extra army battalion to South Korea, two destroyers to Japan, and four littoral combat ships to Singapore.[101] Such relatively minor deployments were unlikely to provide a serious counterbalance to China's preponderance of fighters, frigates, and submarines in the region. In Obama's last months, a RAND Corporation study, *War with China*, warned that Beijing's improved capabilities now meant a US victory was no longer certain in a conflict that "could involve inconclusive fighting with steep losses on both sides."[102]

In Obama's second term, Washington's strategic position in Asia was buffeted by partisan shifts among its allies that revealed some underlying weakness in both its regional position and its system of world power. For nearly seventy years, US hegemony had rested in large part on its control over the axial points at both ends of the strategic Eurasian continent. At the western axis, NATO has long provided a strong multilateral anchor that transcended any sudden shifts in parties or personalities among the twenty-eight European member states. By contrast, the eastern end along the Pacific littoral has never had a regional defense agreement and thus rested on separate bilateral ententes with just four nations—Australia, Japan, South Korea, and the Philippines. In Obama's last years, Washington's position was strengthened by the ascent of pro-American conservatives in South Korea and Japan, but weakened, perhaps seriously, by the election of a fiery populist in the Philippines sympathetic to China.

The May 2016 elections elevating Rodrigo Duterte from tough-talking mayor of Davao, the country's most violent city, to the Philippine presidency brought a sudden chill to once-close relations.[103] At the ASEAN conference in Laos that September, Duterte reacted profanely to Obama's oblique criticism of the thousands of extrajudicial killings under his ongoing drug war, saying, "Who does he think he is? I am no American puppet. I am the president of a sovereign country and I am not answerable to anyone except the Filipino people. *Putang ina mo* [Your mother's a whore], I will swear at you."[104] Obama reacted with his characteristic cool by calling Duterte "a colorful guy." But he also took the uncommon step of canceling their bilateral meeting, opening a breach between the leaders that resisted repair.[105]

A month later as US and Filipino marines landed on a rain-swept Luzon beach in one of twenty-eight joint military maneuvers held every year, Duterte stated: "This year would be the last. For as long as I am there, do not treat us like a doormat because you'll be sorry for it. I will not speak with you. I can always go to China." Within days, Philippine defense secretary Delfin Lorenzana announced that joint naval exercises in the South China Sea were henceforth suspended and the hundred Americans operating drones against Muslim rebels on southern Mindanao Island would leave once the Philippines acquired comparable capacity.[106]

The truly critical blow, however, came in late October during Duterte's state visit to China. To a burst of applause from an audience of officials in Beijing's Great Hall of the People, the symbolic seat of China's ruling Communist Party, he said, "Your honors, in this venue, I announce my separation from the United States . . . both in military, but economics also." At a Philippine-Chinese trade forum that same day, Duterte asked, "What is really wrong with an American character?" Americans are, he continued, "loud, sometimes rowdy, and they have this volume of their voice . . . not adjusted to civility. . . . They are the more forward commanding voice befitting obedience." Evoking some deep Filipino racialist tropes, Duterte then mocked a flat, nasal American accent and rued the time he was questioned at Los Angeles Airport by a "black" officer with "black" uniform, "black" shoes, and "black" gun. Moving from rhetoric to substance, Duterte quietly capitulated to Beijing's relentless pressure for bilateral talks to settle their competing claims in the South China Sea, virtually abrogating Manila's recent slam-dunk win on that issue before the Permanent Court of Arbitration in The Hague.[107]

China reciprocated. After Beijing's usual rituals—smiling girls with flowers and marching soldiers with bayonets—President Xi Jinping proclaimed, "China and the Philippines are neighbors across the sea and the two peoples are blood brothers." Sealing that bond with cash, Beijing signed deals giving Manila US $22.5 billion in trade and low-interest loans.[108]

The breach in the seventy-year Philippine-US alliance was both breathtaking and confusing. More than 30 percent of remittances from overseas workers, the country's largest source of foreign exchange totaling nearly US $30 billion in 2015, comes from Filipinos in the United States.[109] Unlike many peoples around the globe, Filipinos have an abiding affection for America, with 92 percent expressing approval of their former colonial power in a 2015 Pew poll—by far the highest figure for any country in the world, including the United States itself.[110]

Yet Filipino admiration coexists with layer upon layer of resentment over being a distinctly subordinate partner in a long imperial alliance. Colonial pacification during the Philippine-American War ravaged the countryside and killed at least two hundred thousand in a population of just seven million, leaving a "postmemory"—that is, a "trans-generational transmission of traumatic knowledge"—marked by strong nationalism inflected with resentments ready to surface at any slight.[111] As America's bastion in the Western Pacific on the eve of World War II, the Philippines became a twice-fought battleground, suffering the utter devastation of its capital Manila and a million deaths in a population of just sixteen million.[112] During the Cold War, the presence of massive US bases led to incidents between American soldiers and Filipinos, shootings and sexual assaults that highlighted the country's sense of compromised sovereignty.[113] As de facto dictator from 1972 to 1986, Ferdinand Marcos used Washington's need for those installations to mute its criticism of his abysmal human rights record, angering the democratic opposition who concluded the bases only served American interests.[114] Ten years after the Philippine Senate canceled the bases agreement in 1991, both nations cooperated closely during the war on terror, but that ended badly in 2015 when that spectacularly bungled CIA operation left forty-four Filipino troops dead in a firefight with Muslim militias.[115]

Although a simple clash of executive egos sparked the diplomatic rupture between Duterte and Obama, the geopolitical consequences are potentially profound. Along the four thousand miles of the Pacific littoral, the Philippines alone sits astride the South China Sea, providing the optimal strategic position to check China's claim to those international waters. President Duterte lacks the authority, and probably even the ambition, to completely abrogate the strong ties built so painstakingly and painfully over the past 120 years. Indeed, after tilting dramatically toward Beijing, Duterte leaned back toward Washington after the November 2016 elections, quickly congratulating Trump on his victory and appointing the developer of Manila's Trump Tower as his special envoy to Washington. Struggling to contain North Korea's nuclear threat, President Trump reciprocated, telephoning Duterte in April 2017 to praise his "unbelievable job on the drug problem" and dismiss Obama's concerns about the thousands killed. As talk turned to Kim Jong-un's missile tests, the transcript reveals Trump flexing his nuclear muscles in a vain effort to shake Duterte's reliance on China.

> Duterte: As long as those rockets and warheads are in the hands of Kim Jong-un we will never be safe…He is not stable, Mr. President…He has even gone against China, which is the last country he should rebuke…
>
> Trump: Well, he has got the powder but he doesn't have the delivery system. All his rockets are crashing…
>
> Duterte: At the end of the day, the last card, the ace has to be with China…
>
> Trump: We have a lot of firepower over there. We have two submarines—the best in the world—we have two nuclear submarines…
>
> Duterte: I will try to make a call to President Xi Jinping …to tell him that if we will remain…peaceful, China has the card. The other op-

tion is a nuclear blast...

Trump: We can't let a madman with nuclear weapons let [*sic*] on the loose like that. We have a lot of firepower, more than he has times 20, but we don't want to use it. You will be in good shape...

Duterte: I will try to make a call tomorrow to China.[116]

Duterte had clearly decided China's power, not America's military might, was the key to his country's security. Even if his successor aligns again with Washington, a six-year hiatus in the alliance would allow Beijing to consolidate its military position in the region's waters and make its claim to them an undeniable reality.

Ironically for a liberal like Obama, his Asia policy fared best among conservative allies cast in a Cold War mode. And irony upon irony, the fulcrum for Washington's pivot to Asia was none other than Japanese prime minister Shinzō Abe, the unapologetic nationalist leading his country's military resurgence. After returning to office in 2012, Abe spent the next four years confronting China over competing claims to the Senkaku Islands in the East China Sea, courting Southeast Asian allies with arms and aid as part of an expansive foreign policy, and asserting the "vital significance" of the Japan-US alliance in securing Asia's "safety and prosperity."[117] Complementing a five-year expansion of Japan's military budget, already the world's fifth largest, Abe unilaterally undermined Japan's pacifist constitution in 2014 via what he dubbed the doctrine of "collective self-defense," and quickly won Washington's approval for revisions to the mutual security treaty that would allow Japan to project force regionally, far beyond its borders.[118] Abe was also a strong supporter of Obama's pivot to Asia, embracing the Trans-Pacific Partnership and welcoming increased US troop deployments.[119] Seventy years after the cataclysmic end to their bloody Pacific War, Japan was host to 47,000 American troops who occupied eighty-seven installations, including the Yokosuka naval base that is home port for the Seventh Fleet and airfields at Misawa, Yokota, and Kadena that house 130 air force fighters.[120] In sum, Japan remained the firm axial anchor in America's continuing bid to control Eurasia.

With his once-bold geopolitical pivot to Asia stalled, Obama left a legacy of contradictory half-measures: insufficient attention to the Middle East to restore some semblance of stability and woefully inadequate commitment of forces for Asia to contain rather than provoke China. Bilateral interactions with Beijing remained troubled, as the Chinese leadership pressed for what one foreign policy analyst called a "new model of great power relations" that conceded it a "sphere of influence and military advantage in Asia in return for Chinese support of Washington's key global issues."[121]

To meet China's military challenge, Obama had struggled to shore up America's waning hegemony through a final diplomatic surge with mixed results. The nuclear treaty with Iran to prevent another major war in the Middle East held firm, but ongoing conflicts in Afghanistan, Syria, and Iraq slowed the long-term shift in strategic forces to Asia. With the exception of the Philippines, Obama maintained good relations with key Asian allies, although the failure of his signature trade pact would eventually weaken bilateral alliances along the Pacific littoral. By the end of his term, Obama, like the other grandmasters before him, found his bold geopolitical vision, so enticing in the abstract, had been compromised by political complexities at home and abroad.

In the transition to the Trump administration, the fragility of these relations with key Asian allies was immediately apparent. Right after the stunning upset in the November 2016 elections, Japan's Abe broke with the subordinate role of prime ministers past by moving quickly to repair the damage from Trump's unsettling campaign rhetoric, particularly his demands for full payment of the cost of basing troops in Japan and his call for the country to build its own nuclear weapons. Only twenty-four hours after polls closed in America, Abe was on the phone telling Trump that "a strong U.S.-Japan alliance . . . supports peace and stability in the Asia-Pacific region." Abe was also a vocal defender of the TPP, saying its failure would assure the success of Beijing's sixteen-nation regional partnership that excludes America, "leaving China the economy with the largest gross domestic product." A week later, he became the first foreign leader to meet the president-elect, emerging from a ninety-minute sit-down in New York's gilded Trump Tower to announce, "Trump is a leader who can be trusted." While Trump's views of Japan were badly outdated, almost a flashback to the 1980s, one of his top advisers now admitted, "Frankly, the prime minister has been more assertive and forthright in trying to make . . . changes to Japan's global posture."[122] In a striking inversion of past patterns within this strategic alliance, Abe was the seasoned master and Trump the raw apprentice.

Just as Obama's personal clash with Duterte was unprecedented in the seventy-year history of their nations' alliance, so President Trump's contretemps with Australian prime minister Malcolm Turnbull was equally extraordinary. During the round of introductory phone calls every new president makes to close allies, Trump bridled at Turnbull's insistent reminder about a US commitment to take 1,250 refugees and cut short the call. "China and those wishing to weaken the strongest alliance in the Pacific will see opportunity in this moment," commented the head of Canberra's National Security College. Indeed, reflecting the country's growing economic dependence on mineral exports to China, public opinion had shifted dramatically in recent years, with 45 percent of those polled in 2016 saying Australia should distance itself from America. While he was still patching up this contretemps with Australia, President Trump also roiled the once rock-solid alliance with South Korea by calling its free-trade agreement "horrible," insisting that it pay for the antimissile system the United States installed to block North Korean attacks, and, to top it all off, insulting the country's history by asserting incorrectly that it was once "a part of China." Reeling from Trump's gratuitous blasts, Seoul's leading newspaper, *Chosun Ilbo*, published an editorial in May 2017 expressing the "shock, betrayal and anger many South Koreans have felt." In presidential elections that month, liberal leader Moon Jae-in scored a solid win after campaigning for the country to "learn to say no" to America.[123]

Along the entire Pacific littoral, these shifts in the tenor of strategic alliances with Australia, Japan, South Korea, and the Philippines reveal a little-noticed yet central aspect in the waning of US power—the loss of control over a global network of presidents and prime ministers who long served as Washington's loyal subordinate elites. During the Cold War, obeisance was the order of the day and those who harbored nationalist, anti-American sentiments often became the target of CIA-sponsored coups, electoral manipulation, or, when required, assassination plots.[124] But now America's hegemony has proved, like Britain's before it, to be a "self-liquidating concern," as bipolar power becomes multipolar and developing nations develop, allowing once subordinate elites like Abe, Duterte, Moon, and Turnbull to become unimaginably more insubordinate, weakening one of Washington's key means of control on the Pacific littoral and beyond.[125]

While Washington's ties to its Asian allies waxed and waned, the pressure of Beijing's military expansion was relentless. By building the infrastructure for military bases in the Arabian and South China Seas, along with a complementary blue-water navy of carriers and jet fighters, China is forging a future capacity to surgically and strategically impair American military containment, someday breaching that encircling armada of carriers, cruisers, drones, fighters, and submarines, and so sparing it a future confrontation with the full global might of the US military. At the same time, Beijing is contesting Washington's dominion over space and cyberspace.

Simultaneously, Washington has been building a triple-tier architecture for continued global hegemony with a strength, scope, and sophistication unprecedented in the history of world empires. Beneath the earth and seas, the NSA has penetrated the fiber-optic networks of global telecommunications to monitor both national leaders and their restive millions, creating a surveillance apparatus unequaled in both breadth of geographical reach and depth of social penetration. On the surface of the earth, the Pentagon has revived the classical imperial array of naval bastions and battleships, though now in the form of "lily-pad" bases, aircraft carriers, and littoral combat ships.

From sky to space, the Pentagon has launched thousands of drones—light and lumbering, hand-held and carrier-based, lethal and experimental—to command both terrestrial battlespace and that "ultimate strategic high ground." Washington has ringed Eurasia with dozens of drone bases for surveillance and extrajudicial killing, while weaponizing space with stratospheric drones, upgraded satellites, and a space surveillance network of sensors and telescopes. In theory at least, this vast technological apparatus should preserve Washington's grip on the world island and extend its dominion over the destiny of the entire planet.

In short, the world's two most powerful nations, China and the United States, seem to have developed rival geopolitical strategies to guide their struggle for global power. Whether Beijing can succeed in unifying Asia, Africa, and Europe into that world island or Washington can maintain its control of the Eurasian continent from its axial positions on the Pacific littoral and in Western Europe will not become clear for another decade or two.

There is as well a larger, darker question looming over this twenty-first century edition of superpower politics. We still cannot say whether the outcome of this latter-day Great Game will be decided through an intense but peaceable commercial competition or a more violent denouement akin to history's last comparable imperial transition over two hundred years ago—that is, the protracted warfare, at the start of the nineteenth century, between Napoleon's "continental system" and Britain's maritime strategy.[126] Now at the start of a new century, we cannot predict with any certainty whether history will favor Eurasia's emerging land power or the established global hegemon, the would-be master of air, sea, and space. But it does seem certain that we are starting to see the broad parameters of an epochal geopolitical contest likely to shape the world's destiny in the coming decades of this still nascent twenty-first century.

Chapter Eight

Five Scenarios
for the End of the American Century

W ill there be a soft landing for America thirty or forty years from now? Don't bet on it. The demise of the United States as the pre-eminent global power could come far more quickly than anyone imagines. Despite the aura of omnipotence empires often project, most are surprisingly fragile, lacking the inherent strength of even a modest nation-state. Indeed, a glance at their history should remind us that the greatest of them are susceptible to collapse from diverse causes, with fiscal pressures usually a prime factor. For the better part of two centuries, the security and prosperity of their homeland has been the main obligation for most stable states, making foreign or imperial adventures an expendable option, usually allocated no more than 5 percent of the domestic budget. Without the financing that arises almost organically inside a sovereign nation, empires are famously predatory in their relentless hunt for plunder or profit—witness the Atlantic slave trade, Belgium's rubber lust in the Congo, British India's opium commerce, the Third Reich's rape of Europe, or the Soviet exploitation of Eastern Europe.

When their revenues shrink, empires become brittle. Consider the collapse of the Soviet sphere as its command economy imploded. Or recall the rapid dissolution of the British Empire after World War II as London faced an irresolvable conflict between "domestic recovery and [its] imperial commitments."[1] So delicate is their ecology of power that, when things start to go truly wrong, empires regularly unravel with unholy speed: just a year for Portugal, two years for the Soviet Union, eight years for France, eleven years for the Ottomans, seventeen years for Great Britain, and, in all likelihood, just twenty-seven years for the United States, counting from the crucial year 2003.

Future historians are likely to identify George W. Bush's rash invasion of Iraq in that year as the start of America's downfall. But instead of the bloodshed that marked the end of so many past empires, with cities burning and civilians slaughtered, this twenty-first-century imperial collapse could come relatively quietly through the invisible tendrils of economic contraction or cyberwarfare.

But have no doubt: when Washington's global dominion finally ends, there will be painful daily reminders of what the loss of power will mean for Americans in every walk of life. As a half-dozen European nations have discovered, imperial decline tends to have a remarkably demoralizing impact on a society, often bringing at least a generation of economic privation. As the economy cools, political temperatures rise, sparking serious domestic conflict.

Available economic, educational, and technological data indicate that, when it comes to US global power, negative trends are likely to aggregate rapidly by 2020 and could reach a critical mass no later than 2030. The American Century, proclaimed so triumphantly at the start of World War II, may already be tattered and fading by 2025 and, except for the finger pointing, could be over by 2030.

Significantly, in 2008, well before China's challenge was clear to all, the National Intelligence Council, Washington's top analytic unit, admitted for the first time that America's power was on a downward trajectory. In one of its futuristic reports, *Global Trends 2025*, the Intelligence Council cited "the transfer of global wealth and economic power now under way—roughly from West to East . . . without precedent in modern history" as the main cause for the decline of the "United States' relative strength—even in the military realm." But like many in Washington, these intelligence analysts anticipated a long, soft landing, and harbored hopes the country would somehow "retain unique military capabilities . . . to project military power globally" for decades to come.[2]

Only four years later, its next projection, *Global Trends 2030*, was a bit more pessimistic about the future. "By 2030, no country—whether the U.S., China, or any other large country—will be a hegemonic power," the council concluded. Although the "Pax Americana . . . is fast winding down" and the country's "relative decline vis-à-vis the rising states is inevitable," Washington's all-powerful military would allow it to "remain 'first among equals' among the other great powers in 2030." China might "become a global superpower," but "U.S. military capabilities are unmatched by any other plausible combination of power and are likely to remain so for decades to come."[3]

No such luck. A more realistic reading of current projections suggests that the United States will likely find itself in second place to China in economic output sometime around 2030, and possibly behind India a couple of decades after that. Similarly, Chinese innovation in military technology is on a trajectory toward world leadership sometime around 2030, just as America's current supply of brilliant scientists and engineers retires, without adequate replacement by an ill-educated younger generation.

A decade before that in 2020, the Pentagon will, according to current plans, throw a military Hail Mary pass for a dying empire. It will launch that lethal triple-canopy of advanced aerospace robotics that represents Washington's last best hope of retaining global power in excess of its waning economic influence. By that year, however, China's global network of communications satellites, backed by the world's most powerful supercomputers, will also be close to fully operational, providing Beijing with an independent platform for the weaponization of space and a powerful communications system for missile or cyber strikes into every quadrant of the globe.

Wrapped in imperial hubris, the White House, like Whitehall or the Quai d'Orsay in their day, still seems to imagine that American decline will be gradual, gentle, and partial. In his 2010 State of the Union address, President Obama offered a resounding rejection of any "second place for the United States of America."[4] On cue, Vice President Biden ridiculed the very idea that "we are destined . . . to be a great nation that has failed because we lost control of our economy and overextended."[5]

As the 2016 presidential election showed, ordinary Americans, watching their jobs head overseas, have a more realistic view than their cosseted leaders. As early as 2010, an opinion poll found that 65 percent of Americans believed the country was "in a state of decline."[6] By then, Australia and Turkey, traditional military allies, were using their American-manufactured weapons for joint air and naval maneuvers with China.[7] By then, America's closest economic partners were backing away from Washington's opposition to China's rigged currency rates. As the president flew back from his Asian tour that November, a gloomy *New York Times* headline summed up the moment this way: "Obama's Economic View Is Rejected on World Stage, China, Britain and Germany Challenge U.S., Trade Talks with Seoul Fail, Too."[8]

Viewed historically, the question is not whether the United States will lose its unchallenged global power, but just how precipitous and wrenching the decline will be. After crunching masses of data and traveling the world for closed-door seminars with power elites on four continents, the National

Intelligence Council offered some rather modest scenarios for a changing world in its *Global Trends 2030*. In its worst case marked by "stalled engines," Europe unravels, the North American energy revolution falters, conflicts erupt, and "all players do relatively poorly." Under its best possible scenario, China, the United States, and Europe collaborate to stop a regional conflict in, say, South Asia, thereby drawing Beijing more fully into a revitalized international system. After comparing present trends with past global transitions in 1815, 1919, 1945, and 1989, the council came to the reassuring conclusion that "replacement of the United States by another global power and erection of a new international order seems the least likely outcome."[9]

Instead of Washington's wishful thinking, let's use the National Intelligence Council's own futuristic methodology to suggest four more realistic scenarios for how, whether with a bang or a whimper, US global power could end by 2030 (along with four accompanying assessments of just where we are today). Our future scenarios are arranged by increasingly adverse outcomes: an evolving world order, economic decline, military misadventure, and World War III. To these four futuristic hypotheticals, we need to add another major force for change whose likely impact might not be fully manifest by 2030, but will certainly be far more evident by 2040: climate change. Indeed, this troubling trend is on such an undeniable trajectory that we need to treat it less like a fifth scenario and more as a likely array of facts that will be the background to whatever happens to American power. While these scenarios are hardly the only possibilities when it comes to such a decline or even collapse, they offer a window into a world heading in that direction.

World Order: Present Situation

A slow decline in America's status within an evolving world order offers the most benign prospect for the future of its global power. In the aftermath of President George W. Bush's dismal intervention in Iraq, Washington's foreign policy elites have begun to admit, albeit begrudgingly, that the world is changing. In its 2012 report, *Global Trends 2030*, the National Intelligence Council identified half-a-dozen "game-changers" that might modify the current US-dominated world order. As a multipolar world takes shape, "Western dominance of global structures such as the U.N. Security Council, World Bank, and IMF [International Monetary Fund] probably will have been transformed by . . . the changing hierarchy of new economic players." With the fading of "strong alliances" among the Western or G-7 nations that once amplified its power, Washington's influence, circa 2030, will be determined by its ability to "work with new partners to reinvent the international system."[10]

In ways the council did not fully comprehend, US hegemony has developed as a delicately balanced ecology of power surprisingly vulnerable to disequilibrium.[11] By the dawn of the twenty-first century, Washington exercised its global sway through ententes with major powers, leadership in international organizations, and fifty formal military alliances with nations large and small.[12] But after expending its economic and diplomatic capital in an Iraq war replete with false intelligence and lurid acts of torture, Washington's leadership began to wane. As Zbigniew Brzezinski put it, this "unilateral war of choice against Iraq precipitated a widespread delegitimation of U.S. foreign policy even among its friends."[13] Meanwhile, new powers were gaining a competitive edge. European, Russian, and Chinese leaders have grown more assertive since 2003, challenging Washington's ability to set the international agenda.

During a decade of misbegotten warfare, signs of America's fading leadership came in rapid succession: the failure to win majority support from the UN Security Council for its 2003 invasion of Iraq; the raucous booing of American envoys by delegates at the Bali climate conference in 2007; and Obama's exclusion from key meetings at the Copenhagen climate summit in 2009.[14] A year later, the downward trend continued at the 2011 session of G-20 powers when Washington pressed Europe, unsuccessfully, to solve its fiscal crisis internally and thus avoid aid from China or the International Monetary Fund that would diminish US influence.[15] While wasting funds equivalent to the Marshall Plan (that actually rebuilt a ravaged Europe after World War II) on a futile attempt at the reconstruction of corruption-plagued Afghanistan, Washington no longer had the wherewithal for another effort of that scale.[16]

In the wake of the Iraq War and the Abu Ghraib torture scandal, Washington, like London in its day, found its control over key subordinate allies becoming ever more tenuous. While a CIA coup or covert operation had once sufficed to remove a nettlesome leader, the most visible American attempts to control these elites now began to fail. After Washington spent eight years pacifying Iraq at a cost of 4,800 lives and a trillion dollars, its "ally" in Baghdad, Prime Minister Nouri al-Maliki, suddenly asserted his nation's sovereignty in 2011, forcing Washington to withdraw all its troops and curtail plans for making its 104-acre Baghdad embassy a bastion for American power in the Middle East.[17] That rebuke was but one among many signs of fading influence worldwide.

During the quarter century since the collapse of Washington's bipartisan foreign policy consensus at the end of the Cold War, the wrenching partisan back-and-forth between the internationalism of the Democrats versus the uni-lateralism of the Republicans culminated in the insular "America First" posture of the Trump White House. By then, there were already some negative, long-term trends that limited the influence of any US leader on the world stage—including, America's declining share of the world economy, an erosion of its technological primacy, and those increasingly independent subordinate elites.

Apart from these adverse factors beyond anyone's control, Washington's global power also rested on strategic elements that its leaders could manage to extend their hegemony: notably, the NATO alliance and US-Japan security treaty at the axial ends of Eurasia, trade treaties that reinforced such alliances, scientific research to sustain its military's continuing technological edge, leadership in international issues, and promotion of democratic principles. After President Trump, during his May 2017 tour, chastised stone-faced NATO leaders for failure to pay their "fair share" and refused to affirm the alliance's core principle of collective defense, Chancellor Angela Merkel told German voters that "we must fight for our future on our own, for our destiny as Europeans."[18] America's control over the axial ends of the Eurasian landmass was crumbling. By degrading NATO, alienating Asian allies, and canceling trade treaties, the Trump White House was demolishing the key pillars of a delicately balanced architecture that had sustained Washington's preeminent position for seventy years, unwittingly accelerating the move toward a new world order.

Evolving World Order: Scenario 2030

While Washington's global reach will no doubt recede further during the 2020s, there will be, circa 2030, a broad spectrum of possibilities for its smaller yet still significant role within a changing world order. Several of the more likely scenarios might take shape as follows:

At one extreme, we cannot rule out the rise of a new global hegemon. But there does not seem to be any single state with the requisite mix of appealing ideology, administrative apparatus, and military power that would be capable of replacing the United States as the planet's sole superpower. Imperial transitions driven by the hard power of guns and money often require the soft-power salve of cultural suasion as well, much as the shift from British to US dominion over Latin America around 1900 sparked sweeping cultural realignments on three continents.[19]

Every sustainable modern empire has had some source of universal appeal for its foreign subjects. Spain offered Christianity, Britain free markets and fair play, and the United States democracy, human rights, and the rule of law. Searching the world for possible successors, both China and Russia have inward-looking, self-referential cultures, recondite non-Roman scripts, nondemocratic political structures, and underdeveloped legal systems that will deny them key instruments for global dominion. In addition, there is no reason to believe that Russia, an economically rickety petro-state with a large military, will be capable of developing into a Soviet-style superpower again by 2030. China might well break the grip of American power but seems unlikely to replace it. For the first time in four centuries, there is no single state on the horizon to assume the mantle of world power from a fading global hegemon.

In a modest scenario involving more evolution than revolution, the current world order of law and international institutions might move toward a more transnational organization through shared governance of the global commons—the threatened environment, depleted seas, scarce water, and a warming Arctic rich in resources.[20] As political scientist G. John Ikenberry has argued, even if the American ability to shape world politics declines, "the liberal international order will survive and thrive," particularly its core principles of multilateral governance, free trade, human rights, and respect for sovereignty.[21] Indeed, even Washington's chief rival Beijing seems to embrace much of this liberal order, accepting the UN and World Trade Organization while simply ignoring other elements like the Permanent Court of Arbitration. Rather than wholesale rejection, Beijing has challenged what it views as pro-Western organizations by building its own parallel world order—the Shanghai Cooperation Organization instead of NATO, its Asian Infrastructure Investment Bank in lieu of the IMF, and its Regional Comprehensive Economic Partnership to replace the TPP trade pact.

Although the United States played a central role in forging global governance through law, treaties, and international organizations, that system might well retain sufficient strength to weather even a marked decline of American power. As citizens of a culturally diverse nation, US diplomats have a proven facility for forming effective personal relationships around the globe, allowing them influence in excess of raw power. While advances in aerospace and cyberspace may yet condemn the American heavy-metal armada of aircraft carriers and strategic bombers to the fate of the battleship, Washington will likely continue to maintain a significant military leverage for at least another decade or two.

Within such a moderate scenario, a new global oligopoly might emerge between 2020 and 2030, with rising powers China, Russia, India, and Brazil collaborating with receding powers like Britain, Germany, Japan, and the United States to enforce an ad hoc global dominion, akin to the loose alliance of European empires that ruled half of humanity circa 1900.

In a darker, dystopian version of this future world order, a coalition of transnational corporations, multilateral military forces like NATO, and an international financial leadership self-selected at Davos and Bilderberg might forge a supranational nexus to supersede any nation or empire. With denationalized corporations and elites ruling such a world from their secure urban enclaves—Geneva, London, Manhattan, Shanghai, or Sydney—the multitudes would be relegated to urban and rural wastelands. By 2030, there will be 662 cities worldwide with populations of over a million, including forty-one megacities with more than ten million inhabitants. By then, half of humanity will want for adequate water supplies and over a third of the earth's farmland will suffer degraded soils, threatening food security for many of the world's poor.[22]

While these elites take in the view from the fiftieth floors of their glittering metropoles, the two billion poor packed into fetid slums of the global South by 2030 will, says urbanist Mike Davis, make "the 'feral, failed cities' of the Third World . . . the distinctive battlespace of the twenty-first century"—and, agreeing with him fully, the US military is already preparing for such a future of endless urban warfare. As darkness settles over some future super-favela, "the empire can deploy Orwellian technologies of repression," while "hornet-like helicopter gun-ships stalk enigmatic enemies in the narrow streets of the slum districts. . . . Every morning the slums reply with suicide bombers and eloquent explosions."[23] Yet even this dismal vision leaves room for Washington to play a residual role, mediating international conflicts and monitoring the global commons beyond these human cesspits.

If the international order were, however, to weaken markedly, then instead of near anarchy, we might see the rise of regional hegemons in a return to something reminiscent of the international system that operated in the seventeenth century before modern empires took shape. In a 2017 scenario for the planet's future, the National Intelligence Council hypothesized that, by the early 2020s, Washington's retreat from the world stage, as Beijing and Moscow advanced, might lead to "the international system devolving toward contested regional spheres," with each power asserting "their right to privileged economic, political and security influence within their regions." In this neo-Westphalian world order, with its endless vistas of micro-violence and unchecked exploitation, each hegemon would dominate its immediate region—Brasilia, South America; Washington, North

America; Beijing, East and Southeast Asia; Moscow, Eastern Europe; New Delhi, South Asia; Tehran, Central Asia; Ankara, the Middle East; and Pretoria, southern Africa.[24]

With a bow to Secretary of State John Hay's "open door" policy at the start of the twentieth century, we might style this a future world order of "backdoor empires." Indeed, a number of such regional blocs have already formed, from the European Union to Latin America's Mercosur (Mercado Común del Sur).[25] To coordinate these blocs, a broader configuration for global governance might emerge beyond the current club of North Atlantic powers. Thus, the G-8 of older economies would give way to a G-20 of rising nations or something akin to the Shanghai Cooperation Organization, with the global economic agenda now set in part in Beijing and New Delhi rather than solely in London and New York. While its global power would diminish, Washington would still have considerable influence as a regional hegemon for North America and an arbiter of the residual international order.

Economic Decline: Present Situation

Consider the global economy and you immediately find a far darker prospect for the future of US power. This is especially true if you focus on the three main threats to its position in that economy: the loss of clout thanks to a shrinking share of gross world product; the decline of American technological innovation; and the possible end of the dollar's privileged status as the global reserve currency.

Forecasters have long predicted a continuing contraction of Washington's economic power. Back in 2003, Goldman Sachs projected that China would become the world's second-largest economy by 2025 and surpass the United States in 2041. By 2007, it had moved that latter date up to 2027, and suggested India would challenge America for the number two position at least by 2050.[26] In fact, China became the world's second-largest economy in 2010.[27] That same year it also became the world's leading manufacturing nation, ousting the United States from a position it had held for over a century.[28] By April 2011, the IMF was projecting that China would overtake the United States in real GDP to become the world's largest economy in just five more years.[29]

When China's growth started slowing, so did the predictions. In April 2015, the US Department of Agriculture suggested that the American economy would grow by nearly 50 percent over the next fifteen years, while China's would triple and come close to surpassing America's in 2030.[30] British forecasters pushed their estimate back to predict China would become the world's biggest economy in 2031.[31]

Whatever the specific year in which China surges ahead, the trends were all negative. Meanwhile, American leadership in technological innovation was clearly on the wane. In 2008, the United States still held the number two spot behind Japan in worldwide patent applications with 232,000, although China at 195,000 was closing fast, thanks to a blistering 400 percent increase since 2000.[32] By 2014, China actually took the lead with nearly half the world's total, an extraordinary 801,000 of them compared to just 285,000 for Americans.[33] In a harbinger of further decline, in 2009 the United States hit rock bottom among forty nations surveyed by the Information Technology and Innovation Foundation when it came to "global innovation-based competitiveness" during the previous decade.[34]

Putting some meat on these bare statistics, in 2010 China's Defense Ministry launched the world's fastest supercomputer, the Tianhe-1A—so powerful, said one expert, that it "blows away the existing No. 1 machine" in America. This was no fluke. China produced the world's fastest machine for the next seven years, until in 2016 it finally won in the way that really matters: with a supercomputer that had microprocessor chips made in China. By then, it also had the most supercomputers in the world with 167 compared to 165 for the United States and only 29 for Japan.[35] With supercomputing now critical for everything from codebreaking to the production of consumer products, China's edge has wide-ranging implications.

Add to this evidence that the American education system, that critical source of future scientists and innovators, has been falling behind its competitors. In 2012, the Organization for Economic Cooperation and Development (OECD) tested 510,000 fifteen-year-olds in thirty-four developed nations, finding those in Shanghai came first in math, science, and reading, while those in Massachusetts, "a strong-performing U.S. state," placed seventeenth in reading, twentieth in science, and twenty-seventh in math. The OECD also found that American students "have particular weaknesses in performing mathematics tasks with higher cognitive demands, such as . . . interpreting mathematical aspects in real-world problems."[36] Secretary of Education Arne Duncan rued these results as "a picture of educational stagnation." The National Intelligence Council noted that the country's educational advantage "has been cut in half in the past 30 years," meaning that without major investments in schools Americans "will increasingly bring only mediocre skills to the workplace."[37]

Why should anybody care about a bunch of fifteen-year-olds with backpacks, braces, and attitude? Because by 2030 those teenage test-takers will be the mid-career scientists and engineers determining whose computers survive a cyberattack and whose satellites evade a missile strike.

And those tenth-grade failings can be traced right up to the level of the PhD. After leading the world for decades in twenty-five- to thirty-four-year-olds with university degrees, the United States sank to twelfth place in 2012.[38] That same year, the World Economic Forum ranked the United States at a mediocre forty-seventh among 144 nations in the quality of its university math and science instruction. Two years later, its position slid to fifty-first.[39]

Significantly, a survey of some 150 major American universities in 2010 found that more than half of all graduate students in the sciences were foreigners: 70 percent in electrical engineering, 63 percent in computer science, and 52 percent in materials engineering.[40] Many of these students will head home after their schooling is completed and not stay in the United States, as once would have been the case. As one American space expert noted in 2009, "China's core space scientific . . . cadre is about two decades younger than its counterparts in the United States and Russia, which are now retiring," giving Beijing an "expanding pool of young, talented, and motivated space scientists."[41] By 2030, America could well face a critical shortage of scientific talent.

Similarly, in September 2010 the US National Academies warned that unless the country recovers its technological edge by investing in education and research, "the nation's ability to provide financially and personally rewarding jobs for its own citizens can be expected to decline at an accelerating pace."[42] With rising social disparities pushing the United States down to number fifty-six in income equality worldwide, its families increasingly lack the resources to close this talent gap by investing in their children's education.[43]

Doubling down on this deficiency, from 2010 to 2013 Congress imposed the sharpest cuts to science since the end of the space race in the 1960s, accelerating the slide in research and development (R&D) from 2 percent of GDP in the 1970s to only 0.78 percent by 2014.[44] While Beijing's soaring investment in R&D was on track to surpass the United States by 2026, Washington was reducing its research funding, both civil and military, from $160 billion in 2006 to $140 billion in 2015—cuts that will certainly shrink the nation's pool of talented young scientists.[45] By 2030, America's current generation of engineers and scientists will retire without sufficient replacements, and the country could by then lack the economic wherewithal to compete for substitutes internationally.

Such negative trends are encouraging ever sharper criticism of the dollar's role as the world's reserve currency. One of the prime benefits of global power is being on the winning side of a grand imperial bargain: you get to send the nations of the world bundles of brightly colored paper, whether British pound notes or US Treasury bills, and they happily hand over goods of actual value like automobiles, minerals, or oil. By any means fair or foul, empires will always maneuver to keep that deal running. At the peak of its power during the Cold War, the United States exported the cost of its Vietnam debacle to allies by unilaterally ending the dollar's convertibility to gold in 1971. This meant Washington would henceforth settle its debts for imports of machines and minerals not in gold, as required by the Bretton Woods agreement, but with bundles of pretty paper. The dollar's position recovered remarkably quickly in 1974 when Saudi Arabia agreed that oil would be sold in US currency, allowing Washington to close its trade deficit a decade later by pressing Germany and Japan to accept the dollar's unilateral devaluation. This meant it would be sending them even less of that pretty paper. By 2005, analysts could argue that "the core advantage of the U.S. economy . . . is the peculiar role of the U.S. currency," which allows it "to keep hundreds of thousands of troops stationed all over the world," import goods cheaply, and enjoy "limitless spending power" funded by "its twin deficits (fiscal and trade)."[46]

"Other countries are no longer willing to buy into the idea that the U.S. knows best on economic policy," said Kenneth S. Rogoff, former chief economist at the IMF.[47] With the world's central banks holding an astronomical $4 trillion in US Treasury notes by 2009, Russian president Dimitri Medvedev insisted that it was time to end "the artificially maintained unipolar system" based on "one big centre of consumption [and] one formerly strong reserve currency."[48] Simultaneously, China's central bank governor called for the creation of a global reserve currency "disconnected from individual nations" (that is, the US dollar)—a proposal Washington roundly rejected.[49]

Take these as signposts of a world to come, and of a possible attempt, as economist Michael Hudson has argued, "to hasten the bankruptcy of the U.S. financial-military world order." Foreigners watching America become the world's biggest debtor nation, without any of the austerity measures it had imposed on others in similar situations, began to see "the IMF, World Bank, World Trade Organization and other Washington surrogates . . . as vestiges of a lost American empire no longer able to rule by economic strength, left only with military domination. If China, Russia and their allies have their way, the U.S. will no longer . . . have the money for unlimited military spending."[50]

In November 2015, Christine Lagarde, managing director of the IMF, stood before television cameras in Washington for an announcement whose historic import was lost among the acronyms. "The IMF's executive board decided," she said, "that the Renminbi qualified for the SDR basket under existing criteria." In effect, China's currency had pushed aside the Euro and the British pound to join the US dollar as a global reserve currency used to store national assets or settle international debts. *New York Times* analyst Neil Irwin pointed out, "This is akin to what happened about a century ago, when the United States dollar gradually supplanted the British pound." For China, it thus represented "a crucial piece of the nation's rise to superpower status." With this recognition of the Renminbi, China and the Chinese could now start to share the power and privilege that once allowed Washington to impose economic sanctions on Russia, Iran, and North Korea while enjoying a strong currency and low interest rates.[51]

Economic Decline: Scenario 2030

All these negative trends lead to a scenario for the state of US power circa 2030 that might look something like this:

For the majority of Americans, the 2020s will likely be remembered as a demoralizing decade of rising prices, stagnant wages, and fading international competitiveness. After years of swelling deficits fed by incessant warfare in distant lands, in 2030 the US dollar finally loses its special status as the world's dominant reserve currency. As the National Intelligence Council had warned so presciently back in 2012, "The fall of the dollar as the global reserve currency and substitution by another or a basket of currencies would be one of the sharpest indications of a loss of U.S. global economic position, strongly undermining Washington's political influence." This change, it added, would be "equivalent to the [pound] sterling's demise as the world's currency, contributing to the end of the British Empire in the post-World War II period."[52]

Suddenly, there are punitive price increases for American imports ranging from clothing to computers. And the costs for all overseas activity surges as well, making travel for both tourists and troops prohibitive. Unable to pay for swelling deficits by selling now-devalued Treasury notes abroad, Washington is finally forced to slash its bloated military budget. Under pressure at home and abroad, its forces begin to pull back from hundreds of overseas bases to a continental perimeter. Such a desperate move, however, comes too late.

Faced with a fading superpower incapable of paying its bills, China, India,

Iran, Russia, and other powers provocatively challenge US dominion over the oceans, space, and cyberspace. From the start of the American Century in 1945, Washington's "command of the commons" had allowed it, said strategic analyst Barry Posen, "more useful military potential for a hegemonic foreign policy than any other offshore power has ever had," able to see across the surface of the globe and protect its soldiers and sailors wherever they might operate.[53]

By 2030, China's satellites and anti-satellite missiles have broken America's long command over space as the ultimate strategic high ground. Russia's renewed submarine fleet was challenging the US Navy in the North Atlantic. China's armada of aircraft carriers had already made the South China Sea, as the Pentagon had predicted back in 2016, a "Chinese lake." And Beijing's steely admirals are determined to push that watery dominion ever deeper into the Pacific toward Hawaii.[54]

Meanwhile at home, a witches' brew of political and economic change is crippling Washington's capacity to project its power overseas. As its population ages, the country's social welfare costs climb from 4 percent of GDP in 2010 toward a projected 18 percent by 2050, confronting Washington with the same choice between domestic welfare and overseas military operations that London faced in the 1950s. Just as the National Intelligence Council had predicted, "rising entitlement costs" to sustain an aging population will "consume an increasing portion of the Federal budget," driving defense's share of GDP downward from 7 percent during the Cold War and 5 percent in the decade after 2001 to only 2 percent in 2030, forcing a relentless retrenchment of the US global presence.[55]

Amid soaring prices, ever-rising unemployment, and a continuing decline in real wages throughout the 2020s, domestic divisions widen into violent clashes and divisive debates, often over symbolic, insubstantial issues. Riding a political tide of disillusionment and despair, President Trump's political heir, with his second term mired in the country's deepest recession in two decades, rallies the dispossessed white working class with thundering rhetoric. During mass rallies at stadiums shrouded with huge flags in Cincinnati, Cleveland, Toledo, and St. Louis, the president denounces "those tired Europeans" at the IMF who dared dethrone "the almighty dollar" as the global reserve currency. As his attack rolls through a roster of ethnic enemies culminating in the "tricky Chinese" who "stole our technology" and then "shipped American jobs to Asia," the crowd leaps to its feet for full-throated shouts of "USA! USA!" He demands respect for American authority and threatens military retaliation or economic reprisal. With its alliances in tatters and its military demoralized by defeat in Afghanistan, the world pays next to no attention while the American Century ends in silence.

Military Misadventure: Present Situation

As its economic and diplomatic influence fades, Washington's ever-increasing reliance on a military response to challenges creates countless opportunities for setbacks that might damage its global stature. However counterintuitive, as their power wanes, empires often plunge into ill-advised military misadventures, providing countless possibilities for defeat or even disaster. This phenomenon is known among historians of empire as "micro-militarism" and seems to involve psychologically compensatory efforts to salve the sting of retreat or defeat by occupying new territories, however briefly or catastrophically.[56]

While rising empires are often judicious, even rational in their application of armed force for conquest and control of overseas dominions, fading empires are inclined to ill-considered displays of power, dreaming of bold military masterstrokes that would somehow recoup lost prestige and power. Often irrational even from an imperial point of view, these micromilitary operations can yield hemorrhaging expenditures or humiliating defeats that only accelerate the process already under way.

Embattled empires through the ages have suffered an arrogance that drives them to plunge ever deeper into military misadventures until defeat becomes debacle. In 413 BCE, a weakened Athens sent two hundred ships full of soldiers to the slaughter in Sicily. In 1921, a dying imperial Spain dispatched twenty thousand troops to be massacred by Berber guerrillas in Morocco. In 1956, a fading British Empire destroyed its prestige by attacking Egypt's Suez Canal. And in 2001 and 2003, the United States occupied Afghanistan and invaded Iraq, creating client regimes that were soon battered by resurgent Islamic rebels. With the hubris that marks empires over the millennia, Washington has extended its commitment to the pacification of Afghanistan indefinitely, courting disasters large and small in this guerilla-infested, nuclear-armed graveyard of empires.

Military Misadventure: Scenario 2020

So irrational, so unpredictable is "micro-militarism" that seemingly fanciful scenarios are soon outpaced by actual events. With the US military stretched thin from North Africa to Japan and tensions rising in Israel, Syria, and the

Koreas, possible combinations for a disastrous military crisis abroad are multifold. So let's just pick one possible scenario:

It's late spring 2020 and a drawn-down US garrison in the city of Kandahar in southern Afghanistan is unexpectedly overrun by an ad hoc alliance of Taliban and Islamic State guerrillas. While US aircraft are grounded in a blinding sandstorm, the guerrillas summarily execute their American captives, filming the gruesome event for immediate upload on the Internet. Speaking to an international television audience, President Trump thunders against "disgusting Muslim murderers" and swears he will "make the desert sands run red with their blood." In fulfillment of that promise, an angry American theater commander sends B-1 bombers and F-35 fighters to demolish whole neighborhoods of Kandahar believed to be under Taliban control. In an aerial coup de grâce, AC-130U "Spooky" gunships then rake the rubble with devastating cannon fire. The civilian casualties are beyond counting.

Soon, mullahs are preaching jihad from mosques across Afghanistan. Afghan army units, long trained by American forces to turn the tide of the war, begin to desert en masse. In isolated posts across the country, clusters of Afghan soldiers open fire on their American advisers. Meanwhile, Taliban fighters launch a series of attacks on scattered US garrisons, sending American casualties soaring. In scenes reminiscent of Saigon in 1975, US helicopters rescue American soldiers and civilians from rooftops in Kabul and Kandahar.

Meanwhile, angry over the massive civilian casualties in Afghanistan, the anti-Muslim diatribes tweeted almost daily from the Oval Office, and the years of depressed energy prices, OPEC's leaders impose a harsh new oil embargo aimed at the United States and its allies. With refineries running dry in Europe and Japan, the world economy trembling at the brink of recession, and gas prices soaring across the country, Washington flails about for a solution. The first call is to NATO, but the alliance is dysfunctional after four years of President Trump's erratic diplomacy. Even the British, alienated by his inattention to their concerns, rebuff appeals for support.

Facing an uncertain reelection in November 2020, the Trump White House makes its move, sending marines and special operations forces to seize oil ports in the Persian Gulf. Flying from the Fifth Fleet's base in Bahrain, navy SEALs and army rangers occupy the Ras Tanura refinery in Saudi Arabia, the ninth largest in the world; Kuwait's main oil port at Shuaiba; and Iraq's at Umm Qasr. Simultaneously, the light carrier USS *Iwo Jima* steams south at the head of a task force that launches helicopters delivering six thousand special forces to seize the al-Ruwais refinery in Abu Dhabi, the world's fourth largest, and the megaport at Jebel Ali in Dubai, a twenty-square-mile complex so massive that troops can only occupy the oil facilities.

From its first hours, the operation goes badly wrong. The troops seem lost inside the unmapped maze of pipes that honeycomb the oil ports. The refinery staff prove stubbornly uncooperative, sensing that the occupation will be short-lived. On day two, Iranian Revolutionary Guard commandos, who had been training for this moment since the breakdown of the nuclear accord, storm ashore at the Kuwaiti and Emirati refineries with remote-controlled charges. Unable to use their superior firepower in such a volatile environment, American troops are reduced to firing futile bursts at the departing speed boats as oil storage tanks and gas pipes explode spectacularly.

Three days later, as the USS *Gerald Ford* approaches an Iranian island, over a hundred speedboats suddenly appear, swarming the carrier in a practiced pattern of high-speed crisscrosses. Every time lethal bursts from the carrier's MK-38 chain guns rip through the lead boats, another pair emerges from the flames to come closer and closer. Concealed by clouds of smoke, one reaches an undefended spot beneath the conning tower near enough for a revolutionary guardsman to attach a magnetic charge to the hull with a fateful click. With a deafening roar, a gaping hole erupts at the waterline, crippling the carrier and forcing the Pentagon to withdraw its capital ships from the Persian Gulf.

As black clouds billow skyward from the Gulf's oil ports and diplomats rise at the UN to bitterly denounce American actions, commentators worldwide reach back to the 1956 debacle that marked the end of the British Empire to brand this "America's Suez."

World War III: Present Situation

After a quarter century as the world's unchallenged hegemon, Washington and its national security mandarins have only recently been forced to face the possibility of a major global war, a World War III if you will.

In the summer of 2010, military tensions between the United States and China began to rise in the Western Pacific, previously considered an American "lake." Just as Washington once played upon its alliance with London to appropriate much of Britain's global power after World War II, so China was now using the profits from its export trade with the United States to fund a sustained expansion of its military, eventually enabling a challenge to American dominion over the waterways of Asia and the Pacific. In 2016, China's actual military budget was about $219 billion, already approaching half the

US appropriation of $522 billion, and its defense spending was on track to surpass America's around 2040.[57]

With its growing resources, Beijing has been laying claim to a maritime arc of islands and waters from Korea to Indonesia long dominated by the US Navy. In August 2010, after Washington expressed a "national interest" in the South China Sea and conducted naval exercises there to reinforce that claim, Beijing's *Global Times* responded angrily that "the U.S.-China wrestling match over the South China Sea issue has raised the stakes in deciding who the real future ruler of the planet will be."[58] Four years later, Beijing escalated its territorial claim to these waters, building a nuclear submarine facility on nearby Hainan Island,[59] and accelerating its dredging of seven artificial atolls for military bases in the Spratly Islands.[60] When the Permanent Court of Arbitration at The Hague ruled, in 2016, that these atolls gave it no territorial claim to the surrounding seas, Beijing's Foreign Ministry dismissed the decision out of hand, effectively ending the prime nonmilitary means of resolving this conflict.[61]

To counter China's presence on the high seas, the Pentagon began sending a succession of carrier groups on "freedom of navigation" cruises into the South China Sea.[62] More broadly, it began shifting much of its air and sea assets to a string of bases from Japan to Australia in a bid to strengthen America's strategic position along the Asian littoral.

Simultaneously, China has conducted what the Pentagon called in a 2010 report "a comprehensive transformation of its military," focused on improving the ability of the People's Liberation Army (PLA) "for extended-range power projection." With the world's "most active land-based ballistic and cruise missile program," Beijing could target "its nuclear forces throughout . . . most of the world, including the continental United States." Meanwhile, accurate missiles provide the PLA with "the capability to attack ships, including aircraft carriers, in the western Pacific Ocean." China had begun to contest US dominion over cyberspace and space, with plans to dominate "the information spectrum in all dimensions of the modern battlespace."[63]

China's army has developed a sophisticated cyberwarfare capacity through its Unit 61398 and allied contractors that "increasingly focus . . . on companies involved in the critical infrastructure of the United States—its electrical power grid, gas lines, and waterworks." After identifying that unit as responsible for a series of intellectual property thefts, Washington took the unprecedented step, in 2013, of filing criminal charges against five active-duty Chinese cyber officers.[64]

By 2012, China had also launched fourteen satellites into "a hybrid constellation in three kinds of orbits," with "more satellites in high orbits and . . . better anti-shielding capabilities than other systems." Four years later, Beijing announced that it was on track to "cover the whole globe with a constellation of thirty-five satellites by 2020," becoming the world's second power after the United States with a fully operational satellite system.[65] Playing catch-up to match the sheer scale of Washington's network, in August 2016 China achieved a bold breakthrough in communications security by launching the world's first quantum satellite that transmits photons, believed to be "invulnerable to hacking," rather than relying on more easily compromised radio waves.[66]

To check China in these two new domains of military conflict, Washington has been building a new digital defense network of advanced cyberwarfare capabilities and air/space robotics. Between 2010 and 2012, the Pentagon extended drone operations into the exosphere with successful tests of the X-37B unmanned space shuttle, creating an arena for future warfare unlike anything that has gone before.[67] By 2020, if all goes according to plan, the Pentagon will field that triple-tier shield of unmanned drones—reaching from stratosphere to exosphere, armed with agile missiles, linked by an expanded satellite system, and operated through robotic controls.

Weighing this balance of forces, the RAND Corporation's 2016 study *War with China* projected that, by 2025, "China will likely have more, better, and longer-range ballistic missiles and cruise missiles; advanced air defenses; latest generation aircraft; quieter submarines; more and better sensors; and the digital communications, processing power, and C2 [cyber security] necessary to operate an integrated kill chain." In the event of all-out war, RAND suggested the United States would suffer heavy losses to its carriers, submarines, missiles, and aircraft from Chinese strategic forces, and would sustain "degradation" of its computer systems and satellites from "improved Chinese cyberwar and ASAT [anti-satellite] capabilities." Even though American forces would counterattack with "modernized versions of the . . . force-projection capabilities on which it has relied for some decades," their "growing vulnerability" means Washington's victory would not be certain. There might well be no "clear winner" in such a conflict.[68]

Make no mistake about the weight of these words. For the first time, a top strategic think tank, closely aligned with the US military and long famous for its influential strategic analysis, was seriously contemplating a major war with China that the United States would not win.

World War III: Scenario 2030

The technology of space and cyberwarfare is so new, so untested that even the most outlandish scenarios currently concocted by strategic planners may soon be superseded by a reality still hard to conceive. In its 2015 nuclear war exercise, the Air Force Wargaming Institute used sophisticated computer modeling and coding technologies to imagine "a 2030 scenario where the Air Force's fleet of B-52s . . . upgraded with . . . improved standoff weapons" patrol the skies ready to strike. Simultaneously, "shiny new intercontinental ballistic missiles" stand by for launch. Then, in a bold tactical gambit, B-1 bombers with "full Integrated Battle Station (IBS) upgrade" slip through enemy defenses for a devastating nuclear strike.[69]

That scenario was no doubt useful for air force planners, but it does not say much about the future of US global power, absent a decisive thermonuclear war. Similarly, the RAND *War with China* study compared military capacities across the board, without any assessment of the particular strategies that either side might use to its advantage. In its 2017 report *Global Trends 2035*, the National Intelligence Council was somewhat more specific about the way future wars will be fought. Instead of a direct military clash that seeks to defeat an enemy by overwhelming its forces on the battlefield, emerging forms of warfare will employ "remote strikes using standoff precision weapons, robotic systems, and information attacks" to achieve victory by destroying or disrupting "critically important . . . infrastructure . . . on which the enemy military depends."[70]

We might not have access to the Wargaming Institute's computer modeling, RAND's renowned analytical capacity, or the Intelligence Council's limitless resources, but we can carry the unblinking realism of these think tanks one step further by imagining a future conflict against China with an unfavorable outcome for America. As the dominant power, Washington must spread its defense across all military domains, making its strength, paradoxically, a source of weakness. As the challenger, China has the asymmetric advantage of identifying and exploiting a few strategic flaws in Washington's otherwise overwhelming military superiority. Beijing is probably decades away from matching the full might of Washington's global military, but it could, through a combination of cyberwar, space warfare, and supercomputing, find ways of crippling US military communications and thus blinding its strategic forces. So, here's one possible strategic scenario for World War III:

It's 11:59 p.m. on a Thanksgiving Thursday in 2030. For months, tensions have been mounting between Chinese and US Navy patrols in the South China Sea. Washington's attempts at using diplomacy to restrain China have proven an embarrassing failure among longtime allies with NATO crippled by years of diffident American support, Britain now a third-tier power, Japan functionally neutral, and other international leaders cool to Washington's concerns after suffering years of its cyber-surveillance. With the American economy too diminished for effective imposition of sanctions, Washington plays the last card in a weak hand, deploying six of its remaining eight carrier groups to the Western Pacific.

Instead of intimidating China's leaders, the move makes them more bellicose. Flying from air bases in the Spratly Islands, their jet fighters soon begin buzzing US Navy ships in the South China Sea, while Chinese frigates play chicken with two of the aircraft carriers on patrol, crossing ever closer to their bows.

Then tragedy strikes. At 4:00 a.m. on a foggy October night, the massive carrier USS *Gerald Ford* slices through aging Frigate-536 *Xuchang*, sinking the ship with its entire crew of 165. In one of history's eerie echoes, the accident occurs just miles from where an Australian aircraft carrier, the HMAS *Melbourne*, had cut off the bow of an American destroyer, the USS *Frank E. Evans*, in 1969, killing seventy-four American sailors. But this time it wasn't close allies facing the need to cover up an embarrassing incident. Instead of admitting that its frigate's captain was at fault, Beijing demands an apology and reparations. When Washington refuses, China's fury comes fast.

At the stroke of midnight on Thanksgiving eve, as cyber-shoppers storm the portals of Best Buy for deep discounts on the latest consumer electronics from Bangladesh, navy personnel staffing the Space Surveillance Telescope at Exmouth, Western Australia, choke on their coffee as their panoramic screens of the southern sky suddenly blip to black.[71] Thousands of miles away at the US Cyber Command operations center in Texas, air force technicians detect malicious binaries that, though hacked anonymously into American weapons systems worldwide, show the distinctive digital fingerprints of China's People's Liberation Army.[72]

In what historians would later call the "Battle of Binaries," CyberCom's supercomputers launch their killer counter-codes. While a few of China's provincial servers lose routine administrative data, Beijing's quantum satellite system, equipped with super-secure photon transmission, proves impervious to hacking. Meanwhile, an armada of bigger, faster supercomputers slaved to Shanghai's cyberwarfare Unit 61398 blasts back with impenetrable logarithms of unprecedented subtlety and sophistication, slipping into the US satellite system through its antiquated microwave signals.

The first overt strike is one nobody at the Pentagon predicted. Flying at 60,000 feet above the South China Sea, several US carrier-based MQ-25 Stingray drones, infected by Chinese malware, suddenly fire all the pods beneath their enormous delta wingspans, sending dozens of lethal missiles plunging harmlessly into the ocean below, effectively disarming these formidable weapons.[73]

Determined to fight fire with fire, the White House authorizes a retaliatory strike. Confident their satellite system is impenetrable, air force commanders in California transmit robotic codes to a flotilla of X-37B space drones, orbiting 250 miles above the earth, to launch their Triple Terminator missiles at several of China's communication satellites.[74] There is zero response. In near panic, the navy orders its Zumwalt-class destroyers to fire their lethally accurate RIM-174 killer missiles at seven Chinese satellites in nearby geostatial orbits, but launch codes suddenly prove inoperative.[75]

As Beijing's viruses spread uncontrollably throughout the US satellite architecture, the country's second-rate supercomputers fail to crack the Chinese malware's devilishly complex code. With stunning speed, GPS signals crucial to the navigation of American ships and aircraft worldwide are compromised.

Across the Pacific, US Navy deck officers scramble for their sextants, struggling to recall those long-ago navigation classes at Annapolis. Steering by sun and stars, carrier squadrons abandon their stations off the China coast and head for the safety of Hawaii.

An angry president orders a retaliatory strike on a secondary Chinese target, Longpo Naval Base at Hainan Island. Within minutes, the commander of Andersen Air Base on Guam launches a battery of super-secret X-51 "Waverider" hypersonic missiles that soar to 70,000 feet and then streak across the Pacific at 4,000 mph—far faster than any Chinese fighter or air-to-air missile.[76] Inside the White House situation room the silence is stifling as everyone counts down the thirty short minutes before the tactical nuclear warheads are to slam into Longpo's hardened submarine pens, shutting down Chinese naval operations in the South China Sea. Midflight the missiles suddenly nose-dive into the Pacific.

In a bunker buried deep beneath Tiananmen Square, President Xi Jinping's handpicked successor Sun Zhengcai, even more nationalistic than his mentor, is outraged that Washington would attempt a tactical nuclear strike anywhere on Chinese soil. When China's State Council wavers at the thought of open war with America, the president quotes the ancient strategist Sun Tzu: "Victorious warriors win first and then go to war, while defeated warriors go to war first and then seek to win." Amid applause and laughter, the vote is unanimous. War it is!

Almost immediately, Beijing escalates beyond secret cyber attacks to overt acts of war. Dozens of China's next-generation SC-19 missiles lift off for strikes on key American communications satellites, scoring a high ratio of kinetic kills on these hulking units. After the Pentagon scrapped the more resilient F-6 system of dispersed, wirelessly linked components back in 2013, its communication satellites remained surprisingly vulnerable to such strikes.

Suddenly, Washington loses secure communications with hundreds of military bases and its fighter squadrons worldwide are grounded. Dozens of F-35 pilots already airborne are blinded as their helmet-mounted avionic displays go black, forcing them down to 10,000 feet for a clear view of the countryside. Without any electronic navigation, they must follow highways and landmarks back to their base like bus drivers in the sky.

Midflight on regular patrols around the Eurasian landmass, two dozen RQ-180 surveillance drones suddenly become unresponsive to satellite-transmitted commands and fly aimlessly toward the horizon, crashing when their fuel is exhausted. With surprising speed, the United States loses control of what its air force has long called the ultimate high ground.[77]

With intelligence flooding the Kremlin about crippled American capacity, Moscow, still a close Chinese ally, sends a dozen Severodvinsk-class nuclear submarines beyond the Arctic Circle bound for permanent, provocative patrols between New York and Newport News. Simultaneously, a half-dozen Grigorovich-class missile frigates from Russia's Black Sea fleet, escorted by an undisclosed number of attack submarines, steam for the western Mediterranean to shadow the US Sixth Fleet.

Within a matter of hours, Washington's strategic grip on the axial ends of Eurasia—the keystone to its global dominion for the past eighty-five years—is broken. Every weapon begets its own nemesis. Just as musketeers upended mounted knights, tanks smashed trenchworks, and dive bombers sank battleships, so China's superior cybercapability had blinded America's once-dominant system of communication satellites, giving it victory in this war of microwave-linked militaries. Without a single combat casualty on either side, the superpower that dominated the planet for nearly a century is defeated in World War III.

Climate Change: The Current Situation

Whatever the future might hold for any of these scenarios, there is one game changer hovering just over the horizon that will have an undeniable impact on the world and America's place in it: the devastating consequences of climate change. Unlike the other scenarios, climate change is on such a clear scientific trajectory that there is no need for speculation about its impact. All we need to do is add up the numbers and reflect upon what such damage and disruption might mean for the United States, if not by 2030, then almost certainly by 2040.

The thousands of scientists who contribute their research to the Intergovernmental Panel on Climate Change (IPCC), a UN body that won the Nobel Peace Prize in 2007, have produced four periodic assessments over the past quarter century that offer a dismal prospect for the planet's future. In their latest 2014 report, IPCC scientists stated that the "warming of the climate system is unequivocal" and would be marked, if rigorous limits on the emissions of greenhouse gases into the atmosphere were not instituted, by a rise in global mean temperature by the year 2100 of 3.7° to 4.8°C (or 6.6° to 8.6°F), with "the likelihood of severe, pervasive, and irreversible impacts for people and ecosystems."[78]

By the end of the twenty-first century, in other words, such marked warming will have serious and undoubtedly devastating consequences for all humans who live on this planet. With a likely temperature increase of 4.0°C or more, the world faces, says the IPCC, "large risks to food security and compromised normal human activities, including growing food or working outdoors in some areas for parts of the year due to the combination of high temperature and humidity." More specifically, "a large fraction of terrestrial, freshwater and marine species faces increased extinction risk"; carbon stored in the biosphere will mean "deforestation and ecosystem degradation"; rising sea levels will bring coastal "submergence, flooding and erosion"; and inland populations will experience "water scarcity" or "major river floods." In addition to these negative long-term trends, climate change will also bring population displacement from "extreme weather events, such as floods and droughts," along with "emerging hotspots of hunger" and increased "risks of violent conflict."[79] Giving these abstractions real meaning, local universities have advised Boston's mayor that a "worst-case scenario" for polar ice melt would raise sea levels by ten feet in 2100, putting 30 percent of the city permanently under water.[80]

As grave as all this will be for life on the planet, the year 2100 is at least four generations into the future—simply too far away to feel meaningful for many Americans. Immersed in the challenges of daily life, most people can at best plan for events a couple of decades ahead, when their infant child is in college or they are retired. So it might be more realistic to ask what climate change could mean for American society and a wider world circa 2040—a question the National Intelligence Council tried to answer in two major reports.

From a consensus of scientific models, the council warned, in a September 2016 analysis, that climate change would, within twenty years, bring "increasingly disruptive extreme weather events" like "floods, droughts, cyclones, and heat waves" leading to "famine, supply chain breakdown, or damage to infrastructure." In its *Global Trends 2035* report released a few months later, the council predicted that accelerating climate change will deliver a devilish mix of storm surges, food shortages from soil degradation, "extreme weather events such as heat waves, droughts, and floods," and the "spread of human and animal infectious diseases." While the global commons of arable land, adequate food, and clean water are being squeezed by climate change, world population will expand by 20 percent from 7.3 billion in 2016 to 8.8 billion by 2035. Among the "vulnerable populations in Africa, Asia, and the Middle East," those "struggling to survive such disruptions could . . . turn violent, migrate . . . or die." By 2050, environmental change will displace at least 200 million people, unleashing mass migrations.[81]

Although research on "political and security outcomes is still sparse," the council found that recent events reveal a number of "pathways" that would impact on the international security environment in the future. In 2014, Nigeria's president sent troops to quell violence between farmers and herders fighting over "dwindling well water." A year later, the first "hurricane-strength storm . . . in recorded history" struck war-torn Yemen, bringing rains that bred desert locust swarms, which, in turn, threatened to devastate its agriculture. At the same moment, insurgents in Mali used "deepening desertification, worsened by persistent drought," to recruit fighters through a program of "food for jihad." Meanwhile, the surprisingly quick warming of the Arctic regions threatens to rupture the Russia–China oil pipeline that runs over melting permafrost and also to spark friction between Russia and Canada over control of the Arctic shelf. In the developed world, Europe's 2003 heat wave, the hottest in 350 years, killed more than seventy thousand and Russia's sizzling summer of 2010 caused eleven thousand deaths in Moscow alone. Australia's 2014 hot spell was the longest in its recorded history. Two leading European insurance companies, Lloyd's and Allianz, predict that "climate-change-driven losses" are soaring and could reduce capital for economic growth. At the end of 2016, climate scientists were startled that it was the third year in a row with record-breaking temperatures, with the planet warming by a half-degree Fahrenheit in just three years. These trends, reported the *New York Times*, confirmed earlier scientific predictions about escalating climate change, including a projected sea-level rise of 15 to 20 feet that would submerge many of the world's coastal cities "without heroic efforts to fortify them."[82]

In the United States, the national security implications of even a gradual intensification of climate change over the next two decades, said the Intelligence Council, "could be severe." Broader systemic effects will be seen in "more acidic oceans, degraded soil and air-quality, and rising sea levels, resulting in sustained direct and indirect effects on U.S. national security." The council suggested that specific changes might include "a massive release of gases from melting permafrost, persistent megadroughts, extreme shifts in critical ecosystems, emerging reservoirs of new pathogens, or the sudden breakup of immense ice sheets." But the council's two reports seem to avoid any details about what the fiscal costs or social consequences of all this might be.[83] "I saw the effects of climate change firsthand in our northernmost state, Alaska," said President Obama, offering some vivid details at the Paris climate conference in 2015, "where the sea is already swallowing villages and eroding shorelines; where permafrost thaws and the tundra burns; where glaciers are melting at a pace unprecedented in modern times."[84]

Without going north to Alaska, Obama could have cited changes closer to home along the Atlantic and Gulf coastlines where iconic cities hug the shore, vulnerable to steadily rising seas and worsening storm surges. Hurricane Katrina's flooding socked New Orleans for $40 billion in 2005, while Hurricane Sandy did at least $50 billion of damage to New York City in 2012. As for south Florida, home to over five million people, its highest natural elevation is a ridge only twelve-feet high, and most of Miami is less than five feet above sea level. Many of its streets already flood waist-deep after every rainfall, and some hurricane in the near future is going to bring a devastating tidal surge to that city. By 2016, what is now called "sunny-day flooding" was already common along the East Coast from Norfolk, Virginia, to Fort Lauderdale, Florida, prompting government scientist William Sweet to say of this threat: "It's not a hundred years off—it's now."[85]

Sooner or later, the costs of such damage for the American economy could be crippling. In the words of the Army Corps of Engineers, the vulnerable coastal areas are "economic drivers for the whole country," with ports handling $800 billion of goods annually and "estuarine areas" accounting for 49 percent of gross domestic product. But the Corps of Engineers, like the Intelligence Council, stopped short of detailing what the full scope of climate-related damage might add up to. While avoiding any total for protecting the full 3,600 miles of the Atlantic and Gulf coastlines, the corps has estimated the cost of "storm damage risk reduction" for just one hundred miles of Louisiana shoreline at $2.2 billion.[86]

Offering some broader estimates, the Union of Concerned Scientists has estimated that the insured value of property in Florida's threatened coastal counties is $2.9 trillion. In 2012, as insurance companies were already starting to back away from this and other at-risk areas, the National Flood Insurance Program had issued 5.6 million policies covering $1.25 trillion in assets, while only taking in $3.6 billion in premiums and racking up a $20 billion debt—an uneconomic and possibly unsustainable imbalance. In Virginia, for example, 60 percent of the state's population of 8.2 million, along with major defense installations like Langley Air Base and the Norfolk shipyards, are found within a tidal shoreline that faces eighteen inches of sea-level rise over the next twenty years and massive costs for remediation.[87]

While such a two-decade rise could probably be managed, storm surges, like the one that made Sandy so destructive for the New Jersey shoreline and New York City, will likely do serious damage to low-lying cities along the Atlantic and Gulf Coasts—Boston, New York, Baltimore, Norfolk, Savannah, Jacksonville, Miami, Tampa, and New Orleans. A real estate analytics firm estimated that, as of 2016, there were 6.8 million homes along the eastern coasts vulnerable to "hurricane storm surge inundation" with total reconstruction costs of $1.5 trillion. Since these cities are engines of economic growth, the country will face several trillion dollars in costs for the elaborate engineering projects to build barriers—estimated at $30 billion for a network of seawalls around New York City, $5 billion for a fifteen-foot-high "sea belt" structure for Boston, and $100 to $200 million for some eighty-eight smaller metropolitan areas like Stamford, Connecticut.[88] And all of this will simply put off the inevitable as the waters continue to rise.

And keep in mind that this represents only one aspect of the future impact and costs of climate change. Imagine, for instance, the costs that will someday be associated with predicted megadroughts, lasting thirty-five years or longer, that could settle into the Southwest and Midwest and someday, for instance, make the city of Phoenix uninhabitable.[89]

More immediate climate changes by 2040 will likely have mingled consequences for America. With climatic zones ranging from the tropical in south Florida to the arctic in northern Alaska, the loss of arable land in the arid Southwest might be offset by an extended growing season further north. As a continental nation, the United States can also mitigate oceanic surges far more successfully than island nations like Indonesia, Japan, Ireland, and England. Even though America might weather these storms better than many nations, it will still face many trillions of dollars in outlays for prevention and repair—straining the federal budget (which was $3.5 trillion in 2016) and forcing a sustained shift in funds from foreign operations to domestic priorities. Combined with the rising social costs of an aging population, climate change mitigation will likely accelerate Washington's fiscal retreat from global hegemony.

Climate Change: Scenario circa 2040

If we pick up where the Corps of Engineers and the Intelligence Council left off, as early as 2040 such trends could prove profoundly disruptive for an American-led world order. It would, for instance, be possible to imagine a climate-change scenario for Washington's retreat that might go like this:

As natural disasters cripple governmental capacity worldwide, local conflicts over water and food erupt. Meanwhile, countless millions of rural residents are uprooted by drought and flooded lowlands, overwhelming Third World cities and sending millions of refugees trudging out of the dry zone across North Africa and the Middle East toward a well-watered Europe. Should NATO have survived these tumultuous decades, it would be forced to focus on regional security concerns, leaving the rest of the world to Washington. While states weaken even more across the Greater Middle East, insurgents gain power by organizing tribes and ethnic groups to fight for what food and water remains.

Unable to cope with a whirlwind of conflicts in Africa and Asia, Washington starts pulling military forces back into its own hemisphere, struggling to control refugees fleeing catastrophic storms in the Caribbean and dwindling harvests in Central America. Adding to the fiscal strains of an aging population, the United States will face heavy costs from wildfires in the West, recurring droughts across the continent, storm surges that periodically inundate a half-dozen major metropolitan areas, and vast engineering efforts to shore up hurricane-battered coastlines.

These trends would weaken the grip of any would-be world leader while pushing the locus of both problems and power downward within an increasingly devastated global system toward emerging regional hegemons—Istanbul in the Middle East, New Delhi in South Asia, Pretoria in southern Africa, and so on around the globe. While Washington will remain the preeminent power in North America and might retain significant influence in

Latin America as well, it would soon be forced to pull back from its chain of military bases along the Asian littoral toward a mid-Pacific defense line, anchored at Hawaii. With Beijing holding a preponderance of the planet's population and resources within the vast Eurasian continent, its world island strategy of integrated infrastructure, finance, and trade would likely make China the preeminent power on a disintegrating planet.

Without a shot fired or a single diplomatic contretemps, world power would silently shift away from Washington by sheer force of geopolitics and "extreme weather." By 2040, Beijing could emerge not as the sole superpower but rather as a primus inter pares, a first among equals, or more precisely the first among many regional hegemons on a planet in increasing chaos. But first it would still be.

A Changing World

Even if future events prove duller than any of these scenarios, every significant trend points toward a striking decline in American global power by 2030. While torture and surveillance have weakened its moral authority, Washington is also losing its grip on the instruments long essential for the exercise of hegemony—loyal subordinate elites, lethal covert operations, technological innovation, and geopolitical dominion over Eurasia. As allies worldwide adjust to China's rise, maintaining eight hundred or more overseas military bases will become politically and economically unsustainable, sooner or later forcing a staged withdrawal on a still-unwilling Washington. With both the United States and China in a race to weaponize space and cyberspace, tensions between the two powers are bound to rise, making military conflict by 2030 at least feasible, if hardly guaranteed.

Complicating matters even more, the economic, military, and technological trends outlined above will not operate in tidy isolation. As happened to European empires after World War II, these negative forces will undoubtedly prove synergistic—cascading in thoroughly unexpected ways to create crises for which Washington is likely to prove remarkably unprepared. If the worst happens and the country spins into a sudden downward spiral, Americans might well experience a generation or more of economic privation.

All of these scenarios extrapolate existing trends into the future on the assumption that the American people, blinded by decades of historically unparalleled power, cannot or will not take steps to slow the erosion of their global position. If the country is in fact on a twenty-seven-year descent from

2003 to 2030, then Washington has already frittered away more than half that time with wars that distracted Americans from long-term problems and, like water tossed onto desert sands, wasted trillions of much-needed dollars.[90]

If only thirteen years are left, then the odds of wasting this remaining time still seem high. In the aftermath of the 2016 presidential election, the country's leadership is likely to be inward looking for four or eight years, unaware of how its unconventional approach to foreign policy would damage or even dismantle the delicately balanced array of strategic forces that have sustained US hegemony for over seventy years. "This is probably what it felt like to be a British foreign service officer after World War II, when you realize, no, the sun actually *does* set on your empire," a mid-level State Department officer remarked in the muddled first months of the Trump administration. "America is over. And being part of that, when it's happening for no reason, is traumatic."[91]

The American system is flooded with corporate money meant to jam up the works. There is little suggestion that any issues of any real significance—including endless wars, a bloated national security state, the starved education system, a decaying infrastructure, and climate change—will be addressed with sufficient seriousness to assure the sort of soft landing that might maximize the country's chances in a changing world.

Yet the possibility also remains that, even at this late hour, the American people could come together—as they did during World War II or the Cold War—to build a more just society at home and a more equitable world abroad.

Europe's empires are gone and America's hegemony is going. Setting aside all the excesses and exploitation, the British Empire's century of dominance from 1815 to 1914 left behind a global economy, dozens of parliamentary democracies, and the ideal of dominion as trusteeship. Similarly, the American almost-century since 1945 has brought with it viable international institutions, global economic integration, the rule of law, the advance of human rights, the spread of democracy, a period of relative peace, and a decline of disease and world poverty.

With the ticking of history's clock, time is growing short for the United States to have anything akin to Britain's success in shaping a succeeding world order that protects its interests, preserves its prosperity, and bears the imprint of its best values. Now that the American Century is ending, we can only wonder what kind of shadow it will cast across the globe for future generations.

Acknowledgments

Any work that canvasses a topic as broad as the history of a global empire rests upon countless contributions, some remembered, many forgotten. For the latter, I apologize to anyone inadvertently overlooked. For the others, these few words are poor recompense for the rich insights you shared during this lifelong voyage of discovery.

Much of this work was written at the behest of the well-known editor Tom Engelhardt. For more than a decade now my writing days away from university have been interrupted by his phone calls, urging me to climb down from my ivory tower and share my findings with the global audience he has built for his innovative website, *TomDispatch*. At first, I was reluctant. But as one who believes in the humble footnote as the foundation for a historian's integrity, I found that Tom's practice of hyperlinking keywords to full-text sources had transformed the Internet from a repository of rumors into an authoritative medium. Instead of an audience of a dozen or less for an article in an academic journal, one of my essays for *TomDispatch* reached a readership of several hundred thousand in English, Spanish, and French. As these short essays grew into more substantial chapters for this book, both Tom and his colleague Nick Turse were careful, critical editors. For the ideas and the global audience that they have provided me, I am grateful.

During these same years, I was also working with Francisco Scarano, Mike Cullinane, and Courtney Johnson, close colleagues at the University of Wisconsin, in launching a research project on "Empires in Transition." As the project's meetings moved from Madison to Sydney and Manila to Barcelona, our network of contributors grew to some 140 scholars on four continents. At Sydney University, Warwick Anderson added imperial medicine to our ever-expanding research agenda. Our close collaborators at Pompeu Fabra University in Barcelona, Josep Fradera and Stephen Jacobson, contributed their deep knowledge of Spanish imperial history. Some of the many insights developed through these collaborations are found in these pages.

Apart from this general assistance, others helped in more specific ways. Some portions of chapter 1 appeared, in modified form, in my contributions to the two volumes *Colonial Crucible* and *Endless Empire*, which our empires research project published with the University of Wisconsin Press. Parts of chapter 2 originally appeared in essays published, with the help of my colleague Brett Reilly, in *TomDispatch* during 2010 and 2011. The brief discussion of the origins of the US surveillance state in chapter 4 was first developed at much greater length in another book for the University of Wisconsin Press, *Policing America's Empire*. My arguments in all three of these books benefited from that press's insightful publications director, Dr. Gwen Walker.

A far different version of chapter 3 appeared in the journal *Comparative Studies in Society and History* in October 2016. I am indebted to that journal's editor David Akin for some useful suggestions. In drafting chapter 6, I am grateful to Professor Eduardo Tadem of the University of the Philippines for suggesting that a close examination of the tragic massacre of Filipino troops in Mindanao could cast light on the limits of Washington's agile global strategy of drones and special operations forces. My brief account of that event was enriched by insights from my old friends Edilberto and Melinda de Jesus. During a visit to Switzerland in the summer of 2015, my wife's uncle, David Hove, kindly shared the story, recounted in chapter 7, of his monthlong drive across the vast Eurasian landmass, from Peking (Beijing) to Paris. In preparing these chapters for publication, I received generous assistance from a talented group of graduate students at the University of Wisconsin, including Erin Cantos, Joshua Gedacht, and Brett Reilly. Whenever I write, I am reminded of a deep debt to my high school English teacher, Bob Cluett, who gave a me both a love of this craft and the skills to pursue it.

Finally, on a more personal note, many of the ideas in this book were first developed in conversation at the breakfast table over the *New York Times* with my wife and partner, Mary McCoy. Not only did she help me develop these thoughts but she has sustained me through the many solitary hours that it takes to think and write. Hence, this long overdue dedication.

Madison, Wisconsin
March 2017

Notes

Introduction

1. "Edward L. Katzenbach, Jr., 55, Ex-Defense Official, Is Suicide," *New York Times*, April 24, 1974.
2. "E.L. Katzenbach, Civic Leader, Dies," *New York Times*, December 19, 1934.
3. Major Michael J. Muolo, *Space Handbook: A War Fighter's Guide to Space*. vol. 1 (Maxwell Air Force Base: Air University Press, 1998), 18; UPI, "Rocket Achieves 3 Orbits in Test," *New York Times*, February 12, 1965; UPI, "Air Force Rocket Put into 4 Orbits," *New York Times*, May 7, 1965; UPI, "Titan 3-C Orbits Satellites for Pentagon Radio Net," *New York Times*, June 17, 1966; UPI, "U.S. Plugs 8 Radio Gaps with Single Rocket Shot," *New York Times*, January 19, 1967.
4. "Edward L. Katzenbach, Jr.," *New York Times*, April 24, 1974; personal communication from E. Thomas Katzenbach, son of Edward L. Katzenbach Jr., March 6, 2017; Douglas Martin, "Nicholas Katzenbach, 90, Dies," *New York Times*, May 10, 2012.
5. E. Lawrence Katzenbach 3d, "Sonnet," *New York Times*, March 24, 1976.
6. Roy L. Swank, MD, and Walter E. Marchand, MD, "Combat Neuroses, Development of Combat Exhaustion," *Archives of Neurology and Psychiatry* 55 (March 1946): 236–47.
7. See Nina S. Adams and Alfred W. McCoy, eds., *Laos: War and Revolution* (New York: Harper & Row, 1970).
8. The 34 percent figure was cited in US Executive Office of the President, Special Action Office for Drug Abuse Prevention, *The Vietnam Drug User Returns: Final Report* (Washington, DC: US Government Printing Office, 1974), ix, 29. See also Alfred W. McCoy, *The Politics of Heroin: CIA Complicity in the Global Drug Trade* (New York: Lawrence Hill Books, 2003), 258.
9. Tom Tripodi, *Crusade: Undercover against the Mafia and KGB* (New York: Brassey's Inc., 1993).
10. Frances Stonor Saunders, *The Cultural Cold War: The CIA and the World of Arts and Letters* (New York: New Press, 1999), 136–37; David H. Price, *Cold War Anthropology: The CIA, the Pentagon, and the Growth of Dual Use Anthropology* (Durham, NC: Duke University Press, 2016), 243.
11. Saunders, *The Cultural Cold War*, 210–11, 234–41; Deborah Davis, *Katherine the Great: Katherine Graham and* The Washington Post (New York: Harcourt Brace

Jovanovich, 1979), 129–31.

12. Carl Bernstein, "The CIA and the Media," *Rolling Stone*, October 20, 1977; Lance Morrow, "44 Years Later, a Washington, D.C. Death Unresolved," *Smithsonian Magazine*, December 2008, www.smithsonianmag.com/history/44-years-later-a-washington-dc-death-unresolved-93263961; Don Oberdorfer, "JFK Had Affair with Artist, Smoked 'Pot,' Paper Alleges," *Washington Post*, February 23, 1976; Christopher Marquis, "Cord Meyer Jr. Dies at 80; Communism Fighter at C.I.A.," *New York Times*, March 16, 2001, www.nytimes.com/2001/03/16/us/cord-meyer-jr-dies-at-80-communism-fighter-at-cia; Graeme Zielinski, "Key CIA Figure Cord Meyer Dies," *Washington Post*, March 15, 2001, www.washingtonpost.com/archive/local/2001/03/15/key-cia-figure-cord-meyer-dies/fc90ef11-4137-4582-9f01-c7c13461e1bf/.

13. Saunders, *Cultural Cold War*, 341–42.

14. Seymour M. Hersh, "C.I.A. Aides Assail Asia Drug Charge: Agency Fights Reports That It Ignored Heroin Traffic among Allies of U.S.," *New York Times*, July 21, 1972.

15. Zielinski, "Key CIA Figure Cord Meyer Dies."

16. US Department of Justice, Federal Bureau of Investigation, New Haven, Title: Alfred William McCoy, Character: Security Matter—Communist, Field Office File #: 100-207191, Date: August 14, 1972, released under Freedom of Information Request No. 341419 of November 28, 1990.

17. James M. Markham, "The Politics of Heroin in Southeast Asia," *New York Times Book Review*, September 3, 1972, 1.

18. According to a report by Vientiane correspondent John Everingham, in the weeks preceding publication of *The Politics of Heroin*, an Air America helicopter flew this district chief, a Hmong named Gair Su Yang, to a US operations base where he was "interrogated for more than an hour by a short, fat American" who asked angrily "if it's true the American helicopters carried away our opium." Afraid that "they will send a helicopter to arrest me, or Vang Pao soldiers to shoot me," the district chief said, "I didn't know if it was true or not." The CIA then released a report of the interrogation saying the district chief "denies making any statement regarding officers arriving at Long Pot to collect opium harvest for transport back to [the main CIA airbase] Long Tieng in American helicopters." See John Everingham, "Laotian District Chief Intimidated by CIA—Move Seen as Attempt to Discredit Writers and Publisher," Release #409, Dispatch News Service International, Washington, DC, August 15, 1972; John Everingham, "Let Them Eat Bombs," *Washington Monthly*, September 1972, 10–16, www.unz.org/Pub/WashingtonMonthly-1972sep-00010.

19. US Senate, Select Committee to Study Governmental Operations with Respect to Intelligence Activities, 94th Congress, 2d Session, *Foreign and Military Intelligence, Book I: Final Report* (Washington, DC: Government Printing Office, Report No. 94-755, 1976), 205, 227–33.

20. Peter Burroughs, "David Fieldhouse and the Business of Empire," in Peter Burroughs and A. J. Stockwell, eds., *Managing the Business of Empire: Essays in Honour of David Fieldhouse* (London: Frank Cass, 1998), 7.

21. Jeff Gerth and Joel Brinkley, "Marcos Wartime Role Discredited in U.S. Files," *New York Times*, January 23, 1986.

22. Alfred W. McCoy, "Coup! The Real Story Behind the February Revolt," *Veritas* (Manila), October 1986; Alfred W. McCoy, *Closer Than Brothers: Manhood at the Philippine Military Academy* (New Haven, CT: Yale University Press, 1999), chapter 7.

23. Alfred W. McCoy, "The RAM Boys," *National Midweek* (Manila), September 21, September 28, and October 12, 1988; Alfred W. McCoy, "The RAM Boys," *Philippine Daily Inquirer* (Manila), January 1–8, 1990; Alfred W. McCoy, "Philippine Military Reformists: Specialists in Torture," *Los Angeles Times*, February 4, 1990.

24. Alfred W. McCoy, "Torture at Abu Ghraib Followed CIA's Manual," *Boston Globe*, May 14, 2004, http://archive.boston.com/news/globe/editorial_opinion/oped/articles /2004/05/14/torture_at_abu_ghraib_followed_cias_manual/.

25. Alfred W. McCoy, *A Question of Torture: CIA Interrogation, from the Cold War to the War on Terror* (New York: Metropolitan Books, 2006).

26. US Senate, Senate Select Committee on Intelligence, *Committee Study of the Central Intelligence Agency's Detention and Interrogation Program: Findings and Conclusions; Executive Summary* (Washington, DC: US Senate, December 3, 2014).

27. See Alfred W. McCoy, *Policing America's Empire: The United States, the Philippines, and the Rise of the Surveillance State* (Madison: University of Wisconsin Press, 2009), 16, 39.

28. US Senate, 94th Congress, 2nd Session *Final Report of the Select Committee to Study Governmental Operations with Respect to Intelligence Activities*, book 3, 3–4, 7–8, 3–16; *Final Report of the Select Committee to Study Governmental Operations with Respect to Intelligence Activities*, book 2, 5, 15–20, 67, 77, 86–89, 98–104 (Washington, DC: Government Printing Office, 1976).

29. See Alfred W. McCoy, "Welcome Home, War! How America's Wars Are Systematically Destroying Our Liberties," *TomDispatch*, November 12, 2009, www.tomdispatch.com/blog/175154/.

30. See, for example, Amy Kaplan and Donald E. Pease, eds., *Cultures of United States Imperialism* (Durham, NC: Duke University Press, 1993).

31. Alfred W. McCoy and Francisco Scarano, eds., *Colonial Crucible: Empire in the Making of a Modern American State* (Madison: University of Wisconsin Press, 2009); Alfred W. McCoy, Josep Ma. Fradera, and Stephen Jacobson, eds., *Endless Empire: Spain's Retreat, Europe's Eclipse, America's Decline* (Madison: University of Wisconsin Press, 2012).

32. Henry R. Luce, "The American Century," *Life*, February 17, 1941, 61, 64.

33. Francis Fukuyama, "The End of History?," *National Interest* 16 (Summer 1989): 3–18; James Atlas, "What Is Fukuyama Saying? And to Whom Is He Saying It?," *New York Times Magazine*, October 22, 1989, www.nytimes.com/1989/10/22/magazine/what -is-fukuyama-saying-and-to-whom-is-he-saying-it.html.

34. Office of the Director of National Intelligence, National Intelligence Council, *Global Trends 2030: Alternative Worlds* (NIC 2012-001, December 2012), i–iii, 105, www.dni.gov/files/documents/GlobalTrends_2030.pdf.

35. Adam Tooze, *The Wages of Destruction: The Making and Breaking of the Nazi Economy* (London: Penguin Books, 2007), 339, 613, 634.

36. See, for example, Will Durant and Ariel Durant, *The Lessons of History* (New York:

Simon & Schuster, 1968); Ezra F. Vogel, *Japan as Number One: Lessons for America* (Cambridge, MA: Harvard University Press, 1979); Jon Woronoff, *Japan as (Anything but) Number One* (New York: M.E. Sharp, 1990).

Chapter One: The World Island and the Rise of America

1. Joseph S. Nye Jr., *Is the American Century Over?* (Malden, MA: Polity Books, 2015), 50, 57, 114, 125–26.

2. Henry Kissinger, *World Order* (New York: Penguin Press, 2014), 247–76, 280–84, 322–27, 374; Michiko Kakutani, "Long View of History Includes Today," *New York Times*, September 8, 2014, www.nytimes.com/2014/09/09/books/in-world-order-henry-kissinger-sums-up-his-philosophy.html; James Traub, "Book Review: 'World Order' by Henry Kissinger," *Wall Street Journal*, September 5, 2014, www.wsj.com/articles/book-review-world-order-by-henry-kissinger-1409952751.

3. H. J. Mackinder, "The Geographical Pivot of History (1904)," *Geographical Journal* 170, no. 4 (December 2004): 320–21.

4. H. J. Mackinder, "The Geographical Pivot of History," *Geographical Journal* 23, no. 4 (December 1904): 434–37; H. J. Mackinder, *Democratic Ideals and Reality* (New York: Henry Holt, 1919), 79–85.

5. Mackinder, "Geographical Pivot of History," 432–34.

6. Mackinder, *Democratic Ideals and Reality*, 67.

7. Ibid., 82, 186.

8. Mackinder, "Geographical Pivot of History," 434–36.

9. Mackinder, "Geographical Pivot of History" (December 2004 reprint), 314–16.

10. Ibid., 316–20.

11. Mackinder, "Geographical Pivot of History," 435.

12. For example, the US publisher Rand McNally & Company issued its *Indexed Atlas of the World: Historical, Descriptive and Statistical* (Chicago, 1897) with a "Map of the World on Mercator's Projection" showing North and South America prominently displayed at the center and a divided Eurasia pushed to the map's margins. Throughout much of the twentieth century, the company's folding or pull-down schoolroom version, "Rand McNally's Cosmopolitan World Map," usually measuring about 30 by 50 inches, made this self-referential array the standard view of the world for millions of American schoolchildren.

13. Klaus Dodds and James D. Sidaway, "Halford Mackinder and the 'Geographical Pivot of History': A Centennial Perspective," *Geographical Journal* 170, no. 4 (December 2004): 292–97.

14. Mackinder, *Democratic Ideals and Reality*, 72–73, 110–11, 165, 171.

15. Paul Kennedy, "The Pivot of History," *Guardian*, June 19, 2004, www.theguardian.com/world/2004/jun/19/usa.comment.

16. Mackinder, *Democratic Ideals and Reality*, 78–79.

17. Zbigniew Brzezinski, *The Grand Chessboard: American Primacy and Its Geostrategic Imperatives* (New York: Basic Books, 1998), 38–39; Edmund A. Walsh, S. J., "The Mystery of Haushofer," *Life*, September 16, 1946, 107–20; Henning Heske, "Karl

Haushofer: His Role in German Politics and in Nazi Politics," *Political Geography Quarterly* 6, no. 2 (1987): 135–44.

18. Karl Haushofer, *Geopolitics of the Pacific Ocean: Studies on the Relationship between Geography and History* (Lewiston, ME: Edwin Mellen Press, 2002), 2.

19. Walsh, "Mystery of Haushofer," 108, 110, 118; Heske, "Karl Haushofer," 138–39.

20. John Darwin, *After Tamerlane: The Global History of Empire since 1405* (New York: Bloomsbury Press, 2008), 469–71.

21. Halford J. Mackinder, "The Round World and the Winning of the Peace," *Foreign Affairs* 21, no. 4 (1943): 595–605.

22. Alfred W. McCoy, "Circles of Steel, Castles of Vanity: The Geopolitics of Military Bases on the South China Sea," *Journal of Asian Studies* 75, no. 4 (2016): 989–95.

23. Ibid., 989–90.

24. Ibid., 980, 994.

25. Darwin, *After Tamerlane*, 469.

26. "Ramstein Air Force Base in Kaiserslautern, Germany: US Military Bases in Germany," MilitaryBases.com, http://militarybases.com/ramstein-air-base-air-force-base-in-kaiserslautern-germany/.

27. Jovito Salonga, *A Journey of Struggle and Hope* (Quezon City, Philippines: Regina Publishing, 2001), 445; Nick Cullather, *Illusions of Influence: The Political Economy of United States–Philippines Relations, 1942–1960* (Stanford, CA: Stanford University Press, 1994), 79–80; Stephen Rosskamm Shalom, *The United States and the Philippines: A Study of Neocolonialism* (Philadelphia: Institute for the Study of Human Issues, 1981), 63–66, 109–10; Alfredo Bengzon and Raul Rodrigo, *A Matter of Honor: The Story of the 1990–91 RP-US Bases Talks* (Manila: Anvil, 1997), 16–18, 41–42; Gerald R. Anderson, *Subic Bay: From Magellan to Mt. Pinatubo* (Dagupan, Philippines: Lazer, 1991), 76–89.

28. Darwin, *After Tamerlane*, 470–71.

29. Andrew Marshall, "Terror 'Blowback' Burns CIA," *Independent*, October 31, 1998, www.independent.co.uk/news/terror-blowback-burns-cia-1182087.html.

30. "Interview with Zbigniew Brzezinski," *Le Nouvel Observateur* (Paris), January 15–21, 1998, 76, www.voltairenet.org/article165889.html; Brzezinski, *The Grand Chessboard*, 38–39; Zbigniew Brzezinski, *Strategic Vision: America and the Crisis of Global Power* (New York: Basic Books, 2013), 130–31.

31. Kennedy, "The Pivot of History."

32. Nick Turse, "America's Secret Empire of Drone Bases: Its Full Extent Revealed for the First Time," *TomDispatch*, October 16, 2011, www.tomdispatch.com/blog/175454/tomgram%3A_nick_turse%2C_mapping_america%27s_shadowy_drone_wars; Nick Turse, "The Crash and Burn Future of Robot Warfare," *TomDispatch*, January 15, 2012, www.tomdispatch.com/archive/175489/; Eric Schmitt, "In the Skies over Iraq, Silent Observers Become Futuristic Weapons," *New York Times*, April 18, 2003, www.nytimes.com/2003/04/18/international/18PRED.html; David Cenciotti, "Future Drone's World Capital? Sigonella, Italy," *Aviationist*, February 9, 2012, http://theaviationist.com/2012/02/09/future-drones-world-capital-sigonella-italy/; Gaynor Dumat-ol Daleno, "New Drone to Be Deployed to Guam," *sUAS News*, March 6,

2015, www.suasnews.com/2015/03/34634/new-drone-to-be-deployed-to-guam/.

33. Tyler Rogoway, "Why the USAF's Massive $10 Billion Global Hawk UAV Is Worth the Money," *Foxtrot Alpha*, September 9, 2014, http://foxtrotalpha.jalopnik.com/why -the-usafs-massive-10-billion-global-hawk-uav-was-w-1629932000; "Northrop Grumman's Global Hawk Unmanned Aircraft Sets 33-Hour Endurance Record," Space War, March 31, 2008, www.spacewar.com/reports/Northrop_Grumman _Global_Hawk_Unmanned_Aircraft_Sets_33_Hour_Flight_Endurance_Record _999.html.

34. Eric Schmitt, "Russia Expands Submarine Fleet as Rivalry Grows," *New York Times*, April 21, 2016.

35. Kyodo, "Trump Urges Japan to Pay More to Maintain U.S. Military Bases Here," *Japan Times*, May 5, 2016, www.japantimes.co.jp/news/2016/05/05/national/politics -diplomacy/trump-urges-japan-pay-maintain-u-s-military-bases/#.WCqZbHc -LuM; Jesse Johnson, "Trump Rips U.S. Defense of Japan as One-Sided, Too Expensive," *Japan Times*, August 6, 2016, www.japantimes.co.jp/news/2016/08/06 /national/politics-diplomacy/trump-rips-u-s-defense-japan-one-sided-expensive/# .WCqW3Xc-LuM; Carol Morello and Adam Taylor, "Trump Says U.S. Won't Rush to Defend NATO Countries If They Don't Spend More on Military," *Washington Post*, July 21, 2016, www.washingtonpost.com/world/national-security/trump-says -us-wont-rush-to-defend-nato-countries-if-they-dont-spend-more-on-military /2016/07/21/76c48430-4f51-11e6-a7d8-13d06b37f256_story.html.

36. William Appleman Williams, *Empire as a Way of Life* (New York: Oxford University Press, 1980), 170, quoted in Andrew J. Bacevich, *American Empire: The Realities and Consequences of U.S. Diplomacy* (Cambridge, MA: Harvard University Press, 2002), 243.

37. Mark Twain, "To the Person Sitting in Darkness," *North American Review*, February 1901, 174–76.

38. William Graham Sumner, *War and Other Essays* (New Haven, CT: Yale University Press, 1911, 292, 322, 326, 331–32, 347–48.

39. "Remarks by the President in the State of the Union Address," The White House, Office of the Press Secretary, January 27, 2010, www.whitehouse.gov/the-press -office/remarks-president-state-union-address.

40. E. J. Dionne Jr., "Off-Message Biden Recasts the Obama Agenda," *Washington Post*, February 4, 2010.

41. Cullen Murphy, *Are We Rome? The Fall of an Empire and the Fate of America* (Boston: Houghton Mifflin, 2007), 1–6; Vaclav Smil, *Why America Is Not a New Rome* (Cambridge, MA: MIT Press, 2010), ix–xii.

42. Anne-Marie Slaughter, preface to Mr. Y, *A National Strategic Narrative* (Washington, DC: Woodrow Wilson Center, 2011), 2, www.wilsoncenter.org/sites/default /files/A%20National%20Strategic%20Narrative.pdf; Robert Kagan, "Not Fade Away: The Myth of American Decline," *New Republic*, January 10, 2012, www.tnr. com/article/politics/magazine/99521/america-world-power-declinism; Schuyler Null, "In Search of a New Security Narrative: National Conversation Series Launches at the Wilson Center," *New Security Beat*, Woodrow Wilson International Center

for Scholars, April 13, 2011, www.newsecuritybeat.org/2011/04
/in-search-of-new-security-narrative.html.

43. Niall Fergusson, *Colossus: The Price of America's Empire* (New York: Penguin Press, 2004), 14–15.

44. Ian Tyrrell, "American Exceptionalism in an Age of International History," *American Historical Review* 96, no. 4 (1991): 1031–35; Julian Go, "The Provinciality of American Empire: 'Liberal Exceptionalism' and U.S. Colonial Rule, 1898–1912," *Comparative Studies in Society and History* 49, no. 1 (2007): 74–108.

45. Richard W. Leopold, "The Emergence of America as a World Power: Some Second Thoughts," in John Braeman, Robert H. Bremner, and Everett Walters, eds., *Change and Growth in Twentieth Century America* (New York: Harper & Row, 1966), 13–14.

46. William Appleman Williams, *The Tragedy of American Diplomacy* (New York: Dell, 1962), 24, 37–38, 43–45; Bradford Perkins, "*The Tragedy of American Diplomacy*: Twenty-Five Years After," *Reviews in American History* 12, no. 1 (1984): 1–3; Bacevich, *American Empire*, 23–31.

47. William Appleman Williams, "Fred Harvey Harrington: Committed, Tough and Foxy Educator and Liberal," unpublished manuscripts, ca. 1985, Special Collections & Archives, Oregon State University, http://scarc.library.oregonstate.edu/coll /williams/manuscripts/page7.html; Williams, *The Tragedy of American Diplomacy*, 232–34, 244–59; Perkins, "*The Tragedy of American Diplomacy*," 9–11, 17n43.

48. Walter LaFeber, *The New Empire: An Interpretation of American Expansion, 1860–1898* (Ithaca, NY: Cornell University Press, 1963), 127–30, 218–29, 242–83, 285–300, 333–51.

49. For examples of their close collaboration, see Lloyd C. Gardner, Walter F. LaFeber, and Thomas J. McCormick, *Creation of the American Empire*, vol. 1, *U.S. Diplomatic History to 1901* (New York: Rand McNally & Co., 1973); and William Appleman Williams, Thomas McCormick, Lloyd C. Gardner, and Walter LaFeber, *America in Vietnam: A Documentary History* (New York: W. W. Norton & Company, 1989).

50. Arthur M. Schlesinger Jr., *The Cycles of American History* (Boston: Houghton Mifflin, 1986), 143; Joseph Fry, "From Open Door to World Systems: Economic Interpretations of Late Nineteenth Century American Foreign Relations," *Pacific Historical Review* 65, no. 2 (1996): 278.

51. Alejandro Colas, *Empire* (Cambridge: Polity Press, 2007), 5–11, 162–78.

52. Chalmers Johnson, *The Sorrows of Empire: Militarism, Secrecy, and the End of the Republic* (New York: Metropolitan Books, 2004), 5.

53. Bacevich, *American Empire*, 2–3, 232–33.

54. Fergusson, *Colossus*, 2–19.

55. Niall Fergusson, "A World without Power," *Foreign Policy*, no. 143 (2004): 32–39.

56. Paul Kennedy, *The Rise and Fall of the Great Powers: Economic Change and Military Conflict from 1500 to 2000* (New York: Vintage, 1989), 528–40.

57. Paul Kennedy, "The Eagle Has Landed," *Financial Times*, February 2, 2002.

58. Michael Ignatieff, "The Burden," *New York Times Magazine*, January 5, 2003, 22–23.

59. Charles S. Maier, *Among Empires: American Ascendancy and Its Predecessors* (Cambridge, MA: Harvard University Press, 2006), 14–15, 32–33.

60. Max Boot, "American Imperialism? No Need to Run Away from Label," *USA Today*, May 6, 2003; Andrew J. Bacevich, ed., *The Imperial Tense: Prospects and Problems of American Empire* (Chicago: Ivan R. Dee, 2003), xii–xiii.

61. Max Boot, *The Savage Wars of Peace: Small Wars and the Rise of American Power* (New York: Basic Books, 2002), xx, 351–52.

62. Eliot A. Cohen, "History and the Hyperpower," *Foreign Affairs* 83, no. 4 (July–August 2004): 56.

63. Schlesinger, *The Cycles of American History*, 141, quoted in Bacevich, *American Empire*, 30.

64. Cohen, "History and the Hyperpower," 49–63; Stockholm International Peace Research Institute, *SIPRI Yearbook, 2006: Armament, Disarmament, and International Security* (New York: Oxford University Press, 2006), 301.

65. Bacevich, *American Empire*, 244; Boot, "American Imperialism?"

66. Hannah Arendt, *The Origins of Totalitarianism* (New York: Meridian, 1958), 222–66.

67. Darwin, *After Tamerlane*, 16–17.

68. Piers Brendon, *The Decline and Fall of the British Empire* (New York: Vintage Books, 2010), 605.

69. Alfred McCoy, Francisco Scarano, and Courtney Johnson, "On the Tropic of Cancer: Transitions and Transformations in the U.S. Imperial State," in Alfred W. McCoy and Francisco Scarano, eds., *Colonial Crucible: Empire in the Making of a Modern American State* (Madison: University of Wisconsin Press, 2009), 24–26.

70. Andrew J. Bacevich, "New Rome, New Jerusalem," in Bacevich, ed., *The Imperial Tense*, 98–101.

71. Stephen Skowronek, *Building a New American State: The Expansion of National Administrative Capacities, 1877–1920* (Cambridge: Cambridge University Press, 1982), 26, 45–56; Daniel P. Carpenter, "The Multiple and Material Legacies of Stephen Skowronek," *Social Science History* 27, no. 3 (2003): 465–74; Richard R. John, "Ruling Passions: Political Economy in Nineteenth-Century America," *Journal of Public Policy* 18, no. 1 (2006): 1–20; Richard Franklin Bensel, *Yankee Leviathan: The Origins of Central State Authority in America, 1859–1877* (Cambridge: Cambridge University Press, 1990), 5–17.

72. McCoy, Scarano, and Johnson, "On the Tropic of Cancer," 3–33.

73. Paul Sutter, "Tropical Conquest and the Rise of the Environmental Management State: The Case of U.S. Sanitary Efforts in Panama," in McCoy and Scarano, eds., *Colonial Crucible*, 317–26.

74. Mariola Espinosa, "A Fever for Empire: U.S. Disease Eradication in Cuba as Colonial Public Health," in McCoy and Scarano, eds., *Colonial Crucible*, 288–96.

75. Ray Stannard Baker, "General Leonard Wood: A Character Sketch," *McClure's*, February 1900, 368–79.

76. James A. Field Jr., "American Imperialism: The Worst Chapter in Almost Any Book," *American Historical Review* 83, no. 3 (1978): 652–53.

77. George W. Baer, *One Hundred Years of Sea Power: The U.S. Navy, 1890–1990* (Stanford, CA: Stanford University Press, 1994), 21–22, 30–33; Theodore Roosevelt's

speech to the Great White Fleet, February 1909, Theodore Roosevelt Birthplace National Historic Site, www.theodorerooseveltcenter.org/Research/Digital-Library /Record.aspx?libID=o283081.

78. Gregory Barton, "Informal Empire: The Case of Siam and the Middle East," in McCoy, Fradera, and Jacobson, eds., *Endless Empire*, 247–48.

79. Fred T. Jane, *Jane's Fighting Ships: All the World's Fighting Ships* (London: William Clowes and Sons, 1900), 68–70; Clark G. Reynolds, *Navies in History* (Annapolis, MD: Naval Institute Press, 1998), 104–20.

80. Niall Fergusson, *Empire: The Rise and Demise of the British World Order and the Lessons for Global Power* (New York: Basic Books, 2002), 201–4; Brendon, *The Decline and Fall of the British Empire*, 98–99. The figure of 99,000 soldiers includes only those units serving in the regular British army that were funded by Great Britain's defense budget. Counting troops paid by India, the British Empire had a standing army of some 386,000 men. See T. A. Heathcote, "The Army of British India," in David Chandler, ed., *The Oxford History of the British Army* (Oxford: Oxford University Press, 1994), 379; *The World Almanac and Encyclopedia, 1899* (New York: Press Publishing, 1899), 342; John Darwin, email to author, August 10, 2011.

81. Brendon, *The Decline and Fall of the British Empire*, xviii–xx, 660–62.

82. Ronald Robinson, "Non-European Foundations of European Imperialism: Sketch for a Theory of Collaboration," in Roger Owen and Bob Sutcliffe, eds., *Studies in the Theory of Imperialism* (London: Longman, 1972), 138–39.

83. David M. Kennedy, "The Origins and Uses of American Hyperpower," in Andrew J. Bacevich, ed., *The Short American Century: A Postmortem* (Cambridge, MA: Harvard University Press, 2012), 16, 28–29, 32; Christopher Chase-Dunn, Andrew K. Jorgenson, Thomas Reifer, and Shoon Lio, "The Trajectory of the United States in the World-System: A Quantitative Reflection," *Sociological Perspectives* 48, no. 2 (2005): 233–54; William H. Branson, Herbert Giersch, and Peter G. Peterson, "Trends in United States International Trade and Investment since World War II," in Martin Feldstein, ed., *The American Economy in Transition* (Chicago: University of Chicago Press, 1980), 191; Walter LaFeber, "Illusions of an American Century," in Bacevich, *The Short American Century*, 163.

84. Kennedy, "The Origins and Uses of American Hyperpower," 33.

85. S. Gozie Ogbodo, "An Overview of the Challenges Facing the International Court of Justice in the 21st Century," *Annual Survey of International & Comparative Law* 18, no. 1 (2012): 93–113.

86. G. John Ikenberry, "The Future of the Liberal World Order: Internationalism after America," *Foreign Affairs* 90, no. 3 (May/June 2011): 61.

87. Elliott V. Converse III, *Circling the Earth: United States Plans for a Postwar Overseas Military Base System, 1942–1948* (Maxwell Air Force Base: Air University Press, 2005), 88, 101, 208–10.

88. Darwin, *After Tamerlane*, 470–71.

89. US Department of Commerce, *Statistical Abstract of the United States 1961* (Washington, DC: Government Printing Office, 1961), 239–44; "U.S. Has 300 Bases on Foreign Soil," *Chicago Daily Tribune*, September 11, 1954; Walter Trohan, "U.S.

Strategy Tied to World Air Superiority," *Chicago Daily Tribune*, February 14, 1955.

90. Elliott V. Converse III, *History of Acquisition in the Department of Defense*, vol. 1, *Rearming for the Cold War, 1945–1960* (Washington, DC: Historical Office, Office of the Secretary of Defense, 2012), 457–64, 490–500, 522–30; Baer, *One Hundred Years of Sea Power*, 343.

91. Ikenberry, "The Future of the Liberal World Order," 57–59.

92. John Gallagher and Ronald Robinson, "The Imperialism of Free Trade," *Economic History Review* 6, no. 1 (1953): 5.

93. Arnold J. Toynbee, *America and the World Revolutions* (New York: Oxford University Press, 1962), 105–13; "U.S. Has 300 Bases on Foreign Soil," *Chicago Daily Tribune*, September 11, 1954; Trohan, "U.S. Strategy Tied to World Air Superiority," *Chicago Daily Tribune*, February 14, 1955; James R. Blaker, *United States Overseas Basing: An Anatomy of the Dilemma* (New York: Praeger Publishers, 1990), table 2.

94. Tim Weiner, *Legacy of Ashes: The History of the CIA* (New York: Random House, 2008), 29–30, 39–40, 44–54, 61–70, 84–87, 92–105, 133–40, 142, 187–89, 321–22; William Rosenau, *US Internal Security Assistance to South Vietnam: Insurgency, Subversion and Public Order* (New York: Routledge, 2005), 18–26; David E. Sanger, "War President Takes on Riddles of Cyberwarfare," *New York Times*, December 18, 2016.

95. LaFeber, "Illusions of an American Century," 169–70; Dov H. Levin, "Partisan Electoral Interventions by the Great Powers: Introducing the PEIG Dataset," *Conflict Management and Peace Science* (August 2016): 1–19.

96. Weiner, *Legacy of Ashes*, 157, 322–23, 717; Samuel P. Huntington, *The Third Wave: Democratization in the Late Twentieth Century* (Norman: University of Oklahoma Press, 1991), 16–21; Robert Kagan, *The World America Made* (New York: Knopf, 2012), 23–24; John Charmley, *Churchill's Grand Alliance: The Anglo-American Special Relationship, 1940–1957* (New York: Harcourt Brace, 1995), 97.

97. Julian Go, *Patterns of Empire: The British and American Empires, 1688 to Present* (Cambridge: Cambridge University Press, 2011), 170.

98. The World Bank, World Development Indicators, GDP (Current US$), 1987–91, http://data.worldbank.org/indicator/NY.GDP.MKTP.CD?page=5; Chase-Dunn et al., "The Trajectory of the United States in the World-System."

99. For figures on overseas bases, see Report of the Defense Secretary's Commission, *Base Realignments and Closures* (Washington, DC: Department of Defense, 1988), 15; for fighters and missiles, US Department of the Air Force, *United States Air Force Statistical Digest, FY 1998* (Washington, DC: Government Printing Office, 1999), 92; for naval strength, US General Accounting Office, *Navy Aircraft Carriers: Cost-Effectiveness of Conventionally and Nuclear-Powered Carriers* (Washington, DC: US General Accounting Office, 1998), 4.

100. "Table 3.1: Outlays by Superfunction and Function: 1940–2009," in Office of Management and Budget, *Historical Tables, Budget of the United States Government, Fiscal Year 2005* (Washington, DC: Government Printing Office, 2004), 50, www.whitehouse.gov/sites/default/files/omb/budget/fy2005/pdf/hist.pdf.

101. Dana Priest and William M. Arkin, "Top Secret America," *Washington Post*, July 18, 19, 20, and 21, 2010.

102. Scott Shane, "New Leaked Document Outlines U.S. Spending on Intelligence Agencies," *New York Times*, August 30, 2013; Barton Gellman and Greg Miller, "'Black Budget' Summary Details U.S. Spy Network's Successes, Failures and Objectives," *Washington Post*, August 29, 2013, www.washingtonpost.com/world/national-security/black-budget-summary-details-us-spy-networks-successes-failures-and-objectives/2013/08/29/7e57bb78-10ab-11e3-8cdd-bcdc09410972_story.html; Office of the Under Secretary of Defense (Comptroller)/Chief Financial Officer, *Overview: United States Department of Defense, Fiscal Year 2013 Budget Request* (Washington, DC: Department of Defense, February 2012), 1.1, comptroller.defense.gov/Portals/45/Documents/defbudget/fy2013/FY2013_Budget_Request_Overview_Book.pdf.

103. US Special Operations Command, *USSOCOM Fact Book 2015*, 12, www.socom.mil/Documents/2015%20Fact%20Book.pdf; Bob Woodward, "Secret CIA Units Playing a Central Combat Role," *Washington Post*, November 18, 2001, www.washingtonpost.com/wp-dyn/content/article/2007/11/18/AR2007111800675.html.

104. Greg Miller and Julie Tate, "CIA Shifts Focus to Killing Targets," *Washington Post*, September 1, 2011, www.washingtonpost.com/world/national-security/cia-shifts-focus-to-killing-targets/2011/08/30/gIQA7MZGvJ_story.html; Bureau of Investigative Journalism, "Get the Data: Drone Wars," www.thebureauinvestigates.com/category/projects/drones/drones-graphs/.

105. James Risen and Eric Lichtblau, "Bush Lets U.S. Spy on Callers without Courts," *New York Times*, December 16, 2005; James Risen and Eric Lichtblau, "Extent of E-Mail Surveillance Renews Concerns in Congress," *New York Times*, June 16, 2009.

106. Thom Shanker, "San Antonio Built Community Coalition to Land Cyberwarfare Headquarters," *New York Times*, October 31, 2009; Thom Shanker and David E. Sanger, "Privacy May Be a Victim in Cyberdefense Plan," *New York Times*, June 12, 2009.

107. David Alexander, "Pentagon to Treat Cyberspace as 'Operational Domain,'" Reuters, July 14, 2011, www.reuters.com/article/2011/07/14/us-usa-defense-cybersecurity-idUSTRE76D5FA20110714.

108. Eric Schmitt and Thom Shanker, "U.S. Weighed Use of Cyberattacks to Weaken Libya," *New York Times*, October 18, 2011; David E. Sanger, "Obama Ordered Wave of Cyberattacks against Iran," *New York Times*, June 1, 2012; David E. Sanger and Mark Mazzetti, "U.S. Drew Up Cyberattack Plan in Case Iran Nuclear Dispute Led to Conflict," *New York Times*, February 17, 2016; David E. Sanger and William J. Broad, "Trump Inherits Secret Cyberwar on North Korea," *New York Times*, March 5, 2017; Joel Brenner, introduction to *America the Vulnerable: Inside the New Threat Matrix of Digital Espionage, Crime, and Warfare* (New York: Penguin Press, 2011); Ian Traynor, "Russia Accused of Unleashing Cyberwar to Disable Estonia," *Guardian*, May 16, 2007, www.guardian.co.uk/world/2007/may/17/topstories3.russia; Lolita C. Baldor, "Pentagon Takes Aim at China Cyber Threat," Associated Press, August 19, 2010, http://archive.boston.com/news/nation/washington/articles/2010/08/19/pentagon_takes_aim_at_china_cyber_threat/; Lolita C. Baldor, "U.S., China to Cooperate More on Cyber Threat," Associated Press, http://cnsnews.com/news/article/us-china-cooperate-more-cyber-threat.

109. Ann Scott Tyson, "Increased Security in Fallujah Slows Efforts to Rebuild," *Washington Post*, April 19, 2005.

110. Laura Blumenfeld, "Spurred by Gratitude, 'Bomb Lady' Develops Better Weapons for U.S.," *Washington Post*, December 1, 2007; Robert Parry, "Mobile Labs to Target Iraqis for Death," consortiumnews.com, December 13, 2007, https://consortiumnews.com/2007/121307.html.

111. Richard Tomkins, "Biometrics Play Important Role in Afghanistan," *Human Events*, February 23, 2010, www.humanevents.com/article.php?id=35735; Richard A. Oppel Jr., "NATO Apologizes for Killing Unarmed Afghans in Car," *New York Times*, April 21, 2010.

112. *The 9/11 Commission Report: Final Report of the National Commission on Terrorist Attacks on the United States* (Washington, DC: Government Printing Office, 2004), 189–90, 210–14; Richard Whittle, *Predator: The Secret Origins of the Drone Revolution* (New York: Henry Holt, 2014), 78–80, 88–89, 98–104, 147–49, 157–61, 190–94, 243–59.

113. "Air Force Report," *Air Force News*, October 27, 2008, www.youtube.com/watch?v=ureJE68i5q4&feature=related.

114. Nick Turse, "The Drone Surge: Today, Tomorrow, and 2047, " *TomDispatch*, January 24, 2010, www.tomdispatch.com/archive/175195/nick_turse_the_forty_year_drone_war.

115. Peter W. Singer, "Do Drones Undermine Democracy?," *New York Times*, January 22, 2012.

116. Elisabeth Bumiller and Thom Shanker, "War Evolves with Drones, Some Tiny as Bugs," *New York Times*, June 20, 2011.

117. HQ, USAF/XPXC, Future Concepts and Transformation Division, *The U.S. Air Force Transformation Flight Plan, 2004* (Washington, DC, 2004), 48, 53, www.iwar.org.uk/rma/resources/usaf/transformation-flight-plan-2004.pdf.

118. Air Force Space Command, *Strategic Master Plan, FY06 and Beyond* (Washington, DC, 2006), 8, 11, 36, www.wslfweb.org/docs/final%2006%20smp--signed!v1.pdf; United States Strategic Command, "Joint Functional Component Command for Space," www.stratcom.mil/factsheets/7/JFCC_Space/.

119. William J. Broad, "Surveillance Suspected as Spacecraft's Main Role," *New York Times*, May 23, 2010; Paul Rincon, "X-37B US Military Spaceplane Returns to Earth," BBC News, December 3, 2010, www.bbc.co.uk/news/science-environment-11911335; Alicia Chang, "Unmanned Air Force Space Plane Lands in Calif.," Associated Press, June 16, 2012, www.washingtontimes.com/news/2012/jun/16/unmanned-air-force-space-plane-lands-calif/.

120. Gregg Easterbrook, "Undisciplined Spending in the Name of Defense," Reuters, January 20, 2011, http://blogs.reuters.com/gregg-easterbrook/2011/01/20/undisciplined-spending-in-the-name-of-defense/; National Geospatial-Intelligence Agency, *Geospatial Intelligence Standards: Enabling a Common Vision* (Washington, DC: National Geospatial-Intelligence Agency, November 2006), www.fas.org/irp/agency/nga/standards.pdf; National Geospatial-Intelligence Agency, *National System for Geospatial Intelligence (NSG): Statement of Strategic Intent* (Washington, DC: National Geospatial-Intelligence Agency, March 2007), https://knxup2.hsdl.org/?abstract

&did=19363; Priest and Arkin, "Top Secret America," *Washington Post*, December 20, 2010.

121. Office of the Secretary of Defense, *Military and Security Developments Involving the People's Republic of China, 2010* (Washington, DC: Department of Defense, August 2010), i, 1–3, 7, 25–26, 30, 34–37; Thom Shanker, "Pentagon Cites Concerns in China Military Growth," *New York Times*, August 17, 2010; "China Launches New Global Positioning Satellite," Reuters, July 31, 2010, www.reuters.com/article /idUSTRE67005R20100801.

122. Marc Kaufman and Dafna Linzer, "China Criticized for Anti-Missile Test," *Washington Post*, January 19, 2007.

123. Tim Prudente, "In the Era of GPS, Naval Academy Revives Celestial Navigation," *Los Angeles Times*, October 25, 2015, www.latimes.com/nation/la-na-celestial -navigation-20151025-story.html.

124. Andrew Jacobs, "China's Space Program Bolstered by First Docking," *New York Times*, November 4, 2011.

Chapter Two: "Our S.O.B.s"–America and the Autocrats

1. Robert Mackey et al., "All Leaked Cables Were Made Available Online as WikiLeaks Splintered," *New York Times*, September 1, 2011.

2. Lisa Hajjar, "Suleiman: The CIA's Man in Cairo," Al Jazeera, February 7, 2011, www .aljazeera.com/indepth/opinion/2011/02/201127114827382865.html.

3. "Memorandum of Discussion at the 229th Meeting of the National Security Council, Tuesday, December 21, 1954," (Top Secret, Eyes Only) US Department of State, *Foreign Relations Series of the United States, 1952–1954*, vol. 2, *National Security Affairs, Part 2* (Washington, DC: Government Printing Office, 1984), 838.

4. "Memorandum of Discussion at the 410th Meeting of the National Security Council, Washington, June 18, 1959," in US Department of State, *Foreign Relations of the United States, 1958–1960. East Asia–Pacific Region; Cambodia; Laos.* vol. 16 (Washington, DC: Government Printing Office, 1992), 97–102; Matthew F. Holland, *America and Egypt: From Roosevelt to Eisenhower* (Westport, CT: Praeger Publishers, 1996), ix.

5. David D. Kirkpatrick, "Egypt Erupts in Jubilation as Mubarak Steps Down," *New York Times*, February 12, 2011; David E. Sanger, "When Armies Decide," *New York Times*, February 20, 2011; Jeremy M. Sharp, *Egypt: Background and U.S. Relations* (Washington, DC: Congressional Research Service, February 26, 2016), 23.

6. Embtel 496, Embassy Manama to Embassy Baghdad, July 25, 2008, WikiLeaks Cablegate Archive, Reference ID: 08MANAMA496, http://wikileaks.org/cable/2008 /07/08MANAMA496.html.

7. Robinson, "Non-European Foundations of European Imperialism," 138–39.

8. Brett Reilly, "Cold War Transition: Europe's Decolonization and Eisenhower's System of Subordinate Elites," in McCoy, Fradera, and Jacobson, eds., *Colonial Crucible*, 344–59; Frank Baldwin, "America's Rented Troops: South Koreans in Vietnam," *Bulletin of Concerned Asian Scholars* 7, no. 4 (1975): 33–40.

9. Edward Miller, *Misalliance: Ngo Dinh Diem, the United States, and the Fate of South Vietnam* (Cambridge, MA: Harvard, 2013), 1–6; Edward Geary Lansdale, *In the Midst of Wars: An American's Mission to Southeast Asia* (New York: Harper & Row, 1972), 154–58.

10. Lansdale, *In the Midst of Wars*, 171–76, 333–34.

11. McCoy, *The Politics of Heroin*, 155–61, 203–9.

12. US Department of Defense, *The Pentagon Papers: The Defense Department History of United States Decisionmaking on Vietnam*, Senator Gravel Edition, vol. 1 (Boston: Beacon Press, 1971), 242–69.

13. Pierre Asselin, *Hanoi's Road to the Vietnam War, 1954–1965* (Berkeley and Los Angeles: University of California Press, 2013), 6–7.

14. Monique Brinson Demery, *Finding the Dragon Lady: The Mystery of Vietnam's Madame Nhu* (New York: Perseus Books Group, 2013), 1; Miller, *Misalliance*, 310–11.

15. Miller, *Misalliance*, 321–23; "Interview with Lucien Conein," May 7, 1981, *Vietnam: A Television History*, Open Vault, WGBH-TV, http://openvault.wgbh.org/catalog/V_17B091E22675449F9D3E61ABF070482F.

16. Anne Blair, *Lodge in Vietnam: A Patriot Abroad* (New Haven, CT: Yale University Press, 1995), 159; David Halberstam, *The Best and the Brightest* (New York: Random House, 1993).

17. Dan Slater, *Ordering Power: Contentious Politics and Authoritarian Leviathans in Southeast Asia* (Chicago: University of Chicago, 2010), 259–62.

18. Frank Snepp, *Decent Interval* (Lawrence: University Press of Kansas, 2002), 433–38; Evan Thomas, "The Last Days of Saigon," *Newsweek*, April 30, 2000, www.newsweek.com/last-days-saigon-157477.

19. Anand Gopal, *No Good Men among the Living* (New York: Henry Holt, 2014), 30–34.

20. William R. Polk, "Legitimation Crisis in Afghanistan," *Nation*, April 19, 2010, www.thenation.com/article/legitimation-crisis-afghanistan/.

21. Catherine Lutz and Sujaya Desai, "US Reconstruction Aid for Afghanistan: The Dollars and Sense," January 5, 2015, Watson Institute for International Studies, Brown University, http://watson.brown.edu/costsofwar/files/cow/imce/papers/2015/US%20Reconstruction%20Aid%20for%20Afghanistan.pdf.

22. "Corruption Perceptions Index 2009," Transparency International, www.transparency.org/research/cpi/cpi_2009/0/.

23. James Risen, "U.S. Inaction Seen after Taliban P.O.W.'s Died," *New York Times*, July 10, 2009; Elizabeth Rubin, "Karzai in His Labyrinth," *New York Times Magazine*, August 4, 2009, www.nytimes.com/2009/08/09/magazine/09Karzai-t.html.

24. Sabrina Tavernise and Helene Cooper, "Afghan Leader Said to Accept Runoff after Election Audit," *New York Times*, October 19, 2009, www.nytimes.com/2009/10/20/world/asia/20afghan.html.

25. Ben Farmer, "US Diplomat Claims UN Tried to Gag Him," *Telegraph*, October 4, 2009, www.telegraph.co.uk/news/6259530/US-diplomat-claims-UN-tried-to-gag-him.html.

26. "Abdullah Pulls Out of Afghan Vote," BBC News, November 1, 2009, http://news.bbc.co.uk/2/hi/south_asia/8336388.stm.

27. "Afghan President Blames UN, Other Foreigners for Vote," *Washington Post*, April

1, 2010.

28. Alissa J. Rubin, "Karzai's Words Leave Few Choices for the West," *New York Times*, April 4, 2010, www.nytimes.com/2010/04/05/world/asia/05karzai.html.

29. Alissa J. Rubin and Helene Cooper, "In Afghan Trip, Obama Presses Karzai on Graft," *New York Times*, March 28, 2010, www.nytimes.com/2010/03/29/world/asia/29prexy.html.

30. Helene Cooper and Mark Landler, "U.S. Now Trying Softer Approach to Afghan Leader," *New York Times*, April 9, 2010, www.nytimes.com/2010/04/10/world/asia/10prexy.html.

31. Rajiv Chandrasekaran, "As U.S. Assesses Afghan War, Karzai a Question Mark," *Washington Post*, December 13, 2010, www.washingtonpost.com/wp-dyn/content/article/2010/12/12/AR2010121203747.html?sid=ST201012120420.

32. Matthew Rosenberg and Carlotta Gall, "Kerry Pushes for Solutions to Afghanistan's Election Crisis," *New York Times*, July 12, 2014; Ali M. Latifi and Shashank Bengali, "Delays, Fights Marred Afghanistan's Recount," *Los Angeles Times*, August 28, 2014, www.latimes.com/world/afghanistan-pakistan/la-fg-afghanistan-election-recount-delays-20140828-story.html.

33. Mujib Mashal, "Amid Afghan Chaos, Karzai Keeps Power in Play," *New York Times*, August 6, 2016.

34. Aluf Benn, "WikiLeaks Cables Tell the Story of an Empire in Decline," *Haaretz*, December 1, 2010, www.haaretz.com/wikileaks-cables-tell-the-story-of-an-empire-in-decline-1.328145.

35. "US Embassy Cables: Bomb al-Qaida Where You Want, Yemen Tells US, but Don't Blame Us If They Strike Again," *Guardian*, December 3, 2010, www.guardian.co.uk/world/us-embassy-cables-documents/225085; "US Embassy Cables: Profile of 'Intellectually Curious' but 'Notoriously Mercurial' Gaddafi," *Guardian*, December 7, 2010, www.guardian.co.uk/world/us-embassy-cables-documents/167961; "US Embassy Cables: King Hamad and Bahrain's Relationship with the US," *Guardian*, February 15, 2011, www.guardian.co.uk/world/us-embassy-cables-documents/237626.

36. Helene Cooper, "With Egypt, Diplomatic Words Often Fail," *New York Times*, January 30, 2011.

37. Scott Anderson, "Fractured Lands," *New York Times Magazine*, August 14, 2016, 13–14; Gregory A. Barton, "Informal Empire," 256–61; Geoff Simons, *Iraq: From Sumer to Saddam* (London: Macmillan, 1994), 147–89; D. K. Fieldhouse, *Western Imperialism in the Middle East 1914–1958* (New York: Oxford University Press, 2006), 69–116, 245–336.

38. Anderson, "Fractured Lands," 23–24.

39. Bryan Denton and Michael R. Gordon, "At the Mosul Front, Smoke Screens and Suicide Bombers," *New York Times*, October 18, 2016; Tim Arango, "Flee Their City or Stay? For Mosul Residents, Both Choices Seem Bleak," *New York Times*, October 22, 2016; Robert F. Worth, "Weakened ISIS Still Able to Sow Deadly Mayhem," *New York Times*, December 26, 2016; Anderson, "Fractured Lands," 23–24, 44.

40. "US Embassy Cables: Tunisia—a US Foreign Policy Conundrum," *Guardian*, December 7, 2010, www.theguardian.com/world/us-embassy-cables-documents/217138.

41. Embtel 2543, Embassy Cairo to State, December 21, 2008, WikiLeaks Cablegate Archive, Reference ID: 08CAIRO2543, http://wikileaks.org/cable/2008/12 /08CAIRO2543.html.

42. Embtel 874, Embassy Cairo to State, April 16, 2008, WikiLeaks Cablegate Archive, Reference ID: 08CAIRO783, http://wikileaks.org/cable/2008/04/08CAIRO783.html.

43. "Obama Interview: The Transcript," BBC News World Service, June 2, 2009, www.bbc.co.uk/worldservice/news/2009/06/090602_obama_transcript.shtml.

44. Hajjar, "Suleiman: The CIA's Man in Cairo."

45. Scott Shane and David D. Kirkpatrick, "Military Caught between Mubarak and Protesters," *New York Times*, February 11, 2011; Geoffey Wheatcroft, "America's Unraveling Power," *New York Times*, February 11, 2011; Scott Shane, "As Islamists Gain Influence, Washington Reassesses Who Its Friends Are," *New York Times*, July 10, 2012.

46. Anderson, "Fractured Lands," 41–42, 54; Sharp, *Egypt*, 15, 23–25.

47. Thomas L. Friedman, "Up with Egypt," *New York Times*, February 8, 2011.

48. Charlie Savage, " U.S. Diplomats Noted Canadian Mistrust," *New York Times*, December 2, 2010.

49. 09 ANKARA 1717, From: Turkey Ankara, To: Afghanistan Kabul, January 20, 2010, WikiLeaks Reference ID: 10ANKARA87_a, https://wikileaks.org/plusd/cables /10ANKARA87_a.html.

50. Scott Shane and Andrew W. Lehren, "Leaked Cables Offer Raw Look at U.S. Diplomacy," *New York Times*, November 29, 2010; "WikiLeaks: Phobias, Flamenco Dancing, and a 'Voluptuous Blonde' Nurse: Inside the Wacky World of Colonel Gaddafi," *Daily Mail*, December 8, 2010, www.dailymail.co.uk/news/article-1336783/WikiLeaks -Colonel-Gaddafis-phobias-flamenco-dancing-voluptuous-blonde-nurse.html.

51. Deptel 37561, State to Embassy Bujumbura, April 16, 2009, WikiLeaks Cablegate Archive, Reference ID: 09STATE37561, http://wikileaks.org/cable/2009/04 /09STATE37561.html.

52. Deptel 105048, State to Embassy Manama, October 8, 2009, WikiLeaks Cablegate Archive, Reference ID: 09STATE105048, http://wikileaks.org/cable/2009/10 /09STATE105048.html.

53. Associated Press, "Kyrgyzstan: Ex-Leader Convicted over Crackdown," *New York Times*, July 26, 2014; Borut Grgic, "Democratic Change It's Not," *New York Times*, May 31, 2010; Mark Landler, "Clinton Moves to Ease Tensions over Key Kyrgyz Base," *New York Times*, December 3, 2010; David Trilling, "Letter from Bishkek: How Did Kurmanbek Bakiyev's Presidency Fail?," *Foreign Affairs*, April 12, 2010, www.foreignaffairs.com/articles/russia-fsu/2010-04-12/letter-bishkek.

Chapter Three: Covert Netherworld

1. John Prados, *Safe for Democracy* (Chicago: Ivan R. Dee, 2006), 500–567; David Johnston, "Bush Pardons 6 in Iran Affair, Aborting a Weinberger Trial," *New York Times*, December 25, 1992.

2. Transparency International, "Plundering Politicians and Bribing Multinationals Undermine Economic Development, Says TI," press release, March 24, 2004,

www.transparency.org/news/pressrelease/plundering_politicians_and_bribing _multinationals_undermine_economic_develo; Michela Wrong, *In the Footsteps of Mr. Kurtz: Living on the Brink of Disaster in Mobutu's Congo* (London: Fourth Estate, 2000), 250–55; "DR Congo War Deaths 'Exaggerated,'" BBC News, January 20, 2010, news.bbc.co.uk/2/hi/africa/8471147.stm.

3. "Afghan President's Brother, Ahmad Wali Karzai, Killed," BBC News, July 12, 2011, www.bbc.co.uk/news/world-middle-east-14118884; James Risen, "Reports Link Karzai's Brother to Afghanistan Heroin Trade," *New York Times*, October 4, 2008; Dexter Filkins, Mark Mazzetti, and James Risen, "Brother of Afghan Leader Said to Be Paid by CIA," *New York Times*, October 28, 2009.

4. Elisabetta Povoledo, "Italy Gasps as Inquiry Reveals Mob's Long Reach," *New York Times*, December 12, 2014.

5. Weiner, *Legacy of Ashes*, 321.

6. UN Office for Drug Control and Crime Prevention, *World Drug Report 2000* (Oxford: Oxford University Press, 2000), 5, 12–14, 143–48; UN International Drug Control Programme, *World Drug Report* (Oxford: Oxford University Press, 1997), 132, 162–63.

7. Lieutenant Colonel Lucien Conein (former CIA operative in Saigon), interview with author, McLean, Virginia, June 18, 1971.

8. Frederick Wakeman, *Policing Shanghai, 1927–1937* (Berkeley and Los Angeles: University of California Press, 1996), 25–39; Frank J. Prial, "Secret Group Linked to Killing of French Detective," *New York Times*, July 29, 1981.

9. Bryan Christy, "Ivory Worship," *National Geographic* 222, no. 4 (October 2012): 46, 52–55; David Western, "The Undetected Trade in Rhino Horn," *Pachyderm* 11 (1989), 26–28.

10. International Opium Commission, *Report of the International Opium Commission*, vol. 2 (Shanghai: North-China Daily News & Herald, 1909), 44–66, 356; US Department of Commerce, Bureau of Foreign and Domestic Commerce, *Statistical Abstract of the United States 1915* (Washington, DC: Government Printing Office, 1916), 713.

11. David Musto, *The American Disease: Origins of Narcotic Control* (New Haven, CT: Yale University Press, 1973), 5; David T. Courtwright, *Dark Paradise* (Cambridge, MA: Harvard University Press, 1982), 9–28; Virginia Berridge and Griffith Edwards, *Opium and the People* (New Haven, CT: Yale University Press, 1987), 21–35, 274; UN Office on Drugs and Crime, *Bulletin on Narcotics: A Century of International Drug Control* (Vienna: UN, 2010), 54–58.

12. Ethan A. Nadelmann, "Global Prohibition Regimes," *International Organization* 44, no. 4 (1990): 484–513.

13. Musto, *The American Disease*, 37–52.

14. Alan A. Block, *East Side, West Side* (New Brunswick, NJ: Transaction Publishers, 1983), 133–34; Alan A. Block, "European Drug Traffic and Traffickers between the Wars," *Journal of Social History* 23, no. 2 (1989): 315–37.

15. UN Office for Drug Control and Crime Prevention, *World Drug Report 2000*, 5, 13–14, 143–48; UN International Drug Control Programme, *World Drug Report*

(1997), 162–63.

16. See Alfred W. McCoy, "The Stimulus of Prohibition," in Michael K. Steinberg, Joseph J. Hobbs, and Kent Mathewson, eds., *Dangerous Harvest: Drug Plants and the Transformation of Indigenous Landscapes* (New York: Oxford University Press, 2004), 24–111.

17. US Department of Justice, Office of Justice Program, Bureau of Justice Statistics, "Prisoners in 1988," *Bureau of Justice Statistics* (Washington, DC: Government Printing Office, 1989), 1; US Department of Justice, Office of Justice Programs, Bureau of Justice Statistics, *Sourcebook of Criminal Justice Statistics 1990* (Washington, DC: Government Printing Office, 1991), 604; Ethan A. Nadelmann, "U.S. Drug Policy," *Foreign Policy*, no. 70 (1988), 99; Adam Liptak, "U.S. Prison Population Dwarfs That of Other Nations," *New York Times*, April 23, 2008; "Editorial: Thirty-Five Years of Rockefeller 'Justice,'" *New York Times*, May 27, 2008.

18. US Cabinet Committee on International Narcotics Control, *World Opium Survey 1972* (Washington, DC, July 1972), 7, 11, A11–15; UN Office on Drugs and Crime, *2008 World Drug Report* (Vienna: UNODC, 2008), 25.

19. Christopher S. Wren, " U.N. Report Says Tens of Millions Use Illicit Drugs," *New York Times*, June 26, 1997; UN International Drug Control Programme, *World Drug Report* (1997), 31, 32, 124, 132, 162–63; UN Office for Drug Control and Crime Prevention, *World Drug Report 2000*, 5, 13–14, 70, 143–48.

20. UN Office on Drugs and Crime, *2007 World Drug Report* (Vienna: UNODC, 2007), 170.

21. US Senate, 100th Congress, 2d Session, Committee on Foreign Relations, Subcommittee on Terrorism, Narcotics and International Operations, *Drugs, Law Enforcement and Foreign Policy* (Washington, DC: Government Printing Office, December 1988), 73–75.

22. Ibid., 75.

23. Mort Rosenblum, "Hidden Agendas," *Vanity Fair*, March 1990, 120.

24. US Senate, *Drugs, Law Enforcement and Foreign Policy*, 42–49.

25. Gary Webb, "Day One: Backers of CIA-Led Nicaraguan Rebels Brought Cocaine to Poor L.A. Neighborhoods in Early '80s to Help Finance War—and a Plague Was Born," *San Jose Mercury News*, August 18, 1996; Gary Webb, "Day Two: How a Smuggler, a Bureaucrat and a Driven Ghetto Teen-ager Created the Cocaine Pipeline, and How Crack was 'Born' in the San Francisco Bay Area in 1974," *San Jose Mercury News*, August 19, 1996; Gary Webb, "Day Three: The Impact of the Crack Epidemic on the Black Community and Why Justice Hasn't Been for All," *San Jose Mercury News*, August 20, 1996. For a book-length exposition of this case, see Gary Webb, *Dark Alliance: The CIA, the Contras, and the Crack Cocaine Explosion* (New York: Seven Stories Press, 1998).

26. Between the time I downloaded this report from the CIA website on November 1, 1998, and reviewed it on October 12, 2015, these forty-eight paragraphs were replaced by a notice reading "[Paragraphs 913 to 961 removed]." See US Central Intelligence Agency, Office of the Inspector General, *Allegations of Connections between CIA and Contras in Cocaine Trafficking in the United States* (1) (96-0143-IG), vol. 2, *The Contra*

Story, pars. 913–61, www.fas.org/irp/cia/product/cocaine2/contents.html.

27. Ibid.

28. Ibid., pars. 914, 916–17, 921.

29. Ibid., par. 916.

30. Ibid., par. 922.

31. Ibid., par. 925.

32. Ibid., par. 930.

33. Ibid., par. 936.

34. Ibid., pars. 938–39, 942.

35. Ibid., par. 943.

36. Ibid., par. 927.

37. Ibid., pars. 932–33.

38. Ibid., pars. 949–50.

39. Ibid., par. 951.

40. Ibid., par. 952.

41. Ibid., par. 953.

42. Tracy L. Snell, *Correctional Populations in the United States, 1991* (Washington, DC: Government Printing Office, NCJ-147729, August 1993), 6; US Department of Justice, "Prisoners in 1988," *Bureau of Justice Statistics*, 1; US Department of Justice, *Sourcebook of Criminal Justice Statistics 1990*, 604; Nadelmann, "U.S. Drug Policy," 83–108, 99; Adam Liptak, "Inmate Count Dwarfs Other Nations," *New York Times*, April 23, 2008; "Editorial: Thirty-Five Years of Rockefeller 'Justice.'"

43. Christopher Uggen, Ryan Larson, and Sarah Shannon, "6 Million Lost Voters: State-Level Estimates of Felony Disenfranchisement, 2016," The Sentencing Project, October 6, 2016, www.sentencingproject.org/publications/6-million-lost-voters -state-level-estimates-felony-disenfranchisement-2016/.

44. National Security Archive, "The Iran-Contra Affair 20 Years On," November 24, 2006, http://nsarchive.gwu.edu/NSAEBB/NSAEBB210/.

45. Webb, "Day One"; "Editorial: Another CIA Disgrace: Helping the Crack Flow," *San Jose Mercury News*, August 21, 1996.

46. Adam Pertman, "CIA-Dug Link Stories Outrage Blacks in L.A.," *Boston Globe*, October 6, 1996; Tim Golden, "Though Evidence Is Thin, Tale of C.I.A. and Drugs Has a Life of Its Own," *New York Times*, October 21, 1996; Michael A. Fletcher, "Black Caucus Urges Probe of CIA-Contra Drug Charge," *Washington Post*, September 13, 1996; Peter Kornbluh, "The Storm over 'Dark Alliance,'" *CJR*, January/February 1997, 33–35.

47. Roberto Suro and Walter Pincus, "The CIA and Crack: Evidence Is Lacking of Alleged Plot," *Washington Post*, October 4, 1996; Golden, "Though Evidence Is Thin"; Jesse Katz, "Tracking the Genesis of the Crack Trade," *Los Angeles Times*, October 20–22, 1996.

48. Geoff Dyer and Chloe Sorvino, "$1tn Cost of Longest US War Hastens Retreat from Military Intervention," *Financial Times*, December 15, 2014, www.cnbc. com/2014/12/15/-for-us-cost-1tn.html.

49. Joel Brinkley, "Money Pit: The Monstrous Failure of US Aid to Afghanistan," *World Affairs*, January/February 2013, www.worldaffairsjournal.org/article/money-pit

-monstrous-failure-us-aid-afghanistan.

50. Michael S. Schmidt and Eric Schmitt, "U.S. Broadens Fight against ISIS with Attacks in Afghanistan," *New York Times*, February 1, 2016.

51. US Department of State, Bureau of International Narcotics Matters, *International Narcotics Control Strategy Report* (Washington, DC: Government Printing Office, 1986).

52. Lawrence Lifschultz, "Dangerous Liaison," *Newsline* (Karachi), November 1989, 49–54; David Rohde, "Warlord Rule Is Re-emerging in Some Towns," *New York Times*, November 16, 2001; James Dao, "Afghan Warlord May Team Up with Al Qaeda and Taliban," *New York Times*, May 30, 2002; Charles G. Cogan, "Partners in Time," *World Policy Journal* 10, no. 2 (1993): 76, 79.

53. US Cabinet Committee on International Narcotics Control, *World Opium Survey 1972*, 10–11, 47; US Department of State, Bureau of International Narcotics Matters, *International Narcotics Control Strategy Report, April 1994* (Washington, DC: Government Printing Office, 1994), 4; "Afghanistan," *Geopolitical Drug Dispatch*, no. 3 (January 1992): 1, 3.

54. Mathea Falco, "Asian Narcotics," *Drug Enforcement* (February 1979): 2–3; US Cabinet Committee on International Narcotics Control, *World Opium Survey 1972*, A-7, A-14, A-17; *International Narcotics Control Strategy Report* (1994), 4; William French Smith, "Drug Traffic Today—Challenge and Response," *Drug Enforcement* (Summer 1982): 2–3; *International Narcotics Control Strategy Report 1986*, 480.

55. Pakistan Narcotics Control Board, *National Survey on Drug Abuse in Pakistan* (Islamabad: Pakistan Narcotics Control Board, 1986), iii, ix, 23, 308; Zahid Hussain, "Narcopower," *Newsline* (Karachi), December 1989, 17; UN Office for Drug Control and Crime Prevention, *World Drug Report 2000*, 78, 150.

56. *International Narcotics Control Strategy Report 1986*, 480–81.

57. US Department of State, Bureau of International Narcotics Matters, *International Narcotics Control Strategy Report* (Washington, DC: Government Printing Office, March 1988), 177–78.

58. Arthur Bonner, "Afghan Rebel's Victory Garden," *New York Times*, June 18, 1986, www.nytimes.com/1986/06/18/world/afghan-rebel-s-victory-garden-opium.html.

59. Tim Golden, "Afghan Ban on Growing of Opium Is Unraveling," *New York Times*, October 22, 2001, www.nytimes.com/2001/10/22/world/a-nation-challenged-war-and-drugs-afghan-ban-on-growing-of-opium-is-unraveling.html.

60. Kathy Evans, "The Tribal Trail," *Newsline* (Karachi), December 1989, 26.

61. Barnett R. Rubin, Testimony before the Subcommittee on Europe and the Middle East, Foreign Affairs Committee, US House of Representatives, "Answers to Questions for Private Witnesses," March 7, 1990, 18–19; James Rupert and Steve Coll, "U.S. Declines to Probe Afghan Drug Trade," *Washington Post*, May 13, 1990, www.washingtonpost.com/archive/politics/1990/05/13/us-declines-to-probe-afghan-drug-trade/f07eadd2-3d25-4dd5-9e8c-05beed819769/.

62. Lawrence Lifschultz, "Inside the Kingdom of Heroin," *Nation*, November 14, 1988, 495–96.

63. Rupert and Coll, "U.S. Declines to Probe Afghan Drug Trade."

64. *Dealing with the Demon: Part II*, directed by Chris Hilton (Sydney: Aspire Films PL,

1995). Distributed in the United States by Icarus Films, http://icarusfilms.com /new97/dealing_w.html.

65. US Department of State, Bureau of International Narcotics Matters, *International Narcotics Control Strategy Report* (Washington, DC: Government Printing Office, March 2000), 56; United Nations International Drug Control Programme, *Afghanistan: Annual Survey 2000* (Islamabad: UN, 2000), 15.

66. Tim Weiner, "A Nation Challenged: Drug Trade; with Taliban Gone, Opium Farmers Return to Their Only Cash Crop," *New York Times*, November 26, 2001, www.nytimes.com/2001/11/26/world/nation-challenged-drug-trade-with-taliban -gone-opium-farmers-return-their-only.html; Daniel Balland, "Nomadic Pastoralists and Sedentary Hosts in the Central and Western Hindukush Mountains, Afghanistan," in Nigel J. R. Allan, Gregory W. Knapp, and Christoph Stadel, eds., *Human Impact on Mountains* (Lanham, MD: Rownman & Littlefield, 1988), 265–70; Nigel Allan, "Modernization of Rural Afghanistan," in Louis Dupree and Linette Albert, eds., *Afghanistan in the 1970s* (New York: Praeger Publishers, 1974), 117–18.

67. United Nations Information Service, "Opium Production in Myanmar Declines," press release (UNIS/NAR/760), August 27, 2002, www.unis.unvienna.org/unis/en /pressrels/2002/nar760.html; United Nations International Drug Control Programme, *Strategic Study #4* (Islamabad: UN, 1999), 2; *Afghanistan: Annual Survey 2000*, 23.

68. *World Drug Report 2000*, 7–11; United Nations Office for Drug Control and Crime Prevention, *Strategic Study #3: The Role of Opium as a Source of Informal Credit* (Islamabad: UN, 1999), http://david-mansfield.tumblr.com/page/4.

69. Dexter Filkins, "A Nation Challenged: Kabul; Afghans Round Up Hundreds in Plot against Leaders," *New York Times*, April 4, 2002, www.nytimes.com/2002/04/04 /international/asia/04AFGH.html.

70. Ahmed Rashid, *Taliban: Militant Islam, Oil and Fundamentalism in Central Asia* (New Haven, CT: Yale University Press, 2000), 118–20.

71. United Nations International Drug Control Programme, *World Drug Report* (1997), ii; United Nations, *Report of the International Narcotics Control Board for 1999* (New York: UN, 2000), 370–71, 49; Alain Labrousse and Laurent Laniel, "The World Geopolitics of Drugs, 1998/1999," *Crime, Law & Social Change* 36, nos. 1–2 (2001): 62.

72. *Afghanistan: Annual Survey 2000*, iii; Barry Bearak, "At Heroin's Source Taliban Do What 'Just Say No' Could Not," *New York Times*, May 24, 2001, www.nytimes.com /2001/05/24/world/at-heroin-s-source-taliban-do-what-just-say-no-could-not.html.

73. *Afghanistan: Annual Survey 2000*, 21–23; United Nations International Drug Control Programme, *Afghanistan: Annual Survey 2001* (Islamabad: UN, 2001), iii, 11, 15–17; Weiner, "A Nation Challenged," *New York Times*; David Mansfield, *A State Built on Sand: How Opium Undermined Afghanistan* (Oxford: Oxford University Press, 2016), 108–9.

74. Barbara Crossette, "Taliban Open a Campaign to Gain Status at U.N.," *New York Times*, September 21, 2000, www.nytimes.com/2000/09/21/world/taliban-open -a-campaign-to-gain-status-at-the-un.html.

75. US Department of State, Bureau of Public Affairs, Secretary Colin L. Powell, "Statement at Press Briefing on New U.S. Humanitarian Assistance for Afghans," May 17, 2001, https://2001-2009.state.gov/secretary/former/powell/remarks/2001/2928.htm.

76. R. W. Apple Jr., "A Nation Challenged: Washington Letter; Pondering the Mystery of the Taliban's Collapse," *New York Times*, November 30, 2001, www.nytimes.com /2001/11/30/us/nation-challenged-washington-letter-pondering-mystery-taliban -s-collapse.html.

77. United Nations, Office for Drug Control and Crime Prevention, *Global Illicit Drug Trends 2002* (New York: UN, 2002), 41.

78. United Nations General Assembly, *Report of the Secretary General: Emergency International Assistance for Peace, Normalcy and Reconstruction of War-Stricken Afghanistan* (56th Session, Agenda item 20 [f], December 7, 2001), 9.

79. Mansfield, *A State Built on Sand*, 109, 126–27, 137.

80. Gopal, *No Good Men among the Living*, 15–19.

81. Barnett R. Rubin, "Putting an End to Warlord Government," *New York Times*, January 15, 2002, www.nytimes.com/2002/01/15/opinion/putting-an-end-to-wa rlord-government.html; Bob Woodward, *Bush at War* (New York: Simon & Schuster, 2002), 35, 139–43, 194, 253, 298–99, 317; Bob Woodward, "CIA Led Way with Cash Handouts," *Washington Post*, November 18, 2002, www.washingtonpost.com /wp-dyn/articles/A3105-2002Nov17.html.

82. Michael R. Gordon and Steven Lee Myers, "A Nation Challenged: Reinforcements; Allies Building Force to Keep Order in a Vacuum," *New York Times*, November 16, 2001, www.nytimes.com/2001/11/16/world/nation-challenged-reinforcements -allies-building-force-keep-order-vacuum.html.

83. Rubin, "Putting an End to Warlord Government."

84. Tim Golden, "The World: A War on Terror Meets a War on Drugs," *New York Times*, November 25, 2001, www.nytimes.com/2001/11/25/weekinreview/the -world-a-war-on-terror-meets-a-war-on-drugs.html.

85. Doris Buddenberg and William A. Byrd, eds., *Afghanistan's Drug Industry* (Vienna: UN Office on Drugs and Crime, and The World Bank, 2006), 25–28, www .unodc.org/pdf/Afgh_drugindustry_Nov06.pdf.

86. James Risen, "Poppy Fields Are Now a Front Line in Afghan War," *New York Times*, May 16, 2007, www.nytimes.com/2007/05/16/world/asia/16drugs.html.

87. Ashraf Ghani, "Where Democracy's Greatest Enemy Is a Flower," *New York Times*, December 11, 2004, www.nytimes.com/2004/12/11/opinion/where-democracys -greatest-enemy-is-a-flower.html.

88. Carlotta Gall, "Another Year of Drug War, and the Poppy Crop Flourishes," *New York Times*, February 17, 2006, www.nytimes.com/2006/02/17/international /asia/17poppy.html.

89. Carlotta Gall, "Opium Harvest at Record Level in Afghanistan," *New York Times*, September 3, 2006, www.nytimes.com/2006/09/03/world/asia/03afghan.html.

90. Martin Jelsma and Tom Kramer, *Downward Spiral: Banning Opium in Afghanistan and Burma* (Amsterdam: Transnational Institute, 2005), 4–9; David Rhode and David E. Sanger, "How a 'Good War' in Afghanistan Went Bad," *New York Times*,

August 12, 2007; Kirk Semple and Tim Golden, "Afghans Pressed by U.S. on Plan to Spray Poppies," *New York Times*, October 8, 2007; Anna Bawden, "US Backs Down over Afghan Poppy Fields Destruction," *Guardian*, December 7, 2007, www.theguardian.com/world/2007/dec/07/afghanistan.usa.

91. UN Office on Drugs and Crime, *Afghanistan Opium Survey 2007* (Islamabad: UNODCCP, 2007), iii–iv, 7, 39, 60, 71, 77, 86. www.unodc.org/documents/crop -monitoring/Afghanistan-Opium-Survey-2007.pdf.

92. Gretchen Peters, *How Opium Profits the Taliban* (Washington, DC: US Institute of Peace, 2009), 23, www.usip.org/sites/default/files/resources/taliban_opium_1. pdf; UN Office on Drugs and Crime, *Afghanistan Opium Survey 2008* (Vienna: UNODC, 2008), 2–3; Brian Steward, "The New Afghan Battle Plan, Bribing the Taliban," CBC News, January 27, 2010, www.cbc.ca/news/world/the-new-afghan-battle-plan-bribing-the-taliban-1.893983; "Afghanistan Crossroads: Taliban Pay vs. Afghan Forces Pay," *Afghanistan Crossroads*, CNN blog, posted December 9, 2009, at 10:08 am, http://afghanistan.blogs.cnn.com/2009/12/09/taliban-pay-vs-afghan-forces-pay.

93. Steven Lee Meyers and Thom Shanker, "Pentagon Considers Adding Forces in Afghanistan," *New York Times*, May 3, 2008, www.nytimes.com/2008/05/03/world /asia/03military.html.

94. Mansfield, *A State Built on Sand*, 100–101, 110–11, 104; UN Office on Drugs and Crime, *Afghanistan Opium Survey 2015* (Vienna: UNODC, 2015), 12.

95. J. Edward Conway, "Analysis in Combat: The Deployed Threat Finance Analyst," *Small Wars Journal*, July 5, 2012, http://smallwarsjournal.com/printpdf/12915; US Department of Treasury, Press Center, "Fact Sheet: Combating the Financing of Terrorism, Disrupting Terrorism at Its Core," September 8, 2011, www.treasury.gov /press-center/press-releases/Pages/tg1291.aspx.

96. C. J. Chivers, "Afghan Attack Gives Marines a Taste of War," *New York Times*, February 13, 2010, www.nytimes.com/2010/02/14/world/asia/14marja.html.

97. Rob Norland, "U.S. Turns a Blind Eye to Opium in an Afghan Town," *New York Times*, March 20, 2010, www.nytimes.com/2010/03/21/world/asia/21marja.html.

98. Alissa J. Rubin, " In Marja, a Vice President Speaks with Warmth but Reaps Cool," *New York Times*, March 1, 2010, www.nytimes.com/2010/03/02/world/asia /02marja.html.

99. Alfred W. McCoy, "Can Anyone Pacify the World's Number One Narco-State? The Opium Wars in Afghanistan," *TomDispatch*, March 30, 2010, www.tomdispatch .com/blog/175225/alfred_mccoy_afghanistan_as_a_drug_war.

100. Matthew Rosenberg and Rod Norlund, "U.S. Scales Back Plans for Afghan Peace," *New York Times*, October 2, 2012, www.nytimes.com/2012/10/02/world/asia/us -scales-back-plans-for-afghan-peace.html.

101. Joseph Goldstein, "Taliban Make Gains across 3 Provinces in Afghanistan," *New York Times*, July 28, 2014, www.nytimes.com/2015/07/29/world/asia/taliban -make-gains-across-3-provinces-in-afghanistan.html.

102. James Rosen, "U.S. Inspector: Billions in Failed Programs Wasted in Afghanistan," *McClatchyDC*, September 12, 2014, www.mcclatchydc.com/news/nation-world

/national/national-security/article24773107.html; Editorial, "Afghanistan's Un-ending Addiction," *New York Times*, October 27, 2014; Special Inspector General for Afghanistan Reconstruction, *Poppy Cultivation in Afghanistan* (Arlington, VA: Special Inspector General for Afghanistan Reconstruction, October 2014), 1–12, www.sigar.mil/pdf/Special%20Projects/SIGAR-15-10-SP.pdf.

103. UN Office on Drugs and Crime, *Afghanistan Opium Survey 2013: Summary Findings* (Vienna: UNODC, 2013), 3–7, www.unodc.org/documents/crop-monitoring/Afghanistan/Afghan_report_Summary_Findings_2013.pdf.

104. Special Inspector General for Afghanistan Reconstruction, *Poppy Cultivation in Afghanistan*, 2.

105. The $320 million estimate was calculated as follows. According to Gretchen Peters, the Taliban's fixed tax rates collected $425 million from a 2008 opium crop worth $4 billion, based on the UN's estimate for the comparable 2007 crop. (See Peters, *How Opium Profits the Taliban*, 23; UNODC, *Afghanistan Opium Survey 2008*, 1.) Applying this same Taliban tax rate of 10.6 percent to the UN's estimate of $3 billion value for the 2013 opium crop yields revenues of $319 million. (See Special Inspector General for Afghanistan Reconstruction, *Poppy Cultivation in Afghanistan*, 2.) A study for the Congressional Research Service reports that the total Taliban income for 2012 was between $400 and $620 million, thereby making $319 million in opium revenues well over half the Taliban's total income. (See Liana Rosen and Kenneth Katzman, *Afghanistan: Drug Trafficking and the 2014 Transition* [Washington, DC: Congressional Research Service, May 2014], 1, http://fas.org/sgp/crs/row/R43540.pdf.)

106. Special Inspector General for Afghanistan Reconstruction, *Poppy Cultivation in Afghanistan*, 10.

107. UN Office on Drugs and Crime, *Afghanistan Opium Survey 2014: Cultivation and Production* (Vienna: UNODC, 2014), 6–7, www.unodc.org/documents/crop-monitoring/Afghanistan/Afghan-opium-survey-2014.pdf.

108. Elizabeth Chuck, "As Heroin Use Grows in U.S., Poppy Crops Thrive in Afghanistan," NBC News, July 7, 2015, www.nbcnews.com/news/world/heroin-use-grows-u-s-poppy-crops-thrive-afghanistan-n388081.

109. Joseph Goldstein, "Taliban's New Leader Strengthens His Hold with Intrigue and Battlefield Victory," *New York Times*, October 5, 2015.

110. Alissa J. Rubin, "Afghan Forces Rally in Kunduz, but Fight Is Far from Decided," *New York Times*, October 2, 2015.

111. David Jolly and Taimoor Shah, "Afghan Province Teetering to the Taliban, Draws in Extra U.S. Forces," *New York Times*, December 14, 2015.

112. Rod Nordland and Joseph Goldstein, "Afghan Taliban's Reach Is Widest Since 2001, U.N. Says," *New York Times*, October 12, 2015.

113. Mujib Mashal, "Taliban Kill at Least 22 Afghan Police Officers," *New York Times*, October 21, 2015.

114. Jolly and Shah, "Afghan Province Teetering to the Taliban."

115. Mujib Mashal and Taimoor Shah, "Last Refuge from Taliban May Prove No Refuge at All," *New York Times*, December 28, 2015; David Jolly, "U.S. to Send More

Troops to Aid Afghan Forces Pressed by Taliban," *New York Times*, February 10, 2016; Mujib Mashal, "Afghan Troops Retreat under Pressure from Taliban," *New York Times*, February 20, 2016; Mujib Mashal, "Facing the Taliban and His Past, an Afghan Leader Aims for a Different Ending," *New York Times*, February 29, 2016; Rod Nordland and Taimoor Shah, "A 5th District in Helmand Province Falls to the Taliban," *New York Times*, March 16, 2016.

116. Rod Nordland, "Violence and Corruption in the World's Heroin Heartland," *New York Times*, April 7, 2016; Rod Nordland, "General Plants Flowers in Helmand, but Taliban Lurk," *New York Times*, April 10, 2016.

117. Mujib Mashal and Taimoor Shah, "Airstrikes Barely Holding Off Taliban in Helmand, Afghan Officials Say," *New York Times*, August 9, 2016; Mujib Mashal, "Afghanistan Forces Struggle to Hold Firm against Taliban in South," *New York Times*, August 15, 2016.

118. Mark Landler, "Obama Says He Will Slow Troop Reductions in Afghanistan," *New York Times*, July 7, 2016; Missy Ryan and Thomas Gibbons-Neff, "U.S. Widens War in Afghanistan, Authorizes New Action against Taliban," *Washington Post*, June 10, 2016, www.washingtonpost.com/news/checkpoint/wp/2016/06/09/defense-official-u-s-to-begin-striking-taliban-advise-regular-afghan-soldiers-again/.

119. UN Office on Drugs and Crime, "After Six Years on the Rise, Afghan Opium Crop Cultivation Declines: New UNODC Survey," press release, October 14, 2015, www.unodc.org/unodc/en/press/releases/2015/October/after-six-years-on-the-rise--afghan-opium-crop-cultivation-declines_-new-unodc-survey.html.

120. David Mansfield, "Where Have All the Flowers Gone? The Real Reasons for the Drop in the Poppy Crop in Afghanistan in 2015," *Alcis*, October 20, 2015, https://stories.alcis.org/where-have-all-the-flowers-gone-7de7b34e8478#.af0gf3vu8; David Mansfield, "Helmand on the Move: Migration as Response to Crop Failure," research brief, Afghanistan Research and Evaluation Unit, October 2015, www.areu.org.af/Uploads/EditionPdfs/1521E-%20Helmand%20on%20the%20Move%20Migration%20as%20a%20Response%20to%20Crop%20Failure.pdf.

121. Azam Ahmed, "Tasked with Combating Opium, Afghan Officials Profit from It," *New York Times*, February 16, 2016.

122. UN Security Council, "Report of the Analytical Support and Sanctions Monitoring Team on Specific Cases of Cooperation between Organized Crime Syndicates and Individuals, Groups, Undertakings and Entities Eligible for Listing under Paragraph 1 of Security Council Resolution 2160 (2014): S/2015/79," February 2, 2015, 9–10, www.un.org/ga/search/view_doc.asp?symbol=S/2015/79.

123. Ahmed, "Tasked with Combating Opium."

124. David Mansfield, "The Devil Is in the Details: Nangarhar's Continued Decline into Insurgency, Violence, and Widespread Drug Production," *Afghan Research and Evaluation Unit Brief*, February 2016, 1–3, 6–9, 12–13.

125. UN Office on Drugs and Crime, *Afghanistan Opium Survey 2015: Executive Summary* (Vienna: UNODC, October 2015), 7, www.unodc.org/documents/crop-monitoring/Afghanistan/Afg_Executive_summary_2015_final.pdf.

126. Ahmed, "Tasked with Combating Opium."

127. UN Office on Drugs and Crime, *Afghanistan Opium Survey 2014: Socio-economic Analysis* (Vienna: UNODC, March 2015), 8, 11, www.unodc.org/documents /crop-monitoring/Afghanistan/Afghanistan_Opium_Survey_Socio-economic _analysis_2014_web.pdf.

128. Rosen, "U.S. Inspector: Billions in Failed Programs Wasted in Afghanistan."

Chapter Four: A Global Surveillance State

1. Alfred W. McCoy, "Welcome Home, War! How America's Wars Are Systematically Destroying Our Liberties," *TomDispatch*, November 12, 2009, www.tomdispatch. com/blog/175154/tomgram%3A_alfred_mccoy%2C_surveillance_state%2C_u.s.a.

2. James C. Scott, *Seeing Like a State: How Certain Schemes to Improve the Human Condition Have Failed* (New Haven, CT: Yale University Press, 1998), 1–3, 11–22, 24, 29–33, 44–45, 59–61, 64–72, 373.

3. G. Tilghman Richards, *The History and Development of Typewriters* (London: HMSO, 1964), 23–25; Lewis Coe, *The Telegraph: A History of Morse's Invention and Its Predecessors in the United States* (Jefferson, NC: McFarland, 1993), 89.

4. Joel D. Howell, *Technology in the Hospital: Transforming Patient Care in the Early Twentieth Century* (Baltimore, MD: Johns Hopkins University Press, 1995), 33–34, 40–42; Charles J. Austin, *Information Systems for Health Services Administration* (Ann Arbor, MI: Health Administration Press, 1992), 13–21; F. H. Wines, "The Census of 1900," *National Geographic*, January 1900, 34–36; Friedrich W. Kistermann, "Hollerith Punched Card System Development (1905–1913)," *IEEE Annals of the History of Computing* 27, no. 1 (2005): 56–66; Emerson W. Pugh, *Building IBM: Shaping an Industry and Its Technology* (Cambridge, MA: MIT Press, 1995), 1–36; "The Electric Tabulating Machine Applied to Cost Accounting," *American Machinist*, August 16, 1902, 1073–75; S. G. Koon, "Cost Accounting by Machines," *American Machinist*, March 26, 1914, 533–36; Douglas W. Jones, "Punched Cards: A Brief Illustrated Technical History," http://homepage.divms.uiowa.edu/~jones /cards/history.html; Mark Howells, "Counting the Lost Census: The Infant Stage of Modern Technology," *Ancestry* 18, no. 2 (March/April 2000): 53–55.

5. Helmut Gernsheim and Alison Gernsheim, *The History of Photography from the Camera Obscura to the Beginning of the Modern Era* (New York: McGraw-Hill, 1969), 403–9.

6. Wayne A. Wiegand, *Irrepressible Reformer: A Biography of Melvil Dewey* (Chicago: ALA Editions, 1996), 14–24; Wayne A. Wiegand and Donald G. Davis Jr., *Encyclopedia of Library History* (New York: Routledge, 1994), 147–50; John Comaromi and M. Satija, *Dewey Decimal Classification: History and Current Status* (New York: Sterling Pub Private, 1988), 4–9; Leo E. LaMontagne, *American Library Classification with Special Reference to the Library of Congress* (Hamden, CT: Shoe String Press, 1961), 52–60, 63–99, 179–233.

7. Elizabeth Bethel, "The Military Information Division: Origin of the Intelligence Division," *Military Affairs* 11, no. 1 (Spring 1947): 17–24.

8. Alphonse Bertillon, *Alphonse Bertillon's Instructions for Taking Descriptions for the*

Identification of Criminals and Others by the Means of Anthrometric Indications (New York: AMS Press, 1977), 6, 17, 91–94; Frank Morn, *"The Eye That Never Sleeps": A History of the Pinkerton National Detective Agency* (Bloomington: Indiana University Press, 1982), 124–27; E. R. Henry, *Classification and Uses of Fingerprints* (London: HMSO, 1900), 61; Henry T. F. Rhodes, *Alphonse Bertillon: Father of Scientific Detection* (London: George G. Harrap, 1956), 71–109; Jürgen Thorwald, *The Century of the Detective* (New York: Harcourt, 1965), 20–26.

9. Donald C. Dilworth, ed., *Identification Wanted: Development of the American Criminal Identification Systems, 1893–1943* (Gaithersburg, MD: International Association of Chiefs of Police, 1977), 1–3, 6–8, 60–68, 78–79, 82–83, 103–6, 131, 161–66; Henry, *Classification and Uses of Fingerprints*, 4–7, 61–69; Bertillon, *Alphonse Bertillon's Instructions*, 10–12; *Police Chiefs News Letter* 2, no. 3 (March 1934): 2; *Police Chiefs News Letter* 3, no. 7 (July 1936): 2; Richard Polenberg, *Fighting Faiths: The Abrams Case, the Supreme Court, and Free Speech* (New York: Viking Adult, 1987), 165.

10. Gamewell Fire Alarm Telegraph Co., *Emergency Signaling* (New York: Gamewell Fire Alarm Telegraph Co., 1916), chaps. 2–7; William Maver Jr., *American Telegraphy and Encyclopedia of the Telegraph: Systems, Apparatus, Operation* (New York: Maver Publishing, 1903), 440–53; Paul Ditzel, *Fire Alarm!* (New Albany, IN: Fire Buff House Publishers, 1990), 5, 16–28, 40–42; William Werner, *History of the Boston Fire Department and Boston Fire Alarm System* (Boston: Boston Sparks Association, 1974), 177–84.

11. Robert W. Little Jr. and Blaine Bruggeman, *History of the York Fire Department, 1776–1976* (Marceline, MO: Walsworth, 1976), 83; Richard Heath, *Mill City Firefighters: The First Hundred Years, 1879–1979* (Minneapolis, MN: Extra Alarm Association of the Twin Cities, 1981), 32, 45, 69–71; Ditzel, *Fire Alarm!* 27; U.S. Bureau of the Census, *Abstract of the Twelfth Census of the United States, 1900* (Washington, DC: Government Printing Office, 1904), 421–22.

12. Ronald Robinson, "Non-European Foundations of European Imperialism: Sketch for a Theory of Collaboration," in Roger Owen and Bob Sutcliffe, eds., *Studies in the Theory of Imperialism* (London: Longman, 1972), 132–33, 138–39.

13. Brian McAllister Linn, *The Philippine War: 1899–1902* (Lawrence: University of Kansas Press, 2000), 127, 191; Brian McAllister Linn, "Intelligence and Low-Intensity Conflict in the Philippine War, 1899–1902," *Intelligence and National Security* 6, no. 1 (1991): 90–96. See testimony by Colonel Arthur L. Wagner, former head of the Military Intelligence Division, in US Senate, 57th Congress, 1st Session, doc. no. 331, part 3, *Affairs in the Philippine Islands: Hearings before the Committee on the Philippines of the United States Senate* (Washington, DC: Government Printing Office, 1902), 2850–51.

14. Joan M. Jensen, *Army Surveillance in America, 1775–1980* (New Haven, CT: Yale University Press, 1991), 112; Marc B. Powe, "American Military Intelligence Comes of Age," *Military Review* 40, no. 12 (1975): 18–21; Kenneth Campbell, "Major General Ralph H. Van Deman: Father of Modern American Military Intelligence," *American Intelligence Journal* 8 (Summer 1987): 13; Michael E. Bigelow, "Van De-

man," *Military Intelligence* 16, no. 4 (1990): 38.

15. Ralph E. Weber, ed., *The Final Memoranda: Major General Ralph H. Van Deman, USA Ret., 1865-1952, Father of U.S. Military Intelligence* (Wilmington, DE: SR Books, 1988), 7-8; Linn, "Intelligence and Low-Intensity Conflict in the Philippine War," 100-108; Brian McAllister Linn, *The U.S. Army and Counterinsurgency in the Philippine War, 1899-1902* (Chapel Hill: University of North Carolina Press, 1989), 155-56.

16. Thomas H. Barry, Brigadier General US Volunteers, Chief of Staff to the Commanding General, Department of Northern Luzon, March 11, 1901, Entry 4337, RG 395, National Archives and Records Administration (hereafter, NARA).

17. Weber, *The Final Memoranda*, 8-18; John Moran Gates, *Schoolbooks and Krags: The United States Army in the Philippines, 1898-1902* (Westport, CT: Praeger Publishers, 1973), 250-51; Linn, "Intelligence and Low-Intensity Conflict in the Philippine War," 104-5; Captain R. H. Van Deman, For the Information of the Division Commander, December 9, 1901, Philippine Insurgent Records, Special Documents, Publication 254, Microreel 80, Folder 1303, NARA.

18. *Khaki and Red*, September 1927, 5-8, 9; *Khaki and Red*, September 1932, 12; *Philippines Free Press*, May 11, 1918, 3.

19. Heath Twitchell Jr., *Allen: The Biography of an Army Officer, 1859-1930* (New Brunswick, NJ: Rutgers University Press, 1974), 4-6, 19, 24, 26, 36-59, 65-67, 75-84, 86, 290.

20. McCoy, *Policing America's Empire*, 104-6, 129.

21. "Family History of M.Q." [ca. 1900], Box 7, File: 1900 Oct., Henry T. Allen Papers, Manuscript Division, US Library of Congress. Although the document only gives the author's name as "Captain Pyle, P.S.," army records show that a Frank L. Pyle joined the Philippine Scouts as a second lieutenant on June 27, 1902, while retaining the permanent rank of sergeant in Troop D, US First Cavalry. See Military Secretary's Office, *Official Army Register for 1905* (Washington, DC: Military Secretary's Office, 1904), 359, and Hartford Beaumont, letter to Honorable Henry C. Ide, December 7, 1904, Book 21:II, Dean C. Worcester Papers, Harlan Hatcher Library, University of Michigan.

22. Leonard Wood, "Diaries, 1921-27," August 15, 1923, Leonard Wood Papers, Manuscript Division, US Library of Congress.

23. Mark Twain, "Passage from 'Outlines of History' (suppressed) Date 9th Century," in Jim Zwick, ed., *Mark Twain's Weapons of Satire: Anti-imperialist Writings on the Philippine-American War* (Syracuse, NY: Syracuse University Press, 1992), 78-79.

24. Stephen Skowronek, *Building a New American State: The Expansion of National Administrative Capacities, 1877-1920* (Cambridge: Cambridge University Press, 1982), 8-18, 39-46.

25. Theodore Kornweibel Jr., *"Seeing Red": Federal Campaigns against Black Militancy, 1919-1925* (Bloomington: Indiana University Press, 1998), 7, 184; Jeffrey M. Dorwart, *Conflict of Duty: The U.S. Navy's Intelligence Dilemma, 1919-1945* (Annapolis, MD: Naval Institute Press, 1983), 7; Charles H. McCormick, *Seeing Reds: Federal Surveillance of Radicals in the Pittsburgh Mill District, 1917-1921* (Pittsburgh, PA: University of Pittsburgh Press, 1997), 3, 12-13; Rhodri Jeffreys-Jones, *The FBI: A*

History (New Haven, CT: Yale University Press, 2007), 65–72.

26. *Washington Evening Star*, February 20, 1940, Personal Name Information Files: John R. White, Entry 21, RG 350, NARA; H. H. Bandholtz, "Provost Marshal General's Department," April 30, 1919, *United States Army in the World War 1917–1919: Reports of the Commander-in-Chief, Staff Sections and Services* (Washington, DC: Center of Military History, 1991), 313–28; Robert Wright Jr., *Army Lineage Series: Military Police* (Washington, DC: Center of Military History, 1992), 8–9.

27. Major General J. G. Harbord, letter to Brigadier General H. H. Bandholtz, August 31, 1921; Brig. Gen. H. H. Bandholtz, Proclamation, September 2, 1921; A Proclamation by the President of the United States, n.d.; Bandholtz, Copy Telegram No. 2, To: Adjutant General, n.d.; Minutes, Twenty-Ninth Consecutive and Fourth Biennial Convention of District No. 5, United Mine Workers of America, First Day, Pittsburg, Pa., September 6, 1921; Brigadier General H. H. Bandholtz, To: the Adjutant General, September 12, 1921, Reel 9, Harry H. Bandholtz Papers, Michigan Historical Society; Institute for the History of Technology and Industrial Anthropology, *The Battle of Blair Mountain (West Virginia): Cultural Resource Survey and Recording Project* (Morgantown, WV, 1992), 35–50; Clayton D. Laurie and Ronald H. Cole, *The Role of Federal Military Forces in Domestic Disorders, 1877–1945* (Washington, DC: Center of Military History, 1997), 320–24.

28. Joan Jensen, *The Price of Vigilance* (Chicago: Rand McNally & Co., 1968), 287–89; Harold M. Hyman, *To Try Men's Souls: Loyalty Tests in American History* (Berkeley and Los Angeles: University of California Press, 1959), 323–24; McCormick, *Seeing Reds*, 202; Kornweibel, "*Seeing Red*," 174–75; David Kahn, *The Reader of Gentlemen's Mail: Herbert O. Yardley and the Birth of American Codebreaking* (New Haven, CT: Yale University Press, 2004), 94–103; Roy Talbert Jr., *Negative Intelligence: The Army and the American Left, 1917–1941* (Jackson: University Press of Mississippi, 1991), 208–11; Ralph Van Deman, December 15, 1928, Office of Chief of Staff, Cross Reference Card, Microform 1194, RG 350, NARA; US Senate, Select Committee to Study Governmental Operations with Respect to Intelligence Activities, 94th Congress, 2d Session, *Supplementary Reports on Intelligence Activities*, book 6 (Washington, DC: Government Printing Office, 1976), 105–6; Regin Schmidt, *Red Scare: FBI and the Origins of Anticommunism in the United States, 1919–1943* (Copenhagen: Museum Tusculanum Press, 2000), 324–28, 368.

29. Talbert, *Negative Intelligence*, 255–59; US Senate, 94th Congress, 2d Session, *Final Report of the Select Committee to Study Governmental Operations with Respect to Intelligence Activities*, book 2 (Washington, DC: Government Printing Office, 1976), 33–38.

30. Associated Press, "Hundreds Named as Red Appeasers," *New York Times*, June 9, 1949; "Never Were or Would Be Reds, Fredric March and Wife Assert," *New York Times*, June 10, 1949; Richard Halloran, "Senate Panel Holds Vast 'Subversives' Files Amassed by Ex-Chief of Army Intelligence," *New York Times*, September 7, 1971; California Legislature, *Fifth Report of the Senate Fact-Finding Committee on Un-American Activities, 1949* (Sacramento: California State Printing Office, 1948), 411, 448–49, 488–537; Patrick McGilligan and Paul Buhle, *Tender Comrades: A*

Backstory of the Hollywood Blacklist (New York: St. Martin's Press, 1997), 368–69. The famous Appendix 9 of HUAC's 1944 report, which included a similarly massive list of communists, was unknown to the public and restricted to a narrow circle of government investigators as late as 1951. See Edward L. Barrett Jr., *The Tenney Committee: Legislative Investigation of Subversive Activities in California* (Ithaca, NY: Cornell University Press, 1951), 20–22.

31. Halloran, "Senate Panel Holds Vast 'Subversives' Files."

32. Talbert, *Negative Intelligence*, 270–71; Halloran, "Senate Panel Holds Vast 'Subversives' Files"; R. R. Roach to D. M. Ladd, July 13, 1945; D. M. Ladd to E. A. Tamm, October 29, 1945; Colonel F. W. Hein to Commanding Officer 115th CIC Detachment, March 8, 1951; A. H. Belmont to D. M. Ladd, November 9, 1951; Colonel H. S. Isaacson to Major General A. R. Bolling, November 27, 1951; Director to SAC San Diego, December 11, 1951; V. P. Keay to A. H. Belmont, January 22, 1952; Santoiana to Director, January 22, 1952; SAC San Diego to Director, February 4, 1952; SAC SF to Director, n.d.; Subject: Van Deman, Ralph Henry, Files 65-37516, 94-37515, Federal Bureau of Investigation, Washington, DC.

33. Tim Weiner, *Enemies: A History of the FBI* (New York: Random House, 2013), 77, 86–90, 134–35.

34. David Burnham, "Truman's Wiretaps on Ex-New Deal Aide Cited," *New York Times*, February 1, 1986, www.nytimes.com/1986/02/01/us/truman-wiretaps-on-ex-new-deal-aide-cited.html.

35. Robin W. Winks, *Cloak and Gown 1939–1961: Scholars in the Secret War* (New York: Harvill Press, 1987), 60, 74–75, 104, 111, 113–14.

36. Ibid., 104–5.

37. James William Gibson, *Perfect War: The War We Couldn't Lose and How We Did* (New York: Random House, 1986), 305–15; Robert Lester, *A Guide to the Microfilm Edition of the Records of the Military Assistance Command Vietnam: Part 3. Progress Reports on Pacification in South Vietnam, 1965–1973* (Bethesda, MD: University Publications of America, 1990), 2–5; R. W. Komer, *Organization and Management of the "New Model" Pacification Program—1966–1969* (Santa Monica, CA: Rand Corporation, May 7, 1970), 198–204, 207–8, 243.

38. Richard A. Hunt, *Pacification: The American Struggle for Vietnam Hearts and Minds* (Boulder, CO: Westview Press, 1990), 185–86, 194–95, 197–99, 260–61; Lester, *A Guide to the Microfilm Edition of the Records of the Military Assistance Command Vietnam*, 2.

39. US Senate, 94th Congress, 2d Session, *Final Report of the Select Committee to Study Governmental Operations with Respect to Intelligence Activities*, book 3 (Washington, DC: Government Printing Office, 1976), 3–4, 7–8.

40. Weiner, *Enemies*, 178, 249–50; Michael O'Brien, "The Exner File—Judith Campbell Exner, John F. Kennedy's Mistress," *Washington Monthly*, December 1999, www.highbeam.com/doc/1G1-58170292.html; Kitty Kelley, "The Dark Side of Camelot," *People Magazine* 29, no. 8 (January 29, 1988), http://archive.people.com/people/archive/jpgs/19880229/19880229-750-113.jpg.

41. Ronald Kessler, *The Secrets of the FBI* (New York: Crown Publishing, 2011), 37–41.

42. Anthony Summers, "The Secret Life of J Edgar Hoover," *Guardian*, December 31, 2011, www.theguardian.com/film/2012/jan/01/j-edgar-hoover-secret-fbi.

43. Seymour M. Hersh, "Huge C.I.A. Operation Reported in U.S. against Antiwar Forces, Other Dissidents in Nixon Years," *New York Times*, December 22, 1974; Seymour M. Hersh, "C.I.A. Admits Domestic Acts, Denies 'Massive' Illegality," *New York Times*, January 16, 1975; John M. Crewdson, "Triumph and Defeat: The C.I.A. Record," *New York Times*, June 11, 1975; "Summary of Rockefeller Panel's C.I.A. Report," *New York Times*, June 11, 1975; John M. Crewdson, "File Said to Indicate C.I.A. Had a Man in White House," *New York Times*, July 10, 1975; Seymour M. Hersh, "Report on C.I.A. Is Praised, but Recommendations Are Called Weak," *New York Times*, June 12, 1975; Anthony Lewis, "The Teller of Truth," *New York Times*, July 10, 1975; Nicholas M. Horrock, "F.B.I. Is Accused of Political Acts for Six Presidents," *New York Times*, December 4, 1975; Nicholas M. Horrock, "C.I.A. Panel Finds 'Plainly Unlawful' Acts That Improperly Invaded American Rights," *New York Times*, June 11, 1975; Victor S. Navasky, "FBI," review of *FBI*, by Sanford J. Ungar, *New York Times*, March 14, 1976.

44. Hersh, "Huge C.I.A. Operation Reported"; "Text of Ford Plan on Intelligence Units and Excerpts from his Executive Order," *New York Times*, February 19, 1976; "Excerpts from Senate Intelligence Report," *New York Times*, April 29, 1976; Nicholas M. Horrock, "Senate Passes Bill to Bar Bugging in U.S. without Court Order," *New York Times*, April 21, 1978.

45. Dana Priest and William M. Arkin, "Top Secret America," *Washington Post*, July 18–21, 2010.

46. Philip Shenon, "Threats and Responses," *New York Times*, September 10, 2002; Eric Lichtblau, "Administration Plans Defense of Terror Law," *New York Times*, August 19, 2003; Eric Lichtblau, "Secret Warrant Requests Increased in 2003," *New York Times*, May 3, 2004; Eric Lichtblau, "Large Volume of F.B.I. Files Alarms U.S. Activist Groups," *New York Times*, July 18, 2005. Nat Hentoff, "Rescued by Dick Armey from Big Brother," *Washington Times*, July 29, 2002; Dan Eggen, "Under Fire, Justice Shrinks TIPS Program," *Washington Post*, August 10, 2002; Cynthia Crossen, "Early TIPS Corps Did More Harm Than Good in Hunt for Subversives," *Wall Street Journal*, October 2, 2002; Nat Hentoff, "The Death of Operation TIPS," *Village Voice*, December 18, 2002.

47. Tim Weiner, "Look Who's Listening," *New York Times*, January 20, 2002; Weiner, *Legacy of Ashes*, 482–83.

48. James Risen and Eric Lichtblau, "How the U.S. Uses Technology to Mine More Data More Quickly," *New York Times*, June 8, 2013, www.nytimes.com/2013/06/09/us/revelations-give-look-at-spy-agencys-wider-reach.html?_r=0.

49. National Security Agency, Office of Inspector General, "Working Draft," March 24, 2009, 7–13, *Washington Post*, apps.washingtonpost.com/g/page/world/national-security-agency-inspector-general-draft-report/277/.

50. James Bamford, "Every Move You Make," *Foreign Policy*, September 7, 2016, http://foreignpolicy.com/2016/09/07/every-move-you-make-obama-nsa-security-surveillance-spying-intelligence

-snowden/.

51. Robert S. Mueller, III, Testimony: "FBI Oversight," US Senate Committee on the Judiciary, May 2, 2006, www.fas.org/irp/congress/2006_hr/050206mueller.html; Ellen Nakashima, "FBI Show Off Counterterrorism Database," *Washington Post*, August 30, 2006; Barton Gellman and Laura Poitras, "U.S., British Intelligence Mining Data from Nine U.S. Internet Companies in Broad Secret Program," *Washington Post*, June 7, 2013, http://articles.washingtonpost.com/2013-06-06/news/39784046_1 _prism-nsa-u-s-servers.

52. Risen and Lichtblau, "How the U.S. Uses Technology."

53. James Risen and Eric Lichtblau, "Bush Lets U.S. Spy on Callers without Courts," *New York Times*, December 16, 2005, www.nytimes.com/2005/12/16/politics /16program.html.

54. Leslie Cauley, "NSA Has Massive Database of Americans' Phone Calls," *USA Today*, May 11, 2006, http://usatoday30.usatoday.com/news/washington/2006-05-10-nsa _x.htm.

55. Gellman and Poitras, "U.S., British Intelligence Mining Data."

56. Eric Lichtblau, "In Secret, Court Vastly Broadens Powers of N.S.A.," *New York Times*, July 7, 2013; Grant Gross, "Surveillance Court Renews NSA Phone Records Program," *Computer World*, January 3, 2014, www.computerworld.com/article/2487309 /government-it/surveillance-court-renews-nsa-phone-records-program.html.

57. Xan Rice, "Internet: Last Piece of Fibre-Optic Jigsaw Falls into Place as Cable Links East Africa to Grid," *Guardian*, August 17, 2008, www.theguardian.com/technology /2008/aug/18/east.africa.internet; International Telecommunications Union, "ITU Releases Latest Tech Figures & Global Rankings," press release, October 7, 2013, www.itu.int/net/pressoffice/press_releases/2013/41.aspx#.V05902ZrXpf.

58. Floor Boon, Steven Derix, and Huib Modderkolk, "NSA Infected 50,000 Computer Networks with Malicious Software," *NRC Handelsblad*, November 23, 2013, www. nrc.nl/nieuws/2013/11/23/nsa-infected-50000-computer-networks-with-malicious-software.

59. On telephones, see Series R1–R12, 783, and for mail see Series R163–171 and R172–187, 804–6, in US Census Bureau, Bicentennial Edition, *Historical Statistics of the United States, Colonial Times to 1970* (Washington, DC: Government Printing Office, 1975).

60. Federal Bureau of Investigation, "A Brief History of the FBI," www.fbi.gov/about-us /history/brief-history.

61. John O. Koehler, *Stasi: The Untold Story of the East German Secret Police* (Boulder, CO: Westview Press, 2000), 8–9; Belinda Cooper, "A Nation of Spies," *New York Times*, April 25, 1999.

62. "Introverted? Then NSA Wants You," *FCW*, *Circuit* blog, posted by Camille Tuutti on April 16, 2012 at 12:11 pm, https://fcw.com/blogs/circuit/2012/04 /fedsmc-chris-inglis-federal-workforce.aspx.

63. Charlie Savage and Scott Shane, "Top-Secret Court Castigated N.S.A. on Surveillance," *New York Times*, August 22, 2013.

64. James Risen and Laura Poitras, "N.S.A. Examines Social Connections of U.S. Citi-

zens," *New York Times*, September 29, 2013.

65. Senator Ron Wyden, "Wyden, Udall Statement on the Disclosure of Bulk Email Records Collection Program," press release, July 2, 2013, www.wyden.senate.gov /news/press-releases/wyden-udall-statement-on-the-disclosure-of-bulk-email -records-collection-program.

66. Glenn Greenwald, "NSA Collecting Phone Records of Millions of Verizon Customers Daily," *Guardian*, June 6, 2013, www.guardian.co.uk/world/2013/jun/06/nsa -phone-records-verizon-court-order.

67. Barton Gellman and Ashkan Soltani, "NSA Infiltrates Links to Yahoo, Google Data Centers Worldwide, Snowden Documents Say," *Washington Post*, October 30, 2013, www.washingtonpost.com/world/national-security/nsa-infiltrates-links-to-yahoo -google-data-centers-worldwide-snowden-documents-say/2013/10/30/e51d661e -4166-11e3-8b74-d89d714ca4dd_story.html.

68. Steve Mansfield-Devine, "Biometrics at War: The US Military's Need for Identification and Authentication," *Biometric Technology Today*, no. 5 (May 2012): 5–6.

69. Zach Howard, "Police to Begin iPhone Iris Scans amid Privacy Concerns," Reuters, July 20, 2011, www.reuters.com/article/2011/07/20/us-crime-identification -iris-idUSTRE76J4A120110720; Nathan Hodge, "General Wants to Scan More U.S. Irises, Fingerprints," *Wired*, January 29, 2009, www.wired.com/dangerroom /2009/01/biometrics-need/.

70. Charlie Savage, "Facial Scanning Is Making Gains in Surveillance," *New York Times*, August 21, 2013.

71. Charlie Savage, "Report, Evidence Redacted, Ties Snowden to Russian Agencies," *New York Times*, December 23, 2016; Glenn Kessler, "Clapper's 'Least Truthful' Statement to the Senate," *Washington Post*, June 12, 2013, www.washingtonpost.com /blogs/fact-checker/post/james-clappers-least-untruthful-statement-to-the-senate /2013/06/11/e50677a8-d2d8-11e2-a73e-826d299ff459_blog.html?utm_term =.396004be0e7b.

72. James Bamford, "They Know Much More Than You Think," *New York Review of Books*, August 15, 2013, www.nybooks.com/articles/2013/08/15/nsa-they-know -much-more-you-think/.

73. National Security Agency, "Driver 1: Worldwide SIGINT/Defense Cryptologic Platform" (2012), in Boon, Derix, and Modderkolk, "NSA Infected 50,000 Computer Networks."

74. Glenn Greenwald, "XKeyscore: NSA Tool Collects 'Nearly Everything a User Does on the Internet,'" *Guardian*, July 31, 2013, www.theguardian.com/world/2013/jul /31/nsa-top-secret-program-online-data.

75. Nicole Perlroth, Jeff Larson, and Scott Shane, "N.S.A. Able to Foil Basic Safeguards of Privacy on Web," *New York Times*, September 6, 2013.

76. Ewen MacAskill, Julian Borger, Nick Hopkins, Nick Davies, and James Ball, "GCHQ Taps Fibre-Optic Cables for Secret Access to World's Communications," *Guardian*, June 21, 2013, www.guardian.co.uk/uk/2013/jun/21/gchq-cables-secret -world-communications-nsa.

77. Bamford, "Every Move You Make"; Richard Norton-Taylor, "Not So Secret: Deal at

the Heart of UK-US Intelligence," *Guardian*, June 24, 2010, www.guardian.co.uk /world/2010/jun/25/intelligence-deal-uk-us-released; "Minutes of the Inauguration Meeting British Signal Intelligence Conference, 11–27 March 1946," National Security Agency, "UKUSA Agreement Release 1940–1956," www.nsa.gov/news-features /declassified-documents/ukusa/.

78. Scott Shane, "No Morsel Too Miniscule for All-Consuming N.S.A.," *New York Times*, November 2, 2013; Ewen MacAskill and Julian Borger, "New NSA Leaks Show How US Is Bugging Its European Allies," *Guardian*, June 30, 2013, www.guardian.co.uk/world/2013/jun/30/nsa-leaks-us-bugging-european-allies; Laura Poitras, Marcel Rosenbach, Fidelius Schmid, Holger Stark, and Jonathan Stock, "How the NSA Targets Germany and Europe," *Der Spiegel*, July 1, 2013, www.spiegel.de/international/world/secret-documents-nsa-targeted-germany -and-eu-buildings-a-908609.html.

79. Simon Romero and Randal C. Archibold, "Brazil Angered over Report N.S.A. Spied on President," *New York Times*, September 3, 2013; Alissa J. Rubin, "French Condemn Surveillance by N.S.A.," *New York Times*, October 22, 2013; Alison Smale, "Anger Growing among Allies on U.S. Spying," *New York Times*, October 24, 2013; Alison Smale, "Indignation over U.S. Spying Spreads in Europe," *New York Times*, October 25, 2013; Alison Smale, Melissa Eddy, and David E. Sanger, "Data Suggest Push to Spy on Merkel Dates to '02," *New York Times*, October 28, 2013; David E. Sanger, "In Spy Uproar, 'Everyone Does It' Just Won't Do," *New York Times*, October 26, 2013; Mark Mazzetti and David E. Sanger, "Tap on Merkel Provides Peek at Vast Spy Net," *New York Times*, October 31, 2013; Joe Cochrane, "N.S.A. Spying Scandal Hurts Close Ties between Australia and Indonesia," *New York Times*, November 20, 2013; Ian Austen, "Ire in Canada over Report N.S.A. Spied from Ottawa," *New York Times*, November 29, 2013.

80. Peter Allen, "Obama in Crisis Call with French President after WikiLeaks Documents Reveal NSA Spied on Him and Two of His Predecessors," *Daily Mail*, June 23, 2015, www.dailymail.co.uk/news/article-3136659/New-WikiLeaks-documents -reveal-NSA-eavesdropping-THREE-French-presidents.html; Reuters, "NSA Tapped German Chancellery for Decades, WikiLeaks Claims," *Guardian*, July 8, 2015, www.theguardian.com/us-news/2015/jul/08/nsa-tapped-german-chancellery -decades-wikileaks-claims-merkel.

81. James Ball and Nick Hopkins, "GCHQ and NSA Targeted Charities, Germans, Israeli PM and EU Chief," *Guardian*, December 20, 2013, www.theguardian.com /uk-news/2013/dec/20/gchq-targeted-aid-agencies-german-government-eu -commissioner; James Glanz and Andrew W. Lehren, "U.S. and Britain Extended Spying to 1,000 Targets," *New York Times*, December 21, 2013.

82. Steven Erlanger, "Outrage in Europe Grows over Spying Disclosure," *New York Times*, July 2, 2013.

83. James Bamford, *The Shadow Factory: The Ultra-Secret NSA from 9/11 to the Eavesdropping on America* (New York: Doubleday, 2008), 141–42.

84. Glenn Greenwald, *No Place to Hide: Edward Snowden, the NSA, and the U.S. Surveillance State* (New York: Henry Holt, 2014), 142–43.

85. Glenn Greenwald, Ryan Gallagher, and Ryan Grim, "Top-Secret Document Reveals NSA Spied on Porn Habits as Part of Plan to Discredit 'Radicalizers,'" *Huffington Post*, November 26, 2013, www.huffingtonpost.com/2013/11/26/nsa-porn -muslims_n_4346128.html.

86. Edward Snowden, "An Open Letter to the People of Brazil," *Folha de S. Paulo*, December 16, 2013, www1.folha.uol.com.br/internacional/en/world/2013/12/1386296 -an-open-letter-to-the-people-of-brazil.shtml.

87. Bamford, "Every Move You Make."

88. David Rosen, "Is Success Killing the Porn Industry," *Alternet*, May 27, 2013, www.alternet.org/sex-amp-relationships/success-killing-porn-industry.

89. "Press Releases," TopTenReviews, March 12, 2007, available at "Pornography Statistics," Family Safe Media, www.familysafemedia.com/pornography_statistics.html.

90. Danny Hakim and William K. Rashbaum, "Spitzer Is Linked to Prostitution Ring," *New York Times*, March 10, 2008; Nico Pitney, "Spitzer as Client 9: Read Text Messages from Spitzer to Prostitute," *Huffington Post*, March 28, 2008, www.huffingtonpost .com/2008/03/10/spitzer-as-client-9-read-_n_90787.html.

91. Angelique Chrisafis, "French Budget Minister Accused of Hiding Swiss Bank Account," *Guardian*, December 27, 2012, www.theguardian.com/world/2012/dec/27 /french-budget-minister-swiss-account; Angelique Chrisafis, "France's Former Budget Minister Admits Lying about Secret Offshore Account," *Guardian*, April 2, 2013, www.theguardian.com/world/2013/apr/02/jerome-cahuzac-france-offshore -account?INTCMP=SRCH.

92. Alison Smale, "Surveillance Revelations Shake U.S.-German Ties," *New York Times*, August 26, 2013; David E. Sanger and Mark Mazzetti, "Allegation of U.S. Spying on German Leader Puts Obama at Crossroads," *New York Times*, October 25, 2013; Smale, "Anger Growing among Allies."

93. Erlanger, "Outrage in Europe Grows"; Rubin, "French Condemn Surveillance."

94. Martin Shultz, "Arrival and Doorstep by Martin Schulz, President of the European Parliament, Prior to the European Council Taking Place on 24 October 2013 in Brussels," clip and transcript, TV Newsroom—European Council of the EU, http://tvnewsroom.consilium.europa.eu/video/shotlist/arrival-and-doorstep -ep-president-schulz4.

95. Simon Romero, "Brazil's Leader Postpones State Visit to Washington over Spying," *New York Times*, September 17, 2013, www.nytimes.com/2013/09/18/world /americas/brazils-leader-postpones-state-visit-to-us.html; "Brazil Will Have Its Own National-Made Secure Communications Satellite by 2016," *MercoPress*, November 29, 2013, http://en.mercopress.com/2013/11/29/brazil-will-have-its -own-national-made-secure-communications-satellite-by-2016.

96. Jonathan A. Obar and Andrew Clement, "Internet Surveillance and Boomerang Routing: A Call for Canadian Sovereignty," *TEM 2013: Proceedings of the Technology & Emerging Media Track – Annual Conference of the Canadian Communication Association*, Victoria, June 5–7, 2012, 1–8.

97. Julian E. Barnes and Nathan Hodge, "Military Faces Historic Shift," *Wall Street Journal*, January 6, 2012; US Department of Defense, *Sustaining U.S. Global Leadership:*

Priorities for 21st Century Defense (Washington, DC: US Department of Defense, January 2012), 2–5, www.defense.gov/news/Defense_Strategic_Guidance.pdf.

98. Thom Shanker and David E. Sanger, "Privacy May Be a Victim in Cyberdefense Plan," *New York Times*, June 12, 2009.

99. Armed Forces News Service, "Gates Established US Cyber Command, Names First Commander," US Air Force, May 21, 2010, www.stratcom.mil/news/2010/161 /Gates_establishes_US_Cyber_Command_and_names_first_commander/; David Alexander, "Pentagon to Treat Cyberspace as 'Operational Domain,'" Reuters, July 14, 2011, www.reuters.com/article/2011/07/14/us-usa-defense-cybersecurity -idUSTRE76D5FA20110714.

100. Eric Schmitt and Thom Shanker, "U.S. Weighed Use of Cyberattacks to Weaken Libya," *New York Times*, October 18, 2011; David E. Sanger, "Obama Order Sped Up Wave of Cyberattacks Against Iran," *New York Times*, June 1, 2012; Joel Brenner, *America the Vulnerable: Inside the New Threat Matrix of Digital Espionage, Crime, and Warfare* (New York: Penguin Press, 2011), 102–5; Ian Traynor, "Russia Accused of Unleashing Cyberwar to Disable Estonia," *Guardian*, May 16, 2007, www.guardian.co.uk/world/2007/may/17/topstories3.russia; Lolita C. Baldor, "Pentagon Takes Aim at China Cyber Threat," Associated Press, August 19, 2010, http://archive.boston.com/news/nation/washington/articles/2010/08/19/pentagon _takes_aim_at_china_cyber_threat/; Lolita C. Baldor, "U.S., China to Cooperate More on Cyber Threat," Associated Press, May 7, 2012, http://cnsnews.com/news /article/us-china-cooperate-more-cyber-threat.

101. Shane, "New Leaked Document Outlines U.S. Spending on Intelligence Agencies."

102. Mattea Kramer and Chris Hellman, "'Homeland Security': The Trillion-Dollar Concept That No One Can Define," *TomDispatch*, February 28, 2013, www.tomdispatch.com/blog/175655/.

103. David E. Sanger, "Obama Panel Said to Urge N.S.A. Curbs," *New York Times*, December 13, 2013.

104. Bamford, "Every Move You Make."

105. Ibid.

106. MacAskill and Borger, "New NSA Leaks"; Poitras et al., "How the NSA Targets Germany and Europe"; James Bamford, "The NSA Is Building the Country's Biggest Spy Center (Watch What You Say)," *Wired*, March 15, 2012, www.wired. com/2012/03/ff_nsadatacenter/.

107. Bamford, *The Shadow Factory*, 338–39; Wolfgang Gruener, "Cray's New Super-computer XC30 Delivers 66 TFlops/Cabinet," *Tom's Hardware*, November 12, 2012, www.tomshardware.com/news/cray-xc30-supercomputer,19014.html.

108. Bamford, "Every Move You Make."

109. Ibid.; Charlie Savage, "N.S.A. Culled Fewer Phone Records in '16: 151 Million," *New York Times*, May 3, 2017; Charlie Savage, "Fight Brews Over Warrantless Surveillance," *New York Times*, May 7, 2017

110. James Risen and Laura Poitras, "N.S.A. Report Outlined Goals for More Power," *New York Times*, November 23, 2013.

111. Sam Perlo-Freeman, Elisabeth Sköns, Carina Solmirano, and Helen Wilandh,

Trends in World Military Expenditure, 2012 (Stockholm: Stockholm International Peace Research Institute, 2013), 2; Åsa Johansson et al., "Looking to 2060: Long-Term Global Growth Prospects: A Going for Growth Report," in *OECD Economic Policy Papers, No. 3* (Paris: OECD Publishing, 2012), Fig. 10, 23.

112. International Monetary Fund, "World Economic Outlook Database," April 2011 edition, www.imf.org/external/pubs/ft/weo/2011/01/weodata/index.aspx; Mark Weisbrot: "2016: When China Overtakes the US," *Guardian*, April 27, 2011, www.theguardian.com/commentisfree/cifamerica/2011/apr/27/china-imf-econ omy-2016; Michael Mandelbaum, *The Frugal Superpower: America's Global Leadership in a Cash-Strapped Era* (New York: Public Affairs, 2010), 20, 46–52, 185.

113. Shane, "New Leaked Document Outlines U.S. Spending on Intelligence Agencies," *New York Times*, August 30, 2013.

Chapter Five: Torture and the Eclipse of Empires

1. Ron Baer, *See No Evil: The True Story of a Ground Soldier in the CIA's War on Terrorism* (New York: Three Rivers Press, 2002), 268–69.

2. *The 9/11 Commission Report: Final Report of the National Commission on Terrorist Attacks upon the United States* (New York: W. W. Norton, 2004), 90–93.

3. Christopher Simpson, *Science of Coercion: Communication Research & Psychological Warfare, 1945–1960* (New York: Oxford University Press, 1994), 9.

4. Central Intelligence Agency, "Proposed Study on Special Interrogation Methods," February 14, 1952, CIA Behavior Control Experiments Collection (John Marks Donation), National Security Archive, Washington, DC [hereafter, NSA].

5. US Senate, 94th Congress, 2d Session, *Final Report of the Select Committee to Study Governmental Operations with Respect to Intelligence Activities,* book I (Washington, DC: Government Printing Office, 1976), 387–88.

6. Woodburn Heron, "The Pathology of Boredom," *Scientific American* 196 (January 1957): 52–56.

7. D. O. Hebb, "This Is How It Was," Canadian Psychological Association, ca. 1980 (copy provided to author by Mary Ellen Hebb).

8. Lawrence E. Hinkle Jr., "A Consideration of the Circumstances under Which Men May Be Interrogated, and the Effects That These May Have upon the Function of the Brain" (n.d., ca. 1958), 1, 5, 6, 11–14, 18, File: Hinkle, Box 7, CIA Behavior Control Experiments Collection (John Marks Donation), NSA; Lawrence E. Hinkle Jr. and Harold G. Wolff, "Communist Interrogation and Indoctrination of 'Enemies of the States': Analysis of Methods Used by the Communist State Police (A Special Report)," *Archives of Neurology and Psychiatry* 76 (1956): 115–74.

9. Joseph Margulies, *Guantánamo and the Abuse of Presidential Power* (New York: Simon & Schuster, 2006), 120–25; United Press, "Officers to Study 'Brainwash' Issue," *New York Times*, August 23, 1954; United Press, "Red Tactics Spur Code for P.O.W.'s," *New York Times*, August 14, 1955; Anthony Leviero, "New Code Orders P.O.W.s to Resist in 'Brainwashing,'" *New York Times*, August, 18, 1955; Dwight D. Eisenhower, "Executive Order 10631—Code of Conduct for Members of the

Armed Forces of the United States," August 17, 1955, American Presidency Project, University of California at Santa Barbara, www.presidency.ucsb.edu/ws/index .php?pid=59249.

10. "KUBARK Counterintelligence Interrogation" (July 1963), File: Kubark, Box 1: CIA Training Manuals, NSA, 87–90. The term *KUBARK* is an agency cryptonym denoting the CIA itself.

11. McCoy, *A Question of Torture*, chap. 3. To reach the figure of 46,776 Phoenix deaths, I took the total of 40,994 cited by Saigon authorities in 1971 and added 5,782 more, the difference between the US figure of 20,587 that William Colby gave in mid-1971 and the US figure of 26,369 released in 1972.

12. Central Intelligence Agency, Inspector General, "Special Review: Counterterrorism Detention and Interrogation Activities (September 2001–October 2003)," May 7, 2004, 10; Central Intelligence Agency, "Human Resources Exploitation Training Manual—1983," Box 1, CIA Training Manuals, NSA.

13. Erik Holst, "International Efforts on the Rehabilitation of Torture Victims," in June C. Pagaduan Lopez and Elizabeth Protacio Marcelino, eds., *Torture Survivors and Caregivers: Proceedings of the International Workshop on Therapy and Research Issues* (Quezon City: University of the Philippines Press, 1995), 8–14, 190–91, 291–316, 356–57.

14. US Senate, 100th Congress, 2d Session, Treaty Doc. 100-20, *Message from the President of the United States Transmitting the Convention against Torture and Other Cruel, Inhuman or Degrading Treatment or Punishment* (Washington, DC: Government Printing Office, 1988), iii–iv; Ahcene Boulesbaa, *The U.N. Convention on Torture and the Prospects for Enforcement* (The Hague: Martinus Nijhoff, 1999), 19.

15. United Nations Treaty Collection, Convention Against Torture, Status as at: 18-11-2016, https://treaties.un.org/Pages/ViewDetails.aspx?src=IND&mtdsg_no=IV -9&chapter=4&clang=_en.

16. *Congressional Record, Proceedings and Debates of the 103d Congress, Second Session*, vol. 140—Part I (Washington, DC: Government Printing Office, 1994), February 2, 1994, 827; Foreign Relations Authorization Act, PL 103–236, Title V, Sec. 506, 108 Stat. 463 (1994), 18 USC§ 2340-2340A.

17. Richard A. Clarke, *Against All Enemies: Inside America's War on Terror* (New York: Free Press, 2004), 24.

18. Robert G. Kaiser, "Congress-s-s: That Giant Hissing Sound You Hear in Capitol Hill Giving Up Its Clout," *Washington Post*, March 14, 2004.

19. John Yoo, "How the Presidency Regained Its Balance," *New York Times*, September 17, 2006.

20. US Senate Committee on Armed Services, 110th Congress, 2d Session, *Inquiry into the Treatment of Detainees in U.S. Custody* (Washington, DC: Government Printing Office, 2008), xiii, www.democrats.com/senate-armed-services-committee-report -on-torture; George W. Bush, The White House, Washington, For: The Vice President, "Subject: Humane Treatment of Taliban and al Qaeda Detainees," February 7, 2002, www.pegc.us/archive/White_House/bush_memo_20020207_ed.pdf.

21. Alfred W. McCoy, *Torture and Impunity: The U.S. Doctrine of Coercive Interrogation*

(Madison: University of Wisconsin Press, 2012), 28–31.

22. Jane Mayer, "The Black Sites: A Rare Look Inside the CIA's Secret Interrogation Program," *New Yorker*, August 13, 2007, www.newyorker.com/reporting/2007/08/13/070813fa_fact_mayer; US Senate, *Inquiry into the Treatment of Detainees in U.S. Custody*, xiii.

23. Stephen Grey, *Ghost Plane: The True Story of the CIA Torture Program* (New York: St. Martin's Press, 2006), 87, 181, 227, 269–308; Scott Shane, "C.I.A. Expanding Terror Battle under Guise of Charter Flights," *New York Times*, May 31, 2005.

24. Douglas Jehl, "Report Warned C.I.A. on Tactics in Interrogation," *New York Times*, November 9, 2005.

25. Jay Bybee, Office of the Assistant Attorney General, "Memorandum for Alberto R. Gonzales, Counsel to the President, Re: Standards of Conduct for Interrogation under 18 U.S.C. §§ 2340-2340A," August 1, 2002, 1, www.justice.gov/olc/file/886061/download; U.S. Senate, *Inquiry into the Treatment of Detainees in U.S. Custody*, xv–xvi, xxi.

26. Jay Bybee, Office of the Assistant Attorney General, "Memorandum for John Rizzo, Acting General Counsel of the Central Intelligence Agency," August 1, 2002, 5–6, 11, 17, www.washingtonpost.com/wp-srv/nation/pdf/OfficeofLegalCounsel_Aug2Memo_041609.pdf.

27. Steven G. Bradbury, Office of Legal Counsel, "Memorandum for John A. Rizzo Senior Deputy General Counsel, Central Intelligence Agency, Re: Application of 18 U.S.C. §§ 2340-2340A to the Combined Use of Certain Techniques in the Interrogation of High Value al Qaeda Detainees," May 10, 2005, 60, www.washingtonpost.com/wp-srv/nation/pdf/OfficeofLegalCounsel_May10Memo.pdf.

28. Steven G. Bradbury, Office of the Principal Deputy Assistant Attorney General, Office of Legal Counsel, "Memorandum for John A. Rizzo Senior Deputy Counsel, Central Intelligence Agency, Re: Application of United States Obligations Under Article 16 of the Convention Against Torture to Certain Techniques That May Be Used in the Interrogation of High Value al Qaeda Detainees," May 30, 2005, 38, http://nsarchive.gwu.edu/torture_archive/docs/Bradbury%20memo.pdf.

29. Mark Mazzetti, "U.S. Says C.I.A. Destroyed 92 Tapes of Interrogations," *New York Times*, March 3, 2009.

30. Bradbury, "Memorandum for John A. Rizzo," May 10, 2005, 53–56.

31. Bradbury, "Memorandum for John A. Rizzo," May 30, 2005, 37.

32. Jan Crawford Greenburg, Howard L. Rosenberg, and Ariane De Vogue, "Sources: Top Bush Advisors Approved 'Enhanced Interrogation,'" ABC News, April 9, 2008, www.abcnews.go.com/TheLaw/LawPolitics/story?id=4583256; CIA, "Special Review," 5, 24, 45, 101.

33. US Senate, *Inquiry into the Treatment of Detainees in U.S. Custody*, xix; William J. Haynes II, General Counsel, Department of Defense, For: Secretary of Defense, "Subject: Counter-Resistance Techniques," November 27, 2002, www.washingtonpost.com/wp-srv/nation/documents/dodmemos.pdf; Mark Mazzetti and Scott Shane, "Notes Show Confusion on Interrogation Methods," *New York Times*, June 18, 2008.

34. US Senate, *Inquiry into the Treatment of Detainees*, xix; Hayes, For: Secretary of

Defense, November 27, 2002; Mazzetti and Shane, "Notes Show Confusion."

35. M. Gregg Bloche and Jonathan H. Marks, "Doctors and Interrogators at Guantanamo Bay," *New England Journal of Medicine* 353, no. 1 (July 7, 2005): 7; Jonathan H. Marks, "The Silence of the Doctors," *Nation*, December 8, 2005, www.thenation.com/article/silence-doctors/.

36. Neil A. Lewis, "Red Cross Finds Detainee Abuse in Guantánamo," *New York Times*, November 30, 2004.

37. Ricardo S. Sanchez, "Memorandum for: C2, Combined Joint Task Force Seven, Baghdad, Iraq 09335, Subject: CJTF-7 Interrogation and Counter-Resistance Policy," *Truthout*, September 14, 2003, http://truth-out.org/archive/component/k2/item/53410:gen-ricardo-sanchez-orders-torture-in-iraq-his-memo.

38. Eric Schmitt and Carolyn Marshall, "In Secret Unit's 'Black Room,' a Grim Portrait of U.S. Abuse," *New York Times*, March 19, 2006.

39. Phil Klay, "What We're Fighting For," *New York Times*, February 12, 2017; US State Department, Canonical ID: 06KUWAIT913_a, From: Kuwait City, Kuwait, "Regional CT Strategy for Iraq and Its Neighbors: Results and Recommendations from March 7–8 COM Meeting," March 18, 2006, WikiLeaks, Public Library of US Diplomacy, wikileaks.org/plusd/cables/06KUWAIT913_a.html.

40. Terrence McCoy, "How the Islamic State Evolved in an American Prison," *Washington Post*, November 4, 2014, www.washingtonpost.com/news/morning-mix/wp/2014/11/04/how-an-american-prison-helped-ignite-the-islamic-state/.

41. Martin Chulov, "ISIS: The Inside Story," *Guardian*, December 11, 2014, www.theguardian.com/world/2014/dec/11/-sp-isis-the-inside-story.

42. Public Law 109-366, Oct. 17, 2006, Military Commissions Act of 2006, § 950v (12) (B) (i) (IV).

43. US House of Representatives, 105th Congress, 1st Session, Report 105-204, *Expanded War Crimes Act of 1997: Report Together with Dissenting Views*, July 25, 1997, 2–3.

44. Antonio Taguba, preface to Farnoosh Hāshemian, *Broken Laws, Broken Lives: Medical Evidence of Torture by U.S. Personnel and Its Impact* (Cambridge, MA: Physicians for Human Rights, June 2008), viii.

45. Scott Wilson, "Obama Reverses Pledge to Release Photos of Detainee Abuse," *Washington Post*, May 14, 2009, www.washingtonpost.com/wp-dyn/content/article/2009/05/13/AR2009051301751.html.

46. Greg Miller, "Cheney Assertions of Lives Saved Hard to Support," *Los Angeles Times*, May 23, 2009, http://articles.latimes.com/2009/may/23/nation/na-cheney23.

47. "Statement of President Barack Obama on Release of OLC Memos," The White House, Press Office, April 16, 2009, www.whitehouse.gov/the_press_office/Statement-of-President-Barack-Obama-on-Release-of-OLC-Memos/.

48. Peter Baker and Scott Shane, "Pressure Grows to Investigate Interrogations," *New York Times*, April 21, 2009; Editorial, "How the Obama Administration Should Deal with Torture's Legacy," *Washington Post*, April 24, 2009, www.washingtonpost.com/wpdyn/content/article/2009/04/23/AR2009042303476.html.

49. McCoy, *Torture and Impunity*, 255–56.

50. Jose A. Rodriguez Jr., *Hard Measures: How Aggressive CIA Actions after 9/11 Saved American Lives* (New York: Threshold Editions, 2012).

51. US Senate Select Committee on Intelligence, *Committee Study of the Central Intelligence Agency's Detention and Interrogation Program: Executive Summary* (Washington, DC: US Senate, December 3, 2014).

52. Ibid., 49–57.

53. Mark Mazzetti and Matt Apuzzo, "C.I.A. Director Rebuts Report, Calling Interrogators 'Patriots,'" *New York Times*, December 12, 2014.

54. Sheri Fink, James Risen, and Charlie Savage, "New Details of C.I.A. Torture, and a New Clash," *New York Times*, January 20, 2017; US Senate Select Committee on Intelligence, *Committee Study of the Central Intelligence Agency's Detention and Interrogation Program: Findings and Conclusions* (Washington, DC: US Senate, December 3, 2014), 11.

55. Ibid., 3–5, 9–11; US Senate Select Committee on Intelligence, *Committee Study of the Central Intelligence Agency's Detention and Interrogation Program: Executive Summary*, 17–48, 204–9, 405–8.

56. Rebecca Gordon, "The Al-Qaeda Leader Who Wasn't: The Shameful Ordeal of Abu Zubaydah," *TomDispatch*, April 24, 2016, www.tomdispatch.com/blog/176132/; US Senate Select Committee on Intelligence, *Committee Study of the Central Intelligence Agency's Detention and Interrogation Program: Executive Summary*, 21.

57. Dick Cheney, *In My Time: A Personal and Political Memoir* (New York: Threshold Editions, 2011), 357–59.

58. Ali H. Soufan, *The Black Banners: The Inside Story of 9/11 and the War against al-Qaeda* (New York: W. W. Norton, 2011), 547; McCoy, *Torture and Impunity*, 256–59.

59. US Senate, Committee on the Judiciary, 111th Congress, 1st Session, *What Went Wrong: Torture and the Office of Legal Counsel in the Bush Administration*, Testimony of Ali Soufan, May 13, 2009, www.judiciary.senate.gov/meetings/what-went-wrong-torture-and-the-office-of-legal-counsel-in-the-bush-administration; Soufan, *The Black Banners*, 377, 395–96.

60. Hinkle and Wolff, "Communist Interrogation and Indoctrination,'" 115–74.

61. Jason Leopold and Ky Henderson, "Tequila, Painted Pearls, and Prada—How the CIA Helped Produce 'Zero Dark Thirty,'" *Vice News*, September 9, 2015, https://news.vice.com/article/tequila-painted-pearls-and-prada-how-the-cia-helped-produce-zero-dark-thirty.

62. PBS, "Secrets, Politics, Torture," *Frontline*, May 19, 2015, www.pbs.org/wgbh/frontline/film/secrets-politics-and-torture/.

63. Jane Mayer, "The Unidentified Queen of Torture," *New Yorker*, December 18, 2014, www.newyorker.com/news/news-desk/unidentified-queen-torture.

64. Glenn Greenwald and Peter Maas, "Meet Alfreda Bikowsky, the Senior Officer at the Center of the CIA's Torture Scandals," *Intercept*, December 19, 2014, https://theintercept.com/2014/12/19/senior-cia-officer-center-torture-scandals-alfreda-bikowsky/; Center for Legitimate Government, "CIA Torture Queen Bought $825K House While Torturing Her Way to the Top," *CLG Newsletter*, December 20,

2014, www.legitgov.org/CLG-Exclusive-CIA-Torture-Queen-Bought-825K-House-While-Torturing-Her-Way-Top.

65. Jenna Johnson, "Trump Says 'Torture Works,' Backs Waterboarding and 'Much Worse,'" *Washington Post*, February 17, 2016, www.washingtonpost.com/politics/trump-says-torture-works-backs-waterboarding-and-much-worse/2016/02/17/4c9277be-d59c-11e5-b195-2e29a4e13425_story.html.

66. Matt Apuzzo and James Risen, "Donald Trump Faces Obstacles to Resuming Waterboarding," *New York Times,* November 29, 2016; Ryan Browne and Nicole Gaouette, "Donald Trump Reverses Position on Torture, Killing Terrorists' Families," CNN, March 4, 2006, www.cnn.com/2016/03/04/politics/donald-trump-reverses-on-torture/index.html.

67. Steve Benen, "Trump Sees Geneva Conventions as 'Out of Date,'" *MSNBC: The Rachel Maddow Show/The Maddow Blog,* July 27, 2016, www.msnbc.com/rachel-maddow-show/trump-sees-geneva-conventions-out-date.

68. Editorial, "Torture and Its Psychological Aftermath," *New York Times*, October 21, 2016.

69. Julie Hirschfeld Davis, "Trump Selects Loyalists on Right Flank to Fill National Security Posts," *New York Times*, November 19, 2016; Julie Pace and Jonathan Lemire, Associated Press, "Trump Makes AG, CIA Picks," *Wisconsin State Journal,* November 19, 2016; Curis Tate, McClatchey News, "Feinstein: Pompeo 'Absolutely Wrong' about Her Report on CIA Interrogation Program," *The State*, November 18, 2016, www.thestate.com/news/politics-government/article115734493.html#2; Lindsay Wise and Bryan Lowry, McClatchey News, "CIA Nominee Mike Pompeo on Torture, Muslims, Terror, Iran, NSA Spying," *Wichita Eagle*, November 18, 2016, www.kansas.com/news/politics-government/article115646238.html.

70. Apuzzo and Risen, "Donald Trump Faces Obstacles"; Charlie Savage, "Trump Poised to Lift Ban on C.I.A. 'Black Site' Prisons," *New York Times*, January 25, 2017; Mark Mazzetti and Charlie Savage, "Leaked Order Could Revive C.I.A. Prisons," *New York Times*, January 26, 2017; "Transcript: ABC News Anchor David Muir Interviews President Trump," ABC News, January 25, 2017, www.abcnews.go.com/Politics/transcript-abc-news-anchor-david-muir-interviews-president/story?id=45047602; M. Gregg Bloche, "When Doctors First Do Harm," *New York Times*, November 23, 2016; "Donald Trump's New York Times Interview: Full Transcript," *New York Times*, November 23, 2016, www.nytimes.com/2016/11/23/us/politics/trump-new-york-times-interview-transcript.html.

71. Office of the Prosecutor, International Criminal Court, *Report on Preliminary Examination Activities 2016*, November 14, 2016, para. 211, p. 47, www.icc-cpi.int/iccdocs/otp/161114-otp-rep-PE_ENG.pdf.

72. Marnia Lazreg, *Torture and the Twilight of Empire: From Algiers to Baghdad* (Princeton, NJ: Princeton University Press, 2008), 3, 255–56.

73. George J. Andreopoulos, "The Age of National Liberation Movements," in Michael Howard, George J. Andreopoulos, and Mark R. Shulman, eds., *The Laws of War: Constraints on Warfare in the Western World* (New Haven, CT: Yale University Press, 1994), 205–6; T. Lightcap and J. Pfiffer, eds., *Examining Torture: Empirical*

Studies of State Repression (London: Palgrave Macmillan, 2014), chap. 1.

74. Edward Peters, *Torture* (Philadelphia: University of Pennsylvania Press, 1996), 139; Adam Shatz, "The Torture of Algiers," *New York Review of Books*, November 21, 2002, 53–57.

75. Peters, *Torture*, 138–40; Shatz, "Torture of Algiers," 53–57; Henri Alleg, *The Question* (New York: G. Braziller, 1958), 54–67; Interview with Saadi Yacef, in "The Battle of Algiers: Remembering History," *The Battle of Algiers*, directed by Gillo Pontecorvo, 1966 (Criterion Collection, DVD, 2004); Paul Aussaresses, *The Battle of the Casbah: Terrorism and Counter-Terrorism in Algeria, 1955–1957* (New York: Enigma, 2002), 120–21, 126–27, 162–63.

76. "Sir Alistair Horne interview," in *The Battle of Algiers*.

77. Alleg, *The Question*, 61; "Henri Alleg interview," in *The Battle of Algiers*; Shatz, "Torture of Algiers," 57.

78. Peters, *Torture*, 138–40; "Benjamin Stora interview," in *The Battle of Algiers*.

79. Lord Parker of Waddington, *Report of the Committee of Privy Counsellors Appointed to Consider Authorised Procedures for the Interrogation of Persons Suspected of Terrorism* (London: Stationery Office, Cmnd. 4901, 1972), 3, 12, 17; S. Smith and W. Lewty, "Perceptual Isolation in a Silent Room," *Lancet* 1959, 2 (September 12, 1959), 342–45; James Meek, "Nobody Is Talking," *Guardian*, February 18, 2005, www.theguardian.com/world/2005/feb/18/usa.afghanistan; "Lancaster Moor Hospital," www.asylumprojects.org/index.php?title=Lancaster_Moor_Hospital,

80. Sir Edmund Compton, *Report of the Enquiry into Allegations against the Security Forces of Physical Brutality in Northern Ireland Arising Out of Events on the 9th August, 1971* (London: Stationery Office, Cmnd. 4823, November 1971), para. 46; Parker of Waddington, *Report of the Committee of Privy Counsellors*, 1–3, 23–24; Piers Brendon, *The Decline and Fall of the British Empire, 1781–1997* (New York: Vintage, 2010), 563–74.

81. Parker of Waddington, *Report of the Committee of Privy Counsellors*, 1, 12; Roderic Bowen, *Report by Mr. Roderic Bowen, Q.C. on Procedures for the Arrest, Interrogation and Detention of Terrorists in Aden* (London: Stationery Office, Cmnd 3165, December 1966), 3–7, 16–24.

82. "Ireland v. The United Kingdom," No. 5310/17, European Court of Human Rights, January 18, 1978, para. 32, 34, 39, 81, 96–97, www.worldlii.org/eu/cases/ECHR /1978/1.html.

83. Ibid., para. 96.

84. Compton, *Report of the Enquiry into Allegations*, para. 1; *Times* (London), October 17, October 19, October 20, 1971.

85. Compton, *Report of the Enquiry into Allegations,* para. 46–52, 64, 92, 98; *Times* (London), November 17 and November 18, 1971, July 9, 1973.

86. *Times* (London), November 9, November 11, March 13, 1972; *Report of an Enquiry into Allegations of Ill-treatment in Northern Ireland* (London: Amnesty International, March 1972), 36–38.

87. *Times* (London), May 14, August 27, September 3, 1976; "Ireland v. The United Kingdom," para. 102, 147, 166–67, 246; Meek, "Nobody Is Talking."

Chapter Six: Beyond Bayonets and Battleships

1. Commission on Presidential Debates, October 22, 2012, Debate Transcript, President Barack Obama and Former Gov. Mitt Romney (R–Mass.), Lynn University, Boca Raton, Florida, www.debates.org/index.php?page=october-22-2012-the-third-obama-romney-presidential-debate.

2. Dwight D. Eisenhower, "Military-Industrial Complex Speech, 1961," http://coursesa.matrix.msu.edu/~hst306/documents/indust.html.

3. Katie Hafner and Matthew Lyon, *Where Wizards Stay Up Late: The Origins of the Internet* (New York: Simon & Schuster, 1999), 13–35.

4. Stockholm International Peace Research Institute, *SIPRI Yearbook 2011: Armaments, Disarmament and International Security; Summary* (Solna, Sweden: SIPRI, 2011), 9–11.

5. Frederick Winterbotham, *The Ultra Secret* (London: Weidenfeld and Nicolson, 1974).

6. Victor B. Anthony and Richard R. Sexton, *The United States Air Force in Southeast Asia: The War in Northern Laos, 1954–1973* (Washington, DC: Center for Air Force History, United States Air Force, 1993), 333.

7. Air Force, Headquarters, Pacific Air Forces, "Corona Harvest: USAF Force Withdrawal from Southeast Asia, 1 January 1970–30 June 1971 (U)," May 31, 1972, 53–54, 76, 78, www.scribd.com/doc/51912794/USAF-Withdrawal-from-Southeast-Asia-1-JANUARY-1970–30-JUNE-1971.

8. Anthony and Sexton, *United States Air Force in Southeast Asia*, 333.

9. US Congress, *Congressional Record—Senate: May 14, 1975* (Washington, DC: Government Printing Office, 1975), 14266.

10. Anthony and Sexton, *United States Air Force in Southeast Asia*, 296–97.

11. Ibid., 336.

12. Anthony and Sexton, *United States Air Force in Southeast Asia*, 336; "Rockeye II Mark 20," US Naval Museum of Armament and Technology, China Lake, California; Greg Goebel, "CBU-2/A: 360 'BLU-3/B Pineapple'" and "CBU-46B/A: 640 'BLU-66/B Pineapple,'" in, [2.2] US Rockeye, SUU-30, & TMD Canisters, *Dumb Bombs & Smart Munitions*, http://www.faqs.org/docs/air/twbomb.html..

13. Channapha Khamvongsa and Elaine Russell, "Legacies of War: Cluster Bombs in Laos," *Critical Asian Studies* 41, no. 2 (2001): 281–306; The National Regulatory Authority for UXO/Mine Action, Lao People's Democratic Republic, "The Unexploded Ordnance (UXO) Problem and Operational Progress in the Lao PDR—Official Figures," June 2, 2010, www.nra.gov.la/resources/Official%20UXO%20Statistic/UXO%20Sector%20Official%20Statistics%20-%20signed.pdf.

14. Mark Landler, "Obama Acknowledges Scars of America's Secret War in Laos," *New York Times*, September 6, 2016.

15. Jacob Van Staaveren, *Interdiction in Southern Laos, 1960–1968* (Washington, DC: Center for Air Force History, 1993), 255–69; "Obituary: Alfred Starbird, Retired General," *New York Times*, July 30, 1983, www.nytimes.com/1983/07/30/obituaries/alfred-starbird-retired-general.html; HQ PACAF, Directorate, Tactical Evaluation, Project Contemporary Historical Examination of Current Operation (hereafter CHECO), "Igloo White July 1968–December 1969 (U)," January 10, 1970, 1–5, www.dtic.mil/dtic/tr/fulltext/u2/a485055.pdf.

16. Andrew Cockburn, *Kill Chain: The Rise of High-Tech Assassins* (New York: Picador, 2016), 23.

17. US Congress, *Congressional Record—Senate: May 14, 1975*, 14265–66; Raphael Littauer and Norman Uphoff, eds., *The Air War in Indochina* (Boston: Beacon Press, 1972), 9–11, 168, 281; James W. Gibson, *The Perfect War: Technowar in Vietnam* (New York: Atlantic Monthly Press, 2000), 396–97; John T. Correll, "Igloo White," *Air Force Magazine*, November 2004, www.airforcemag.com/MagazineArchive/Pages/2004/November%202004/1104igloo.aspx; CHECO, "Igloo White July 1968–December 1969 (U)," 21–28.

18. Gibson, *The Perfect War*, 397; Staaveren, *Interdiction in Southern Laos*, 271–72; Correll, "Igloo White"; Littauer and Uphoff, *The Air War in Indochina*, 154; CHECO, "Igloo White July 1968–December 1969 (U)," 17–19; Bernard C. Nalty, *The War against Trucks* (Washington, DC: Air Force Museums and History Program, 2005), 103.

19. CHECO, "Igloo White July 1968–December 1969 (U)," 30–31; Nalty, *The War against Trucks*, 41, 85–88, 126–27, 217; Thomas P. Ehrhard, "Unmanned Aerial Vehicles in the United States Armed Services: A Comparative Study of Weapon System Innovation" (PhD diss., John Hopkins University, 2000), 162n.

20. Cockburn, *Kill Chain*, 23–24.

21. Ibid., 24; CHECO, "Igloo White July 1968–December 1969 (U)," 20, 35.

22. Gibson, *The Perfect War*, 398–99; Staaveren, *Interdiction in Southern Laos*, 278.

23. Correll, "Igloo White."

24. Military History Institute of Vietnam, *Victory in Vietnam*, trans. Merle Pribbenow (Lawrence: University of Kansas Press, 2002), 320; Correll, "Igloo White."

25. Nalty, *The War against Trucks*, 294, 301–2; Cockburn, *Kill Chain*, 26–31.

26. Anthony and Sexton, *United States Air Force in Southeast Asia*, 106, 239.

27. Richard Whittle, *Predator: The Secret Origins of the Drone Revolution* (New York: Henry Holt, 2014), 21–22, 170–71; Ehrhard, "Unmanned Aerial Vehicles in the United States Armed Services," 413, 417–18. Greg Goebel, "The Lightning Bug Reconnaissance Drones," www.vectorsite.net/twuav_04.html#m3; US Air Force, *The US Air Force Remotely Piloted Aircraft and Unmanned Aerial Vehicle Strategic Vision* (2005), 1–2, www.af.mil/shared/media/document/AFD-060322-009.pdf.

28. Whittle, *Predator*, 22.

29. Rowe Findley, "Telephone a Star," *National Geographic*, May 1962, 638–51; Telesat, "Brief History of Satellite Communications," www.telesat.com/about-us/why-satellite/brief-history.

30. UPI, "Comsat Launches Second Lani Bird," *New York Times*, January 12, 1967; UPI, "U.S. Plugs 8 Radio Gaps with Single Rocket Shot," *New York Times*, January 19, 1967; David N. Spires and Rick W. Sturdevant, "From Advent to Milstar: The U.S. Air Force and the Challenges of Military Satellite Communications," *NASA History Homepage*, para. 65–69, history.nasa.gov/SP-4217/ch7.htm; JPL Mission and Spacecraft Library, "DSCS (Defense Satellite Communications System): Launch Facts," http://space.jpl.nasa.gov/msl/Programs/dscs.html.

31. Stephen Daggett, *Costs of Major U.S. Wars: CRS Report for Congress* (Washington, DC: Congressional Research Service, July 24, 2008), 2, www.fas.org/sgp/crs/natsec

/RS22926.pdf.

32. Laura Blumenfeld, "Spurred by Gratitude, 'Bomb Lady' Develops Better Weapons for U.S.," *Washington Post*, December 1, 2007.

33. Whittle, *Predator*, 25–38, 40–41, 75–89; US Naval Observatory, "NAVSTAR Global Positioning System," *NAVSTAR GPS Operations*, http://tycho.usno.navy.mil /gpsinfo.html.

34. Whittle, *Predator*, 100–104.

35. Gopal, *No Good Men among the Living*, 13–14; Cockburn, *Kill Chain*, 118–20; Whittle, *Predator*, 232–61.

36. Cockburn, *Kill Chain*, 177; Peter W. Singer, "Do Drones Undermine Democracy?," *New York Times*, January 21, 2012, www.nytimes.com/2012/01/22/opinion/sunday /do-drones-undermine-democracy.html.

37. Christopher Drew, "For U.S., Drones Are Weapons of Choice in Fighting Qaeda," *New York Times*, March 16, 2009.

38. Cockburn, *Kill Chain*, 215.

39. Drew, "For U.S., Drones Are Weapons"; Cockburn, *Kill Chain*, 223–25.

40. Bill Roggio, "Charting the Data for US Airstrikes in Pakistan, 2004–2016," *FDD's Long War Journal*, June 16, 2016, www.longwarjournal.org/pakistan-strikes/.

41. Bureau of Investigative Journalism, "Drone Wars, Casualty Estimates," May 21, 2016, www.thebureauinvestigates.com/category/projects/drones/drones-graphs/.

42. Nick Turse, "The Drone Surge: Today, Tomorrow, and 2047," *TomDispatch*, January 24, 2010, www.tomdispatch.com/archive/175195/nick_turse_the_forty_year _drone_war.

43. "The Growing U.S. Drone Fleet," *Washington Post*, December 23, 2011, www .washingtonpost.com/world/national-security/the-growing-us-drone-fleet/2011 /12/23/gIQA76faEP_graphic.html; Peter Finn, "Rise of the Drone: From Calif. Garage to Multibillion-Dollar Defense Industry," *Washington Post*, December 23, 2011, www .washingtonpost.com/national/national-security/rise-of-the-drone-from-calif-garage -to-multibillion-dollar-defense-industry/2011/12/22/gIQACG8UEP_story.html.

44. David Cenciotti, "Future Drone's World Capital? Sigonella, Italy," *Aviationist*, February 9, 2012, http://theaviationist.com/2012/02/09/future-drones-world -capital-sigonella-italy/.

45. Craig Whitlock, "U.S. Military Drone Surveillance Is Expanding to Hot Spots beyond Declared Combat Zones," *Washington Post*, July 20, 2013, www.washingtonpost .com/world/national-security/us-military-drone-surveillance-is-expanding-to-hot -spots-beyond-declared-combat-zones/2013/07/20/0a57fbda-ef1c-11e2-8163 -2c7021381a75_story.html.

46. Craig Whitlock and Greg Miller, "U.S. Moves Drone Fleet from Camp Lemonnier to Ease Djibouti's Safety Concerns," *Washington Post*, September 24, 2014, www.washingtonpost.com/world/national-security/drone-safety-concerns-force -us-to-move-large-fleet-from-camp-lemonnier-in-djibouti/2013/09/24/955518c4 -213c-11e3-a03d-abbedc3a047c_story.html.

47. Peter Kovessy, "Qatar Military Pilots Receiving Drone Training This Month," *Doha News*, September 4, 2014, http://dohanews.co/qatar-armed-forces-training

-drone-operators/; Micah Zenko and Emma Welch, "Where the Drones Are: Mapping the Launch Pads for Obama's Secret Wars," *Foreign Policy*, May 29, 2012, http://foreignpolicy.com/2012/05/29/where-the-drones-are/.

48. Zenko and Welch, "Where the Drones Are."

49. Ibid.

50. Gaynor Dumat-ol Daleno, "New Drone to Be Deployed to Guam," *sUAS News*, March 6, 2015, www.suasnews.com/2015/03/34634/new-drone-to-be-deployed-to-guam/.

51. Cockburn, *Kill Chain*, 252–53; Turse, "The Drone Surge"; Nick Turse, "America's Secret Empire of Drone Bases: Its Full Extent Revealed for the First Time," *TomDispatch*, October 16, 2011,www.tomdispatch.com/blog/175454/tomgram%3A _nick_turse%2C_mapping_america%27s_shadowy_drone_wars; Nick Turse, "The Crash and Burn Future of Robot Warfare: What 70 Downed Drones Tell Us about the New American Way of War," *TomDispatch*, January 15, 2012, www.tomdispatch .com/archive/175489/.

52. "Unmanned Aircraft Systems," AeroVironment, Inc., www.avinc.com.

53. Michael S. Schmidt, "Air Force, Short of Drone Pilots, Uses Contractors to Fight Terror," *New York Times*, September 6, 2016; Jacek Siminski, "Nobody Wants to Fly Drones," *Aviationist*, September 6, 2013, https://theaviationist.com/2013/09/06 /nobody-wants-to-fly-drones/; Pratap Chatterjee, "Are Pilots Deserting Washington's Remote-Control War? A New Form of War May Be Producing a New Form of Mental Disturbance," *TomDispatch*, March 5, 2015, www.tomdispatch.com/blog/175964/.

54. Scott Shane, "C.I.A. Is Disputed on Civilian Toll in Drone Strikes," *New York Times*, August 12, 2011.

55. Cockburn, *Kill Chain*, 248–49; Tom Engelhardt, "The US Has Bombed at Least Eight Wedding Parties since 2001," *Nation*, December 20, 2013, www.thenation .com/article/us-has-bombed-least-eight-wedding-parties-2001/.

56. Cockburn, *Kill Chain*, 1–4.

57. David S. Cloud, "Transcripts of U.S. Drone Attack," *Los Angeles Times*, April 8, 2011, http://documents.latimes.com/transcript-of-drone-attack/.

58. Cockburn, *Kill Chain*, 1–16.

59. Major General Timothy P. McHale, Memorandum for Commander, United States Forces-Afghanistan/International Security Assistance Force, Afghanistan, Subject: Executive Summary for AR15-6 Investigation, February 21, 2010, CIVCAS incident in Uruzgan Province, www.rs.nato.int/images/stories/File/April2010-Dari /May2010Revised/Uruzgan%20investigation%20findings.pdf.

60. Cockburn, *Kill Chain*, 13–16.

61. Kimberly Dozier et al., "A Question of Secrecy vs. Safety," *Wisconsin State Journal*, June 17, 2012; Pew Research Center, "Global Opinion of Obama Slips, International Policies Faulted; Drone Strikes Widely Opposed," June 13, 2012, www.pewglobal. org/2012/06/13/global-opinion-of-obama-slips-international-policies-faulted/.

62. Pew Research Center, "Global Opposition to U.S. Surveillance and Drones, but Limited Harm to America's Image; Chapter 1: The American Brand," July 14, 2014, www.pewglobal.org/2014/07/14/chapter-1-the-american-brand/.

63. Scott Shane, "Drone Strikes Reveal Uncomfortable Truth: U.S. Is Often Unsure

about Who Will Die," *New York Times*, April 23, 2015, nytimes.com/2015/04/24/world/asia/drone-strikes-reveal-uncomfortable-truth-us-is-often-unsure-about-who-will-die.html.

64. Shane, "C.I.A. Is Disputed"; Charlie Savage and Scott Shane, "U.S. Makes Public the Death Toll from Airstrikes," *New York Times*, July 2, 2016.

65. Cockburn, *Kill Chain*, 245; Bryan D. "Doug" Brown, "U.S. Special Operations Command: Meeting the Challenges of the 21st Century," *Joint Force Quarterly*, no. 40 (2006): 38–43, www.dtic.mil/dtic/tr/fulltext/u2/a481635.pdf; Bob Woodward, "Secret CIA Units Playing a Central Combat Role," *Washington Post*, November 18, 2001, www.washingtonpost.com/wpdyn/content/article/2007/11/18/AR2007111800675.html.

66. US Special Operations Command, *USSOCOM Fact Book 2015*, 12, www.socom.mil/Documents/2015%20Fact%20Book.pdf; Nick Turse, "American Special Operations Forces Have a Very Funny Definition of Success," *Nation*, October 26, 2015, www.thenation.com/article/american-special-operations-forces-have-a-very-funny-definition-of-success/; Mark Moyar, Hector Pagan, and Wil R. Griego, *Persistent Engagement in Colombia* (MacDill Air Force Base, Florida: JSOU Press, 2014), 29–30.

67. Edilberto C. de Jesus and Melinda Quintos de Jesus, "The Mamasapano Detour," in Paul Hutchcroft, ed., *Mindanao: The Long Journey to Peace and Prosperity* (Manila: Anvil, 2016), 160, 181.

68. De Jesus and de Jesus, "The Mamasapano Detour," 165; Philippine Senate, Committee on Public Order, "The Committee Report on the Mamasapano Incident," January 24, 2016, 1–2, 22–28, www.philstar.com/headlines/2015/03/18/1434963/document-senate-panels-report-mamasapano-clash; Arlyn dela Cruz, "SAF Chief: I Am Responsible," *Inquirer.net*, January 29, 2015, http://newsinfo.inquirer.net/668715/saf-chief-i-am-responsible.

69. David S. Cloud and Sunshine de Leon, "A Heavy Price Paid for Botched Terrorist Raid by Philippines and U.S.," *Los Angeles Times*, September 10, 2015, www.latimes.com/world/asia/la-fg-botched-terror-raid-20150910-story.html.

70. Philippine Senate, "The Committee Report on the Mamasapano Incident," 1–2, 50, 58; Moro Islamic Liberation Front Special Investigative Commission, "Report on the Mamasapano Incident" (March 2015), 1–5; de Jesus and de Jesus, "The Mamasapano Detour," 161, 165–66.

71. Committee on Public Order, "The Committee Report on the Mamasapano Incident," 94–97, 100–101; Patricia Lourdes Viray, "Senate Report Confirms US Involvement in Mamasapano Operation," *Philstar Global*, March 17, 2015, www.philstar.com/headlines/2015/03/17/1434648/senate-report-confirms-us-involvement-mamasapano-operation; Jeoffrey Maitem, "US Role in Maguindanao Operation Questioned," *Inquirer.net*, January 28, 2015, http://globalnation.inquirer.net/118067/us-role-in-maguindanao-operation-questioned; Julie S. Alipala, "US behind Oplan Exodus," *Inquirer.net*, February 16, 2015, http://globalnation.inquirer.net/118745/us-behind-oplan-exodus; "Napeñas Balked at Giving Whole Truth on US Role in Mamasapano—Poe," *GMA News Online*, March 19, 2015,

www.gmanetwork.com/news/story/455541/news/nation/napenas-balkeat-giving
-whole-truth-on-us-role-in-mamasapano-poe.

72. Philippine National Police, *Board of Inquiry: The Mamasapano Report* (Quezon City: Philippine National Police, 2015), 41–42, 78–79.

73. Ibid.

74. Arlyn dela Cruz, "US Drone Watched Mamsapano Debacle," *Inquirer.net*, February 8, 2015, http://newsinfo.inquirer.net/671237/us-drone-watched-mamasapano -debacle; Carmela Fonbuena, "What Is EDCA? Look at Zambo's PH-US Joint Operations," *Rappler*, May 15, 2014, www.rappler.com/nation/57985-edca-zamboanga -jsotf-joint-operations.

75. Alipala, "US behind Oplan Exodus."

76. De Jesus and de Jesus, "The Mamasapano Detour," 190; Arlyn dela Cruz, "Police Board of Inquiry: SAF Troops Killed Marwan," *Inquirer.net*, September 14, 2015, http:// newsinfo.inquirer.net/721726/board-of-inquiry-saf-troops-killed-marwan; Marlon Ramos and Nikko Dizon, "Duterte Hits Aquino on Mamasapano," *Inquirer.net*, January 25, 2017, newsinfo.inquirer.net/865165/duterte-hits-aquino-on-mamasapano.

77. Philippine National Police, *Board of Inquiry*, 88–89.

78. Cloud and de Leon, "A Heavy Price Paid."

79. David S. Maxwell, Statement, US House of Representatives, 112 Congress, 2d Session, Committee on the Armed Services, Subcommittee on Emerging Threats and Capabilities, *Understanding Future Irregular Warfare Challenges* (Washington, DC: Government Printing Office, 2012), 63–88; Randy David, "The American Role in Mamasapano," *Inquirer.net*, March 22, 2015, http://opinion.inquirer.net/83507 /the-american-role-in-mamasapano.

80. Craig Whitlock and Greg Jaffe, "Obama Announces New, Leaner Military Approach," *Washington Post*, January 5, 2012, www.washingtonpost.com/world/national -security/obama-announces-new-military-approach/2012/01/05/gIQAFWcmcP _story.html?hpid=z1; US Department of Defense, *Sustaining U.S. Global Leadership: Priorities for 21st Century Defense* (Washington, DC: White House, January 2012), 5, http://archive.defense.gov/news/Defense_Strategic_Guidance.pdf.

81. Edward Helmore, "US Air Force Prepares Drones to End Era of Fighter Pilots," *Guardian*, August 22, 2009, www.guardian.co.uk/world/2009/aug/22/us-air-force -drones-pilots-afghanistan.

82. Matthew Rosenberg and John Markoff, "At the Heart of U.S. Strategy, Weapons That Can Think," *New York Times*, October 26, 2016.

83. The definitive French text of the 1919 Paris Convention, which the United States failed to ratify, stated in Article I that the parties recognize "*la soveraineté complète et exclusive sur l'espace atmosphérique au-dessus de son territoire.*" This was narrowly translated in the English text as "complete and exclusive sovereignty over the air space above its territory." By contrast, the 1944 Chicago Convention, which the United States and almost all the world's nations did ratify, kept the same language verbatim for the English text but changed one word in the French text so the broader "*espace atmosphérique*" became "*espace aérien.*" Neither treaty, however, specified the point in the 6,200-mile height of the earth's atmosphere where "air space"

ended and "space" began. Similarly, the basic UN Declaration on Outer Space did not define where airspace or the atmosphere ends and "space" begins. See League of Nations, "No. 297, Convention Relating to the Regulation of Aerial Navigation, Signed at Paris, October 13, 1919," www.worldlii.org/int/other/LNTSer/1922/99 .html; "Convention on International Civil Aviation – Doc 7300, Signed at Chicago on 7 December 1944," www.icao.int/publications/pages/doc7300.aspx; and United Nations General Assembly, "1962 (XVIII). Declaration of Legal Principles Governing the Activities of States in the Exploration and Use of Outer Space," December 13, 1963, www.un-documents.net/a18r1962.htm.

84. US Air Force, "Defense Satellite Communications System," November 23, 2015, www.af.mil/AboutUs/FactSheets/Display/tabid/224/Article/104555/defense -satellite-communications-system.aspx.

85. Barry R. Posen, "Command of the Commons: The Military Foundation of U.S. Hegemony," *International Security* 28, no. 1 (2003): 8–9.

86. Jo Becker and Scott Shane, "Secret 'Kill List' Proves a Test of Obama's Principles and Will," *New York Times*, May 29, 2012; Greg Miller, "Plan for Hunting Terrorists Signals U.S. Intends to Keep Adding Names to Kill Lists," *Washington Post*, October 23, 2012, www.washingtonpost.com/world/national-security/plan-for-hunting-terrorists -signals-us-intends-to-keep-adding-names-to-kill-lists/2012/10/23/4789b2ae-18b3 -11e2-a55c-39408fbe6a4b_story.html.

87. Mark Prigg, "Pentagon Reveals Plans to Mount Laser Weapons on High-Flying Drones to Blast Ballistic Missiles Out of the Sky," *Daily Mail*, January 20, 2016, www.dailymail.co.uk/sciencetech/article-3409105/Pentagon-reveals-plans-mount -laser-weapons-high-flying-drones-blast-ballistic-missiles-sky.html.

88. Jason Sherman, "'Innovative' UAV Demo in Alaska Precursor to Autonomous Swarming Project," *Inside Defense*, June 25, 2015, https://insidedefense.com/daily -news/innovative-uav-demo-alaska-precursor-autonomous-swarming-project; Dr. William B. Roper Jr., "Statement before the Subcommittee on Emerging Threats and Capabilities," US Senate, Armed Services Committee, April 12, 2016, www.armed-services.senate.gov/imo/media/doc/Roper_04-12-16.pdf.

89. Christopher Drew, "Under an Unblinking Eye," *New York Times*, August 3, 2011; Cockburn, *Kill Chain*, 179–81, 255.

90. Cockburn, *Kill Chain*, 253–54, 256; Kimberly Dozier, "Iran Puts U.S. Drone on Television," *Wisconsin State Journal*, December 9, 2011; David Fulghum and Bill Sweetman, "U.S. Air Force Reveals Operational Stealth UAV," *Aviation Week*, December 4, 2009, www.aviationweek.com/aw/; Northrop Grumman, Electronic Systems, "AESA Radar: Revolutionary Capabilities for Multiple Missions," www.es.northropgrumman.com/solutions/aesaradar/assets/review_aesa.pdf.

91. Cockburn, *Kill Chain*, 256; Scott Peterson, "Exclusive: Iran Hijacked US Drone, Says Iranian Engineer," *Christian Science Monitor*, December 15, 2011, www.csmonitor.com/World/Middle-East/2011/1215/Exclusive-Iran-hijacked -US-drone-says-Iranian-engineer.

92. Cockburn, *Kill Chain*, 254; Amy Butler and Bill Sweetman, "Secret New UAS Shows Stealth, Efficiency Advances," *Aviation Week*, December 6, 2013, http://aviationweek

.com/defense/secret-new-uas-shows-stealth-efficiency-advances; "Secret New Stealth Drone Exposed," CNN, December 12, 2013, www.youtube.com/watch ?v=efIyLrqjI8g; "RQ-180," Deagel.com, October 18, 2015, www.deagel.com /AEWandC-ISR-and-EW-Aircraft/RQ-180_a002915001.aspx.

93. Nidhi Subbaraman, "X-47B Navy Drone Completes First Ever Unmanned Carrier Landing," NBC News, July 10, 2013, www.nbcnews.com/technology/x-47b-navy -drone-take-first-stab-unmanned-carrier-landing-6C10591335; "X-47B Historic Drone Carrier Landing," YouTube, www.youtube.com/watch?v=kw3m7bqrQ64; James Drew, "UCLASS Reborn as US Navy Spy-Tanker," *Flight Global*, February 11, 2016, www.flightglobal.com/news/articles/uclass-reborn-as-us-navy-spy-tanker -421844/; Sandra I. Erwin, "Navy Halts Funding for Northrop Grumman's Carrier-Based Combat Drone," *National Defense Magazine*, February 10, 2016, www.nationaldefensemagazine.org/blog/Lists/Posts/Post.aspx?ID=2083; Sam LaGrone, "It's Official: 'MQ-25A Stingray' U.S. Navy's Name for First Carrier UAV," *USNI News*, July 15, 2016, https://news.usni.org/2016/07/15/official-mq-25a -stingray-title-navys-first-carrier-uav.

94. NASA/Dryden Flight Research Center, "Helios Prototype Solar Aircraft Lost in Flight Mishap," *Science Daily*, July 1, 2003, www.sciencedaily.com/releases/2003 /06/030630111917.htm; Aurora Flight Sciences, "DARPA Selects Aurora for Vulture Program," defense-aerospace.com, April 14, 2008, www.defense-aerospace.com /article-view/release/93255/aurora-wins-darpa-contract-for-vulture-program.html.

95. "Blackswift Test Bed Hypersonic Technology Vehicle (HTV-3)," *GlobalSecurity.org*, www.globalsecurity.org/space/systems/x-41-htv-3.htm.

96. Thom Shanker, "Brief Test of Military Aircraft Said to Yield Much Data," *New York Times*, August 12, 2011; Defense Advanced Research Projects Agency, "Hypersonic Vehicle Advances Technical Knowledge," www.defense-aerospace.com/articles -view/release/3/127911/bipartisan-consensus-seen-on-selecting-new-defense-cuts .html.

97. "Darpa Refocuses Hypersonics Research on Tactical Missions," *Aviation Week*, July 8, 2013, http://aviationweek.com/awin/darpa-refocuses-hypersonics-research -tactical-missions; "AFRE (Advanced Full Range Engine Program) Envisions Hybrid Propulsion System Paving the Way to Routine Reusable Hypersonic Flight," Defense Advanced Projects Research Agency, June 24, 2016, www.darpa.mil /news-events/2016-06-24.

98. Sebastian Anthony, "Lockheed Unveils SR-72 Hypersonic Mach 6 Scramjet Spy Plane," *ExtremeTech*, November 6, 2013, www.extremetech.com/extreme/170463 -lockheed-unveils-sr-72-hypersonic-mach-6-scramjet-spy-plane; "Meet the SR-72," Lockheed Martin, November 1, 2013, www.lockheedmartin.com/us/news /features/2015/sr-72.html.

99. William J. Broad, "Surveillance Suspected as Main Role of Spacecraft," *New York Times*, May 23, 2010; Brian Weeden, "X-37B Orbital Test Vehicle Fact Sheet," Secure World Foundation, November 23, 2010, https://swfound.org/media/1791 /swf_x-37b_otv_fact_sheet_updated_2012.pdf; US Air Force, "X-37B Orbital Test Vehicle Fact Sheet," April 17, 2015, www.af.mil/AboutUs/FactSheets/Display

/tabid/224/Article/104539/x-37b-orbital-test-vehicle.aspx.

100. Paul Rincon, "X-37B US Military Spaceplane Returns to Earth," BBC News, December 3, 2010, www.bbc.co.uk/news/science-environment-11911335; Alicia Chang, "Unmanned Air Force Space Plane Lands in Calif.," *Washington Times*, June 16, 2012, www.washingtontimes.com/news/2012/jun/16/unmanned-air-force -space-plane-lands-calif/.

101. Posen, "Command of the Commons," 12–14.

102. Edward Cody, "China Confirms Firing Missile to Destroy Satellite," *Washington Post*, January 24, 2007, www.washingtonpost.com/wp-dyn/content/article /2007/01/23/AR2007012300114.html; Marc Kaufman and Josh White, "Navy Mis- sile Hits Satellite, Pentagon Says," *Washington Post,* February 21, 2008, www .washingtonpost.com/wp-dyn/content/article/2008/02/20/AR2008022000240.html.

103. Defense Advanced Research Projects Agency, "F-6 System," www.darpa.mil/Our _Work/TTO/Programs/System_F6.aspx, /; DARPATech, DARPA's 25th Systems and Technology Symposium, August 8, 2007, Anaheim, California, Teleprompter Script for Dr. Owen Brown, Program Manager, Virtual Space Office, archive.darpa.mil /DARPATech2007/proceedings/dt07-vso-brown-access.pdf.

104. "Lockheed Martin MUOS Satellite Tests Show Extensive Reach in Polar Communi- cations Capability," Lockheed Martin, January 31, 2014, www.lockheedmartin.com /us/news/press-releases/2014/january/131-ss-muos.html; Space and Naval Warfare Systems Command Public Affairs, "Counting Down to Launch: 5th MUOS Satellite Poised to Complete Constellation," Navy News Service, www.globalsecurity.org /space/library/news/2016/space-160622-nns01.htm.

105. US Strategic Command, "USSTRATCOM Space Control and Space Surveillance," January 2014, www.stratcom.mil/factsheets/11/Space_Control_and_Space _Surveillance/.

106. Defense Advanced Research Projects Agency, "Space Surveillance Telescope," www .darpa.mil/Our_Work/TTO/Programs/Space_Surveillance_Telescope_(SST).aspx; David Szondy, "DARPA Ready to Deliver Telescope to Watch the Skies for Space Debris," *New Atlas*, December 11, 2013, www.gizmag.com/sst-delivery/30063/.

107. Cockburn, *Kill Chain*, 169–76.

108. Andrew Tarantola, "To Test a Satellite Dock, the NRL Built a 37-Ton Air Hockey Table," *Gizmodo*, August 7, 2012, http://gizmodo.com/5932150/to-test-a-satellite -dock-the-nrl-built-a-37-ton-air-hockey-table; B. E. Kelm et al., "FREND: Pushing the Envelope of Space Robotics," *Space Research and Satellite Technology* (2008), 239–41, www.nrl.navy.mil/content_images/08Space_Kelm.pdf.

109. US Naval Research Laboratory, "NRL Engineers to Lead Payload Development for Robotic Servicing of Geosynchronous Satellites," April 11, 2106, www.nrl.navy .mil/media/news-releases/2016/NRL-Engineers-to-Lead-Payload-Development -for-Robotic-Servicing-of-Geosynchronous-Satellites.

110. DARPATech, DARPA's 25th Systems and Technology Symposium.

111. Gregg Easterbrook, "Undisciplined Spending in the Name of Defense," Reuters, January 20, 2011, http://blogs.reuters.com/gregg-easterbrook/2011/01/20 /undisciplined-spending-in-the-name-of-defense/; National Geospatial-Intelligence

Agency, *Geospatial Intelligence Standards: Enabling a Common Vision* (November 2006), www.fas.org/irp/agency/nga/standards.pdf.

112. Edward Wong, "China Launches Satellite in Bid to Lead Quantum Research," *New York Times*, August 17, 2016; Elizabeth Gibney, "Chinese Satellite Is One Giant Step for the Quantum Internet," *Nature*, July 27, 2016, www.nature.com/news/chinese -satellite-is-one-giant-step-for-the-quantum-internet-1.20329.

113. Mike Wall, "China Launches New Rocket, Prototype Crew Capsule," *Space.com*, June 27, 2016, www.space.com/33283-china-new-rocket-launch-crew-capsule .html; Paul Mozur and John Markoff, " Is China Outsmarting America in Artificial Intelligence?," *New York Times*, May 28, 2017.

114. A&E Network, "Secrets of Hitler's Wonder Weapons," History Channel, aired September 19, 2003, www.youtube.com/watch?v=I3V01IW9ImQ.

Chapter Seven: Grandmasters of the Great Game

1. US National Intelligence Council, *Global Trends 2030: Alternative Worlds* (Washington, DC: National Intelligence Council, NIC 2012-001, December 2012), iii, 2, 98.

2. Ling Huawei, "What Should China Buy with Its $3.9 Trillion Reserves?," *Market Watch*, June 17, 2014, www.marketwatch.com/story/what-should-china-buy-with -its-39-trillion-reserves-2014-06-17.

3. Nelson Schwartz and Quoctrung Bui, "Hurt by Free Trade and Moving to Extremes," *New York Times*, April 26, 2016; Office of the United States Trade Representative, "U.S.-China Trade Facts," https://ustr.gov/countries-regions/china -mongolia-taiwan/peoples-republic-china.

4. For a widely read discussion of this distinction, see Hannah Arendt, *The Origins of Totalitarianism* (New York: Meridian, 1958), 222–66.

5. Mackinder, "The Geographical Pivot of History," 434.

6. Brzezinski, *The Grand Chessboard*, 31–35.

7. Tracy Powell and Peter Rutimann, "From Peking to Paris,"*Automobile Quarterly* 47, no. 4 (2007): 101–6.

8. Markus Rauh, "Old-Timer Rally from Beijing to Paris," *AODialogue* (January 2008): 12–16, www.aofoundation.org/documents/4_oldtimerrally.pdf; Peter Rutimann, "Peking to Paris, 100 Years Later," *Automobile Quarterly* 47, no. 4 (2007): 107–10.

9. "China Boasts World's Largest Highspeed Railway Network," *Xinhua*, January 30, 2015, http://news.xinhuanet.com/english/photo/2015-01/30/c_133959250.htm; Gerald Olivier et al., "Chinese High-Speed: An Evaluation of Traffic," *International Railway Journal*, February 1, 2015, www.highbeam.com/doc/1G1-402875735.html; "China's Fastest High Speed Train 380A Rolls Off Production Line," *Xinhua*, May 27, 2010, http://news.xinhuanet.com/english2010/sci/2010-05/27/c_13319787.htm.

10. Sarwant Singh, "China High-Speed Rail Juggernaut, While Most of US Stands and Waves—but Not Elon Musk (Part 1)" *Forbes*, July 17, 2014, www.forbes.com/sites /sarwantsingh/2014/07/17/china-high-speed-rail-juggernaut-while-most-of -us-stands-by-and-waves-but-not-elon-musk-part-1/.

11. "Eurasian Land Bridge: Via Container Trains from Europe to China and Back," DB

Schenker, May 31, 2012, www.dbschenker.com/ho-en/news_media/press
/corporate-news/news/2728098/china_train.html; Keith Bradsher, "Hauling New
Treasure Along the Silk Road," *New York Times*, July 20, 2013, www.nytimes.
com/2013/07/21/business/global/hauling-new-treasure-along-the-silk-road.html.

12. Allport Cargo Services, "China to Germany Freight Train Makes Maiden Journey,"
August 6, 2013, http://allportcargoservices.com/retailnews/allport-knowledge
/regulatory-news/china-to-germany-freight-train-makes-maiden-journey
/801621580; Raushan Nurshayeva, "Kazakhs Launch 'Silk Road' China-Europe Rail
Link," Reuters, June 10, 2013, www.reuters.com/article/2013/06/10/us
-kazakhstan-railway-idUSBRE9590GH20130610; Nicholas Brautlecht, "Germany
Plans to Expand Chinese Rail Link as Xi Visits Duisburg," *Bloomberg Technology*,
March 28, 2014, www.bloomberg.com/news/articles/2014-03-28/germany-plans
-to-expand-chinese-rail-link-as-xi-visits-duisburg.

13. Agence France-Presse, "Russia and China Want to Build the Longest High Speed
Railroad in the World to Connect Them," *Business Insider*, October 17, 2014,
www.businessinsider.com/afp-china-russia-mull-high-speed-moscow-beijing
-rail-line-report-2014-10.

14. "China's Xi Jinping Agrees $46bn Superhighway to Pakistan," BBC News, April 20,
2015, www.bbc.com/news/world-asia-32377088; Saleem Shahid, "Gwadar Port
Inaugurated," *Dawn*, March 21, 2007, www.dawn.com/news/238494/gwadar-port
-inaugurated-plan-for-second-port-in-balochistan-at-sonmiani.

15. "China Coming Down the Tracks," *Economist*, January 20, 2011, www.economist.
com/node/17965601?story_id=17965601; "Fears for Little Laos under China's
Kunming-to-Singapore Rail Vision," *Global Construction Review*, January 22, 2014,
www.globalconstructionreview.com/sectors/fears-little-laos-under-chinas-kunming
-singapore-r/.

16. "Kazakhstan–China Oil Pipeline Opens to Operation," *Xinhua*, July 12, 2006, http://
eng.caexpo.org/index.php?m=content&c=index&a=show&catid=10021&id=60094;
"CNPC Announces Kenkiyak–Kumkol Section of Kazakhstan–China Oil Pipeline
Becomes Operational," *Your Oil and Gas News*, July 15, 2009, www.youroilandgasnews
.com/cnpc+announces+kenkiyak-kumkol+section+of+kazakhstan-china+oil
+pipeline+becomes+operational_35798.html.

17. Raushan Nurshayeva and Shamil Zhumatov, "Update 3-China's Hu Boosts Energy
Ties with Central Asia," Reuters, December 12, 2009, http://uk.reuters.com/article
/2009/12/12/china-kazakhstan-idUKGEE5BB01D20091212?sp=true; "Construction of Third Branch of Uzbekistan–China Gas Pipeline Completed," Trend News
Agency, December 23, 2014, http://en.trend.az/casia/uzbekistan/2346917.html.

18. Eric Meyer, "With Oil and Gas Pipelines, China Takes a Shortcut through Myanmar," *Forbes*, February 9, 2015, www.forbes.com/sites/ericrmeyer/2015/02/09
/oil-and-gas-china-takes-a-shortcut/; "The Uncertain Future of the Sino–Myanmar
Pipeline," *Global Intelligence*, August 5, 2013, www.stratfor.com/analysis/uncertain
-future-sino-myanmar-pipeline.

19. Eric Watkins, "China, Russia Agree on Loans for ESPO Pipeline Spur," *Oil & Gas
Journal*, February 17, 2016, www.ogj.com/articles/2009/02/china-russia-agree-on

-loans-for-espo-pipeline-spur.html; Aibing Guo, "CNPC to Start Laying Second China-Russia Oil Pipeline in June," *Bloomberg*, May 12, 2016, www.bloomberg .com/news/articles/2016-05-12/cnpc-to-start-laying-second-china-russia-oil -pipeline-in-june-io48uk3h; Zhang Yu and Lyu Chang, "China-Russia Oil Pipeline Fuels Trade," *ChinaDaily.com.cn*, August 19, 2016, www.chinadaily.com.cn /business/2016-08/19/content_26530568.htm.

20. "Russia Signs 30-Year Gas Deal with China," BBC News, May 21, 2014, www.bbc .com/news/business-27503017.

21. Jane Perlez, "Rush to Join China's New Asian Bank Surprises All, Even the Chinese," *New York Times*, April 3, 2015; Saibal Dasgupta, "Asian Infrastructure Investment Bank Opens in Beijing," Voice of America, January 16, 2016, www.voanews.com /content/asian-infrastructure-development-bank-opens-beijing/3149401.html; Editorial, "China's Trillion-Dollar Foreign Policy," *New York Times*, May 18, 2017; Jessica Meyers, "China's Belt and Road Forum Lays Groundwork for a New Global Order," *Los Angeles Times*, May 15, 2017, www.latimes.com/world/asia/la-fg-china -belt-road-20170515-story.html; Tom Phillips, "EU Backs Away from Trade State- ment in Blow to China's 'Modern Silk Road' Plan," *Guardian*, May 15, 2017, www. theguardian.com/world/2017/may/15/eu-china-summit-bejing-xi-jinping -belt-and-road.

22. Hans M. Kristensen, "China SSBN Fleet Getting Ready—but for What?," Federation of American Scientists, April 25, 2014, http://fas.org/blogs/security/2014/04 /chinassbnfleet/.

23. Rupert Wingfield-Hayes, "China's Island Factory," BBC News, September 9, 2014, www.bbc.co.uk/news/special/2014/newsspec_8701/index.html.

24. Jim Sciutto, "Exclusive: China Warns U.S. Surveillance Plane," CNN Politics, Sep- tember 15, 2015, www.cnn.com/2015/05/20/politics/south-china-sea-navy -flight/; "China Lodges Complaint with U.S. over Spy Plane Flight," Reuters, May 25, 2015, www.reuters.com/article/2015/05/25/us-southchinasea-china-usa -complaint-idUSKBN0OA0DY20150525.

25. "China's Xi Jinping Agrees $46bn Superhighway to Pakistan"; Jeremy Page, "Beijing Agrees to Operate a Key Port, Pakistan Says," *Wall Street Journal*, May 23, 2011, www.wsj.com/articles/SB10001424052702303654804576339323765033308; Ridz- wan Rahmat, "PLAN to Deploy Range of Warships in Indian Ocean, Says China's Defence Ministry," *IHS Jane's Defence Weekly* (Singapore), January 29, 2015, http:// worldaffairsroc.org/news.cfm?story=499&school=0; Andrew Jacobs and Jane Perlez, "U.S. Wary as Chinese Base Rises as a Neighbor in Africa," *New York Times*, February 26, 2017.

26. Editorial, "Pushback in the South China Sea," *New York Times*, May 30, 2015; Javier C. Hernández, "China: U.S. Blamed for Regional Rifts," *New York Times*, July 30, 2015; Derek Watkins, "What China Has Been Building in the South China Sea," *New York Times*, October 27, 2015, nytimes.com/interactive/2015/07/30/world /asia/what-china-has-been-building-in-the-south-china-sea.html; Jane Perlez, "U.S. Admiral Assails China's 'Unilateral' Actions at Sea," *New York Times*, December 16, 2015; Max Fisher and Sergio Peçanha, "What the U.S. Gets for Defending Its

Allies and Interests Abroad," *New York Times*, January 15, 2017; Jeff Himmelman, "A Game of Shark and Minnow," *New York Times Magazine*, October 27, 2013; Ho Binh Minh, "South China Sea: Vietnam Protests after China Lands Plane on Disputed Spratlys," *Sydney Morning Herald*, January 3, 2016, www.smh.com.au/world /south-china-sea-vietnam-protests-after-china-lands-plane-on-disputed-spratlys -20160103-glyd3t.html; "Island Building," Asia Maritime Transparency Initiative, http://amti.csis.org/island-tracker/.

27. Michael Forsythe, "Missiles Deployed on Disputed South China Sea Island, Officials Say," *New York Times*, February 17, 2016; Lucas Tomlinson and Yonat Frilling, "China Sends Surface-to-Air Missiles to Contested Island in Provocative Move," Fox News, February 16, 2016, www.foxnews.com/world/2016/02/16/exclusive -china-sends-suface-to-air-missiles-to-contested-island-in-provocative-move.html#.

28. Michael Forsythe and Jane Perlez, "South China Sea Buildup Strengthens Beijing's Claims," *New York Times*, March 10, 2016.

29. David E. Sanger and Rick Gladstone, "Photos Raise Questions on China's Promise Not to Militarize Disputed Islands," *New York Times*, August 10, 2016; Helene Cooper, "U.S. Demands Return of Drone Seized by China," *New York Times*, December 17, 2016; Jane Perlez and Matthew Rosenberg, "China Agrees to Return U.S. Naval Drone Seized Off Philippines," *New York Times*, December 18, 2016.

30. Simon Denyer, "By 2030, South China Sea Will Be 'Virtually a Chinese Lake,' Study Warns," *Washington Post*, January 20, 2016, www.washingtonpost.com/news /worldviews/wp/2016/01/20/by-2030-south-china-sea-will-be-virtually-a-chinese -lake-u-s-study-warns/; Mike Yeo, "Analysis: Chinese Aircraft Carrier Program Progressing Substantially into the New Year," *DefenseNews*, January 31, 2017, defensenews.com/articles/analysis-chinese-aircraft-carrier-program-progressing -substantially-into-the-new-year.

31. U. Rashid Sumaila and William W. L. Cheung, *Boom or Bust: The Future of Fish in the South China Sea* (Vancouver: OceanAsia Project, University of British Columbia, 2015), 1–3, www.admcf.org/wordpress/wp-content/uploads/2015/11 /FishSCSea03_11-FINAL-FINAL.pdf; John W. McManus, Kwang-Tsao Shao, and Szu-Yin Lin, "Toward Establishing a Spratly Islands International Marine Peace Park: Ecological Importance and Supportive Collaborative Activities with an Emphasis on the Role of Taiwan," *Ocean Development & International Law* 41, no. 3 (2010): 273, http://dx.doi.org/10.1080/00908320.2010.499303.

32. Michael Fabinyi and Neng Liu, "The Social Context of the Chinese Food System: An Ethnographic Study of the Beijing Seafood Market," *Sustainability* 8, no. 3 (2016): figure 1, www.mdpi.com/2071-1050/8/3/244/htm; *Fish to 2030: Prospects for Fisheries and Aquaculture* (Washington, DC: World Bank Report No. 83177-GLB, 2013), vii, 3, www.fao.org/docrep/019/i3640e/i3640e.pdf.

33. Simon Funge-Smith, Matthew Briggs, and Weimin Miao, *Asia-Pacific Fishery Commission (APFIC) Regional Overview of Fisheries and Aquaculture in Asia and the Pacific 2012* (Bangkok: Food and Agriculture Organization of the United Nations, Regional Office for Asia and the Pacific, 2012), 11, 26; Rodger Baker, "Fish: The Overlooked Destabilizer in the South China Sea," Stratfor, February 12, 2016, 4–6,

www.stratfor.com/analysis/fish-overlooked-destabilizer-south-china-sea; Simon Denyer, "How China's Fishermen Are Fighting a Covert War in the South China Sea," *Washington Post*, April 12, 2016, www.washingtonpost.com/world/asia _pacific/fishing-fleet -puts-china-on-collision-course-with-neighbors-in-south-china-sea/2016 /04/12/8a6a9e3c-fff3-11e5-8bb1-f124a43f84dc_story.html.

34. "China's BeiDou Satellite System Expected to Achieve Global Coverage by 2020," *Xinhua*, December 27, 2013, http://news.xinhuanet.com/english/china/2013 -12/27/c_133001847.htm; "DSCS-1," Federation of American Scientists, https:// fas.org/man/dod-101/sys/land/wsh/82.pdf.

35. David Sanger, David Barboza, and Nicole Perlroth, "China's Army Seen as Tied to Hacking against U.S. Order," *New York Times*, February 19, 2013.

36. Mackinder, "The Geographical Pivot of History," 436.

37. "Venezuela's Chavez Calls Obama 'Ignoramus,'" Reuters, March 22, 2009, www .reuters.com/article/2009/03/22/us-venezuela-obama-idUSTRE52L19G20090322 ?feedType=RSS&feedName=topNews&rpc=22&sp=true/Venezuela's.

38. Chris McGreal, "John McCain and Lindsey Graham Attack Obama Ahead of Final Debate," *Guardian*, October 22, 2012, www.theguardian.com/world/2012/oct/22 /mccain-graham-obama-foreign-policy.

39. Glenn Foden, "Cartoon: Obama's Criticism of Walker on Foreign Policy," *Daily Signal*, April 10, 2015, http://dailysignal.com/2015/04/10/cartoon-obamas-criticism -of-walker-on-foreign-policy/.

40. "Carter: Obama's Foreign Policy Accomplishments 'Have Been Minimal,'" Fox News Insider, July 1, 2015, http://insider.foxnews.com/2015/07/01/jimmy-car- ter-president-obamas-foreign-policy-accomplishments-have-been-minimal.

41. Jose A. DelReal, "An Incomplete List of Everyone Donald Trump Insulted in and after the Debate," *Washington Post*, August 7, 2015, www.washingtonpost.com/ news/post-politics/wp/2015/08/07/an-incomplete-list-of-everyone-donald-trump- insulted-in-and-after-the-debate/.

42. Jeffrey Goldberg, "The Obama Doctrine," *Atlantic*, April 2016, www.theatlantic.com /magazine/archive/2016/04/the-obama-doctrine/471525/.

43. Amy Belasco, *Troop Levels in the Afghan and Iraq Wars, FY2001–FY2012: Cost and Other Potential Issues* (Washington, DC: Congressional Research Service, July 2009), 14, www.fas.org/sgp/crs/natsec/R40682.pdf.

44. Mark Landler, "U.S. Troops to Leave Afghanistan by End of '16," *New York Times*, May 28, 2014; Belasco, *Troop Levels in the Afghan and Iraq War*, 12.

45. Goldberg, "The Obama Doctrine."

46. Ibid.

47. "Remarks by President Obama at the University of Yangon," November 19, 2012, The White House, Office of the Press Secretary, www.whitehouse.gov/the-press -office/2012/11/19/remarks-president-obama-university-yangon.

48. Weiner, *Legacy of Ashes*, 87.

49. Dan Roberts and Julian Borger, "Obama Holds Historic Phone Call with Rouhani and Hints at End to Sanctions," *Guardian*, September 28, 2013, www.theguardian

.com/world/2013/sep/27/obama-phone-call-iranian-president-rouhani.

50. Hillary Clinton, "America's Pacific Century," *Foreign Policy*, October 11, 2011, http://foreignpolicy.com/2011/10/11/americas-pacific-century/.

51. "Remarks by President Obama and President Xi Jinping in Joint Press Conference," November 12, 2014, The White House, Office of the Press Secretary, www .whitehouse.gov/the-press-office/2014/11/12/remarks-president-obama-and -president-xi-jinping-joint-press-conference.

52. Azam Ahmed and Julie Hirschfeld Davis, "U.S. and Cuba Reopen Long-Closed Embassies," *New York Times*, July 21, 2015.

53. Goldberg, "The Obama Doctrine"; Josh Lederman and Michael Weissenstein, "In Cuba, Obama Calls for Burying 'Last Remnant' of Cold War," Associated Press, March 22, 2016, http://elections.ap.org/content/cuba-obama-calls-burying-last -remnant-cold-war.

54. Goldberg, "The Obama Doctrine."

55. Alfred W. McCoy, "The Geopolitics of American Global Decline: Washington Versus China in the Twenty-First Century," *TomDispatch*, June 7, 2015, www.tomdispatch .com/post/176007/.

56. Ibid.

57. Peter Baker, "A Barely Veiled Pitch on China's Turf," *New York Times*, July 30, 2015.

58. Center for Strategic and International Studies, "What Does China Really Spend on Its Military?," *China Power*, http://chinapower.csis.org/military-spending/.

59. Susan George, foreword to Manuel Pérez-Rocha, *The Transatlantic Trade and Investment Partnership [TTIP]: Why the World Should Beware* (Washington, DC: Institute for Policy Studies, May 2015), 6–7, www.ips-dc.org/wp-content/uploads /2015/06/TTIP-BEWARE-june2015.pdf.

60. Economist Intelligence Unit, *Foresight 2020: Economic, Industry, and Corporate Trends* (March 2006), 8–9, http://graphics.eiu.com/files/ad_pdfs/eiuForesight2020_WP.pdf.

61. European Commission, "EU Position in World Trade," October 2, 2014, http:// ec.europa.eu/trade/policy/eu-position-in-world-trade/.

62. Gordon Lubold, "Has the White House Bungled a Historic Africa Summit?," *Foreign Policy*, July 9, 2014, http://foreignpolicy.com/2014/07/09/has-the-white-house -bungled-a-historic-africa-summit/.

63. Baker, "A Barely Veiled Pitch on China's Turf."

64. Kevin Granville, "The Trans-Pacific Partnership Trade Deal Explained," *New York Times*, May 11, 2015.

65. Alan Rappeport, "Elizabeth Warren Knocks Obama over Trade Deal Transparency," *New York Times*, April 22, 2015.

66. Dan Kaufman, "Which Side Are You on, Hillary?," *New York Times*, March 13, 2016.

67. Jonathan Weisman, "Trade Accord, Once Blocked, Nears Passage," *New York Times*, June 24, 2015.

68. International Monetary Fund, "4. Report for Selected Country Groups and Subjects," World Economic Outlook Database, April 2014, www.imf.org/external /pubs/ft/weo/2014/01/weodata/weorept.aspx?pr.x=46&pr.y=16&sy=2014&ey =2014&sort=country&ds=.&br=1&c=998&s=NGDPD%2CPPPGDP&grp=1&a=1.

69. European Commission, *Transatlantic Trade and Investment Partnership: The Economic Analysis Explained* (September 2013), 7, http://trade.ec.europa.eu/doclib/docs/2013/september/tradoc_151787.pdf.

70. Jane Perlez and Chris Buckley, "Injecting Risk in China Ties," *New York Times*, January 25, 2017; Andrew Walker, "TTIP: Why the EU-US Trade Deal Matters," BBC News, May 13, 2015, www.bbc.com/news/business-32691589; Andrew Walker, "TTIP: Are US-Europe Trade Talks Tanking?," BBC News, August 29, 2016.

71. Richard Falk, "Henry Kissinger: Hero of Our Time," *Millennium: Journal of International Studies* 44, no. 1 (2015): 156–57, http://mil.sagepub.com/content/early/2015/07/05/0305829815594038.abstract?rss=1.

72. Georg Wilhelm Friedrich Hegel, *Introduction to the Philosophy of History* (Indianapolis: Hackett, 1988), 31, 69.

73. Root's long and distinguished public service career is detailed in the 1,149 pages of Philip C. Jessup's laudatory biography, *Elihu Root* (New York: Dodd, Mead, 1938).

74. Richard W. Leopold, *Elihu Root and the Conservative Tradition* (Boston: Little, Brown, 1954), 12–19.

75. Warren Zimmermann, *First Great Triumphs: How Five Americans Made Their Country a World Power* (New York: Farrar, Straus and Giroux, 2002), 129–31, 134–42.

76. Stephen Skowronek, *Building a New American State: The Expansion of National Administrative Capacities, 1877–1920* (Cambridge: Cambridge University Press, 1982), 26, 45–56.

77. Zimmermann, *First Great Triumphs*, 148, 411–12, 417; Leopold, *Elihu Root and the Conservative Tradition*, 24–46.

78. William J. Johnston, "The Pan-American Conference and the Cuban Crisis," *New York Times*, September 23, 1906; Leopold, *Elihu Root and the Conservative Tradition*, 53–69; Frederick W. Marks, *Velvet on Iron: The Diplomacy of Theodore Roosevelt* (Lincoln: University of Nebraska Press, 1979), 203; Jessup, *Elihu Root*, vol. 1, *1845–1909*, 474–92; Vredespaleis [Peace Palace, The Hague, Netherlands], Verede Door Recht, www.vredespaleis.nl/.

79. Leopold, *Elihu Root and the Conservative Tradition*, 67, 161–64; "Elihu Root—Biographical," nobelprize.org, www.nobelprize.org/nobel_prizes/peace/laureates/1912/root-bio.html.

80. Courtney Johnson, "Understanding the American Empire: Colonialism, Latin Americanism, and Professional Social Science, 1898–1920," in Alfred W. McCoy and Francisco Scarano, eds., *Colonial Crucible: Empire in the Making of the Modern American State* (Madison: University of Wisconsin Press, 2009), 175–90; Jessup, *Elihu Root*, vol. 2, *1905–1937*, 416–17, 486–93.

81. Brzezinski, *The Grand Chessboard*, 38.

82. Andrew Marshall, "Terror 'Blowback' Burns CIA," *Independent*, October 31, 1998, www.independent.co.uk/news/terror-blowback-burns-cia-1182087.html; "Interview with Zbigniew Brzezinski," *Le Nouvel Observateur*, January 15–21, 1998, 76, www.globalresearch.ca/articles/BRZ110A.html; Brzezinski, *The Grand Chessboard*, 38–39; Brzezinski, *Strategic Vision*, 130–31.

83. "Interview with Zbigniew Brzezinski," *Le Nouvel Observateur*.

84. Brzezinski, *The Grand Chessboard*, 35, 39.

85. Barack Obama, *Dreams from My Father: A Story of Race and Inheritance* (New York: Three Rivers Press, 2005), x, 23–25.

86. "Remarks by President Obama to the Australian Parliament," The White House, Office of the Press Secretary, November 17, 2011, www.whitehouse.gov/the-press -office/2011/11/17/remarks-president-obama-australian-parliament.

87. Brzezinski, *The Grand Chessboard*, 123–25.

88. "We're Back: America Reaches a Pivot Point in Asia," *Economist*, November 17, 2011, www.economist.com/node/21538803.

89. Stephen Collinson, "Obama's Pivot to Nowhere," CNN Politics, June 16, 2015, www.cnn.com/2015/06/16/politics/obama-trade-china-asia-pivot/.

90. Fareed Zakaria, "Whatever Happened to Obama's Pivot to Asia?," *Washington Post*, April 16, 2015, www.washingtonpost.com/opinions/the-forgotten-pivot-to -asia/2015/04/16/529cc5b8-e477-11e4-905f-cc896d379a32_story.html.

91. "Australia and the American 'Pivot to Asia,'" Australian Centre on China in the World, Australian National University, July 2015, http://aus.thechinastory.org /archive/australia-and-the-american-pivot-to-asia/.

92. Javier C. Hernández and Floyd Whaley, "Philippine Supreme Court Approves Agreement on Return of U.S. Troops," *New York Times*, January 13, 2016; Floyd Whaley, "Eye on China, U.S. and Philippines Ramp Up Military Alliance," *New York Times*, April 13, 2016; Tina G. Santos, "PH, Chinese Naval Vessels in Scarborough Shoal Standoff," *Philippine Daily Inquirer*, April 11, 2012, http://globalnation .inquirer.net/32341/ph-chinese-naval-vessels-in-scarborough-shoal-standoff; "US, Philippines Sign Military Deal to Counter Chinese Aggression," *Australian*, April 28, 2014, www.theaustralian.com.au/news/world/us-philippines-sign -military-deal-to-counter-chinese-aggression/story-e6frg6so-1226898560016; Lance M. Bacon, "U.S. Negotiating to Rotate Troops to 8 Philippine Bases," *Navy Times*, April 28, 2015, www.navytimes.com/story/military/pentagon/2015/04/28 /us-negotiating-troop-rotation-philippines-catapang-china-base-troops/26512301/; Republic of the Philippines, Department of Foreign Affairs, "Q&A on the Enhanced Defense Cooperation Agreement," *Official Gazette*, April 28, 2014, www.gov.ph /2014/04/28/qna-on-the-enhanced-defense-cooperation-agreement/.

93. Vince Scappatura, "The US 'Pivot to Asia,' the China Spectre and the Australian-American Alliance," *Asia-Pacific Journal* 12, Issue 36, no. 3 (September 6, 2014), http://apjjf.org/2014/12/36/Vince-Scappatura/4178/article.html.

94. Statement of Admiral Jonathan Greenert, US Navy Chief of Operations, *Report to the Senate Armed Services Committee*, March, 27, 2014, 1–5, 20, www.armed -services.senate.gov/imo/media/doc/Greenert_03-27-14.pdf; Chuck Hagel, "The US Approach to Regional Security," The IISS Shangri-La Dialogue: The Asia Security Summit, International Institute for Strategic Studies, Singapore, June 1, 2012, www.iiss.org/en/events/shangri%20la%20dialogue/archive/shangri-la-dialogue -2013-c890/first-plenary-session-ee9e/chuck-hagel-862d.

95. Goldberg, "The Obama Doctrine."

96. Peter Goodman, "More Jobs, but Not for Everyone," *New York Times*, September 29,

2016.

97. Binyamin Appelbaum, "Little-Noticed Fact about Trade: It's No Longer Rising," *New York Times*, October 31, 2016.

98. Alison Smale, "Austria Rjects Far Right in Test of Trump's Effect," *New York Times*, December 5, 2016; Alissa J. Rubin, "A New Wave of Popular Fury May Crash Down in 2017," *New York Times*, December 6, 2016; Pankaj Mishra, "The Globalization of Rage," *Foreign Affairs* 95, no. 6 (November/December 2016): 46–54; Walker, "TTIP: Are US-Europe Trade Talks Tanking?"

99. Jackie Calmes, "Pacific Trade Pact Finds Few Friends on Hustings," *New York Times*, September 2, 2016; Amy Chozick, "Hillary Clinton Opposes Obama's Trans-Pacific Trade Deal," *New York Times*, October 7, 2016; Kevin Zeese and Margaret Flowers, "The TPP Is Dead: The People Defeat Transnational Corporate Power," Global Research, November 12, 2016, www.globalresearch.ca/the-tpp-is-dead-the-people-defeat-transnational-corporate-power/5556548.

100. William Maudlin, "Obama Administration Gives Up on Pacific Trade Deal," *Wall Street Journal*, November 11, 2016, www.wsj.com/articles/obama-administration-gives-up-on-pacific-trade-deal-1478895824.

101. US Senate, Committee on Foreign Relations, 113th Congress, 2d Session, *Re-Balancing the Rebalance: Resourcing U.S. Diplomatic Strategy in the Asia-Pacific Region* (Washington, DC: Government Printing Office, April 17, 2014), 2–3.

102. David C. Gompert, Astrid Stuth Cevallos, and Cristina L. Garafola, *War with China: Thinking Through the Unthinkable* (Santa Monica: RAND Corporation, 2016), iii–iv.

103. Andrew R. C. Marshall and Manuel Mogato, "Philippine Death Squads Very Much in Business as Duterte Is Set for Presidency," Reuters, May 26, 2016, www.reuters.com/article/us-philippines-duterte-killings-insight-idUSKCN0YG0EB.

104. Sheena McKenzie and Kevin Liptak, "After Cursing Obama, Duterte Expresses Regret," CNN Politics, September 6, 2016, www.cnn.com/2016/09/05/politics/philippines-president-rodrigo-duterte-barack-obama/.

105. Carole E. Lee, "Obama Nixes Meeting after Rodrigo Duterte Lobs an Insult," *Wall Street Journal*, September 6, 2016, www.wsj.com/articles/obama-may-cancel-meeting-with-philippine-president-rodrigo-duterte-1473090231.

106. Associated Press, "Philippines to Suspend Joint Exercises and Patrols with US Military," *Guardian*, October 7, 2016, www.theguardian.com/world/2016/oct/07/philippines-suspend-joint-exercises-duterte-anti-us-rhetoric.

107. Barbara Demick and Tracy Wilkinson, "Philippine President Duterte: 'I Announce My Separation from the United States,'" *Los Angeles Times*, October 20, 2016, www.latimes.com/world/asia/la-fg-philippines-us-20161020-snap-story.html; "President Duterte Speech at Philippine China Trade & Investment Forum Beijing China, October 20, 2016," YouTube, www.youtube.com/watch?v=pKUHjTWnqaA; Jane Perlez, "Presidents of Philippines and China Agree to Reopen Talks on Disputed Sea," *New York Times*, October 21, 2016.

108. Demick and Wilkinson, "Philippine President Duterte."

109. Ted P. Torres, "Third Highest Worldwide, OFW Remittances Seen to Hit $29.7B in 2015," *Philstar Global*, December 27, 2015, www.philstar.com/business/2015/12

/27/1536499/third-highest-worlwide-ofw-remittances-seen-hit-29.7-b-2015; "Infographic: Where $26.92B of OFW Remittances Come From," *GMA News Online*, June 9, 2015, www.gmanetwork.com/news/story/500918/money/infographic-where -26-92b-of-ofw-remittances-come-from.

110. "Global Indicators Database: Opinion of the United States," Pew Research Center, www.pewglobal.org/database/indicator/1/survey/all/.

111. Leon Wolff, *Little Brown Brother: How the United States Purchased and Pacified the Philippines* (New York: Doubleday, 1961), 360; Marianne Hirsch, "The Generation of Post Memory," *Poetics Today* 29, no. 1 (2008): 103–28.

112. Gordon L. Rottman, *World War II Pacific Island Guide: A Geo-Military Study* (Westport, CT: Greenwood Press, 2002), 318; David Joel Steinberg, *Philippine Collaboration in World War II* (Ann Arbor: University of Michigan Press, 1967), 113–14.

113. Alfredo Bengzon and Raul Rodrigo, *A Matter of Honor: The Story of the 1990–91 RP-US Bases Talks* (Manila: Anvil, 1997), 19–21.

114. Roberto D. Tiglao, "The Consolidation of the Dictatorship," 50–52; Emmanuel S. De Dios, "The Erosion of Dictatorship," 75–78; Ma. Serena Diokno, "Unity and Struggle," 152–58, 168–70; and A. de Dios, "Intervention and Militarism," 270–72, all in Aurora Javate-De Dios et al., eds., *Dictatorship and Revolution: Roots of People's Power* (Manila: Conspectus, 1988).

115. De Jesus and de Jesus, "The Mamasapano Detour," 159–95.

116. Richard C. Paddock, "Trump Partner Is Philippines' New Trade Envoy to U.S.," *New York Times*, November 10, 2016; Republic of the Philippines, Department of Foreign Affairs, Subject: Phone Call of the President with the POTUS, Date 02 May 2017, *Intercept*, May 23, 2017, theintercept.com/2017/05/23/read-the-full-transcript-of-trumps-call-with-philippine-president-rodrigo-duterte/.

117. James Przystup and Tatsumi Yuki, "The Foreign Policy of Abe Shinzo: Strategic Vision and Policy Implementation," ASAN Forum, February 5, 2015, www .theasanforum.org/the-foreign-policy-of-abe-shinzo-strategic-vision-and -policy-implementation/.

118. Martin Fackler, "Amid Chinese Rivalry, Japan Seeks More Muscle," *New York Times*, December 17, 2013, www.nytimes.com/2013/12/18/world/asia/japan-moves -to-strengthen-military-amid-rivalry-with-china.html; "Japan Cabinet Approves Landmark Military Change," BBC News, July 1, 2014, www.bbc.com/news /world-asia-28086002; Ankit Panda, "US, Japan Agree to New Defense Guidelines," *Diplomat*, April 28, 2015, http://thediplomat.com/2015/04/us-japan-agree-to-new -defense-guidelines/.

119. Julie Hirschfeld Davis and Michael R. Gordon, "U.S. and Japan Tighten Military Cooperation," *New York Times*, April 28, 2015; Linda Sieg and Kaori Kaneko, "Japan's Abe Says TPP Would Have Strategic Significance If China Joined," Reuters, October 6, 2015, www.reuters.com/article/us-trade-tpp-abe-idUSKCN0S004920151006.

120. Reiji Yoshida, "Basics of the U.S. Military Presence," *Japan Times*, March 25, 2008, www.japantimes.co.jp/news/2008/03/25/reference/basics-of-the-u-s-military -presence/#.WCY45Hc-LuM.

121. Victor Cha, "The Unfinished Legacy of Obama's Pivot to Asia," *Foreign Policy*, Sep-

tember 6, 2016, www.foreignpolicy.com/2016/09/06/the-unfinished-legacy
-of-obamas-pivot-to-asia/.

122. Motoko Rich, "Concerned about Security and Trade, Abe Scrambles for Meeting
with Trump," *New York Times*, November 11, 2016; Motoko Rich and Jonathan
Soble, "Trump and Shinzo Abe to Meet to Discuss Japan Security and Trade," *New
York Times*, November 17, 2016; Motoko Rich, "Prime Minister's Visit with Trump
Provides Relief to the Anxious Japanese," *New York Times*, February 14, 2017; "Abe
Warns TPP Impasse Would Shift Focus to China-Inclusive Trade Pact," *Japan Times*,
November 15, 2016, www.japantimes.co.jp/news/2016/11/15/business/economy
-business/abe-warns-tpp-impasse-shift-focus-china-inclusive-trade-pact/#
.WDTew6IrLjA; "Japan PM Is First Foreign Leader to Meet Trump," BBC News,
November 17, 2016, www.bbc.com/news/world-asia-37946613; Reuters, "After New
York Meeting, Abe Confident Trump Can Be Trusted," *Japan Times*, November 18,
2016, www.japantimes.co.jp/news/2016/11/18/national/politics-diplomacy/new
-york-talks-abe-confident-can-build-trust-based-ties-trump/#.WDDoq3c-LuN;
Steve Holland and Kiyoshi Takenaka, "Japan's PM Abe Meets Trump, Say Confident
Can Build Trust," Reuters, November 18, 2016, www.reuters.com/article/us-usa
-trump-japan-idUSKBN13C0C8.

123. Jane Perlez, "A Contentious Call Strains an Alliance," *New York Times*, February 3,
2017; Choe Sang-Hun, "In South Korea Race, One Topic Eclipses Others: Trump,"
New York Times, May 5, 2017; Choe Sang-Hun, "Missile Defense Cost Jolts South
Korea Race," *New York Times*, April 29, 2017; Choe Sang-Hun, "Moon Jae-in De-
clares Victory in South Korea Presidential Election," *New York Times*, May 9, 2017..

124. Reilly, "Cold War Transition," 344–59.

125. Piers Brendon, *The Decline and Fall of the British Empire* (New York: Vintage
Books, 2010), xviii–xx, 660–62.

126. "Continental System," *Encyclopedia Britannica*, www.britannica.com/event/Conti-
nental-System.

Chapter Eight: Five Scenarios for the End of the American Century

1. William Roger Lewis, *Ends of British Imperialism: The Scramble for Empire, Suez,
and Decolonization* (London: I. B. Tauris, 2006), 455.

2. US National Intelligence Council, *Global Trends 2025: A Transformed World*
(Washington, DC: Government Printing Office, November 2008), vi, 97, www.dni
.gov/files/documents/Newsroom/Reports%20and%20Pubs/2025_Global_Trends
_Final_Report.pdf.

3. US National Intelligence Council, *Global Trends 2030: Alternative Worlds* (Washington, DC: National Intelligence Council, December 2012), iii, x–xi, 61, 63, 98,
www.dni.gov/index.php/about/organization/global-trends-2030.

4. "Remarks by the President in State of the Union Address," January 27, 2010, The
White House, Office of the Press Secretary, www.whitehouse.gov/the-press-office
/remarks-president-state-union-address.

5. E. J. Dionne Jr., "Off-Message, Biden Recasts the Obama Agenda," *Washington Post*,

February 4, 2010, www.washingtonpost.com/wp-dyn/content/article/2010/02/03 /AR2010020302913.html.

6. Mark Murray, "Poll: Clear GOP Advantage Ahead of Midterms," NBCNews.com, September 7, 2010, www.nbcnews.com/id/38996574/ns/politics/#.V6JKFGVlzDM.

7. Lale Kemal, "New Questions about Turkey's Secret Military Exercise with China," Atlantic Council, October 6, 2010, www.atlanticcouncil.org/blogs/natosource /new-questions-about-turkeys-secret-military-exercise-with-china; Phil Mercer, "Australia, China Conduct Live-Fire Naval Exercise in Yellow Sea," Voice of America, September 24, 2010, www.voanews.com/content/australia-china-conduct -live-fire-naval-exercise-in-yellow-sea-103780194/126679.html.

8. Sewell Chan, Sheryl Gay Stolberg, and David E. Sanger, "Obama's Economic View Is Rejected on World Stage, China, Britain and Germany Challenge U.S., Trade Talks with Seoul Fail, Too," *New York Times*, November 12, 2010; David Gergen, "Is America Losing Its Influence?," CNN, November 12, 2010, http://edition.cnn .com/2010/OPINION/11/12/gergen.america.economy/.

9. US National Intelligence Council, *Global Trends 2030*, xii–xiv, 110–33.

10. Ibid., vii–xii.

11. G. John Ikenberry, "The Future of the Liberal World Order: Internationalism after America," *Foreign Affairs* 90, no. 3 (May/June 2011): 66.

12. Robert Kagan, *The World America Made* (New York: Knopf, 2012), 58.

13. Brzezinski, *Strategic Vision*, 44–45.

14. Chan, Stolberg and Sanger, "Obama's Economic View Is Rejected on World Stage," *New York Times*, November 12, 2010.

15. Helene Cooper, "U.S. Leverage Is Limited as Greek Debt Drama Dominates G-20 Meeting," *New York Times*, November 4, 2011.

16. Tom Engelhardt, "It's a \$cam! The American Way of War in the Twenty-First Century," *TomDispatch.com*, November 12, 2015, www.tomdispatch.com/blog/176068/.

17. Tim Arango, "U.S. Plans to Cut Its Staff by Half at Iraq Embassy," *New York Times*, February 8, 2012.

18. Peter Baker, "Trump Says America's NATO Allies Aren't Paying Their Fair Share. Is That True?," *New York Times*, May 28, 2017; Alison Smale and Steven Erlanger, "Wary of Trump, Merkel Says U.S. Is Less Reliable," *New York Times*, May 28, 2017.

19. Kagan, *The World America Made*, 92–93; Courtney Johnson, "Alliance Imperialism and Anglo-American Power after 1898: The Origins of Open-Door Internationalism," in McCoy, Fradera, and Jacobson, eds., *Endless Empire*, 122–35.

20. Akira Iriye, "Toward Transnationalism," in Andrew J. Bacevich, ed., *The Short American Century: A Postmortem* (Cambridge, MA: Harvard University Press, 2012), 141; Brzezinski, *Strategic Vision*, 115–19.

21. Ikenberry, "The Future of the Liberal World Order," 57–58, 61–68.

22. Michael Hardt and Antonio Negri, *Empire* (Cambridge, MA: Harvard University Press, 2000), xi–xvii, 179–90, 214–18, 325–48, 393–403; Michael Hardt and Antonio Negri, *Multitude: War and Democracy in the Age of Empire* (New York: Penguin Press, 2005), xii–xiii, 30–32, 59–61, 129–38, 163–76; Brzezinski, *Strategic Vision*, 115–16; US National Intelligence Council, *Global Trends 2035: Paradox of Progress*

(Washington, DC: National Intelligence Council, January 2017), 10, 24, dni.gov /index.php/about/organization/national-intelligence-council-global-trends.

23. Mike Davis, *Planet of Slums* (London: Verso, 2007), 151, 199, 205–6.

24. Brzezinski, *Strategic Vision*, 76–77; US National Intelligence Council, *Global Trends 2035*, 54.

25. Jeffry A. Frieden, "From the American Century to Globalization," in Bacevich, ed., *The Short American Century*, 156.

26. Dominic Wilson and Roopa Purushothaman, *Global Economics Paper No. 99: Dreaming with BRICs: The Path to 2050* (New York: Goldman Sachs, October 1, 2003), 9–10, 21; Dominic Wilson and Anna Stupnytska, *Global Economics Paper No. 153: The N-11: More Than an Acronym* (New York: Goldman Sachs, March 28, 2007), 8, www.chicagobooth.edu/~/media/E60BDCEB6C5245E59B7ADA7C6B1B6F2B.pdf.

27. David Barboza, "China Overtakes Japan to Become No. 2 Global Economic Power," *New York Times*, August 16, 2010.

28. Louis Uchitelle, "Is Manufacturing Falling Off the Radar?," *New York Times*, September 11, 2011.

29. International Monetary Fund, "World Economic Outlook Database," April 2011 edition, www.imf.org/external/pubs/ft/weo/2011/01/weodata/index.aspx; Mark Weisbrot, "2016: When China Overtakes the US," *Guardian*, April 27, 2011, www .guardian.co.uk/commentisfree/cifamerica/2011/apr/27/china-imf-economy-2016.

30. Doug Bolton, "US? China? India? The 10 Biggest Economies in 2030 Will Be . . . ," *Independent*, April 15, 2015, www.independent.co.uk/news/business/us-china-india -the-10-biggest-economies-in-2030-will-be-10178587.html.

31. Andrew Soergel, "America's Days Are Numbered as the World's Top Economy," *U.S. News & World Report*, December 28, 2015, www.usnews.com/news/articles /2015-12-28/americas-days-are-numbered-as-the-worlds-top-economy.

32. World Intellectual Property Organization (WIPO), "WIPO Patent Report: Statistics on Worldwide Patent Activity," http://data.worldbank.org/indicator/IP.PAT.RESD.

33. The World Bank, "Table 5.13: World Development Indicators; Science and Technology," http://wdi.worldbank.org/table/5.13.

34. Robert D. Atkinson and Scott M. Andes, *The Atlantic Century: Benchmarking EU & U.S. Innovation and Competiveness* (Washington, DC: The Information Technology and Innovation Foundation, February 2009), 2, www2.itif.org/2009-atlantic -century.pdf?_ga=1.68285841.1897444338.1470266663.

35. Ashlee Vance, "Chinese Wrest Title from U.S.: Fastest Supercomputer, by Far," *New York Times*, October 28, 2010; John Markoff, "China Crowds Top Computer List," *New York Times*, June 21, 2016.

36. Organisation for Economic Cooperation and Development, Programme for International Student Assessment (PISA), "Results from PISA 2012: United States," www.oecd.org/pisa/keyfindings/PISA-2012-results-US.pdf.

37. US National Intelligence Council, *Global Trends 2030*, 98–99; Stephanie Simon, "PISA Results: 'Educational Stagnation,'" *Politico*, December 3, 2013, www.politico .com/story/2013/12/education-international-test-results-100575.

38. Tamar Lewin, "Once in First Place, Americans Now Lag in Attaining College De-

grees," *New York Times*, July 23, 2010.

39. Klaus Schwab, *The Global Competitiveness Report 2012–2013* (Geneva: World Economic Forum, 2012), 361, http://reports.weforum.org/global-competitiveness-report-2012-2013/; Klaus Schwab, *The Global Competitiveness Report 2014–2015* (Geneva: World Economic Forum, 2014), 379, www.weforum.org/reports/global-competitiveness-report-2014-2015/.

40. Stuart Anderson, "The Importance of International Students to America," *NFAP Policy Brief* (Arlington, VA: National Foundation for American Policy, July 2013), www.nfap.com/pdf/New%20NFAP%20Policy%20Brief%20The%20Importance%20of%20International%20Students%20to%20America,%20July%202013.pdf.

41. James Clay Moltz, "Russia and China: Strategic Choices in Space," in Damon Coletta and Frances T. Pilch, eds., *Space and Defense Policy* (London and New York: Routledge, 2009), 277, 281.

42. Thomas L. Friedman, "Can't Keep a Bad Idea Down," *New York Times*, October 27, 2010; Members of the 2005 "Rising above the Gathering Storm" Committee, *Rising above the Gathering Storm, Revisited: Rapidly Approaching Category 5* (Washington, DC: National Academies Press, 2010), 5, www.nap.edu/catalog/12999/rising-above-the-gathering-storm-revisited-rapidly-approaching-category-5.

43. United Nations Development Program, "Human Development Index 2007 and Its Components," in *Human Development Report 2009,* http://hdr.undp.org/sites/default/files/reports/269/hdr_2009_en_complete.pdf, "Economy > GINI Index: Countries Compared," www.nationmaster.com/graph/eco_gin_ind-economy-gini-index.

44. Jahnke, "Who Picks Up the Tab for Science," *BU Today* (Boston University, 2015), www.bu.edu/research/articles/funding-for-scientific-research/.

45. American Association for the Advancement of Science, "Trends in Federal R&D, FY 1976–2017," www.aaas.org/sites/default/files/DefNon%3B.jpg; American Institute of Physics, "Report: U.S. Global Lead in R&D at Risk as China Rises," February 1, 2016, www.aip.org/fyi/2016/report-us-global-lead-rd-risk-china-rises.

46. Rohini Hensman and Marinella Correggia, "US Dollar Hegemony: The Soft Underbelly of Empire," *Economic and Political Weekly* 40, no. 12 (March 19, 2005): 1093–95.

47. Sewell Chan, "Seismic Shift in Cash Clout," *New York Times*, October 10, 2010.

48. Michael Hudson, "Washington Cannot Call All the Shots," *Financial Times*, June 14, 2009, www.ft.com/cms/s/0/e9104e82-58f7-11de-80b3-00144feabdc0.html#axzz4GNjgozZs.

49. Nicole E. Lewis, "China's Foreign Exchange Reserves: Unintentional Means to a Strategic End," *Huffington Post*, January 13, 2010, www.cfr.org/china/chinas-foreign-exchange-reserves-unintentional-means-strategic-end/p21189.

50. Hudson, "Washington Cannot Call All the Shots."

51. Neil Irwin, "China's Choices as Its Currency Becomes More Global," *New York Times*, December 1, 2015.

52. US National Intelligence Council, *Global Trends 2030*, xii, 105.

53. Posen, "Command of the Commons," 8–9.

54. Nicholas D. Kristof, "As China Looks at World Order, It Detects New Struggles Emerging," *New York Times*, April 21, 2016; Denyer, "By 2030, South China Sea

Will Be 'Virtually a Chinese Lake."

55. Mandelbaum, *The Frugal Superpower*, 20, 46–52, 185; US National Intelligence
Council, *Global Trends 2030*, 99.

56. Stephen Jacobson, "Imperial Ambitions in an Era of Decline: Micromilitarism
and the Eclipse of the Spanish Empire, 1858–1923," in McCoy et al., eds., *Endless
Empire*, 74–91.

57. Andrew Jacobs and Jane Perlez, "U.S. Wary as Chinese Base Rises as a Neighbor in
Africa," *New York Times*, February 26, 2017; Jane Perlez, "China to Raise Military
Spending, Though Less Than in Recent Years," *New York Times*, March 5, 2017; US
Department of Defense, Press Operations, "Department of Defense (DoD) Releases
Fiscal Year 2017 President's Budget Proposal," February 9, 2016, www.defense.gov/
News/News-Releases/News-Release-View/Article/652687/department-of
-defense-dod-releases-fiscal-year-2017-presidents-budget-proposal.

58. Mark Landler, "Offering to Aid Talks, U.S. Challenges China on Disputed Islands,"
New York Times, July 24, 2010; Peter Ford, "China and the US Battle to Assert Presence in South China Sea," *Christian Science Monitor*, August 17, 2010,
www.csmonitor.com/World/Asia-Pacific/2010/0817/China-and-the-US-battle
-to-assert-presence-in-South-China-Sea.

59. Kristensen, "China SSBN Fleet Getting Ready."

60. Wingfield-Hayes, "China's Island Factory."

61. Permanent Court of Arbitration, *In the Matter of the South China Sea Arbitration before
an Arbitral Tribunal Constituted under Annex VII to the United Nations Convention on
the Law of the Sea between the Republic of the Philippines and the People's Republic of
China*, "Award," PCA Case 2013-19, July 12, 2016, 68–77, 116–17, www.pcacases.com
/pcadocs/PH-CN%20-%2020160712%20-%20Award.pdf; Jane Perlez, "Panel Rejects
China's Claims in Sea Dispute," *New York Times*, July 13, 2016; Zhiguo Gao and Bing
Bing Jia, "The Nine-Dash Line in the South China Sea: History, Status, and Implications," *American Journal of International Law* 107, no. 1 (2013): 103–4.

62. Jane Perlez, "Chinese Lease of Australian Port Troubles U.S.," *New York Times*,
March 20, 2016; Jane Perlez, "2 U.S. Carriers Sail in Western Pacific in Show of
Force," *New York Times*, June 19, 2016.

63. Office of the Secretary of Defense, *Military and Security Developments Involving the
People's Republic of China, 2010* (Washington, DC: Department of Defense, August
2010), i, 1–3, 7, 25–26, 30, 34–37.

64. David Sanger, David Barboza, and Nicole Perlroth, "China's Army Seen as Tied to
Hacking against U.S. Order," *New York Times*, February 18, 2013; David E. Sanger,
"Cyberthreat Posed by China and Iran Confounds White House," *New York Times*,
September 16, 2015; David E. Sanger, "U.S. and China Seek Arms Deal for Cyber-
space" *New York Times*, September 20, 2015.

65. "China Launches New Global Positioning Satellite," Reuters, July 31, 2010,
www.reuters.com/article/idUSTRE67005R20100801; "China's Homegrown Navigation System to Have 35-Satellite Constellation by 2020," *China Daily*, June 16, 2016,
www.chinadaily.com.cn/china/2016-06/16/content_25732439.htm.

66. Edward Wong, "China Launches Satellite in Bid to Lead Quantum Research," *New*

York Times, August 17, 2016

67. Broad, "Surveillance Suspected as Spacecraft's Main Role."

68. Gompert, Cevallos, and Garafola, *War with China*, 38–39.

69. Carl Bergquist, "Air Force Wargaming Institute Hosts CSAF Wargame," Air University Public Affairs, Maxwell Air Force Base, October 29, 2009, www.maxwell
.af.mil/News/Display/tabid/10067/Article/421016/air-force-wargaming-institute
-hosts-csaf-wargame.aspx; Lara Seligman, "Air Force Nuclear War Game Tests Future Bomber Fleet," *Defense News*, December 18, 2015, www.defensenews.com
/story/defense/air-space/air-force/2015/12/18/air-force-nuclear-war-game-tests
-future-bomber-fleet/77515594/.

70. US National Intelligence Council, *Global Trends 2035*, 221.

71. David Szondy, "DARPA Ready to Deliver Telescope to Watch the Skies for Space Debris," *New Atlas*, December 11, 2013, http://newatlas.com/sst-delivery/30063/.

72. John Markoff and David Barboza, "Researchers Spy on Computer Spies," *New York Times*, April 5, 2010; David E. Sanger and Peter Baker, "Obama Limits When U.S. Would Use Nuclear Arms," *New York Times*, April 6, 2010.

73. James Drew, "US Navy Descoping Stealth Requirement for Stingray Tanking UAV," *FlightGlobal*, March 11, 2016, www.flightglobal.com/news/articles/us-navy
-descoping-stealth-requirement-for-stingray-t-423039/.

74. Leonard David, "Mystery Mission: Air Force's X-37B Space Plane Nears 1 Year in Orbit," *Space.com*, May 10, 2016, www.space.com/32839-x37b-military-space
-plane-one-year-mission-otv4.html.

75. "Navy Hits Satellite with Heat-Seeking Missile," *Space.com*, February 20, 2008, www.space.com/5006-navy-hits-satellite-heat-seeking-missile.html.

76. Brendan McGarry, "Air Force Getting Closer to Testing Hypersonic Weapon, Engineers Say," *Military.com*, May 19, 2015, www.military.com/daily-news/2015/05/19
/air-force-getting-closer-to-testing-hypersonic-weapon.html.

77. Lt. Col. Mark E. Harter, "Ten Propositions Regarding Space Power: The Dawn of a Space Force," *Air & Space Power Journal*, Summer 2006, www.au.af.mil/au/afri/aspj
/airchronicles/apj/apj06/sum06/harter.html.

78. Intergovernmental Panel on Climate Change, *Climate Change 2014: Synthesis Report; Summary for Policymakers* (November 11, 2013), 4, 8, 83, http://ar5-syr.ipcc
.ch/topic_summary.php.

79. Ibid., 65–73.

80. David Abel, "Climate Change Could Be Even Worse for Boston Than Previously Thought," *Boston Globe*, June 22, 2016, www.bostonglobe.com/metro/2016/06/22
/climate-change-could-have-even-worse-impact-boston-than-previously-expected
/S6hZ4nDPeUWNyTsx6ZckuL/story.html.

81. US National Intelligence Council, *Implications for US National Security of Anticipated Climate Change* (Washington, DC, September 21, 2016), 3, 5, www.dni.gov
/index.php/newsroom/reports-and-publications/214-reports-publications-2016
/1415-implications-for-us-national-security-of-anticipated-climate-change; US National Intelligence Council, *Global Trends 2035*, 8, 170–72, 211.

82. US National Intelligence Council, *Implications for US National Security of Anticipat-*

ed Climate Change, 7–13; Justin Gillis, "For Third Year, the Earth in 2016 Set Heat Record," *New York Times,* January 19, 2017.

83. US National Intelligence Council, *Implications for US National Security of Anticipated Climate Change,* 11–13.

84. "Remarks by President Obama at the First Session of COP21," Paris, France, November 30, 2015, The White House, Office of the Press Secretary, www.whitehouse .gov/the-press-office/2015/11/30/remarks-president-obama-first-session-cop21.

85. Jonathan Corum, "A Sharp Increase in 'Sunny Day' Flooding," *New York Times,* September 3, 2016; Jeff Goodell, "Goodbye, Miami," *Rolling Stone,* June 20, 2013, www.rollingstone.com/politics/news/why-the-city-of-miami-is-doomed-to -drown-20130620.

86. US Army Corps of Engineers, Directorate of Civil Works, *Coastal Risk Reduction and Resilience: Using the Full Array of Measures* (September 2013), 1–2, www .corpsclimate.us/docs/USACE_Coastal_Risk_Reduction_final_CWTS_2013-3.pdf; US Army Corps of Engineers, "Southwest Coastal Louisiana, Coastal Storm Damage Risk Reduction/Ecosystem Restoration," March 30, 2016, www.usace.army.mil /Missions/Civil-Works/Project-Planning/Civil-Works-Review-Board/sw_coastal/.

87. Union of Concerned Scientists, "Overwhelming Risk: Rethinking Flood Insurance in a World of Rising Seas," August 2013 (revised February 2014), www.ucsusa.org/ sites/default/files/legacy/assets/documents/global_warming/Overwhelming -Risk-Full-Report.pdf.

88. Mireya Navarro, "Weighing Sea Barriers as Protection for New York," *New York Times,* November 7, 2012, www.nytimes.com/2012/11/08/nyregion/after -hurricane-sandy-debating-costly-sea-barriers-in-new-york-area.html; Michael Fitzgerald, "How Boston Is—and Should Be—Preparing for Rising Seas," *Boston Globe,* April 4, 2014, www.bostonglobe.com/magazine/2014/04/04/how-boston -and-should-preparing-for-rising-seas/8mF4YVWgAMzDGQexMF35FK /story.html; Joe Joyce, "Boston Developers Plan for Rising Sea Level," CBS Boston, November 18, 2011, http://boston.cbslocal.com/2011/11/18/boston-developers -plan-for-rising-seal-level/; CoreLogic, "CoreLogic Storm Surge Analysis Identifies More Than 6.8 Million US Homes at Risk of Hurricane Storm Surge Damage in 2016," June 1, 2016, www.corelogic.com/about-us/news/corelogic-storm-surge -analysis-identifies-more-than-6.8-million-us-homes-at-risk-of-hurricane-storm -surge-damage-in-2016.aspx.

89. Brian Clark Howard, "Worst Drought in 1,000 Years Predicted for American West," *National Geographic,* February 12, 2015, http://news.nationalgeographic.com /news/2015/02/150212-megadrought-southwest-water-climate-environment/; William deBuys, "Phoenix in the Climate Crosshairs," *TomDispatch,* March 14, 2013, www.tomdispatch.com/blog/175661/william_debuys_exodus_from_phoenix.

90. Linda J. Bilmes and Joseph E. Stiglitz, "The Iraq War Will Cost Us $3 Trillion, and Much More," *Washington Post,* March 9, 2008, www.washingtonpost.com/wp-dyn /content/article/2008/03/07/AR2008030702846.html.

91. Julia Ioffe, "The State of Trump's State Department," *Atlantic,* March 1, 2017, www .theatlantic.com/international/archive/2017/03/state-department-trump/517965/.

Index

About the Author

Alfred McCoy holds the Harrington Chair in History at the University of Wisconsin–Madison. After earning his doctorate in history at Yale University in 1977, his writing has focused on three main topics—the emergence of the modern Philippines, the netherworld of covert operations, and the history of modern empires.

His first book, *The Politics of Heroin in Southeast Asia* (New York, 1972), sparked controversy over the CIA's attempt to block its publication. But it is now regarded as the classic study of global narcotics trafficking, remaining in print for nearly fifty years and translated into nine languages. His book *A Question of Torture: CIA Interrogation, from the Cold War to the War on Terror* (New York, 2006) provided the historical dimension for the film *Taxi to the Dark Side*, which won the Oscar in 2008 for Best Documentary Feature.

Another book, *Policing America's Empire: The United States, the Philippines, and the Rise of the Surveillance State* (Madison, 2009), was awarded the Kahin Prize by the Association for Asian Studies for its exploration of the transformative power of police, information, and scandal in shaping both the modern Philippine state and the US national security apparatus.

In 2012, Yale University awarded him the Wilbur Cross Medal to acknowledge his work as "one of the world's leading historians of Southeast Asia and an expert on Philippine political history, opium trafficking in the Golden Triangle, underworld crime syndicates, and international political surveillance."